Secrets to Success in
COUNTRY MUSIC
THE INSIDERS GUIDE TO LAUNCHING YOUR CAREER

Gabriel Farago

Press

Copyright © 2007 by Gabriel Farago

Published by: Opry of the Sandhills Press
P.O. Box 3323
Shawnee, KS 66203

Second Printing 2008

All rights reserved. No part of this publication may be reproduced, stored in a retrieval system, or transmitted in any form or by any means – for example, electronic, photocopy, recording – without the prior written permission of the publisher. The only exception to this is brief quotations in printed reviews.

ISBN 978-0-9793155-1-0

Library of Congress Control Number 2007900747

Publisher's Cataloging-in-Publication
(Provided by Quality Books, Inc.)

Farago, Gabriel.
   Secrets to success in country music : the insiders guide to launching your career / Gabriel Farago.
   p. cm.
   LCCN 2007900747
   ISBN 978-0-9793155-1-0

   1. Country music--Vocational guidance. 2. Music trade--Vocational guidance.   I. Title.

ML3795.F37 2007   781.642'023'73
                              QBI07-700054

This book has been written to provide information on the country music business and offer ideas and suggestions on how to break into it. It is sold with the understanding that neither the author nor the publisher are engaged in rendering legal, accounting or other such related services. An individual may need to retain an attorney or accountant once they reach a certain plateau in their development.

Printed in the United States of America

DEDICATION

To my mother and father,

and to Uncle Hank.

TABLE OF CONTENTS

(Part I)

Chapter 1 "The Basics"   1
Talent --- Attitude --- Motivation --- "Name," Money, and Connections --- Defining Your Goals --- Establishing "Game Plans" --- Success As A "Club Act" --- Success As A "National Act" --- Making Money With Your Music

Chapter 2 "Finding Investors"   9
Do Your Homework --- Why Look For Backing --- Where to Look --- Your Backer's Return --- Sample Proposals --- Customizing Your Own Proposal

Chapter 3 "Images & Illusions"   19
"Image" Sells The Sizzle --- The "Illusion": An Extension Of Reality --- You Are What You Are --- Defining *Your* Image

Chapter 4 "The Artist (Promo) Pack"   23
Artist Pack Contents --- Your Demo --- Photo --- Narrative Biography --- Press Info --- Video --- Posters --- Website --- Letters of Recommendation

Chapter 5 "Bars, Honky-Tonks & Karaoke"   33
Positive Side Of Club Work --- Negative Aspect Of Club Work --- "King Of Karaoke"

Chapter 6 "The Move to Nashville"   37
"Pro's" Of The Move --- The Down-Side Of The Move --- The Scout Motto: "Be Prepared"

Table of Contents

Chapter 7 "Song-Writing"   41
A Song's Anatomy --- Title --- Theme --- The Unfolding of the Story --- Pay-Off --- Chorus or Refrain

Chapter 8 "Publishing"   45
How A Publisher Works --- Assignment And Ownership Of Songs --- "Mechanical" Royalties --- Splitting Royalties --- Performance Rights Societies --- "Performance" Royalties --- Joining a Performance Rights Society --- Starting Your Own Publishing Company --- Mechanical Licensing --- What About Recording "Cover" Songs? --- What Publishers Look For --- Three Door-Opening Strategies

Chapter 9 "The Major Labels"   51
Advantages Of Being Signed --- "Shopping Yourself" -- Go About It Properly --- "The Code" --- Be Persistent And Creative --- Patience Is A Virtue

Chapter 10 "Your Recording Session"   55
Musicians --- Back-Up Vocalists --- Studios --- Engineer --- Tape --- Cartage

Chapter 11 "Your Producer"   61
Finding A Producer --- What To Look For --- Know What To "Watch Out" For --- Your Producer's Fee

Chapter 12 "Recording A Hit Vocal"   65
Crucial Areas Of Vocal Performance --- Finding Yourself --- Vocal Technique --- A Few Other Points

Chapter 13 "The 'Independent' Approach"   69
"You Pay Your Own Way" --- Vital Areas To Focus On --- Product Release --- Format And Manufacturing --- "Limited" Release --- National Release --- "Custom" Label Vs. "Independent" Label --- Mailings --- Promotions --- Radio In Promotions --- Other Points Regarding Radio Promotions --- Marketing And Distribution --- Bar Coding And Artwork

Table of Contents

Chapter 14 "Radio Airplay" — 81
Getting Airplay --- The Music Director --- Sample Game Plan To Self-Promote

Chapter 15 "Fairs, Festivals & Rodeos" — 87
"You Are The Star" --- Your Performance --- Booking Yourself… A Practical Approach --- "Band Vs. Single-Act" --- "The Drummer Trick" --- Sound Systems --- Lighting --- The "After-Market" --- Performance Fees

Chapter 16 "Merchandising Yourself" — 97
Basic Strategies For Self-Merchandising --- Other Things To Consider

Chapter 17 "What About Branson?" — 101
"Name Act" Or "Lounge Act" --- The Positive Side

Chapter 18 "The Overseas Market & Canada" — 105
Advantages Of Pursuing The Overseas Market --- European Radio --- Opening The Right Doors --- Canada --- Cancon --- Cancon Requirements --- Pursuing Airplay

Chapter 19 "Generating Publicity" — 111
Public Relations Firms – Creating Your Own Publicity (Newspaper Write-Ups --- TV Talk Shows And News --- Radio Interviews --- Fan Clubs --- Talent Contests --- Oprys --- Jamborees --- Other Avenues)

Chapter 20 "Jukeboxes" — 117
"Perks" A Jukebox Offers --- Getting "Added" To The Jukebox

Chapter 21 "Sponsorships & Endorsements" — 119
Landing A Deal --- How "The Trade-Off" Works --- Benefits Of Sponsorships --- Endorsements

Chapter 22 "Showcasing" — 123
The "Professional" (P.R. Firm) Approach --- Setting Up Your Own Showcase --- "Label" Showcases --- Performance (Talent Buyer) Showcases

Table of Contents

Chapter 23 "Managers"   **127**
Typical Duties Of A Manager --- Maybe Another "Colonel Parker"? --- Finding A Manager --- Create Your Own "Pre-Manager" Think-Tank

Chapter 24 "Booking Agents"   **131**
Finding The Right Agent --- Be Your Own Agent --- Making Your "Pitch" --- Six Key Points To Remember…

Chapter 25 "Entertainment Attorneys"   **137**
Contacting An Entertainment Attorney --- How An Entertainment Lawyer Can Help You --- What's In It For The Attorney?

Chapter 26 "Scams, Shams & Charlatans"   **139**
The "Sin Of Omission" --- You Do Have To Pay Your Own Way! --- The "Talent Contest" Or "Audition" Sham --- The "Video" Sham --- The "Consultation" Or "Evaluation" Sham --- The "We'll Pay Half" Sham --- The "Trade Magazine" Sham --- The "Radio Station Talent Scout" Sham --- "The Publisher" Sham --- The "Paying A Fee To Enter Talent Contests" Sham --- The "CD Manufacturer Mail Direct To Radio" Sham --- The "Win A Recording In Nashville" Sham --- The "Internet CD Promo" Sham --- The "Talent Contest on the Internet" Sham --- The "Showcase" Sham --- The "Seminar" Sham --- The "Scholarship" Sham --- Other Things To Look Out For

Glossary of Names & Terms   **151**

Supplements to Part I   **159**
(Samples) Letter of Recommendation --- Press Releases/ Promo Flyers --- Posters --- Narrative Bio's --- Newspaper Write-ups --- Promo Photos --- Backer "Prospectus" --- Artist/Backer Contract --- Performance Contract

TABLE OF CONTENTS

(Part II)

Appendix A
U.S. Country Radio (state-by-state) Listing   175
Canada Country Radio (province-by-province) Listing   201
International Country Radio (nation-by-nation) Listing   205

Appendix B
U.S. Fairs (state-by-state) Listing   233
Canadian Fairs (province-by-province) Listing   271
U.S. Festivals (state-by-state) Listing   279
Canadian Festivals (province-by-province) Listing   313
Meetings/Convention Data   319

Appendix C
Recording Studios   325
Sound Engineers   325
Studio Musicians   326
Back-up Singers   327
Cartage Companies   328
Record Labels   331
Performance Rights Societies   332
Publicists   335
Record Promoters   337
Satellite Radio & Radio Syndicators   337
Rodeo Companies   338
Song Publishers   341
Managers   347
Compilation CD Distributors   350
Talent (Booking) Agents   351

Index   **353**

DISCLAIMER

This book has been written to provide information on the country music business and offer ideas and suggestions on how to break into it. It is sold with the understanding that neither the author nor the publisher are engaged in rendering legal, accounting or other such related services. An individual may need to retain an attorney or accountant once they reach a certain plateau in their development.

Every effort has been made to make this manual as complete and accurate as possible. However, there may be mistakes, both typographical and in content.

The author and Opry of the Sandhills Press shall have neither liability nor responsibility to any person or entity with respect to any loss or damage caused, or alleged to have been caused, directly or indirectly, by the information contained in this book.

ACKNOWLEDGEMENTS

As with any challenge and undertaking in life that we hope bears fruit, one can ask the question, "Where would I be without a little help from my friends?" There have been so many people – music industry personnel, my clients, personal friends – who have influenced the creation of *Secrets to Success in Country Music*, to remember them all would create a practically endless list. However, there are a certain few who stand out and need to be recognized.

In particular, I wish to thank Colleen Kendzierski, who typed this manuscript, for a tremendous job well done. Her patience, technical skills, knowledgeable input and willingness to stick with it have been nothing short of extraordinary. You've been a true blessing, Col! Again, thanks.

In Nashville, special thanks go out to Mr. Harold Bradley, my former producer, mentor and current president of Nashville's Musician's Union. Thanks, Harold, you are my hero and you're the best! To Bob Saporiti, former marketing director of Warner Brothers Records (and record promoter of mine in the 1980's!), thanks for always having an open door. Thank you, Ed Benson, Executive Director of the Country Music Association, for your insights and sharing future plans for the CMA. To Mary Templeton at BMI, thanks for your continuous help and direction. Bert Stein of Gold Mountain Entertainment, thanks so much for your friendship, time and wisdom. Jerry Duncan of Jerry Duncan Promotions, thanks for always taking time out of your busy schedule for me. (Let's make one of my projects your next platinum award!) To Ray Pilszak of Amusement Business Magazine, thanks for always lending your knowledge and your ear. To Charline Wilhite of ASCAP, thanks for being a good listener! To Mark Capps and Soundshop Studios, it's easy to understand why so many hits have been cut there! Thanks for our many great sessions! To John Willis, Bobby Ogdin, Sonny Garrish and my favorite "crew" of Nashville's studio musicians – you guys are awesome! And to David "Noel" Gibson of the Music Craftshop Group, you're an amazing guy; you have my sincerest gratitude for your help and our many years of friendship.

In Canada, to Dale Bohna, my former booking agent and a great friend, thanks for always believing in me, your never-ending enthusiasm and that occasional kick in the butt I needed! Phil Kallsen, Music Director of CKRY-FM up in Calgary, Alberta, thanks for being so informative about Cancon and adding your knowledge to this project.

Karen Johnson and Gary Sprague, thank you both for your useful proofing and valuable comments on my manuscript. Dr. Gary Smith, thank you for your positive input, help and years of friendship. Dr. John Clorius, my former neighbor and lifelong friend, thanks for the encouragement from Day One.

Debbie Woods, thanks for a monumental job typing the Appendices and for understanding me so well – you're a sweetheart.

To Kinkos, thanks for being everywhere all the time! You've provided an excellent service and have been a late night port in the storm (many a night!) through my travels over the years. Special thanks to the Bloomington, Illinois, store, especially to Pat, Jeff, Scott, Adam, Tim, Shawn, Jason, Erin, Joe and, of course, Andy.

To Kenny Ota of AlphaGraphics, thank you for coming on board in the eleventh hour. Your help is sincerely appreciated. Tammy Burke of Morris Publishing, thank you so much for your last minute help.

To David Frantz of FranZart, thank you for this great cover design. I'm sure glad God blessed you with patience as well as talent!

Dave and Carol Erke, you guys are the best neighbors anybody could ever have anywhere! Thanks so much for holding down the fort when I'm away on road trips. To Gyuszi and Terri Szabo, my fellow Hungarian expatriots, thanks for your lifelong friendship. Tom Hoffman, you are the clothier extraordinaire. Thanks for showing a country boy how to dress up! To Karl Grigg, where would I be without your IT skills and sound advice? Your loyalty and friendship have been a blessing and inspiration to me. Thanks so much. To Hobbie, Bogáncs and Dexter, thanks for being my faithful four-legged traveling companions and "studio hounds" through the years. To Cica and my family of "Oak Canyon Ranch cats," you're great buddies and mousers. To David Congdon of Barnes & Noble, thanks for your suggestions and valuable direction. To Pastor Kevin Cunningham, thanks for helping me discover what my life is really all about.

And to my Lord Jesus Christ, thanks for those gifts that made all of this possible.

Gabriel Farago
Nashville, TN

FOREWORD

When Gabriel Farago first asked me to write the Foreword to his book, my initial response was, "A book? I thought you were a singer!" I was referring to the fact that we had charted two of his records in Billboard's Country Top 100 back in the '80's. My late wife Betty and I headed up an independent label and distribution company in Nashville called Nationwide Sound Distributors.

During that time, we had the pleasure of being associated with many talented and memorable people. Some were destined to go a long ways. We were fortunate to be instrumental in launching the careers of two of Country Music's greatest acts -- Alabama and Aaron Tippin.

Having been in the music industry for fifty or so years, people have often asked me, "Joe, what does it take to make it?" Truth is, there is no simple answer. From all my experience, I can tell you this much: It takes a lot more than just talent. I've always said you can have all the talent in the world, but if you don't know what you're doing, you and it will forever remain a well-kept secret! Unfortunately, the average "wanna-be" has no clue about the whole thing. That's the reason for the downfall of many an otherwise promising new act.

Once I read the manuscript to *Secrets to Success in Country Music*, I realized our former client had done his homework -- and then some. Farago's book offers an "inside" look and remarkably informed assessment of what it takes to (as he puts it) "turn talent into treasure." It's filled with hot tips, sound advice and, as I see it, offers real solutions to the real problems that stand in every aspiring artist's way. *Secrets to Success in Country Music* is testament to the fact that the writer has "been there" and knows what he's talking about.

I've always said if somebody ever wrote "the book" on it, they'd make a million dollars. Congratulations, Gabriel Farago, you've scored you a hit with this one!

Joe Gibson

PREFACE

Anyone who has ever tried to make it in Nashville -- or just break into the music business in general -- can relate to the feeling of running into a brick wall time and time again. The scenario is always the same: You get only so far and then that's it! This is especially frustrating to individuals who know they have what it takes, but can't find an opportunity to prove it to the rest of the world. Hence, a saying I've coined, "Talent is like buried treasure; it's not worth anything until it's discovered!"

For whatever reason, there has always been an incredible lack of reliable information on this subject. Myths, misinformation, and "fairy tales" abound. Worst of all, people buy into the assumption that success is something they have very little control over, and that either luck, being in the right place or "who you know" randomly selects those who make it. Nothing could, in reality, be further from the truth!

While there is always an element of good fortune in everything we do, getting a break in the music business means *making it yourself*. Making that break, however, requires a lot of specialized knowledge. In fact, it can arguably be said that "know-how" is more important than talent itself!

Since necessity is the mother of invention, *Secrets to Success in Country Music* has been born. Many would agree it's long overdue. I've written it to remove the shroud of mystery surrounding this area, and to empower aspiring country artists with the facts. Although numerous books have in recent years appeared on the subject of the music business, to me none provide much in terms of practical value. Why? Simply because they all fall into one of three basic categories: (1) Some offer motivation and hype, but woefully lack substance, (2) Others offer complex, technical information which tends to be premature and confusing unless you are already well on your way, (3) Others yet boast endless listings of people who, in reality, are totally inaccessible to the average Joe.

Secrets to Success in Country Music offers a completely different and infinitely more effective approach. Instead of more of the same-old, it deals head on with the key issue: *How to make your talent work for you*.

Part I of the book acts as the *what to* and *how to* section. Within its twenty-six chapters, it focuses on vital career-launching areas, and provides hard-hitting, door-opening strategies and techniques with which to get the job done.

Part II (the "Yellow Pages") *interacts with* Part I as a direct source supplement. It features exhaustive appendices that provide instant access to *thousands* of high-visibility performance venues and radio airplay opportunities in the U.S. and Canada, record labels (majors and successful "indies"), leading managers, booking agents, key overseas country music radio venues and many other critically important areas.

Who will benefit most from this book? Categorically, everyone! All music industry hopefuls will find *Secrets to Success in Country Music* indispensable. Its innovative approach allows it to serve as a lightning-quick reference tool as well as a complete, "big picture," career-launching guide. Professional or beginner, singer, songwriter or musician, everyone can find a wealth of useful information in pursuing their personal goals. So, whether you are just getting started, or are a long-time veteran of the music industry searching for ways to improve yourself (and your earning power!), *Secrets to Success in Country Music* will help take your potential to the max and dramatically increase *your* chances of success!

With that in mind, let's turn the page and get down to "The Basics."

_____Chapter 1

THE BASICS

*"You gotta work, work, work ... and then work some more.
If it was easy, everybody'd be doin' it!"*

Uncle Hank Secord

Talent

Vocal talent, unless you are classically trained, is very difficult to assess or measure since its interpretation is so subjective. If you are an opera singer, your voice can at least be judged by its range, quality and other traditional criteria. No such standard of measure exists, however, for an aspiring country singer. Another thing to think about: Since we all have personal preferences, saying one person is actually *better than* or *has more talent than* the other is, in reality, not valid either. Opinions are not objective or definitive. It's like asking who's the better painter, Picasso or Terry Redlin -- it's all a matter of individual taste.

Practically speaking, it's safe to say "talent" in the country music industry is measured and defined in terms of *who has potential to sell records and make money!*

Realistically, here's what counts:

- **How well you do *what you are trying to do*.**

- **How marketable a record company (or whoever) finds you.**

You are born with what the Good Lord gives you. Although some people seem to be gifted with a natural talent for music and singing more than others, you can't change what you received at birth. That's a done deal! *Talent can, however, be developed.* Here is what it boils down to: Take what you have and hone it to the fullest. Develop your own style and create your own vocal signature. Stick to what you are comfortable with, and don't try to be something or someone that you are not -- it will show. To a great extent, the so-called "talent" you eventually wind up with will be the result of *how much you put into it!*

Attitude

Confidence and a business-oriented approach are as much the cornerstones of success within the music industry as your talent itself. You must genuinely believe in yourself and *honestly feel you have what it takes* to make others believe it, too! Just as important, learn to think in a practical and logical (not just emotional) way in regards to your music. It's okay to dream and reach for the stars, as long as you keep your feet on the ground.

Here's something else to keep in mind regarding attitude. There can be a fine line between confidence and arrogance. *Real* confidence shows and lets the world know you believe in yourself. Arrogance, on the other hand, is a sure turn-off to those around you. Becoming "jaded," often associated with arrogance, is very common among singers and musicians. Typically, it is caused by low achievement, which results in disillusionment. In this business people tend to become frustrated by either setting their goals too low (when they know they're capable of much more), or having overly lofty expectations way too soon.

Motivation

My former manager and backer, Uncle Hank, had lots of motivation. As a young man, while working on the railroad, he once put in 96 hours straight! Small wonder he went on to become a highly-successful contractor. Doc Hall, my veterinarian -- and another *real* worker -- always says, "Remember, there are 21 work days in a week!" (Get it? Three "shifts" per day x 7.) While Doc may be stretching it a bit, he makes a good point: Winners are workers!

It's easy to say, "I have always dreamed of becoming a star," and even easier to just sit around thinking about it. **Motivation is what separates the "wanna-be's" from the "gonna-be's"** to a far greater extent than anyone could imagine. It is *the force* that makes us want to get things done and move on to greater achievements.

Remember, the music business requires a lot of ambition and perseverance. If you are the type of person who cannot discipline yourself enough to do what needs to be done, don't count on going too far. The truth is, to a lot of people, the best part of their music is just having fun. Once things become too much like work, the fun can disappear. Take a good look at yourself and your own level of motivation. If you don't have plenty of drive and willpower, forget about lofty goals. Stick to weekend bands and karaoke instead!

"Name," Money, And Connections

We would be kidding ourselves if we didn't admit that big bucks, well-placed connections and the right "politics" weren't a large part of anyone's success -- be it the music industry or any other! Yes, certain things in life, especially the circumstances into which we are born, are beyond our control. But, the good news is this -- we have the *power to change things*. Here are the realities:

Contrary to what some believe, just having a "name" is no guarantee of success. At best, it may provide a jump-start, but, without the *right stuff*, the effort is going to stall. For example, look at the careers of Loretta Lynn's daughters, Merle Haggard's son Marty, Reba McEntire's brother Pake, Dolly Parton's brother Randy and sister Stella, the late, great Conway Twitty's son Mike and daughter Kathy, -- even Ol' Blue Eyes' son Frank Sinatra, Jr. Though all of these individuals are talented in their own right and have had limited success, they have yet to come close to filling the shoes of their famous "kinfolk."

As far as "money" is concerned, it can be acquired easily enough through motivated and resourceful efforts such as *finding backers*. Attracting investors is an excellent option for a person lacking adequate funding to finance their musical career.

Even the "connections" and "politics" you hear about in the music business will come along if you work hard and are able to prove yourself. So, if you weren't born into a family with a silver spoon in your mouth or aren't the child of a record label's president, *connections can be acquired*.

Remember, *talent* and *motivation* are fundamental prerequisites for success. Many things in life can be learned or bought; however, if you can't sing, neither voice lessons, "name," money nor wishful thinking are going to make a star out of you.

Defining Your Goals

Have you ever noticed how difficult finding a destination can be without good directions? So it is with goals. *You need to know where you are going in order to get there.*

If you don't know what your goals are as yet, here are two tips: (1) Figure out what you enjoy doing with your music, and (2) Ask yourself, "Where do I want to be five or ten years from now with my music?" But regardless of whether you want to go big time or just have fun locally, remember this: The main reason singers succeed *at any level* is because of *their love for it*!

Which brings me to this point: Singers and musicians generally get into the music business for one (or more) of three basic reasons:

- **They love doing it for the sake of doing it.**

- **They want to make it for money and ego.**

- **Some are just interested in expanding their "social horizons" -- there are few better ways to go about this than through the music business.**

Whatever you do, however, be *realistic* about your goals. No matter how much you've always dreamed about becoming a singer, if you can't carry a tune in a bucket you had better look for another line of work!

Here's another point to keep in mind: Unless you are doing it just for fun, don't squander your efforts and energies on low potential goals such as bar band engagements for long. Keep looking to climb the ladder. Opportunities to get ahead are there if you *know how to go about finding them and have the motivation to do what needs to be done*.

Establishing "Game Plans"

Learn how to establish short-term goals as well as long-term ones. They serve two distinct purposes:

<u>Short-Term, Or "Tactical" Goals</u> should offer the immediate fulfillment our egos need. Moreover, they pave the way to our ultimate destination! Short-term goals serve as individual stepping stones or a springboard to the larger goals you have your eyes set on. Here's a tip: Make sure your goals are not *too lofty too soon*, or you're asking for a letdown.

<u>Long-Term, Or "Strategic" Goals</u> are the end result of what you are shooting for. For example, becoming a nationally recognized act or aiming for a number one spot in the charts are both good examples of long-term goals.

The Basics

Goals limited to being a successful local club or "weekend" act will differ from those of an individual aspiring to stardom. Although certain steps in your game plan will over-lap either way, the main thrust will differ considerably. Let's take a look at some key areas.

Success As A "Club Act"

1. **Perfect your vocal skills**. In these venues, you will probably want to liken your voice to or imitate the artist whose songs you will be singing. ("Club" audiences want you to sound like the original.)

2. **Polish up your appearance, stage presence and attitude**. You must come across in a professional manner if you are to be seen as a professional act.

3. **Put a good band together**. Concentrate not only on acquiring talented musicians, but also *reliable* ones. All too often, singers try to put a "super-star band" together only to find a mess of problems that usually start with egos! Remember, these are people that you are going to have to live with as well as perform with, especially if you plan to go on the road.

4. **Assemble an impressive publicity or promo pack**. This should include a good picture of yourself, a website and a recording *of your band* -- not studio musicians. (A club owner wants to know what you're going to sound like *on his stage!*) A professionally-done video is also a great door-opener.

5. **Find a good booking agent**. The best way to do this is through word-of-mouth, talking to club owners, or looking in the yellow pages of your phone book or on the web. See to it that you deal with an agent who books the types of venues or clubs that you are qualified to work.

6. **Make sure that your repertoire contains primarily "cover" or "copy" material**. People who frequent clubs want to hear what is on the radio or their favorite "oldies."

7. **Put a newsletter or web page together** once you have begun establishing yourself and develop a following. Solicit names and addresses of your new fans to send your newsletters to. This serves two purposes: (1) They will appreciate being kept informed as to where you are appearing, and (2) You'll be able to count on a better turn-out. Having a good following is a key consideration to club owners.

Secrets to Success in Country Music

Success As A "National Act"

Overall, the suggested steps under "Success as a Club Act" hold true in this area, as well. The main difference: Forget your "copy" mentality. Otherwise, here are additional areas that need to be addressed:

1. **Become a "big fish in a small pond,"** and use this as a springboard! Create as much "local" success as possible.

2. **Find a backer** to finance your future if you lack the funds.

3. **Do a professional recording session in Nashville.** This must include some strong, original material, *whether you wrote it or not*.

4. **Pursue radio airplay** once you have recorded, even if it is only on a limited or local level -- it gives you a regional star status. Remember, *any* airplay makes you *bigger than life*.

5. **Learn how to use airplay as leverage to obtain bookings** in high-visibility venues such as fairs, rodeos, festivals, theme parks and conventions.

6. **Create and take advantage of any publicity** that presents itself along the way, especially newspaper write-ups, radio interviews, TV talk shows and concerts. *Learn how to make a big deal out of everything*!

7. **Merchandise yourself.** Manufacture and sell CD's, T-shirts and whatever else you have (another reason to acquire adequate funding!).

8. **Find a booking agent** who can put you in the venues you need to be in, or *book yourself*. It's important to be able to "custom-tailor" your bookings.

9. **Find a capable manager** once your development warrants it.

10. **Submit your recordings to the major labels in Nashville.**

11. **If you are a writer** and as yet unpublished, submit originals to the better-known publishing houses, and/or start your own publishing company.

12. **Set up showcases** and contact key individuals for prospective bookings and/or label signings.

13. **Explore the possibilities** of finding an *endorsement* or *sponsorship* deal with a local or regional high-visibility business.

14. **Pursue overseas airplay and bookings**.

15. **Run ads in trade magazines** such as *Billboard* and *Amusement Business*. These magazines are widely read by industry people and talent buyers. Appearing in a nationally-circulated trade magazine is an effective credibility builder.

16. **Learn to recognize and take advantage of opportunities when they knock.** Genuine ones have a nasty habit of not coming around a second time!

There may be other areas you want to pursue. Our intention here is to mention key areas that will need to be addressed eventually.

Making Money With Your Music

Very few singers and musicians ever figure out how to *really* turn their talent into treasure, unless, of course, you consider $100 a weekend serious money! In fact, it is not overly difficult to make a comfortable living *without ever becoming a superstar or even having a record released*.

Although your primary motivation to succeed should be because of your love for music, **be prepared to look upon your music as a business**. Learn to think in terms of successful businessmen. That includes a healthy dose of a "Where is the money in it?" attitude. Though everyone should share the gift they have, problems begin when one *gives it away* too easily. Learn to recognize the monetary value of your talent. This is especially true if you are planning on making it your sole source of bread and butter.

If you're not polished enough to command a price for what you have to offer as yet, that's one thing. Otherwise, don't take your talent for granted -- others may, too! Everyone knows you don't get anywhere in life without *paying your own way*. Chances are, if you have been pursuing your music for a while, you have already invested a lot of time in developing your singing skills, as well as having shelled out a substantial sum for equipment, traveling expenses and who knows what else. Don't be shy. **If you have something to offer with your talent, make sure you are fairly compensated**.

_____Chapter 2

FINDING INVESTORS

"It takes money to make money."
Adage

Next to getting a major label "deal" (contract), probably most every struggling singer's biggest dream is being approached by someone who says, "I'm going to make a star out of you, no matter what it costs," -- and meaning it.

Almost all of country music's stars owe their success to financial backing somewhere along the way. You may be very surprised to learn this because celebrities seldom talk openly about, or reveal, these kind of "behind the scenes" scenarios. The group *Alabama*, for example, owe their legendary success in great part to a Dallas financier. Without his help, they most likely would never have achieved the superstar status they have enjoyed over the years.

Finding a backer is a lot easier than you think if you go about it properly. The key is being able to offer something worthwhile to an investor, *as well as* finding the right person. Remember, the main reason anyone invests -- other than family or close friends trying to help -- is to *make money*! A backer needs to see potential for a return, so the more realistic and lucrative your proposal, the better.

Do Your Homework

Make sure that you have a clearly-defined and thoroughly-outlined proposal before approaching a prospective backer. Regardless of how rich a person may be, *people do not part easily with their money if they are not spending it on themselves!* And this is particularly true if the individual does not understand the business you expect them to invest in. For this reason, the more business-like and knowledgeable you come across, the more likely you will be successful.

Try to project all your money needs in one package so you don't have to go back to your backer later with surprises. Don't be afraid to ask for as much as you think you

Secrets to Success in Country Music

need *providing you can reasonably substantiate your request.* (A fortune to you may be small potatoes to your prospective backer.)

I want to emphasize, *don't be afraid to ask!* The worse thing a person can do is say "No." Forget convenient cop-outs like "I really don't know who to ask." -- what that actually means is "I'm really too afraid to ask!" If you need the backing, get it! Otherwise, if you don't have the courage to ask for help to get started, you don't have the courage needed to succeed. End of story!

Why Look For Backing

Whether you are planning to open a restaurant, paying your way through college or trying to break into the music industry -- somebody's got to foot the bill. A good business person understands that *you need to spend money in order to make money*! Acquiring adequate funding to pursue your career is not only helpful but absolutely essential.

Typical Reasons People Need Backing:

- **Recording session costs.**

- **Independent record (CD) releases.**

- **Buying or leasing a tour bus.**

- **Band and stage equipment.**

- **Weekly retainers (salaries) for band while you are not working.**

- **Sponsoring promotional tours of radio stations.**

- **Manufacturing after-market items for sale, such as T-shirts, baseball caps, etc...**

Where To Look

The most obvious place one should begin to look for backers is among family and friends. They, more than anyone, should be aware of what you have to offer; plus, you have a head start knowing who may be willing *and able* to help you. Also, if you know your potential investor personally, you may be able to custom-tailor your proposal in a manner particularly appealing to them. Other than that, virtually *anyone* who has the financial means to help you is a prospective candidate.

Here are a couple of things to keep in mind: Often the type of person interested in this type of venture is a **maverick or gambler-sort willing to take chances** -- the kind who'll bet thousands of dollars a pop in Vegas and doesn't worry much about it.

An opportunity like this may also be very appealing to **an individual who has money but leads a rather mundane existence**. A person like this may be intrigued, and even star-struck, by the prospect of involvement with a future celebrity. The idea of riding a big tour bus, being amongst screaming throngs of fans, the glitz and the glamour -- might all provide a *vicarious substitute* for an otherwise uneventful lifestyle.

Just remember one thing, though. The music industry has always been viewed as a *high-risk investment*, so conventional wisdom might preclude a lot of otherwise potential candidates. "Typical" investors who feel safe with "sure things" like real estate will probably not be interested.

Suggested Approach:

- **Talk to family or close friends.**

- **Contact business acquaintances.**

- **Get leads from your banker or CPA. (They, if anyone, are familiar with the local "money people.")**

- **Get leads from "fans" eager to help.**

- **Talk to your local country station's program director for leads.**

- **Approach your favorite club owner (if you are playing in a club).**

- **Join your country club (or a civic organization) and do a little elbow-rubbing with the "right crowd."**

- **Approach several individuals suggesting the formation of a corporation, with each contributing a certain amount (their investment returned proportionately).**

- **As a last resort, advertise in a newspaper's classified section, business** journal, or on the web. If you find it necessary to do this, place your ad under the "Personal" or "Investments" categories of the publication. Make the ad read something like:

Talented and highly-motivated singer seeking financial backer for serious, long-term career launching project. Lucrative return.

Include your name and address (preferably a P.O. Box -- if you don't have one, get one) or e-mail address, but not your phone number, to avoid prank calls. Never use your home address, either.

Your Backer's Return

You and your backer's relationship will be of a symbiotic nature -- *you are benefitting each other.* Truthfully though, you need the backer more than he (or she) needs you (at least initially) *because he is the one holding the purse strings.* Chances are he already has the kind of money you'd like to have someday!

Although it shouldn't be necessary to "give yourself away," don't be greedy. Remember, 100% of nothing is nothing, and if the whole thing fizzles, it's the backer's financial loss, not yours.

Your request may range from a few thousand dollars for a basic demo session to a six-figure investment capable of funding a long-term, career-launching game plan. The amount you *recompense* (pay back) should depend on how much you are asking for and the *terms*.

Repayment will always be defined in terms of: (1) *area of return*, (2) *percentage of return*, (3) *time frame (length) of return*.

"Areas" Of Return You Can Offer:

- **Percentage of "net" artist royalties** from product sales -- CD's, cassettes, videos -- if you are signed to a major.

- **Percentage of "independently-manufactured" product sales** (CD's you get made up yourself).

- **Publishing royalties**, if you are the writer. This can be a "one song only" deal or a share of everything you've written (your entire *catalog*).

Finding Investors

- **Sharing revenues from live performance dates such as concerts.**

- **A share of "after-market sales,"** including T-shirts, caps, pictures, etc.

- **A percentage of profits from product sponsorships and endorsements.**

Sample Proposals

Here are some proposals you may wish to consider approaching your backer with. There is no specific rule of thumb regarding investment and return except that it be worthwhile for both you and the investor.

Proposal A

You are looking for $8,500 to do a three or four song recording session in Nashville. A suggested return might be:

1. 10% of your net profits for one year (if a major label signs you during that time-frame), and/or
2. 25% of gross profits from independently-manufactured CD's (future albums), and/or
3. Half of all gross sales going to the backer until the investment is repaid with a continuing 10% of all sales for another year (to sweeten the pie).

In Proposal A, you are offering a combination of three unrelated areas. #1 is contingent strictly upon being signed to a major label. The percentage (10%) can be increased, as well as the length of time, if need be. #2 deals with a financial return from CD's that you (or your backer) pay to manufacture, then sell at concerts, stores or wherever. This is potentially a very profitable area of return providing your product is vigorously marketed, since profits per unit can be as high as 900% (i.e. if *your* CD cost is $1 per unit and selling price is $10 = 900%). Neither #1 nor #2 require you to repay the investor; however, #3 takes a different approach. In this case, you and your backer (evenly) split the profits on product sales until your backer's investment is repaid, then a continuing percentage (10%) will be paid to him for a certain time (one year). This "extra" 10% is the actual profit in the deal for your backer, otherwise, his investment amounts to nothing more than a loan! If your backer invests $5,000, you must sell $10,000 worth of CD's for him to break even (1/2 of $10,000). Then, if within the next year you sell an additional $5,000 worth, your backer's profit will be 10% of $5,000, or $500.

Secrets to Success in Country Music

> **Proposal B**
>
> *You want $60,000 to do a recording session and shoot a video. A suggested return might be:*
>
> 1. 30% of your net profits for one year (if a major label signs you during that time-frame), and/or
> 2. 20% of publishing royalties (providing you are the writer), and/or
> 3. An additional 10% of money earned from concert performances for the next two years.

With Proposal B, you are asking for substantially more, consequently #1 offers a higher percentage of return, should you be signed by a major. In addition, #2 provides a percentage of *mechanical royalties* on publishing (20%), if you are the writer and own the publishing rights to the song. #3 offers a share of potentially-lucrative concert receipts to your backer.

> **Proposal C**
>
> *You want to record an album, release three singles (independently) and shoot a video. The basic cost of recording your album will be approximately $30,000. Three single releases, including promotions, will be approximately $20,000 apiece and your video will cost a minimum of $50,000. (Don't forget video promotional costs and additional money needed in reserve.) You need approximately $175,000. A suggested return might be:*
>
> 1. 25% of all CD's sold within a two-year period (major or independent label), and/or
> 2. 30% of any income from endorsements and sponsorships for two years, and/or
> 3. An additional 15-20% of money earned from concert performances for two years, and/or
> 4. 10% of after-market sales (T-shirts, etc.) for three years.

Proposal C not only deals with a return from CD sales (#1), but after-market sales (#4) as well. #2 offers a percentage of return should you receive a product endorsement (i.e. Reba McEntire for Fritos or Toby Keith for Ford), while #3 offers a percentage of concert revenues.

> **Proposal D**
>
> *You have a very well-to-do backer who totally believes in you and is willing to invest whatever it takes -- $50,000 or $500,000 -- to launch your career. A suggested return might be:*
>
> 1. A flat, one-third of all of your net revenues (what you, the artist, makes) for twenty years, including every area of return.

A deal like Proposal D could sound extremely tempting to an investor (providing he has deep pockets) because it offers an "umbrella"-type return -- he's in on everything. Any savvy businessman likes the potential of seeing a return from as many areas as possible. Although in this deal you're giving up a healthy chunk, look at it like this: *two-thirds of potential millions is still a lot of money!*

Here's one more "proposal" to think about. Since getting a record deal is always (at best) a long shot, an effective approach is a combination of focusing on a *recording session first*, then setting up a *showcase*. For an investment of about $20,000, this avenue can be a real opportunity for the artist, as well as a winner in terms of "cost vs. potential return" in the eyes of your backer. The fact is, a competitive, high-quality recording augmented with a professionally-produced showcase can go far in getting industry (label included) interest. And when you consider the further options a good recording provides along with the visual "sell" your showcase creates, it's more than a worthwhile investment! (Later chapters will provide further, detailed information on putting a plan like this together.)

Customizing Your *Own* Proposal

The figures and percentages in the preceding proposals are hypothetical. Although each could be considered realistic, you alone will have to custom-tailor any proposals for your prospective backers. Whereas one backer may invest $50,000 and be satisfied with a "10% of your royalties for one year if you are signed by a major" deal and nothing more, another may want to tie you up for everything they can for only a $5,000 investment!

Again, it's good to *know* your backer as well as possible. Figure out what motivates him or her and, most of all, how much you can count on them. Here are a few more pointers along that line:

Normally, a backer's *percentage or share* ranges from 10 to 30 percent for any particular area of return. The *length of time* for backer/artist commitments (as with percentages) can vary, however, two to five years could be considered the norm. Should a backer be providing "carte blanche" help -- continual investing until the goal is met, as in Proposal D -- expect a longer commitment, greater percentages and more areas of return to be included as well.

Whatever your proposal and final agreement, it's important to remember that the backer's share should come *after* other related expenses, not "off the top." Percentages due booking agents and managers are deducted first, leaving the *net* earnings for artist and backer to split. (You could always propose that the backer pay those expenses out of *his* share -- it's worth a try!)

It may also be prudent to include a "bail out" clause or *buy out option* in you and your backer's contract. Let's say someone very interested in helping you launch your career came along and wanted to buy your contract. If that individual was in a better position (financially or otherwise) to help, a move like this would be beneficial to you *and* your backer.

Whatever you do, don't over-commit. Even though it may not matter much (at the time) whether you offer 10% or 30%, one-year's or five-year's duration, be careful! In your eagerness to find money (particularly if you work with more than one backer), don't promise more than you can realistically *afford to repay* -- or worse yet -- *more than 100%* of what you take in. If you have three backers and commit 50% to each, you're in big trouble when it's time to pay up!

When dealing with strangers (even friends, for that matter), avoid coming across as overly-desperate or in an "I'll do anything" manner for the money -- or you may have to. (Females especially, *heed this warning*...) Always maintain an air of confidence which says, "If you don't recognize this opportunity, I can find someone else who will!" *Confidence* attracts investors.

Remember, the more articulate and convincingly you come across, the more your chances of success will increase. Put something together that *makes sense*. Always present your proposal (neatly!) on paper -- it looks so much more professional that way. (Check with a lawyer before signing any contracts, *especially* ones you don't understand.)

If your prospective backer turns your proposal down, you can always reapproach him offering additional areas of return, higher percentages or longer commitments. Don't be afraid to bargain a little if you sense a genuine interest. In fact, you might want to *make concessions gradually* instead of all at once. A little haggling shows the backer you are willing to give a fair share of yourself and *may actually increase your profits* if the backer will settle for less than what you are prepared to offer!

Finding Investors

Finally, make sure your backer understands that having cash behind you is a tremendous help in finding a label deal. Although labels seldom admit it, artists with substantial backing have a marked advantage. *Labels look at the big picture when they sign someone.* Considering the basic artist development budget of a label is normally anywhere from $500,000 to one million dollars, it's simply good business for the label to know *outside-funding* is available should the need arise.

If you're good and have serious backing, your chances of stardom increase a zillion percent.

(Sample "backer prospectus" and artist/backer contract/agreement can be found on Pages 169 & 170 in Supplements to Part I.)

_____Chapter 3

IMAGES & ILLUSIONS

"When you're a George Strait or Faith Hill looks-wise, you've won half the battle. The rest of us (as Avis says) 'have to try a little harder!'"

Bill Higgins

The entertainment industry survives in great part by creating *images*. These images and, in turn, the *illusions* they foster, are bought by the public and become the stuff "stars" are made of! In fact, images and illusions affect far more aspects of our daily lives than just entertainment. Think about it. When you buy a new brand of coffee, *you buy it because of what you see or hear* on TV, radio, billboards, magazines, as well as word of mouth from friends. Marketing and advertising agencies spend millions of dollars on creating color schemes, shapes, catchy names and whatever else it takes to make a specific product appeal to the public.

The same concept holds true with packaging talent. **The goal is to present an artist/act in a unique and appealing manner.** Images and illusions, to a great degree, define the basis of the *star quality* that ultimately sells an act.

"Image" Sells The Sizzle

Images and illusions capture people's imagination and attention. That is a key factor in a singer's success. Consider a few well-known examples:

- **Elvis** was cast as a rebel, a real come-on to young people.

- **The Dixie Chicks** are seen as talented, hot babes.

Secrets to Success in Country Music

- **George Strait** is seen as the All-American heartthrob, singing cowboy.

- **LeAnn Rimes** took off being cast as "a teenage Patsy Cline."

- **Reba McEntire** made it being as country and salt-of-the-earth as you can get.

- **Billy Ray Cyrus** took off by portraying machismo.

- **Shania Twain's** appeal is sex (with some vocal talent!).

- **Big & Rich, Gretchen Wilson** come on as "rockin' and rowdy."

- **Faith Hill** offers the ultimate in a beautiful (and sexy) "sweet girl next door that your parents always wanted you to marry" image.

- **Vince Gill** is an interesting combination: Mr. All-around nice guy, super voice, and an affable, almost Gomer Pyle-like personality.

- **Tim McGraw** and **Kenny Chesney** epitomize the "new country" image.

The "Illusion": An Extension Of Reality

While an image is relatively defined, an illusion remains abstract and subject to personal interpretation.

Everyone's image casts an illusion, to a degree. Though illusions are not reality, they attract and capture imaginations, and imaginations create whatever they want. Interestingly, illusions can work two ways: They make people see *what you want them to see*, as well as letting them see *whatever they want to see* in you.

Your image and any illusions it may foster depends on everything from the way you sing to the way you look and act. Little things have lots of impact, particularly *body language*. The way a person licks their lips, moves, brushes their hair, or holds a microphone can create sex appeal even though, physically, he or she may not be overly attractive. Like it or not, we live in an era of sexual connotations. *Sensuality* can be a big selling point.

But here's where an artist needs to be careful. "If the steak isn't as good as the sizzle" as the old saying goes, the illusion can flop. A good example of what I'm talking about was a girl who used to live next door to me. From a distance, when she was out in her swimsuit, she looked striking -- the goddess-type blonde, great tan, everything. But when you got up real close, she just wasn't all that hot. (Know what I mean?) As a singer, an illusion (or *gimmick*) should not be a substitute for talent but merely a *marketable extension* of it. Make sure your illusions *have substance* behind them.

You Are What You Are

It is said that true star quality runs more than skin deep. Be that as it may, "looks" are a definite plus for aspiring artists, *especially women*. **The female gender has always been and is still seen more in terms of physical beauty.** However, ladies, don't let that discourage you if you're not a perfect "10." For example, look at Wynonna Judd and Trisha Yearwood. They are both "big" girls but are cast as extremely attractive, feminine, and even sexy by the way they dress and carry themselves.

Men, on the other hand, are generally seen in terms of *character*. Even though today there has been a growing trend towards the soap-star, youthful "hunk" types, *character* -- whether it be facial or uniqueness of personality -- sells men. It's obvious that neither Garth Brooks' receding hairline nor Randy Travis' stoic "Vladimir the Russian Sailor" look has stood in the way of their stardom. In fact, many women find the characteristics of their appearance very attractive. **Aside from a lucky few with naturally-chiseled good looks, take away the tight jeans, the fancy belt buckles and Stetson hats, and you'll find that most of your stars are quite average-looking people.** One thing you can bet on, though, is that your heroes spend lots of time with a make-up man before they hit center stage or their camera shoot!

Defining Your Image

Finding a successful image means *the* right combination of an artist's voice, physical appearance and personality. It will be the basis of what people see in you. Images are and should be as personal as a signature. They must define you and make a statement. Remember, your image needs to be convincing, so be comfortable with it.

Play up your strong points and downplay your weaknesses. Learn to accept yourself, looks included. If you don't, you will not exude the positive image and "star aura" expected by your audience and fans.

Here's a suggestion: **Experiment with various "looks" and images in front of a mirror or with a VCR.** Figure out what works best *for you*. Don't waste your time and energies worrying about what you think may be shortcomings. Concentrate on accentuating the *positive things* you have to offer. Believe me, they are there.

Secrets to Success in Country Music

The old writing found in St. Paul's Cathedral back in 1692 that says something to the effect of: "Learn to change what you can change, but accept (and deal with) what you cannot...!" says it better than anything else.

Focus on your strengths. *If you've got it, flaunt it -- if you don't, find it!*

_____Chapter 4

THE ARTIST PACK
(Promo Pack)

"Your calling card"

The basis of what you have to offer as a singer is reflected in your artist pack, also referred to as a *promo pack* or *press kit*. This is your calling card -- make sure that it does you justice. Much of the interest you are able to cultivate from record labels, prospective managers, booking agents and buyers will be based upon the strength of this item.

Of course, in reality two factors will determine what comprises *your* package -- your actual *credits* and *available budget*.

Artist Pack Contents

Ideally, your artist pack should include:

1. A professionally-recorded, high-quality "demo."

2. Photo.

3. Narrative biography.

4. Press info (news clippings or such, if you have any).

5. A video.

6. Posters.

7. Website info.

8. Letters of recommendation.

Your Demo

Only a quality recording should be used. Don't even think about apologizing and saying, "I could have done better..." to a potential buyer. Make sure your demo is as good as you are realistically capable of at the time. If pre-recorded, karaoke-type music is all that is available to you, (as a last resort) use that. Better to use a quality, pre-recorded track for your demo than presenting something with an unprofessional or lousy-sounding band.

Make sure your demo reflects *who you are* musically and is *tailored to your goals*. Here is what I mean:

If you are aiming for clubs or bar-type engagements, concentrate on *copy* music. How well you and your band do the *cover songs* that people are used to hearing is what counts. Remember, your own artistic identity is not what is important in these venues. *How well you perform and imitate the hits is*! Club owners want to hear the band you plan on appearing with. Even if you supply a professionally-recorded studio tape, make sure you augment that with one of *you and your own band.*

If your artist pack is intended strictly for record labels or other career-launching directions, stick to primarily original material. Although honky-tonks want copy songs, record labels don't. They are not interested in launching new careers based on "rehash!" Make your *own signature* with your music. Whether you are or are not the writer, do your best to submit only original material.

Should your goal be the many fairs, festivals and rodeos which provide excellent opportunities for developing acts, I'd recommend a combination of both. For venues like these, it is vital that you present yourself as a genuine up-and-coming *Nashville recording artist* with original material because fairs and such like to offer something unique or "special" to their audience. This means featuring something more than just the local band from the corner bar. *However, here's the catch*: People relate to things that they have heard before. If you are still an unknown, it is important that you lean on cover songs *as well as* any originals to keep the audience interested. Combine your offerings with the best of both worlds.

Remember, if you are to be billed as a legitimate Nashville recording artist, it is essential that you are able to present a quality product of *music* actually recorded there.

Photo

Get as professional a picture done as possible. If you don't have the money to invest with a photographer, find a friend who knows something about taking pictures. Remember, the golden rule in promotional photography is *you are the most important element of the picture.* People want to see what you look like. Even though you might be a girl blessed with great legs (or whatever) or a Mr. Hunk, full-length shots are great for secondary photos; initially, however, concentrate on *head and shoulder* shots.

Keep the photos as simple as possible. Although composition of a picture is important, stick to simplicity. Too many "goodies" in the background compete with and distract from you, the focal point!

If you find it necessary to shop around for a photographer, ask to see some of their work. Explain what you want -- a "hip" looking photo. I have found that if you bring along a few examples of CD covers, you can present a better idea of what you are looking for.

A word of caution: Just because a photographer takes great wedding portraits doesn't mean that he or she can fit the bill for a good promotional shot.

It is best to stay away from the typical picture that grandma might like. You know what I am talking about: Grinning from ear to ear like a jackass while you're saying "cheese." It might be a good idea to practice posing in front of a mirror before you go to the photographer. Remember, the way you come across is important -- a picture is worth a thousand words. You would be amazed as to what lengths the stars go for the photos they want you to see.

(Sample photos can be found on Page 168 in Supplements to Part I.)

Narrative Biography

The objective is to tell the reader something of relevance and interest about yourself, preferably in a format that can be skimmed through in fifteen seconds or less.

As yet, readers honestly do not care about how many times you have been married or how many kids you have. Stick to information relevant to only you and your music -- anything outside that, make sure it is pretty doggone interesting. Whatever you do, don't write it up as a boring job resume!

A biography should be informative, interesting and must move right along. Avoid lots of self-serving praise like "She has an unbelievable voice with a four-octave range" or "He has the capacity to hold the audience spellbound with his phenomenal voice and will fill your club night after night."

Avoid the bull. Let a reviewer dole out the compliments. That will present a lot more credibility.

Structure your bio so that it starts in an interesting way. You might want to begin with a humorous angle -- even if you have to "stretch it" a bit to make it sound good. **Always start with your name** (in large, bold letters) and jump right into something like:

"***Tammy Jones*** *remembers the first time she sang a duet with Loretta Lynn. Of course, Loretta was on TV and eight-year old Tammy was at home in her pajamas!*

That was a long time ago. Today, Tammy is priming herself for a shot at Nashville and the big times..."

and so on.

Hopefully, at this point you have established reader interest. Next, go on into a chronological sequence starting with where you were born, what you studied in school, with lots of emphasis on who your greatest musical influences were -- this could include family as well as certain singing stars -- and what you are doing with your music now. Finally, state your goals with something like "*With a little bit of luck, Tammy Jones will soon become a household name to country music fans everywhere.*" At the very end, it might be helpful to tie the whole story together with the introduction in a humorous way, such as, "*And the next time she does a duet with Loretta, she won't be in pajamas!*"

The basic idea is to keep it all simple and interesting. Length should never exceed one typeset or printed page. Format for your bio should be a standard 8 1/2 x 11 sheet with your photo appearing in the upper left-hand corner and taking up anywhere from 1/5 to 1/4 of the page. The actual write-up can begin to the right side of the photo. As mentioned earlier, make sure it starts with your name in bold letters many times larger than the rest of the copy.

A word of caution: **Avoid using fluorescent-colored papers or ink**. This will only distract from what you have to say and will not reproduce well on copiers.

(Sample bios can be found on Pages 165 & 166 in Supplements to Part I.)

Press Info (News Articles)

Any articles, reviews or stories about you and your music should always be included in your promo pack. It is important to reveal what others think of you, particularly those in the media. We live in a media-oriented society -- what the media says is "the way it is" -- or at least that's what we are supposed to think. If you don't have any press releases or reviews as yet (of course, stick to only "good" ones for your promo pack!), create some. Any kind of angle that portrays you in a positive way will work. Consider doing a freebie for the local humane society or volunteer fire department.

Once you have targeted an organization, tell them what you have in mind. I can almost guarantee you that they will be excited and grateful. Next, contact the local media. This includes newspapers, radio and TV. *Aside from making you feel good about doing something worthwhile*, you can count on some valuable publicity, which could include a story in the local paper, PSA's (public service announcements), and interviews on radio and TV.

Let's face it. There is way too much negativity in what we see (or hear!) in the media. It's up to us to change things. We may not be able to control what happens in other countries half-way around the world, but I believe God put a "do-good" ministry in all of us.

This reminds me of something I did along these lines a few years ago. My dog had just had a heart attack, and his prognosis was not good. I adopted him as a little pup at the humane society while traveling through Sioux Falls, South Dakota, ten years earlier. I wanted to show my gratitude for getting a great pet and also kind of wanted to "immortalize" my dog because I did not know how much longer he would be around. So I called the humane society in Sioux Falls (1,100 miles away) and told them I would like to arrange a "ten-year reunion" just for fun -- would they be interested? I thought we could get some real good press and help place animals in new homes along with it.

WOW! What a success! I had contacted the largest of the three TV stations in the area, as well as the daily newspaper. When I arrived a few days later with Hobbie my Doberman, a film crew was eagerly awaiting at the humane society shelter. They went ahead and shot a very interesting (and touching, I might add) two-minute or so story that appeared on the news that night. It was great! What made it even better was the fact that little tidbits of our "reunion" appeared every half hour from 6 PM until news time.

The results were just what I had hoped for: Enormously successful! The publicity turned out to be a blessing for the humane society because they received all kinds of inquiries, donations and phone calls offering to adopt pets. It proved to be an immensely wonderful event for all. (Sadly, my dog died two weeks after we came home.)

To be perfectly honest, the publicity in this whole undertaking had not been one bit for me -- it was for something much more worthwhile. In this case, it was because of my love for God's four-legged critters! It just shows you that by using a little creativity, you can get things done *especially if you believe in what you're doing!* I almost forgot to mention, the Sioux Falls daily newspaper also ran an excellent story on our little reunion, along with a nice color picture of me and my dog! (See Page 167 in Supplements to Part I.)

It is always important to contact the proper source at the venue you are going after. At newspapers, ask to speak with the city, regional or local editor in charge of *human interest stories*. If you've done any professional recording, you might also want to talk to the music editor or music reviewer.

At TV stations, contact the *news department*, and when pursuing radio, ask for the *program director* or *news department*. (Most stations provide a certain number of free daily PSA's -- public service announcements -- for charity and benefit events.)

Video

It could arguably be said that a music video offers more than any other promotional tool in your artist pack. A buyer can see, hear, and in short, actually experience you, the artist. An excellent video is undeniably a very effective sales tool -- however, the word *excellent* is the catch.

If you are considering a video project, first and foremost you must have a strong recording. After all, *the song* is the backbone of every video. If you want a truly competitive CMT or VH1 quality video, it must not only be good, but an absolutely top shelf, professionally-done product. This is another area where a healthy budget makes the difference. (Another reason for backers.) Whereas a professional-quality Nashville recording only costs you in the range of $8,500, a competitive video project begins at somewhere around $50,000! I'm talking about having it done with the major leaguers such as Deaton-Flanigan -- the biggies whose work you watch on TV!

If this kind of "advanced" financing is not in the cards for you as yet, there are a couple of other options. However you go about it, remember that you need a good recording as the basis of the video. I suppose if you can't afford anything else, here again, you could always use a good quality, pre-recorded accompaniment soundtrack (but we all know that you would not go up for any Grammy nominations!).

Let's take a look at a few alternate options for shooting your video:

1. **Contact your local cable TV station.** Become a producer member or approach them with a *trade-off deal*. Here is the offer: You perform free of charge on some shows if they shoot the video footage. Your obvious objective is to get something done with professional people using state-of-the-art equipment. This could prove to be a great door-opener on a local or regional level while expanding your "networking" efforts at the same time.

2. **Contact your local high school or college** to find out if they have any communications courses. Chances are, the instructor might be very interested in attempting a country music video as a special project for his or her students -- particularly if your song or record really impresses them.

3. **Find a friend with a camcorder who has a steady hand** and at least enough common sense not to aim into the sun -- the old standby budget plan! If you work up an interesting little clip, it could serve its purpose until you have enough saved up to do something more professional -- or even help you find a backer.

Actually, producing a clip as in option #3 is quite simple and could be a lot of fun. All you have to do is act out a little skit to your music. The soundtrack can be recorded either through the camcorder's external mike or "direct" input. (Camcorders have an input/output for an outside music source if you are not using the built-in mike.) All you must do is synchronize your singing and acting with the music. Try to lip synch closely where your face is seen; otherwise, your video will turn out like one of those "spaghetti westerns" -- where the American actor's lips and words seldom match the original Italian! With a little creativity you could come up with an effective promotional tool. Make sure the final product is available on DVD.

Posters

This item, as a video, is an option that can add a real touch of professionalism to your artist pack. The underlying theme behind a poster is, again, creating the *illusion of being bigger than life*. It portrays you as a successful up-and-coming new act. People normally associate posters with big names, so they are likely to look at them. Here are some basic criteria for creating a professional-looking poster:

- **Make sure it says "Nashville Recording Artist" visibly at the top.** Of course, if you want to maintain your integrity, make sure that there is some semblance of truth to this. (In other words, you can't just record in Buffalo, not having anything whatsoever to do with Nashville and at the same time be honest about it.) In reality, a Nashville recording artist is someone *who has recorded in Nashville* or *done a vocal overdub to tracks cut in Nashville.* Even if you have done nothing more than spend ten dollars in a recording booth in Nashville, theoretically, you could consider yourself a Nashville recording artist (although that is s-t-r-e-t-c-h-i-n-g it a bit!).

- **Feature an attractive photo of yourself.** Remember, it has to be eye-catching. The photo should be placed either in the upper left-hand section of the poster or smack dab in the middle with printed info appearing over or around it.

- **Include your name in bold letters under "Nashville Recording Artist."**

- **Use the bottom few inches of the poster for two lines practically running the entire width.** These lines should be one or two inches apart, and the beginning of one should say "Appearing At" and the other "Time and Place."

These blank lines serve two purposes:

1. **They provide a place for pertinent information regarding an actual performance.**

2. **The lines are a great place to sign autographs.** For example, "Many thanks to WYRK Radio, signed Charlie Barrett" or "Lots of Love, Tammy Jones."

- **Print a stenciled box** stating *"On Tour -- Nashville's Hottest New Act"* or something similar *in red* on your poster. This can be placed at an angle over the picture or off to the side. For maximum effect, everything should be in black, except the stenciled box. Use red ink to fill in the information on the lines. This will really make it stand out. (Always be conservative in the use of a second color -- the more you use it, the less impact it will have.)

- **If you have ever had a record release or any radio airplay,** you might want to include that information, as well, to associate with. Find a place on the poster to put the name of the song, which is normally printed in quotation marks. If you can't capitalize on that point, you might want to add a little come-on instead, like *"Don't miss this red-hot newcomer everyone is talking about"* to create even more attention. Whatever you do, keep the poster easy to read and well-balanced. In other words, simple, attractive and informative. Best of all, people have a tendency to hang posters up, which provides continuous free advertising.

Believe me, if you have CD's to sell after a performance *and offer a free signed poster* to boot, you will increase sales like crazy!

Another Tip: A signed poster can be extremely effective when targeted at a radio station along with your CD. For example: "Thanks to WFMB for all your help, signed Jeff Wyles." This not only serves as a decorative piece of promotion from you, but psychologically (subliminal suggestion) presents a "done-deal" concept to the radio station and may help in generating credibility for airplay as well.

Here's something else to think about: Whereas old-fashioned colored glossies were quite expensive, posters are not only much more "hip," but also cost-effective. A typical 11 x 17 size, which is available at all quick-print shops, should cost you under $100 for a quantity of two to three hundred. You might ask to see the various types of paper available, although it is my bet that you will prefer a *coated* or *semi-glossy* stock. If your budget can handle it, you might want to contact a *full-service printer*, who can provide posters in much larger sizes, or in color. (Of course, the cost will also increase.) Use your imagination in the layout and design. Feel free to follow the formats in this book. Any print shop will be glad to help you put it together as well. (Samples can be found on Pages 163 & 164 in Supplements to Part I.)

Website

A virtual "given" these days. However, if you don't have one yet, it might be good to wait until you earn a few *legitimate* credits, such as a professionally-done recording. As with any interview or newspaper article, you've got to have something to talk about or show! (Visit author's website at www.gabrielmusicgroup.com.)

Letters of Recommendation

Any time you conclude a performance or show, it's important to obtain a good reference. A solid letter of recommendation is a very effective tool. (Sample found on Page 160 in Supplements to Part I.)

Keep it simple, informative and "easy on the eyes!"

Chapter 5

BARS, HONKY-TONKS & KARAOKE

"I was nineteen years old and it was my first real job as a singer at a place called Pauline's. What a dump, but there were always a lot of chicks. To a shy, skinny kid like me, I thought, 'Wow, this is it!'"

Gabriel Farago

The corner bar is quite often the "proving ground" and first paying engagement a singer finds. A lot of people assume that playing these places is where you get your start if you want to make it in the business. Not so. Playing clubs is no guarantee whatsoever of success in the long run.

As with anything else, performing in bars and clubs has its pro's and con's. How much emphasis you put on these types of venues should depend on *your goals*.

Let's take an objective look:

Positive Side Of Club Work

1. **You can develop your confidence** and acquire valuable experience in front of an audience. Since few people are born entertainers, it provides a place to develop the skills that will be needed later on.

2. **It is possible to make some money**, although you are generally restricted to playing weekends unless you are doing the club circuit on the road. The average pay that you can expect is probably about $50 a night.

3. **Although the possibility of being discovered in a club exists**, your chances of being struck by lightning or winning the lottery are higher!

Negative Aspect Of Club Work

1. **You are forced into copycat situations**. This is the "Catch-22" if you're trying to make it as an artist. The more you sound like Tim McGraw or Shania, the better the crowd and owner like it. You might as well get one thing straight right now: Nobody cares about your *own identity;* they want you to sound like what is on the radio. That's what brings people in and sells drinks!

2. **People go to clubs to party, drink and socialize**. They are seldom there to see a struggling new singer trying to make it doing his or her own thing. Trying to develop as a new act, in a situation like this, might even be a turn-off to the audience. Once again, whatever is hot on the charts and CMT is what the clientele want to hear. Clubs don't offer *captive audiences* unless it is a big name in concert.

3. **There can be a fine line between developing confidence and becoming a legend in your own mind**. Don't be overly flattered when people come up to you in a club saying, "What are you doing here -- why aren't you in Nashville?" Chances are, these people say exactly the same thing to other singers and bands.

Entertainers often kid themselves when they get a good response to a particular song. The truth is, a bar crowd almost always *applauds the song* because of its popularity, or the crowd is just plain "ready to party!" A good beat and flowing booze always makes for a "great" performance. If nothing else, the audience often applauds the frenzy they create for themselves!

Remember, hearing only what you want to hear is a great way of losing touch with reality. Don't be disappointed if Warner Brothers or RCA do not call the next morning just because the crowd went nuts when you did "Old Time Rock 'N' Roll" or "Friends In Low Places."

4. **Your health should always be a consideration in everything you do**. The fact is that the air is always terrible in the average bar. There is probably no better example of *concentrated second-hand smoke* anywhere on the planet!

If I make the honky-tonk route look awfully bleak, it is only because I am trying to be objective. True, some of today's stars got started that way, but it was generally due to a matter of convenience or simply not having the means or know-how to go about it otherwise.

As I had mentioned in the chapter dealing with "Goals," a lot of singers and musicians are not really interested in trying to make it big; they just want to have fun, play some good music, make a few dollars -- and there is nothing wrong with that. What it comes down to is that bars are fine for fun and experience *as long as you know when to get out* if "making it" is your goal.

"King Of Karaoke"

The sing-with-the-tape craze hit in the 1990's like gangbusters! The concept of giving everyone an opportunity to be a star -- at least for a few minutes -- has proven itself to be enormously successful. And there is probably no greater ego trip for the average bar-goer who thinks that he or she can sing.

As with a "bar band" situation, karaoke can be useful in developing your confidence and stage presence, but that is about it. The greatest compliments you can expect to receive are "She sounds just like Gretchen Wilson!", or "If you closed your eyes, you would have sworn it was Alan Jackson!" Voice-wise, there is but one rule -- *imitate the original as closely as possible*. The *original artist* is, in reality, getting the credit, not you!

The only problem I've ever had with karaoke is that **some people take it much too seriously**. I have seen individuals actually change outfits for different songs and really get caught up in what amounts to nothing more than a little fantasy. Imitating, pretending, and maybe even winning a contest is okay, but that's where the ride ends. If you're looking for reality, the truth is *the industry is not interested in "sound-alikes."* Although karaoke may be a great time, it presents a misconception as to what getting ahead in the music business is all about.

Chapter 6

THE MOVE TO NASHVILLE

"Welcome to Music City, USA"

Interestingly, few people in the music business are originally from Nashville. They've come from all over, every state in the union, Canada, Australia and Europe, as well. You'd be surprised as to how many in the industry (including bigshots and superstars) migrated to the Mecca of Country Music from afar.

There are basically *four reasons* people aspiring to succeed within the music industry move to Nashville:

1. **Make it as an artist (singer)**

2. **Make it as a songwriter**

3. **Make it as a session (studio) musician, backup singer or studio engineer**

4. **Get successfully involved in the business end of the industry -- record companies, record production, publishing, artist management, booking agencies, etc...**

Though many accept relocating to "Music City" as a given if they are truly serious, the question arises, is the move in *your* best interest -- and, is the *timing* right? Let's look at reality: *Just moving to Nashville in itself means nothing.* Get your ego under control for a minute and remember there are tens of thousands of talented people wanting to do the same thing. Those (few) who make it in Nashville are usually those who have a mapped out strategy of some kind. Among other things, this means having your financial backing in place. Your chances of success will increase dramatically if you do.

"Pro's" Of The Move

Relocating to Nashville could be considered a virtual must if you are a songwriter. The town is crawling with writers. Just about every club has an "open mike" or writer's night, and your chances of making contacts at these affairs are good. Although you shouldn't count on actually being "discovered" at one of these writer's nights, you are able to showcase what you have to offer in front of lots of other writers and industry people.

You have the opportunity to meet others aspiring to the same goals, and it's a chance to see and hear what the "competition" is coming up with! This also presents a good opportunity to find people to co-write with. Most hit songs these days are co-written, often by more than just two people. Of course, some might complain that the downside of such *writer's nights* is that others may steal your ideas and come up with a song first. (Wouldn't you have a chance to get new ideas, too?!) Look at it like this -- life's a trade-off!

Many people find Nashville offers a much friendlier atmosphere than the other major music centers of New York and L.A. A genuine sincerity seems to prevail with a feeling of "family" and others willing to help you. At least on the surface, people don't seem to look at one another as real competition, but rather as a potential alliance for networking and possibly doing things together down the road.

The most obvious advantage of living in Nashville, however, is **being able to make those all-important personal contacts**. This is difficult from 2,000 or even 200 miles away.

The Down-Side Of The Move

So why not just unequivocally say, "Let's go?"

Surviving in Nashville must be a primary consideration especially if you have a family or others depending on you. Although the musical circle may seem warm enough at first, it gets "cliquish" once you reach a certain point.

Believe it or not, *the city is not just waiting for you (or anyone else) with open arms*. Unless you have a trade or profession, you will most likely fall within the ranks of thousands of other hopefuls (also known as "starving musicians") that trod the sidewalks of Music Row every day. You may need to work as a "pump jockey" or waitress to survive. Whatever you do, don't go with the notion that once you arrive, you'll instantly be discovered and live happily ever after!

Another important point to consider is that **success generally comes very slowly**. You must have a *lion's heart* and *thick skin* to handle the countless rejections you will experience. Be prepared for that, or you will be on the next bus home!

Don't count on making much money as a performer with your music in Nashville itself. There are a lot more musicians and singers than there are club gigs. Chances of landing a weekly spot on the Grand Ole Opry right off the bat aren't real likely.

If you are counting on making a living with your music, unless you break into session or demo work, you'll probably have to go out on the road, as you would otherwise. From this point of view, however, working out of Nashville offers two distinct advantages:

- **A great opportunity to find excellent musicians for your band, and**

- **Being able to legitimately bill yourself as "Direct from Nashville," which is a great selling point in itself.**

Overall, it would be to your advantage to stay home and get as "polished" as you can. Become a "big fish in a small pond" first -- then make your move. The credibility you earn back on a regional level can be extremely helpful in opening the right doors in Nashville later on. Remember, if you can't make it at home, you can't make it anywhere!

The Scout Motto: "Be Prepared"

If you are determined to move to Nashville no matter what, *at least do a minimum of preparation* for the undertaking. If at all possible, go for a visit even if it's just for a few days to get a feel for the town and hopefully establish a few basic contacts. If that is not feasible, call *The Tennessean,* Nashville's daily newspaper. Ask to have a copy of the paper's classifieds sent to you so you can find out what employment opportunities and housing options exist.

Concentrate on landing a job within the industry such as at a record company or publishing house. Even though an initial job in the mailroom might not be very glamorous, it could put you in the midst of the action and help start building your contacts. (Kris Kristofferson, as the story goes, got his start by hiring on as a janitor at Columbia Records.)

Make sure that you have a substantial amount of cash, at least enough to tide you over for a few weeks. It might be embarrassing (and unpleasant, to say the least) to have to spend the night in the city mission or on a park bench waiting for Western Union to open (for your bus fare home!). Remember, all those stories about living on peanut butter and jelly sandwiches are interesting topics for talk shows, but are not nearly as neat when they happen to you, or worse, your family, too.

Use a little "business sense" and put the odds in your favor before you make your move, lest you become victim of an *"Everybody wants to move to Nashville, but just about everybody winds up going home!"* eventuality.

Chapter 7

SONG-WRITING

"It's all in the song."
Harold Bradley

Although this chapter is certainly not intended to be a definitive guide to song-writing, it addresses a few basic points that I believe are of extreme importance to aspiring writers.

A lot of people go into the song-writing process with the notion "As long as I can sing, I can write." Truthfully, the two areas have nothing to do with each other. **Although there are many successful singers who write well, there are as many writers who can't sing and singers who can't write!**

Think about it like this, generally speaking, most singers have been "honing" their craft since they were kids. The average person has probably been singing longer than they can even remember.

Song-writing, on the other hand, is a whole different thing. Most likely your first attempt at writing a song was when you were already somewhat older. It was probably in the form of a love poem talking about a broken heart. That is how it usually begins; however, song-writing takes years to perfect.

Writing a successful song is a process that requires a definite knowledge of how a song needs to be structured *as well as* the inspiration which gave it life. Remember that within the industry, a successful song means a *marketable song* -- one that will sell!

A Song's "Anatomy"

The first step in the creation of a song is finding or picking a theme. There has to be a common thought or thread to inspire the song -- lost love, happy love, your favorite dog, closeness to God, whatever. In country music, the love theme seems to be most prevalent, probably because everyone can relate to it.

Be careful, however, of the way you present the theme. Be sure it is not overly hidden or deeply philosophical, making it hard to understand. It's like telling an inside joke -- only those who know about it will laugh. **With a song the goal is to make people relate**. The more that do, the more likely it will be a success.

Though the song itself may present a great theme, the challenge lies in *not only getting the listener's attention, but holding it.* Let's look at five areas vital to the structure of a good song:

1. **Title**

2. **Theme**

3. **Unfolding of the story**

4. **The "pay-off"**

5. **Chorus or refrain**

Title: *Make it catchy from the git-go*! People do judge a book by its cover. A catchy title can mean a lot. Sum up the theme of the song into as few words and as interestingly as possible. Although there are exceptions, try to stick to titles that are at most six words in length.

Theme: The theme is the heart of the song. *Is it universally appealing; can people identify?* Once again, make sure you pick something relevant. Some themes can be *timely* (the war in Iraq), which could mean *gimmicky* as well. Whereas love, heartbreak and happiness are eternally a part of life (and songs), social issues such as environment, peace on earth, racism and strife need to be capitalized on while they are *hot* in order to be marketable.

The Unfolding Of The Story: Your song must move along and present a situation which "unravels" in the listener's mind. *Is it going anywhere? Does it present "hills and valleys,"* the musical and lyrical highs and lows? Unlike video or movies, when we hear a song (as in reading a book), *we must visualize what is going on.*

The most successful writers are not only those who come up with good ideas, but are able to paint pictures in your mind. The more we are able to visualize the story, the more it affects us spiritually and emotionally. We all know there are songs that can put us in the dumps with gloom and songs that lift us high in the sky with fun and joy.

Country music fans -- more than any others -- pay attention to lyrics, so make sure your song says something.

Pay-Off: *This is what everyone is waiting for*, the point where the song is headed. As Harold Bradley, my former producer, mentor and hero once said to me in the studio, "Gabriel, this is where the song goes to glory." He was talking about the crescendo or climax -- the "pay-off" of the song. Generally, the pay-off is the fulfillment -- the point where it all comes together. However, it can also be in the form of a repetitive theme or chorus that is sung over and over.

Chorus Or Refrain: This area is generally a series of repetitions and usually contains the main theme or "hook" of the song. "The Gambler" by Don Schlitz probably had one of the best choruses ever in the lines *"You've got to know when to hold 'em..."* The chorus or refrain is the part of a song most people remember, the part they sing along with.

Another important point, make sure the song is not *too long.* Occasionally I hear songs from hopeful writers that just go on and on, verse after verse, kind of like Gordon Lightfoot's "Wreck of the Edmund Fitzgerald." While that was a great song, country radio doesn't like those marathon numbers. Keep it short and sweet, close to three minutes, not much longer.

One of the most effective ways of learning how to write a successful song is by carefully scrutinizing hit songs themselves. If you listen objectively, the points we have briefly talked about in this chapter will make even more sense to you. As long as you know what you are listening for, things will come across in a different way and shed new light on your understanding of -- and ability to create -- a good song.

Chapter 8

PUBLISHING

"The gift that keeps on giving"

Publishing is an immensely important and lucrative area of the country music industry. It deals primarily with the *ownership of songs* and *payment of royalties*. You could almost think of a publisher as a "clearing house" of sorts -- writers need publishers to get their songs recorded, while singers (who don't write) need to find good songs!

How A Publisher Works

Publishers, or publishing houses (in the musical sense) represent writers by administering their songs and *pitching* them to major recording artists. If the publisher is successful in its efforts and gets a *cut* (song recorded), it then splits earnings with the writer, usually 50/50. The money a publisher earns comes from several areas that include product sales and performance royalties.

Let's take a look at the two "categories" individuals fall into:

For Singers Who Don't Write

Publishers function by *providing material*. Strong, *career-launching caliber* material is essential to a singer's success. Besides that, it's a known fact publishers have lots of "clout." They can help an artist get signed to a label. Although artists who are both singer and writer offer a more "attractive" package, publishers may still push someone who doesn't write if they feel the individual has potential to cut hit records (theirs, of course!).

Garth Brooks and George Strait are great examples of superstars who *don't* write. You can't get any bigger in the industry than these two. (Great news for all you "non-writers" out there.)

A case in point: Although I am a writer, my first chart single (a song not written by me) belonged to a well-known Nashville publisher. They were excited enough about my "cut" to the extent of putting two of their own promoters (at *their* expense) on the project. The reasoning: help get more airplay, stimulate record sales, and make more money (royalties)!

For Singer/Writers Or Writers Only

Publishers function in three ways:

1. **They can represent the writer** (the song) on an individual, *song-for-song* basis. This means no extended commitment.

2. **The publisher may purchase** an *entire catalog* of songs from a writer or another publisher. These catalogs may contain dozens or even hundreds of *titles* (songs). Sometimes the publisher will, for a fee, simply *administer* catalogs, which means handling and licensing the songs without actually owning them.

3. **Publishers may sign a writer** to an *exclusive writer's contract*. Although the time frame may vary, it's generally for a period of two to three years. All works written during that time belong to the publisher.

Assignment And Ownership Of Songs

It's important to remember that whenever a writer is dealing with a publisher and assigning ("giving") songs to them, the writer *always* retains the *writer's portion*, and assigns the *publishing rights only*. In this way, the writer will always "own" (the actual creation of) the song itself.

Publishing rights are assigned to a publisher for a limited time only. After the stated timeframe, the *rights* to your song revert (go back) to you. This is called a *reversion clause*. Make sure you read your publishing contract thoroughly (even if it's technical and boring) to see that it contains a reversion clause, otherwise the song(s) will belong to the publisher forever! (The only way you can get your songs back then is by buying them back!)

The Nashville Songwriters Association has created an atmosphere in which the rights of a song will go back to the writer within a year if the song has not been cut by a major act.

Publishing

"Mechanical" Royalties

All royalties coming from the sale of product -- records, CD's, cassettes -- are referred to as *mechanical royalties*. These royalties are paid to your publisher through the Harry Fox Agency (or one of several other *licensing* agencies) whose function it is to collect mechanical royalties for publishers. The current royalty rate is 9¢ per song sold (or manufactured). This means that if one of your songs is a cut on a George Strait album that sells 1,000,000 copies, your publisher would receive .09 x 1,000,000 = $90,000. This money (minus Harry Fox's fee) would in turn be split between you and your publisher -- the *writer's portion* and *publisher's portion*. Mechanical royalties are paid to the writer regardless of whether he or she is the artist singing the song.

Splitting Royalties

Since publishing is such big business, it's common to have two, three or even more publishers collecting money from a single song! Here's what often happens. Let's say "Bogáncs Music" is the name of your publishing company and you get a cut on that George Strait album we talked about. It's entirely likely that George Strait's publishing company will want to *split publishing* with Bogáncs Music on that song, even though George had nothing to do with writing it! That means giving up a share, or splitting, your royalties. If you refuse, you may not get your cut (song) on the album. But that's the industry -- a piece of the pie is better than no pie at all.

Splitting royalties can also work conversely. Offering a *publisher's share* of a royalty can be used *to lure* a popular artist's interest to record a particular song.

Performance Rights Societies

We've all seen the initials BMI, ASCAP or SESAC on records, sheet music, or wherever. They stand for *performance rights societies*, whose function is to collect *performance royalties*.

"Performance" Royalties

Performance royalties come from the actual "performance" (not sales) of the music, either "live" (clubs or concerts) or recorded format such as airplay on radio stations, TV or jukeboxes. Unlike mechanical royalties, performance royalties are paid *direct* and *separately* to the publisher and writer. Here's a sweet bonus: If a writer belongs to a performance rights society *and* is the publisher (even if he starts his *own* publishing company), that individual will always receive what is referred to as a 200% (double) royalty -- 100% for writer, 100% for publisher. For performance royalties sake, it's very important *to be affiliated* (with a performance rights society) as a *writer and publisher*. Each performance rights society has its own method of calculating royalties, either basing them on sample loggings (estimated) or actual "performance" counts.

Joining A Performance Rights Society

Without being a member, you will never get a cent for airplay royalties, even if you write what becomes a hit record! It's simple enough. Contact the society you wish to be affiliated with for an application. (Names and addresses in Part II, Appendix C.)

Starting Your Own Publishing Company

Join a performance rights society as a writer first. To become a *publisher member,* pick a name for your company (actually, pick several, in case your preference name already exists), and your society will register it. Although as a *writer* you can affiliate with only *one* performance rights licensing society, as a publisher you can be a member of all three (under three *different* publishing company names).

Mechanical Licensing

This is a technical procedure which allows an artist or label to "officially" release a song on a record. Normally, the record label you are signed to assumes this responsibility, or you can contact the publisher yourself. You will need to provide the *song's title, writer's name, society affiliation, record label, artist name* and *release date*. The publishing company's mechanical licensing department will issue the license, which is, in fact, a letter of consent and agreement that you will pay the current royalty for each record sold (or manufactured).

What About Recording "Cover" (Previously Recorded) Songs?

Technically, recording songs that have already been out poses no problem. This may come as a surprise to many, but songs in that category -- whether they be Elvis' or Garth's biggest hits as well as Johnny Nobody's most obscure release -- are granted "automatic" licensing. The only problem the "cover song" scenario presents (to newcomers) is that **recording well-known songs is actually *counter-productive* to career-launching attempts.** Why? The industry is looking for *new* sounds and identities, not rehash. That's not to say that an *established artist* can't do an update of an older record (i.e. The Judds' "Don't Be Cruel," Alan Jackson's "Summertime Blues," Faith Hill's "Piece of My Heart"), it just means that *new* artists are much better off sticking to previously *unrecorded* material.

To obtain *mechanical licensing* for the "remake" of a song, go through the same procedure as you would with recording brand new material.

What Publishers Look For

If you're looking for a "writer deal," obviously, hit songs! Otherwise, if a writer shows a lot of "raw" potential, he or she may be signed to an exclusive contract even though they may not have anything red-hot right yet. The problem is, getting a large publisher to even listen to your material as a new/unknown writer is tough. It's basically as competitive as getting signed to a major label. Without any track record, or without the credibility and clout of a record company, well-known manager or entertainment lawyer to represent you, you're just another wanna-be.

Here are a few "sneak-in-the-back-door" techniques to get your songs heard:

Three Door-Opening Strategies

1. **Contact a *song-plugger* at the publisher and do your best to convince them you're worth their time!** Dropping a few "names" is always helpful. Just sending a demo without prior agreement will probably get it returned with an "unsolicited" stamp, or simply discarded. Make sure you send nothing but your very best!

2. **If you have the opportunity to "demo" a publisher's song, you have an open-door of sorts.** Publishers are always interested and willing to listen to *quality* cuts of *their* songs. When submitting the demo (either by mail or in person), you have an opportunity to "slip in" a few of your own!

3. **Approach the publisher (song-plugger) with the intent of *soliciting new material for yourself* to record.** If they are willing to work with you, the publisher may request a demo of your voice to help them find the right kind of material. The publisher will "pitch" their songs to

you in one of two ways: putting several songs together (for you to pick up), or giving you an appointment to come in, then playing some selections while you are in their office. Obviously, being there in person is infinitely more preferable.

If you're fortunate enough to meet with the publishing company personally, be gracious and show interest in a few (even if you don't care for any) of their songs. Accept the offer to take a demo of the material you "liked." At some point during your meeting (especially if they haven't heard you yet), ask if they could indulge you by listening to a bit of *your own* material. Use the excuse that you're "looking for something a little more like this." Or, just ask for some feedback on your demo while you're in their office. The objective is to get *your* songs heard. They will quite likely give you a few minutes of their time.

Of course, if you *really are* in the market for songs for yourself, remember that big publishers are reluctant to provide top-shelf material (or often *any* material) to unknowns. Yes, they *do* save their "best" for "name" artists! Their reasoning is why waste a potential hit on a nobody? A hit record could be worth hundreds of thousands, even millions to a publisher! An unknown artist not on a major label isn't likely to cause much of a stir. There is no *performance-royalty* or *mechanical-royalty* incentive to speak of. Plus, "exposing" a hit-potential song could wreck the *original* aspect of it, perhaps discouraging interest from a "name" artist later on.

Interestingly, there have been occasional exceptions to this reasoning. Don Schlitz, writer of Kenny Rogers' monster-hit "The Gambler," released a record of the song himself (on an independent label), making a modest dent in the charts *before* Kenny's. And another example -- a bizarre one, dealing with recording cover material by "unknowns" -- was the song "Suspicion," recorded by Elvis Presley in the early '60's. It was a hit for Elvis, but amazingly, an even bigger hit for an Elvis sound-alike by the name of Terry Stafford a short time later!

(List of publishing companies can be found in Part II, Appendix C.)

Chapter 9

THE MAJOR LABELS

*"It's like a football team. They either
need you or they don't!"*

Jimmy Bowen

It's a virtual given that every singer out there wants a *label deal!* Consequently, record companies are constantly deluged with demos and inquiries from hopefuls. This is for good reason. The major labels set the standard and control the industry.

The likelihood of "making it big" is almost non-existent without being signed to a major label. There are currently about eight "majors" in Nashville and a handful of independent labels that have had somewhat of a success on a national level. A few major artists like Toby Keith and Tracy Lawrence have even started their own labels.

Advantages Of Being Signed

- **Credibility** and recognition within the industry.

- **In-house new artist development budgets** in excess of a million dollars.

- **Almost guarantee of radio airplay,** particularly if the label promotes you properly.

- National/International **marketing** and **distribution.**

- Big artist royalties from gold and platinum **record sales.**

- Professional **promotional teams** behind the artist.

- Typically simultaneous **video release.**

- Potential for enormous **revenues from concerts.**

- Opportunities to find **sponsorships** and **endorsements.**

... And the list goes on.

Disadvantages, in turn, are few in comparison. About the only complaint that one really hears is not getting as much priority as they would like or the fear of being "shelved" in favor of another hot act.

It was rumored that when Billy Ray Cyrus' "Achy Breaky Heart" was released, Polygram put so much money and effort into him that virtually everything else came to a standstill. While this was not true, Polygram was smart enough to realize they had a good thing on their hands and really got behind this new artist. Obviously, it paid off in multiples!

Here is the bottom line: If a major label signs you, your likelihood of stardom just increased a thousand-fold.

"Shopping Yourself" -- Go About It Properly

Knowing *to whom* as well as *how to* send your demo is as important as the demo itself. You have one objective -- get it heard by the right people.

Make sure you send your demo in a neat envelope addressed to the A&R Department. If possible, get a specific A&R person's name. You may also be able to e-mail it via an mp3 file. (A listing of record labels can be found in Part II, Appendix C.)

Include a brief cover letter as well as a professional-looking picture of yourself, preferably a head and shoulder shot. If you don't have a decent photo (or your appearance requires some sprucing up), don't send one -- looks can make a difference. Music industry people *hear with their eyes* as well as their ears*!*

Don't be disappointed if the personnel at labels are somewhat cool or unencouraging if you call. These people are instructed to be that way to help discourage every Tom, Dick and Mary from flooding the mailroom with demo tapes! If you do manage to speak with someone at a label, a typical response you may be given is, *"I'm sorry, we are not accepting new material now"* -- or -- *"Try back in six months."* Don't let that stop you. Your best bet is to send your artist pack anyway -- it just might get through! You can always send another a few months later if returned.

No matter what anyone tells you -- if a label hears something that "knocks them out," they're signing anytime!

"The Code"

In the past, labels have often had a *code*, which was nothing more than a particular number, word or little drawing placed in a certain position on the envelope. Unless your envelope "wore" this code, it would automatically be returned. Once again, the whole idea of the code was to review only those demos expected by previous arrangement.

If you run into this problem, there are several things you can do. First, re-submit your packet a few weeks later to see if it gets through. Should it be returned again, try to call the label and speak with the A&R person that you had originally addressed the packet to or send them an e-mail. If they are impressed with the way you come across, you might convince the A&R individual to request your demo, whereas *they'll give you* the code!

Another idea is to contact a local music biz "insider" or otherwise big shot. This could be a lawyer, country music radio station general manager or music director -- whoever -- to call for you. Because of their position, the code may well be given to them.

If all else fails, the code could probably be broken using "James Bond tactics." I know of a singer who was able to imitate foreign accents very well. One day he convinced the secretary of a major label in Nashville that he was calling from Vienna, Austria. The story continues that he was referred to call Nashville by the label's home branch, which had forgotten to give him the proper code. It must have worked because the next packet was never returned! (We haven't heard his record on the radio yet, but at least he broke the code.)

Be Persistent And *Creative*

In a recent magazine interview, a hot new female star revealed that she had been turned down by a label with her packet being returned bearing an *unsolicited* stamp. She later re-submitted it, but not before writing *solicited material* in the lower left-hand corner of her envelope. She not only got her demo through, but ended up getting signed to the label as a result of her efforts! Sure, that might have been a fluke, but what the heck -- if it worked once, it could work again.

Don't get me wrong. *I am not advocating being deceitful or lying*, but it is a dog-eat-dog world out there, and you have to be resourceful enough to **do whatever it takes** *providing that it is not illegal or immoral* **to get the job done.** "Uncommon resourcefulness" can go a long ways!

Incidentally, if you are fortunate enough to speak with someone in the A&R department, be brief and to the point. These people are extremely busy, so don't try to BS with them all day. If *they're* interested and leading the conversation, that's one thing, otherwise, *make sure you are the one who signs off.* Say something like, "Thanks a lot for your time, Mr. So and So, but I know you're busy so I better let you go. I certainly hope to talk to you again sometime." By doing this, you will have shown yourself to be a considerate person, as well as save them the trouble of shaking you off. Some people don't want to appear rude.

If a label returns your packet, it could be for one of several reasons:

1. **A&R Department is log-jammed with material.**

2. **Label roster is full.**

3. **Label is pre-occupied with existing acts.**

4. **"Code" is needed on envelope.**

5. **No budget.**

Patience Is A Virtue

Whatever you do, don't call back day after day. If you have not heard anything, give it some time. If your demo has not been returned and you are wondering what happened to it, you might give the label a call -- but not for at least one month after you have submitted it. Here's a tip: If you do call a label to inquire about a demo you've submitted, ask if they've *received your demo yet* instead of "have they heard it." Psychologically, this is much less pushy. Remember that bugging these people by phone would be a big mistake, lest they turn a permanently deaf ear on you.

Chapter 10

YOUR RECORDING SESSION

"This is your musical birth."

Karl F. Grigg

Recording a first-class, competitive piece of material must be one of your top priorities if you are trying to make it as an artist. It should not be taken for granted because there are several areas that need to be considered and addressed if you want to get the results you're looking for. Remember, *your recording will mirror what you have to offer as a singer*. It can be the determining factor in getting signed to a record label, the success of your record, or even finding a major investor. Let's look at the essential areas and costs.

Musicians

There are an abundant number of extremely talented musicians available in Nashville. Amongst these, a handful of names often appear over and over again on album credits. They are the ones who are (at least for now) the "hottest" and most in demand. Their particular technique, taste, and overall creativity earns them a position of respectability above others within Nashville's recording scene. Consequently, major producers use them regularly.

What a lot of people do not realize is that *anyone* can hire the exact same musicians the "stars" use on their recordings if they know how to go about it. The process is actually quite simple. But first, let's clear up a big misconception.

Singers returning from doing sessions in Nashville often brag that they recorded with Travis Tritt's or Shania Twain's (or whoever's) "band." Unfortunately, these individuals are misinformed in assuming that "the band" (in reality, the *road musicians*) are the ones playing on these artist's recordings. Not so. **From an industry perspective, there is a big difference between *road* and *session* musicians.**

To underscore this point, road musicians earn in the neighborhood of $30,000 per year, while popular session players easily average six figures! Session players are musically the cream of the crop. They are the creators of the "Nashville sound" on the records you hear. Their style and "licks" are copied not only by musicians that play in local honky-tonks every Saturday night, but also by *those who tour with the stars themselves!*

You may be surprised to know that (except for isolated instances) **even well-known groups such as *Alabama* and *Rascal Flatts* record with studio musicians**. *Only the vocals* are actually performed by the group members themselves during sessions. (Ironically, the group members must then learn the "licks" the session musicians played in order to sound like *their own recordings* in live performances later on!)

If you have a preference for a particular musician whose reputation you're familiar with (for example, legendary steel guitarist Sonny Garrish) or are interested in hiring someone whose style you really like on a Keith Urban or Martina McBride album, look at the names (credits) on the liner. Contact the musician's union to get their phone number (the union will gladly oblige!). Call the individual to find out if they're available. Be prepared to give them the date, time and location (studio), and whether it will be a *master* or *demo* session. Make sure arrangements are made regarding payment -- whether it will be following the session (*paid direct*) or through the union. (You may have to fill out some paperwork at the union or deposit the funds in an escrow account if you are "new" in town.)

Virtually all studio musicians (or "pickers," as they are called in Nashville) are members of the local musician's union, officially referred to as The American Federation of Musicians, Local #257. They are located at 11 Music Circle N., their phone number is (615)244-9514, and their website is www.afm257.org. Union musicians all charge the same fee (regardless of instrument), known as *union scale*. At the time of this writing, *scale* is approximately $325 per individual (*master session* rate), which includes three hours of recording time. In addition to regular scale, the *session leader* (individual who is generally responsible for selecting the rest of the musicians) gets paid *double*. In other words, if the rest of the crew is paid $325 per person, the session leader makes $650! There are even some exceptionally popular musicians that charge *double scale* to begin with. This means should you hire any of these individuals to play, their fee will be $650, session leader or not! (Add $19 extra for each musician for health and welfare, and 10% extra for each musician for pension fund.)

Price-wise, if you are not necessarily planning a national release, doing a *demo scale* or *limited pressing scale session* may be a bit more cost-effective for you. Either would be somewhat cheaper. (Demo scale is approximately $200 per musician.) The truth is, all of these high-caliber session musicians will play their very best for you regardless of whether it is a master or demo session. The main difference is they may not strive for an "ultimate" refinement or bring as many "goodies" for a demo. What I mean by goodies is all kinds of extra processing gear, additional guitars or keyboards, things of that nature.

The only danger, however, in trying to book a top-name "picker" for a demo is if he or she gets called for a master session, your session may be *bumped* for the other. And, although they will generally help find a replacement for your session, you wouldn't have the particular player that you originally wanted which could be a disappointment, if nothing else.

Of course, you are always best off in letting a "real" producer put your session together. However, if you are not working with one, make arrangements with one of the musicians you hire to act in the capacity of *session leader*. They'll then be in charge of making up your *charts* and running the session for you. (A partial listing of some of Nashville's popular studio musicians can be found in Part II, Appendix C.)

Incidentally, sessions in Nashville are booked in *blocks* of time which begin at 10 AM, 2 PM, 6 PM and 10 PM. Within these four hour "blocks," the musicians have three hours of recording time, then an "open" hour in which to go to their next session, eat, or whatever. In this way, a studio musician can do as many as four full sessions per day!

Back-Up Vocalists

Back-up singers are a subtle but important part of recordings. A good share of the records you hear have back-up singers on them. Your source for acquiring them is through AFTRA, which stands for **American Federation of Television and Radio Artists**. This, too, is a union. Their Nashville location is 1108 17th Avenue S., telephone number is (615)327-2944, and website is www.aftra.com.

Like their musician counterparts, back-up singers are available at either *master scale* or *demo scale* rates. The price of these singers is currently $80 per song (or per hour, whichever comes first) for demo, or $120 per song for a master. The *contractor's fee* (the singer who is the leader) will be somewhat higher, although not doubled as with studio musicians. There is also a two song (or two hour) minimum.

How many singers -- and what voices you might need for your session -- will depend on your material and the kind of sound you are looking for. For those wanting a traditional southern gospel sound, a quartet like the legendary Jordanaires might be ideal. If you are looking for a more contemporary sound, you may wish to use a trio including two females and one male. This should all be determined with some planning on your part. Once you are into the session, should you find that you need something different than what you already have, you can always call and get additional people. (A partial listing of popular singers can be found in Part II, Appendix C.)

Both the musician's union and AFTRA have additional expenses you will incur on top of what the musicians and singers charge. These include relatively small fees for health and welfare, and pension fund.

Studios

All-digital studios are now the norm. There are a myriad of top-notch ones in Nashville that can get the job done! Obviously, some are "better" (and considerably more expensive!) than others in that they feature higher quality recording gear in their consoles (boards), microphones, etc. Other than that, virtually any studio in Nashville is capable of recording a hit. If you really want to get technical about it, there are basically three types of studios. (A partial listing of popular studios can be found in Part II, Appendix C.)

> **Tracking Studio**: This is your general-purpose studio, where recording vocals, instrumentation and everything else as a whole is done. *Acoustics* can be a consideration in choosing such a studio because each one has its own particular "sound" or flavor. Incidentally, there is no particular studio where all "the hits" are cut in Nashville. Each has its own list of credits. Finding the right one for you will depend on your budget, the acoustics you are looking for (if you are really fussy) and the ambiance (atmosphere) you prefer.
>
> **Overdub Studio**: Should the recording of additional musical or vocal parts be required once the initial tracking session is completed, it is often done in a smaller and (usually) less costly facility such as this. Generally, however, these are only one-room studios with no isolation (vocal) booths; plus, they might not offer a good *line of sight* for the musicians as found in tracking studios.
>
> The *final mix* of your session will be done either in a regular *tracking* or *overdub* studio -- the choice will be a matter of preference. (*Mixing* is the process where all instrumentation, back-up vocals and your lead vocal are combined and balanced.) The final mix will be what your recording will actually sound like.
>
> **Mastering Studio:** These facilities prepare the final mix for record (CD) production. The mastering studio adds the finishing touches -- this includes proper equalization (highs, lows) to the desired "brightness" of sound, and/or other electronic processing which might enhance the final product. At this phase, everything is given *volume consistency,*

as well. (If the various cuts on an album were recorded at different times and places, volume levels must be adjusted.) Unlike tracking and overdub studios, mastering facilities are not set up to accommodate "live" recording. Their only function is to prepare what has already been recorded for final production.

Generally, a studio rents its facility either on an hourly or daily basis. The hourly rates range widely -- anywhere from $25 to $150 an hour -- perhaps even more for a real high-tech facility. Your best bet cost-wise is to book the studio on a daily basis, which, as the name implies, includes anywhere from 12 to 24 hours of recording time. Prices of *daily rates* also vary widely -- anywhere from $300 to $2,500. However, *this cost does not include the price of an engineer.*

Engineer

The engineer is the individual who runs the soundboard and takes care of the technical aspects of your recording session. Although the engineer doesn't generally act in the capacity of a producer, his "ears" and skill are of paramount importance to the success of the final product. Nashville engineers are also tuned in to the "now" sounds and styles that make for successful country records. Engineers generally charge anywhere from $30 *upwards* per hour -- varying greatly, depending on their reputation and demand. (A partial listing of popular sound engineers can be found in Part II, Appendix C.)

Tape

Most recording sessions are now done on ProTools or a similar (computer-based) digital audio workstation system. If, however, you are using a tape format, you will need a reel of *multi-track tape*: 2" for 24-track, 1" for 32-track (digital), or ½" for 48-track (digital). Typically, cost will be $175 per roll. Studios can supply you with tape. Chances are you will be able to save at least $50 by buying your tape directly from an outlet such as Nashville Tape Supply. Blank CD's, DVD's and hard drives are available at most office supply outlets, as well.

Cartage

This may be a surprise expense to many. A lot of studio musicians, drummers and keyboard players in particular, routinely have their equipment handled by *cartage companies*. These outfits haul the musician's gear to various studios for them. Their service includes delivery, set-up, and pick-up when the session is over. (No more trying to stuff the bass drum into the back seat for these musicians!) The average cartage cost for a session generally ranges from about $200 - $400. (Listing of cartage companies can be found in Part II, Appendix C.)

Chapter 11

YOUR PRODUCER

"Hum your last hit!"

The Fish

Since there are no special qualifications for a producer to "hang out his shingle," it is important to understand what a producer's function is in order to choose the right person for the job. Unfortunately, the concept of "producer" is often murky and lies in a gray area that can result in misunderstanding and disappointment in the least, or "getting taken to the cleaners" at worst! To begin with, in a recording context, the producer puts the session together. This includes help with finding the material, choosing the musicians, preparing the music charts, and then hopefully having some sort of game plan to help perpetuate the artist's efforts thereafter.

It is important to *define the agreement* that you and your producer have ahead of time. It may be possible to have an agreement of a limited nature, which includes producing your recording session only, or, perhaps "shopping" or "pitching" your product to labels as well.

Finding A Producer

The problem newcomers face is that a real hot shot producer won't be interested in working with them unless they are brought to the producer's attention through "inside" sources, or, the artist must be willing *to spend a lot of money!* If you want the "name," you (or your backer) are going to have to pay for it. You don't just walk off the street into a hot producer's office whose name you got off a CD jacket or heard on G.A.C. (Great American Country)! It doesn't work like that.

And forget about looking through long lists of well-known producers -- you're wasting your time!

Your best bet from the git-go is to contact the Nashville Musicians Association (musician's union). Their phone number is (615)244-9514 or call AFTRA at (615)327-2944 for recommendations. Although the Musician's Union or AFTRA may initially be hesitant to offer names (to avoid being accused of favoritism), if you explain your situation, they will most likely lend a sympathetic ear and steer you in the right direction to help you connect with some *legitimate* sources. Feel free to contact the author of this book: (615)944-2230 or gf@gabrielmusicgroup.com.

What To Look For

Your producer should **have access to good material at publishing companies**, especially if you don't write, or are not a *polished* writer. Since it is getting more difficult for outsiders to solicit songs from the big publishing houses, this can be a real consideration. Your producer should also **be familiar with the musicians needed for your session**. Although Nashville abounds with incredibly talented players, some are exceptionally adept in specific areas. It should be up to your producer to find the individuals who really excel in the style or sound you are looking for.

Vocal performance-wise, **you need a good producer's ear and objectivity in the studio**. Although he is not there to teach you how to sing, his job is to bring the best out of what you have to offer -- and that takes a capable individual with excellent communication skills. Remember, we are not necessarily the best judges of "how it should sound," especially when it comes to our own vocals. You should trust and rely on your producer's objectivity. They see you in an entirely different light than you see yourself, and most likely the way other industry people and your future audience will, too!

Getting the *musical charts* done for your session should also be your producer's responsibility. If he is not musically inclined in a technical sense, he will relegate this job to the *session leader*. This process simply entails writing out (in "number" format) the music you are planning to record. Ideally, each musician should have a chart waiting at the studio. Otherwise, the charts must be made up at the beginning of your session and will cut into your recording time. If the charts haven't already been prepared, the musicians must write theirs out (while listening to your demo) once they're at the studio. Either way works, however, if the charts are already prepared, it will save you time (and money!).

Finally, **your producer should be well-connected.** Being able to present your recording to people who can do you some good (i.e. help sign you to a label) could be as important as your recording itself *if you are looking for a record deal*. Along that line, try to find someone with current credits. A producer who was "hot" in 1965 with Porter Wagner, even though he may well understand the "ins" and "outs" of the business, may not be able to serve your best interests nearly as effectively now. Why?

Your Producer

- **The sounds have changed**, meaning that the playing style of studio musicians is different that it was some years ago.

- There is a whole **new bunch of session players** on the scene.

- **The "trend" of material has also changed** over the years.

- **People come and go**. The "power players" -- personnel at major labels and publishing companies -- have changed hands many times since your producer's heyday.

Don't get me wrong. I am not implying that someone who was at his peak name-wise twenty years ago can't do the job. I am just saying that it is likely such an individual may be living in the past with a lot of the tools and perhaps attitudes that he has to work with. You need someone who is tuned into *now*.

At the same time, be cautious of someone with "lots and lots of great (perhaps radical) ideas." If you are not careful, you may be the first person that he tries his great ideas out on -- only to find you may not appreciate being a guinea pig!

Know What To "Watch Out" For

1. **Stay away from potential producers who are *too easily accessible*** and/or have an inordinate amount of time to spend with you. This might be a good indicator that their services are not overly in demand.

2. **Be observant in your meetings**. If a prospective producer is not interrupted by a few phone calls or messages from a secretary now and then, chances are he is not an industry "mover and shaker." Also, look to see if there are "gold" or "platinum" record plaques or awards hanging on the wall. If there are, ask your prospective producer what he had to do with them. Another thought: is the office in a run-down part of town, or is it in an upscale neighborhood?

3. **Ask to hear some of his** work if your producer does not have name recognition, such as on a CD jacket. Find out whatever happened to former clients and, if possible, try to contact a few individuals yourself to get the scoop.

4. **Avoid picking up a prospective producer from an encounter at a restaurant or bar**, whatever you do. No joke, these are favorite feeding-grounds for the sharks of Nashville's sucker game. They can

size wanna-be's up with ease. Like real spies, they actually sit around eavesdropping on conversations (to find new people to hit on!) or "coffee-clutch" most of the day to be visible. To get attention, they often introduce their clients to each other in a loud or boisterous fashion that might draw curious onlookers into conversation. In fact, there are a couple of restaurants in Nashville's Music Row district that always have an inordinately high number of so-called producers and managers eagerly waiting to "help" newcomers. (Sorry, no names...) Remember, those who can *really* help you -- the industry big-shots -- don't hang out offering their services in places like this.

5. **Steer clear of any and all deals in your local newspaper or magazine** concerning *Nashville producers* or *talent scouts* coming to town.

Your Producer's Fee

This cost may run on the low side, from about $500 per song, to a high of (believe it or not) $10,000 per song *if the guy is really hot*! Since there is no hourly rate or scale to go by, a producer charges you pretty much what he wants. Herein lies the "fee" problem: Legitimate producers, as well as con men, charge for their services. *There are no free rides.* If a *legit* producer's fee is high, the reasoning (to justify it) is that they've worked with acts that have had hit records. You are then to assume they could do the same for you. (In reality, this is "sucker" reasoning.)

I know of two producers who struck gold with a couple of their acts a few years back and have since been known to charge $10,000 *per side* (song). Unfortunately, the new acts that they worked with never went anywhere. The only thing these singers got for spending a huge wad of money was a decent recording. And that, in fact, could have been done for a lot less!

It is always a crap shoot. There are no guarantees. Your only hope is that the individual in whom you place your trust is *really going to put forth an effort to help you and carry out his end of the bargain.* My best advice is, aside from the obvious, follow your own gut instinct.

Chapter 12

RECORDING A HIT VOCAL

"Nobody knows a hit 'til they hear it!"

Nashville Adage

Singing "live" differs from recording in a studio. They represent two different schools of thought and approach. For one thing, in a *live performance* scenario, you must, in fact, be thoroughly prepared to perform your song. There is no stopping halfway through and saying to the audience, "Geez -- I screwed up -- could I start over again?" Recording in a studio, however, means *creating the product.* Your final vocal performance, after all the individual *takes* and *retakes*, will reflect the best you are capable of under "controlled" circumstances.

Crucial Areas Of Vocal Performance

- **Your singing must reflect honesty and sincerity** -- in other words, vocal integrity. People, especially record company personnel, see through phony and contrived efforts. Think about some of the hit records you've heard over the years. Whether it be Patsy Cline doing "Sweet Dreams," Lee Greenwood singing "God Bless the U.S.A.," or Tim McGraw rockin' to "Somethin' Like That," the vocals are honest and *believable.*

- **Be vocally consistent**. This ties in with point number one. Make sure you are the "same person" throughout the song. Don't take on different vocal identities or personalities. Although there are obvious changes in emotion and feeling in every song, make sure that you remain the same person.

- **Concentrate on uniqueness of style**. Remember, no one except club owners and karaoke-goers are looking for "rehash."

- **You don't have to sing nasally** or worry about (not having) a southern accent. Although many people associate country music with the south, it has in recent years become universal in geographic origin. "Northerners," as well as Canadians, have become front-line country music superstars. Probably the only area of country music that still leans toward the hard core, nasal twang is traditional "hillbilly" or bluegrass. Other than that, regional accents have no bearing on the potential success of a singer.

What counts most of all is your personal vocal signature. Just about every country music star's records are immediately recognizable by their distinct style. (When was the last time you could not pick out a Brooks & Dunn, Vince Gill or Wynonna song?)

Finding Yourself

We all have our heroes, those who have influenced us in developing our own sound. This is likewise true of *every* country star out there. It is obvious how much George Jones has affected the likes of Alan Jackson, Travis Tritt and practically every "new-traditional" artist around. And, if you listen carefully, you can hear strains of Elvis, Tammy Wynette, Patsy Cline and Hank Williams, Sr., in scores of others, as well.

Remember, when you are a newcomer, no one has any expectations of *what* or *who* you should sound like *before they hear you*. Try to be creative enough to carve out your own niche. Do what is comfortable for you. There are no rules except *do whatever you do the best you can.*

Vocal Technique

"Hit vocals" in country music are determined to a great extent by *how convincingly the artist delivers the lyrics and message* of the song. Here are a few tips:

<u>**Vibrato**</u> -- Although vibrato has often been equated -- correctly or incorrectly -- with having a "good" voice, country singers, particularly those in the traditional or "new-traditional" vein, have a tendency to use very little of it. This is particularly noticeable at the end of stanzas or phrases, where most "purists" have a tendency to hold notes out "straight" (without vibrato). Instead, the end of the line or stanza is cut short, often punctuated with a subtle vocal curl or yodel-ish cry. This is especially noticeable in up-tempo (fast) songs. It is almost a guarantee that if you indulge in a lot of vibrato, you won't come across as "real" country.

Recording A Hit Vocal

In ballads, vibrato is a little easier to get away with. Ricky Van Shelton typified this, as did Gary Morris and the late, great Marty Robbins. Their "big voice" style is similar to pop greats such as Elvis, Tom Jones, Englebert and a host of other Vegas-type acts. Even Vince Gill has quite a bit of vibrato in his ballads. Listen to the difference in that respect to his up-tempo numbers like "Liza Jane" and ballads such as "I Still Believe In You." In contrast, "purest" singers like George Strait, Trace Adkins and Montgomery Gentry use virtually no vibrato.

<u>**Frame Of Mind**</u> -- **With up-tempo songs, get in the groove and have fun!** Don't be afraid to play act (get animated) a little. If it's a tongue-in-cheek "Boy, I'm in trouble with her now" song, let it show in your vocal performance. Imagine yourself on stage turning the crowd on like crazy!

While performing ballads or other emotional tunes, don't hold emotion back. If tears begin to fall because of the way the song makes you feel, so be it. True emotion is hard to "bottle" or fake. It might be helpful to think in terms of being "alone" (in the studio) in cases like that. Do the best you can to forget that anyone, even the producer and engineer, is there. You might request that the lights be dimmed in your vocal booth and/or control room. It's easier to keep from being distracted or intimidated when you are not aware of other people's presence and their stares. It can be understandably difficult to try and really "get into" a song when you feel like you are under a magnifying glass. (This is especially true if you haven't had much studio experience.)

Regardless of anything, *don't hold back in the studio.* Let those vocals out as if you were singing along with the radio on a late night drive! Do whatever it takes to make yourself comfortable. If you are afraid of making a mistake, *don't be!* Make your mistake, then go back and fix it. **If you sing half-heartedly, chances are you will have to do "problem" parts over and over again, which can burn you out and take the *enthusiasm* and *spontaneity* from your voice.** Your "peak" only lasts so long in every song, after which you reach a point of diminishing returns.

Bottom line: Make a statement with your song and get the message across.

A Few Other Points...

As a rule, you're best off starting your session with an *up-tempo* (fast) song. If you begin with a ballad, especially a real sad one, you might fall into a melancholy rut. For most people it's a lot easier to go from feeling "up" (like doing a fun, fast song), to "down" (singing a ballad), than the other way around!

Concentrating on "good" pitch is, of course, obvious. If you encounter a particularly stubborn pitch problem somewhere in a song during your recording session, here is an effective trick: Remove *one* of your headphones while leaving the other in place. This allows you to hear yourself "naturally," as well as with electronic processing at the same time. More often than not, this will remedy it, especially if it is a matter of "ear fatigue." Electronic/digital pitch correction (autotune) systems have become a God-send for many singers, including some very famous ones (no names!), who have problems staying in pitch.

Dress comfortably for your session. You are there to record, not for a photography shoot, so don't worry about what you are wearing. Most likely you will be standing behind a microphone for several hours at a time, so dress accordingly.

Save picture-taking and video-taping until you are done. You don't need any extra distractions to compromise the quality of what you came to do.

Bring some tea, juice or plain bottled water to keep those vocal cords moist and soothe your throat. (A big thermos of warm chamomile tea and honey can't be beat!)

Try to practice singing for at least 45 minutes a day for two weeks prior to your session, especially if you are not performing steadily and your voice is not "in shape." Take it easy the night before, and don't talk excessively. Talking wears your voice out (believe it or not) more than singing because it places much more stress on the throat (rather than the diaphragm).

Another suggestion: **You are best off coming to the studio alone or at most with one person**. And believe it or not, the worst people to bring to a session are usually those who are closest to you, such as parents, husbands, wives or children. In those scenarios, you automatically have the additional burden of worrying about *their* approval.

In truth, what your family and friends think doesn't mean much -- they are not music industry professionals. If you feel funny about saying anything to family members or friends about not coming to your session, ask your producer to do so. If all else fails, you might suggest they stay out in the lobby or go to the closest McDonald's for a couple of hours. Let them know that they are welcome to come in to listen once you are finished, but even then, make sure they are not in anyone's way. Not only can "additional bodies" have a devastating effect on your concentration, but there is a danger of tapping into your producer's energies and attention as well. And whatever you do, leave little kids at home.

Remember, your recording session is a major move. It is the first day of the *rest of your musical life*. Don't let anything compromise it in any way.

Chapter 13

THE "INDEPENDENT" APPROACH

"Getting it done on your own"

Relatively speaking, few aspiring singers ever get signed to a major label. If for no other reason, numerically the odds are overwhelmingly against it. There is a never-ending supply of new talent versus very limited openings on record company rosters. Although you hear new people on the radio all the time, here's a thought to keep things in perspective: For everyone that makes the grade, *thousands* remain "wanna-be's."

Since the competition is so keen at the major label level, artists have a viable alternative through "independent" avenues. While this approach may pale in comparison with what the majors have to offer (such as huge budgets for new artist's development and promotions), it is much better than doing nothing at all. Aside from providing *visibility* and *increased earning potential*, especially on a regional level, a successful independent project is able to serve as a springboard or proving-ground to capture industry attention and interest from the majors.

"You Pay Your Own Way"

The independent approach means spending your own money. Whereas a major label provides minimum artist development budgets starting at half a million dollars, an independent project means putting everything together -- and paying for it all -- yourself. Very rarely does an independent (label) pay expenses (recording, promoting, etc.) or advance monies.

Be that as it may, a properly mapped-out independent project *with adequate funding* can go a long way in launching a new artist's career.

Success via the independent route depends to a great extent on your financial resources. An independent project can range from a few thousand dollars (for a small demo session) to one in six figures for a thorough and extended career-launching attempt on a national scale.

Vital Areas To Focus On

Overall, an independent project must address the "big picture" in order to be effective. That means not just recording, but ambitiously pursuing radio airplay, the proper bookings, publicity opportunities, possible endorsements and sponsorships, marketing and distribution of product, approaching publishers (if you're a writer) and seeking interest from major labels, as well.

One of the greatest shortcomings of independent projects in general has always been not being able to properly develop the act and cash in on further opportunities. Too often, the sole objective of an independent project focuses strictly on being picked up by a major label. Although this does happen, it does so infrequently. **The main effort of any independent project should be an overall strategy to present the artist an opportunity to grow in every possible direction.**

In a nutshell, the following objectives should be your primary goals:

- **Recording high-quality, competitive product** so that, quality-wise, your product is as good as anything released by the majors. It's important to remember that you will be competing head-on with the Keith Urbans and Shania's of the industry.

- **Pursuing radio airplay**, with high-quality product and the proper promotions. Make sure any airplay is "translated" into further door-opening opportunities that should include the right kind of bookings.

- **Pursuing high-visibility performance venues**, which means getting booked into fairs, festivals, rodeos, theme parks -- wherever you can get "star image" billing.

- **Marketing and manufacturing** T-shirts, CD's and other after-market items to generate income from product sales.

- **Capturing media attention and publicity opportunities** to "spread the news!" The objective is to make the artist appear *bigger than life* and become a "household" name to as many country fans as possible.

Product Release

Getting your product *out* so it can begin to work for you is the jumping-off point for any career-launching attempt. Here are several areas that must be addressed if a *national* (or even *regional*) record release is planned:

1. **Manufacture of product.**

2. **Label.**

3. **Mailing of product.**

4. **Promotion of product.**

5. **Distribution (sales) of product.**

Format And Manufacturing

Once you've recorded, you must decide what format (for what purpose) you'll be releasing your product on. Options include "single-song" CD's, album CD's, videos (DVD's), and, yes, cassettes. And believe it or not, there is an outfit in Nashville, *United Record Pressing*, that still makes vinyl records! Let's look at the "pro's" of each.

CD's offer the ultimate technology in reproduction of audio recordings. Because they are digital, they have a purer, cleaner sound than their analog (tape) counterparts. All radio stations are CD formatted. Interestingly, the cassette is unwilling to go away. Why? It has been universally available for five decades! Quite a few cars (and trucks) are still equipped with cassette players. Although the cassette will never compete with a CD, having some in your stockpile of "goodies" couldn't hurt.

Videos are probably the single best promotional tool there is. However, don't substitute them for CD's. Radio is what makes you happen, and it doesn't play videos. The significance of videos in today's market is the fact that an artist's video often appears at the same time their CD is out. Videos give an audience the opportunity to completely experience an artist – not just voice-wise – but everything. And *that* is a great selling point.

Again, a good rule of thumb is to stock every format, especially for sales following your shows. This way you won't disappoint anyone. More on this in Chapter 16, "Merchandising Yourself."

Cost of manufacturing CD's ranges from about $.90 to $1.20 per unit, depending on the artwork and where you go. Typically 1,000 units are considered a minimum order. If you order less than 1,000 – a "short run" – your per unit price can go up dramatically. **Cassettes** are generally a bit more expensive, partly because most manufacturing plants are set up for CD's. **Video** reproduction will vary with *length* and whether it is *VHS* or *DVD*. DVD is the preferred format, but here again, a lot of people still have VHS players at home. Get some of both. Prices should be about $1,400 per 1,000 units of VHS and $1,600 per 1,000 units of DVD.

"Limited" Release

If your efforts will be focused strictly on a local level, or if you have an extremely tight budget to begin with, investing in a few individually-made "single" (one song only) CD's for airplay and a batch of a few hundred CD albums for promo packs and sales are a start. This could kick off a surprisingly effective local or regional promotional and marketing campaign for very little in manufacturing costs. (This is assuming you already have some material recorded and ready for release!) Cheapest approach of all: burn your own CD's on your computer.

Once you've done as much as possible within your budget, *expand your marketing efforts and product line as additional funding becomes available* (profits from sales, or even help from backers).

National Release

If your goal is to pursue a national release, manufacture at least one thousand single CD's. They are a must for professional radio promotions. Include CD "albums" in your plans for *promo kits*, as well as *distribution* and *marketing*.

The bulk of expenses related to a national release will come from promotional (record promoter) costs. Figure about $16,000 to $20,000 *per release* to do it right. (More on this later.)

In general, an artist should always have product on *three formats*:

1. **"Single" (one song only) CD's for radio promotion.**

2. **CD's (albums) for retail sales and promo kits.**

3. **Videos/DVD's for promo kits.**

The "Independent" Approach

"Custom" Label Vs. "Independent" Label

Another important consideration, particularly if your product is to be promoted professionally, is *recognition factor*. A *custom* label is a brand new label created by you and/or your backers. The label name (as well as the artist) will be something as yet unknown.

An *independent* label, on the other hand, has existed for a while and released artists other than you. It is not their first time around.

Overall, independent labels can offer a big advantage if they have a good track record. This is extremely important with regard to generating credibility with radio stations. Another advantage of an independent label is that they most likely have an in-house "team" already assembled for record promotion, distribution and marketing, or can put one together easily enough. A great example of this is NSD Records. Established in 1972, they were instrumental in launching the careers of Alabama, Aaron Tippin and several other chart-busters. (Visit www.nsdrecords.com.)

Perhaps the only tangible advantage that a custom label offers is being able to hand pick the "team" you want *yourself* -- providing you are prepared and *qualified* for the undertaking. In that case, make sure to appoint someone (preferably a promoter) as *project coordinator*. It is vital that everyone is working *in conjunction* toward a common goal. Nothing should be assumed or left to chance; every move must be carefully assigned, planned and coordinated.

Mailings

Once you have manufactured your product and want to promote it, the next step is mailing it to radio stations (or talent buyers). If you are dealing with an independent label that regularly submits product to radio, mailing your CD will be routine to them. However, you might want to check on the following:

1. **Make sure that you send *only one song at a time* if it is intended strictly for radio.** Even the big stars submit only individual song CD's of their new releases. Otherwise, you might face the *possibility of competing with yourself* (if you send several selections) and coming across as an amateur.

2. **Make sure you are not "sandwiched in" amongst several other CD's being sent.** You don't want to become lost in a sea of other contenders. In fact, if your independent label doesn't suggest it, ask them to mail

your product *separately* and also *first class*. Make your product stand out as much as possible. It is well worth the extra cost to go first class all the way!

3. **If cost is an issue, consider compilation CD's.** However, concentrate your efforts on compilation projects for the *overseas market*, or *secondary radio stations* here in the United States.

An established compilation service such as International Music Express most often features a current or former *major-label-act* in their releases. Don't worry about "competition" from the major-label-artist! Their presence is a great benefit. Involvement in a compilation project that includes *major-label-product* enhances a new artist's image and can be a door-opener in itself! (For further information on International Music Express visit www.gabrielmusicgroup.com.)

Promotions

Without good promotions, your product will not even make it to the music director's desk, let alone get listened to or played! The record promoter fulfills a vital role -- he or she is the *salesperson* responsible for:

- **Bringing your product to the music director's attention.**

- **Getting it listened to and (hopefully) placed on the play list.**

- **Keeping your record on the play list for as long as possible.**

Normally, record promoters handle product one of two ways -- either on a *weekly* or a *life-of-the-record basis*. **Typically, the weekly cost of record promotion is $300 per promoter**. This includes calls to as many radio stations as that promoter "works." Most promoters will want five weeks in advance with the weekly program.

The life-of-the-record fee is generally $2,500 - $3,000. Here, the promoter keeps "working" the record as long as there is a continuing interest in it. Either way is a gamble because *no one ever knows* what a record is going to do. If your record takes a nose dive within a few weeks after its release, for all intents and purposes, the record "dies." In short-lived situations like this, you do not make out very well if you paid the $2,500 life-of-the-record fee. There is no refund on the promoter's part. However, should your release take off and last longer than eight weeks (for example, ten weeks x $300 equals $3,000, compared to the $2,500 fee), you would have done better choosing the life-of-the-record plan.

Some may assume that the larger amount of money in the life-of-the-record plan might make the promoters try harder, but that is not necessarily true, either. (*Bonuses* for surpassing goal expectations might be an incentive, instead.) Most reputable promoters won't handle a piece of product if they don't think it has a chance of doing anything. A piece of "junk" looks bad for them. However, every promoter IS interested in working a hit record -- it's a feather in their cap. Overall, *quality* in product is paramount. *Everybody works harder if they believe in what they're doing!*

And remember, don't necessarily blame the promoter(s) if your product doesn't take off like crazy. The record might not be as great as *you want to think it is*, or for whatever reason, is not that well-liked by radio. There have been many instances in which the artist, label and promoters were positive the record would be a smash hit, but radio thought otherwise!

Radio In Promotions

At the time of this writing, there are approximately 2,000 full-time country radio stations in the United States and a little over one hundred in Canada. Of these, approximately 400-450 fall into the category of *reporters* -- stations that "report" their airplay and chart activity exclusively to a *trade magazine* (i.e. *Music Row Magazine*, *R&R*, *Billboard*) with which they are affiliated. The remaining bulk of radio stations are referred to as *non-reporters* or *secondary* stations. For the most part, these are considered *starter stations* -- which do what the name implies -- provide airplay opportunities for new and unknown artists.

Starter stations, as a rule, have a somewhat larger play list than reporters and are not as "selective" in the programming of their material. They are more open-minded with a "try it, you might like it" approach to new acts and independent labels. Also, starter stations are not quite as concerned about the fanatic competition that the major trade-affiliated stations (reporters) find themselves in. However, don't misunderstand what I'm saying. *Quality is still a prerequisite.* No radio station is willing to play sub-standard product.

In years gone by, it was feasible to do record releases and promotions that were concentrated in specific areas (such as the Ohio Valley or Southwest), or even individual states. Now, efforts like this will depend pretty much on *you*. (See *National Music Express,* a new company that offers this option, at www.gabrielmusicgroup.com.) Record promoters focus on the trade magazines and their radio counterparts, not geographic areas. Ideally (if you can afford it) get your product mailed to *every* radio station -- reporter and non-reporter alike. There is always an outside chance that the music director, even at a reporter, will have a bit of spare time and go through some unpromoted stuff. You might be pleasantly surprised. (Just don't count on it!)

In fact, I remember such an occasion involving my second record, *Friends Before Lovers*. One of my promoters had made a routine call to a "heavy" (very influential) *Billboard* reporter in Ohio to check on the status of a major label act he was also working. He hadn't even attempted to pitch me to that station as yet because he felt they were out of my "league," dealing strictly with "Top 30" stuff only. To my promoter's surprise (and delight!), at the end of his call the music director casually inquired "Aren't you going to ask about Gabriel's record? We're on it!" Totally unexpected, and probably just by chance, the music director listened to my record, liked it, and proceeded to play the living heck out of it! It was a great shot in the arm. The "weight" of this station handily improved my chart status (and image) as well!

A growing number of stations subscribe to satellite broadcasting -- programming that is pre-recorded and not done "live" by a DJ on their premises. Except for certain daily slots -- local news and advertising -- what you hear on a "pre-programmed" station is simultaneously playing on dozens of other stations around the country that subscribe to the same company. Getting airplay on these stations, unless you are *part of* the programming, can be difficult under the circumstances. (You may wish to contact a syndicator. A partial listing can be found in Part II, Appendix C.)

However, here is an angle to consider: *Record companies don't supply everyone with new CD's*. Smaller, secondary stations *not subscribing* to pre-programmed music usually have to buy their own product. They might be a good source of potential airplay for you. One of the reasons a lot of the smaller stations subscribe to satellite programming is because they don't have the money to go out and buy brand new releases as they appear. Too, there is always a chance that if the product is really well-liked, it may take off at a "grassroots" level. "Reporters" might hear it and jump on the bandwagon. These things do happen, but not enough to get your hopes way up.

Other Points Regarding Radio Promotions...

Every week, radio stations have deletions or *drops* from their play lists. **The slots that "open" are the ones promoters try to fill**. They want the new "adds" to be theirs. Be careful to avoid potential situations where you will not only be competing with other promoters' product, but with the artists *your own promoter* is carrying, as well.

Here's what I mean. When working with a record promoter (as with a booking agent or manager), you are one amongst many. Try to find out ahead of time how big a workload your promoter is *used to* dealing with. Then, check to see how much product your promoter is going to be carrying when *your* record is released. If the number of records is unusually large, you might be best off waiting for a couple of weeks until his or her obligations ease up.

The "Independent" Approach

There is no guarantee of how much you will actually be pushed by your promoter. Should your promoter be doing independent promotions for any "names" on major labels at the same time, use a little common sense. For the brief conversation your promoter will have with each radio station, whose product do you think, for the most part, is going to get primary attention? As a rule, the label (or individual promoters) will most likely supply you with a *weekly print-out* as to how many calls involving you were completed and what the results were. However, you will never know what actually ensued in each promotional call.

Until recently, "reporters" were called weekly by their affiliated trade publications to determine who was at #1, #2, etc., chart-wise at their stations. For the most part, this information is now monitored electronically. It simplifies the "reporting process" and offers a more honest or reliable indicator of actual airplay. Music directors have sometimes been guilty of reporting *non-existent airplay* -- known as *paper ads* -- as favors. Although this practice made the promoter look good and pumped the ego of the artist, it didn't reflect reality. (Find promoters with a good, solid rep!)

Another important consideration: **what type of radio station is your promoter going after**? Most promoters generally specialize in one or more of the trade publication-affiliated radio stations. If you are already a big star -- or are on your way -- *R&R (Radio & Records)* affiliated stations will be their primary goal. Should you be a new and developing act (particularly one not yet on a major label), your promoter's best shot at getting you airplay will be going after the secondary, non-reporting stations.

Although *Billboard* used to be the final word or "bible" of the industry, this is not the case anymore. *R&R* and *Music Row Magazine* have replaced it as the "standard of measure" regarding *airplay*. *Billboard* is now primarily a retailer's tool dealing with sales, marketing and general industry info.

The number of promoters you use on your project will most likely depend on your budget. **Ideally, you should have a minimum of four to six promoters** -- two working *Music Row Magazine*, two working *R&R*, and one or two working secondary stations. Additional info on this subject is in chapter on "Radio Airplay". (Partial list of popular record promoters can be found in Part II, Appendix C.)

Marketing And Distribution

The question arises: If you are fortunate enough to be getting a lot of positive response from the airplay of your product, *how will you make it available to the public?* This is a consideration worthy of addressing because airplay could prove "embarrassing" to a radio station *if they are playing something that is not available to their listeners*. In fact, it could be a legitimate reason to turn you down. Not only that, but if you are counting on *making money* with your recordings, you've got to figure out a way to get them sold!

Some years back, most of Nashville's independent labels had their own, however modest, distribution network. A few of the more successful ones actually made arrangements with major labels to distribute their product, which almost made the independent appear as a subsidiary, or division of the major. This is not the case anymore.

There are basically three *realistic* approaches in the area of marketing and distribution that you can consider pursuing *yourself*:

1. **Some companies will, "from scratch", manufacture and distribute your product through their wholesaler's network**. You present them with your "master" (CD), and for a fee, say $30,000, they will take care of manufacturing, distributing, sales, billing, collecting -- everything.

2. **Another option is if a company is willing to manufacture a certain amount of your product, then sell it and keep a percentage**. This is very similar to the *per inquiry* concept used on TV where a record or book is advertised along with instructions on how to order, whether it's calling an 800-number or whatever. The advertiser then either makes arrangements with another outfit to *drop ship* the product for a certain fee or does it themselves.

3. **Perhaps the safest and most practical approach for an artist on a small independent or custom label is to *sell on consignment*.** In a nutshell, you receive a percentage or share of the product sold but are responsible to take back what is left on the shelves. The easiest way to go about this is to deal with the prospective store directly, or contact the distributor responsible for servicing that particular store (or chain). With consignment deals, *wholesale* prices (what you can expect to be paid by a wholesaler or distributor) currently range from $6.75 to $7.00 for CD's and $4.30 to $4.50 for cassettes.

What it all comes down to is unless you have an extremely hot piece of product that wholesalers want to handle, or have plenty of cash to pay for their service, marketing and distributing efforts will be done primarily by yourself. This will include selling your product after performances and on a "one-on-one" basis to various stores. Most likely, your independent (or "mom and pop" stores) will be the easiest nut for you to crack. Although there are exceptions, the chain stores normally have to clear whatever they do with the home office, which could mean a mountain of red tape. Bear in mind, also, if a large chain like WalMart, K-Mart or Target was interested in handling your product and placed a rather large order, you may have a real problem fulfilling it. (*Barnes & Noble* and *Borders* will handle product from "local" artists. Make sure it's *bar coded*.)

Bar Coding And Artwork

It's absolutely necessary to *bar code* your product. This provides stores easy access for information on inventory, price, re-ordering and whatever else need be known. If you sell product in stores other than music outlets, you might need a Universal Product Code (UPC). Their website is www.uccouncil.org. Otherwise, virtually any CD manufacturer can hook you up with the necessary bar code.

Here's another important consideration: **Make sure the artwork is as appealing and professionally done as the quality of the recording itself**. People *hear* with their eyes! The music industry has become a very visual world. The "look" of your product makes a lot of difference. There are several commercial artists on Music Row that can supply album cover artwork. Prices vary. Check yellow pages in Nashville telephone book or websites under "record production" or "commercial/graphic artists.

Cover design for CD's is just plain "whatever"! While in years gone by album covers (and the labels on the vinyl records themselves) followed a definite format, today's products are unique in every way. Virtually anything goes. If you are totally clueless, glean ideas from other artwork, then come up with something of your own. Otherwise, that's what graphic artists are for. Let me recommend David Frantz of FranZart. He did this book cover as well as all of the artwork for my Christian CD, "Holy Ghost Power." (See www.gabrielmusicministries.com.) Contact David at d.j.frantz@gmail.com.

_____Chapter 14

RADIO AIRPLAY

"If you can't hear it, it's not happening!"

Dan Souder

In many ways, radio airplay is *the* indicator of "having made it." It is a recording artist's life blood. Without this exposure, they would not sell product or draw at concerts. Airplay and "heaviness" of rotation is a barometer of an artist's success nationally or in any given area. To a great degree, it also reflects the effort a record company puts into them.

Getting Airplay

Unless you are on a *major label,* getting airplay under normal circumstances is extremely difficult. Any possibilities will depend primarily on these six areas:

Label - The most important consideration is being signed to a major label or at least a strong independent. The recognition factor of the label spells credibility *even before the product is heard.* Although "being signed" to a major is not a guarantee of a "Top 10" record, the chances of airplay are greatly improved. Some radio stations have a policy of not even considering material that is not on a major label. In a case like that, no matter how good your product, it's a moot point.

Nashville Quality - Your product must be competitive quality-wise with whatever else a radio station is programming. No music director in his or her right mind is going to play a piece of product that just doesn't cut the mustard. Remember, every station's greatest nemesis is "button-pushing." If enough people do this (change stations), the ratings fall. The better the ratings, the more successful the station is in securing advertisers -- this is what supports radio. Consequently, it is vital that a station airs only quality material. Unless your product is as "good" as what's in the charts, they can't take the chance.

Format - Another area to look at is the actual format of the radio station itself. While some stations consider themselves "young country" -- concentrating on the new country sounds -- others prefer a more "traditional" format. Radio likes to play it safe by not going beyond what their listeners are expecting to hear. For this reason, *young country* stations will stay away from recordings of Hank Williams, Sr., or Johnny Cash, while traditional ones will avoid the high energy sounds of a Tim McGraw or Gretchen Wilson.

Promoters - A very major factor in getting airplay is the number and individual *effectiveness* of the promoters on your project. Find promoters who have a good track record and are well-liked by music directors. Some people are more *believable* or just plain hit it off better personality-wise than others.

Time Of Year - The holidays, particularly Christmastime, have always been a bad release time for new artists. In addition to the normal competition one would expect from other records on the market, you are up against the additional obstacle of Christmas songs which will further cut down (room-wise) on the play list. A few years back, the major labels released their product during certain time frames, which were often predictable. In this manner, independents took advantage of the "gaps" and scheduled releases of their product during those periods. The objective, of course, was to catch the music director's attention when they were not preoccupied priority-wise with major label product. Another tip: Avoid March and October because of *arbitrons* (ratings sweeps).

Up-Tempo Or Ballad - Radio gets about five times as many ballads as fast songs sent to them. As a new act, your chances of getting airplay are far greater if your first record is a good feeling, toe-tapping tune!

The Music Director

Without meaning to sound irreverent, a radio station's *music director* is "god" as far as what that station plays. If the product in question does not meet with his or her criteria, it goes in the dumpster.

Once again, *any hope of serious consideration requires strong, Nashville-recorded product*. I cannot emphasize enough how important it is to present *outstanding product* as well as *effective promotions*.

Sample Game Plan To Self-Promote

Promoting yourself to radio can be done effectively, however, you must be extremely knowledgeable about how to do it. This, for the most part, means a "select," station-by-station approach.

Contact the radio station and ask to speak with the music director. If you are told that the station does not have one as such, ask to speak with the individual acting in that capacity. Avoid dealing with the other jocks, even if it's a "friend referred a friend" type situation. Always stick to the music director. Should the receptionist ask, "Is this a music call?" you're better off if you answer, "No, it is a personal call." *Music calls* mean calls from professional record promoters. Let me explain why this is important.

Every *reporter* (radio station) has a certain time frame during which the music director takes music calls from promoters, which are, in fact, sales calls. The promoter is "selling" the records he or she is handling. Examples may be 8-10 AM Mondays or 1-3 PM every Wednesday. That time frame is a literal feeding frenzy for promoters whether they be *in-house* major label promoters (employed strictly by the record company) or "independent" ones. It is crucial for promoters to speak with the music directors and convince them to listen to and (hopefully) play the various records they are "pushing." The point is, if your communication is interpreted as a music call, you will have a tough time getting through.

Introduce yourself, then tell the music director that you have done a professional quality (once again, preferably Nashville) recording you would appreciate any feedback on. You might also mention that you live in that particular state (or even a nearby town), using that as a little extra leverage. However, play that angle by ear, because people often take "locals" with a grain of salt. Fortunately, others look at a situation like that in a more positive "I knew him or her back when" way.

Never ask a music director to play your product on the air in your initial conversation. Let that come up later (hopefully) as *their* idea. Asking for airplay can ruin your chances of even getting your music listened to. Wait until the music director hears it, comments on it and suggests that himself. If the music director likes your product and is willing to play it, he or she may ask if the song is *published* and *licensed*. This is a technicality that you may run across, so make sure you know who the publisher is and whether it's licensed by ASCAP, BMI or SESAC. (The term "licensed" is actually a misnomer when used in this context. What is actually meant is *performance rights society*!)

If the music director doesn't offer very positive feedback once they've heard your recording, there is no sense even thinking about bringing up the airplay issue. (From a psychological point of view, why should you be turned down?) On the other hand, if the music director indicates that he or she likes your recording but probably would not be able to play it for whatever reason, see if it would be possible to at least get it aired on a "make it or break it" type program. This would still give listeners an opportunity to hear you and call in. (Some stations place a lot of emphasis on the results of these "hit or miss" shows!)

Another vital point to remember is to **submit only one song at a time**. Even if you have more material recorded, regardless of how interested a music director may seem, submit only one song. If you must, tell the music director the other songs are not mixed yet or the producer is holding them back. Use any excuse, just stick to the *one song at a time* concept.

You ask why? **The last thing you need is *competition with yourself* on top of the competition from other artists**. Also, an opportunity to hear several of your songs *confuses the issue*. What if the music director happens to like one of the other songs in your batch and falls out of "synch" with the particular song you are promoting *to other radio stations as well*? To be professional and consistent, you've got to stick to the *one-song* approach. Radio stations routinely receive new releases in the form of a single and not as a *suggested cut* from a complete album.

Once you are getting airplay anywhere, make sure that fact is known to other music directors you approach. These people all know each other, and the fact that others are already "on you" (playing you) substantiates the fact that your product must be good enough for serious consideration! This approach can also open doors if you go back to a station that has previously turned you down. *Just remember not to ask for airplay*. Let them bring it up, or find an opening to hint around when they tell you how much they like it.

Make sure you don't pester the music director. If you bug a station too much, there is always a (slight) possibility that you may be told you are getting airplay just to get you off their back. Worse yet, they may never want to talk to you again! Also, beware of *paper ads*, bogus reports of airplay to the trades (to appease promoters and improve "chart status"), while it's, in fact, not really occurring! In other words, in this type of scenario, it's possible you are being "reported" but actually not being played at all! If this is the case, no one on that market will be familiar with you, and any self-promoting efforts *based on airplay* will do you no good. Luckily, this isn't common anymore.

Although you probably won't run into this, do not encourage -- or even allow -- a station to play an inferior piece of product even if *they* want to! There is a very good reason for this. A cassette, for example, does not compete favorably with the purer, cleaner sound of a CD. The difference is really going to stick out.

Since all radio stations play only CD's these days, you must present your music in that format. Although prices are coming down because of advances in technology, the cost of *individually-made* CD's remains relatively high. They can be obtained at any recording studio, typically at a cost of $2 to $5 a piece, or burn your own! Do a little checking around. Don't forget to offer some CD's to radio stations for promotional give-aways. They will appreciate it, and that will be a good chance to brown-nose a bit.

One more suggestion: Should you be turned down by a radio station -- as you often will be -- accept that graciously and without hard feelings. In doing so, you will demonstrate that you are a true professional. The next time you come back, you can count on an open door!

Remember, airplay -- any airplay at all -- creates *attention* and builds the *credibility* needed to make you *bigger than life*.

(A complete state-by-state and province-by-province listing of country music stations can be found in Part II, Appendix A.)

_____Chapter 15

FAIRS, FESTIVALS & RODEOS

"If you want to know what it feels like to be a star before you become one, you've come to the right place!"

Bill Higgins

These venues could well be considered *gold mines* by singers and entertainers. **Aside from doing a major concert in an arena, fairs provide probably the best exposure one could hope for.** In short, performances in fairs, rodeos, festivals, theme parks, exhibitions and conventions are some of the most publicity-garnering, credibility-building and lucrative venues you will ever come across!

"You Are The Star"

Unlike bars and lounges where people go to socialize and dance, you are the focal point at these kinds of engagements. People are there because they want to be entertained by you. It is the ultimate situation as far as gratification is concerned. The crowd is there to watch you, listen to you, cry with you, laugh with you, and applaud for you. You have a captive audience! And if you're good, you can have every one of them eating out of your hands.

And here's a bonus. **At the end of your show, people will be interested in taking a piece of you home with them. That means everything from getting your autograph to buying pictures, CD's, T-shirts and whatever else may bear your name, music and likeness.** If nothing more, your new fans will be happy just hanging around basking in your presence -- hopeful to be in a snapshot with you. To this type of audience, *you are* the new Brad Paisley or Carrie Underwood on the way up!

Your Performance

Fairs, rodeos, festivals and theme parks are traditionally family-oriented venues. Performers who go over best are ones with *lots of personality, energy* and a *good stage presence*. These audiences want to be entertained and see a show.

Stay away from "raunchy" humor. Although that may work in nightclubs, a family audience can be embarrassed easily and made to feel uncomfortable with a few off-color remarks. A clean-cut, down-to-earth presentation is the order of the day.

Booking Yourself... A Practical Approach

Successfully convincing a fair buyer to book you is your obvious goal. Don't be "run of the mill" like everybody else -- *find something special about you and your act to offer*. Remember, there are lots of singers to choose from, and bar bands are a dime a dozen.

The objective is to reflect either *the fact* or *illusion* that you are an *up-and-coming country music star*. Anything less than that spells "nice local singer" -- and won't buy much. So put together an impressive artist (promo) pack. The better your promo pack, the better your chances of being booked.

Suggested Steps: (Also see chapter on "Booking Agents".)

1. **Contact the fair to find out who the talent buyer is. (State-by-state and province-by-province listings can be found in Part II.)**

2. **Submit your artist pack, but call first to establish personal contact with the talent buyer and let him or her know your promo pack is being sent.**

3. **Try to determine a date and time you can speak again regarding interest and (hopefully) confirmation of the date.**

4. **If you are hired, get a written commitment to that effect from the fair and close the deal as soon as possible. As in any other sales situation, the longer it drags on, the less likely your prospects become.**

5. **If you are turned down, don't be afraid to (politely) ask why. Most likely it will be for one of the following reasons:**

Fairs, Festivals & Rodeos

- *The time slots your act would have been considered for have already been booked.*

- *There are no stages or other places available for you to perform.*

- *No sound systems are available.*

- *Your fee may simply be too high.*

- *They may already have committed all of their entertainment budget money!*

It is up to you to convince the buyers that your presence will be a *draw* for the fair and worth the extra cost or effort for them. I personally remember salvaging many an initially turned-down fair date. The best way to accomplish this is by being convincing about what you have to offer and knowledgeable about *logistics*.

Suggestions That Turn "No" Into "Yes"

1. **Make sure the talent buyer knows that you can be *flexible in your availability*,** meaning the days and times of your performances.

2. **If the main stage (or any other stages on the fairgrounds) are already booked and unavailable, suggest obtaining a flat-bed trailer as an alternate stage. Quite often local merchants or businesses will donate one free of charge. If need be, suggest scheduling your performance in a different location on the fairgrounds.**

3. **Make sure the buyer knows that you are *self-contained*, which means you are able to provide your own sound system and lighting.** (You may have to rent if you don't already own one.)

4. **Offer extra shows! This will let the fair get more "mileage" out of you and your fee.**

5. **Re-negotiate your asking price.**

6. **Suggest that the fair get outside funding or sponsorships for your event, such as from a car dealership, supermarket, or any other "high-visibility" local business. This provides free advertising *for the sponsor*, and they know the value of that!**

(If the fair is unable or unwilling to go this route for you, you can pursue the outside funding approach yourself.)

If your fee is the problem, tell the talent buyer that you will discuss it with your manager (even if you don't have one!). This is your opportunity to compromise and come back with a reduced fee. (The "manager" concept, even if you don't really have one, is not only useful to lean on for fee haggling but might build extra credibility in the eyes of the buyer.)

If that approach still does not work, simply tell the talent buyer -- and this should do the trick, if anything -- that you really want or need this job and it has to be *worth something* to them! **As a last resort, if all else fails and *you have product to sell*,** you could perform for nothing *just to promote yourself and make some sales!*

Should the problem not be a matter of price but simply logistics (available time or space), here are a couple of sample approaches you might consider:

"Mr. Smith, if you are willing to get a flat-bed truck, we could use our own sound system and provide a whole new attraction near the back gate to keep people from leaving early."

or,

"Mr. Smith, we would be willing to play a dance following the grandstand concert or rodeo, since it is over with pretty early."

Always make sure the suggestions or counter-offers you present are seen as beneficial to the fair. Otherwise, use your head and a little common sense. You might be surprised as to how a little resourcefulness can turn a good many "no" into a "yes." If it's obviously a lost cause, make sure that you do not become overbearing or arrogant. After all, there is always next year to think about, and you want to leave a good, professional impression in the buyer's mind.

"Band Vs. Single-Act"

You will most likely have the option of performing with either a back-up band or singing to pre-recorded music tracks. "Tracks" have become very popular recently because they provide good quality, yet are inexpensive and easy-to-use accompaniment. **Many singers, especially those who are used to being one-man bands, actually prefer working with tracks because of the simplicity and practicality.**

Fairs, Festivals & Rodeos

Let's face it, the musicians on these "tracks" are always good, there is no worry about a band member not showing up (or getting drunk) and the drummer is always on beat! Anyone who has ever dealt with bands knows what I'm talking about.

If you plan on working with tracks, see to it that your music is on a CD format, which is much "cleaner" than tape. Make sure you run your tracks and vocals through a *butt-kickin'* sound system.

The obvious down-side of singing to accompaniment tracks is a conspicuous lack of bodies on stage and, in general, a lack of excitement normally associated with a band. Ideally, there is no substitute for good, *live* music whenever possible. In fact, if you are being considered for a major event, the fair may insist on a band as your back-up. If this is the case and you don't have one, don't worry. Getting a band can be a lot easier than you think.

Simply check out all your better local groups, pick the one you feel best-suited and approach them. Offer them $100 per person to be your back-up, and you should not have any problem at all. This fee should also include rehearsing your originals (if you have any), as well as going over the cover material you will be singing. Most any band would be interested in working for you in a situation like this because *it gives them the opportunity to share the limelight.* Instead of playing in a smoky old bar for four or five hours and getting paid a mere $50 as usual, they have a chance to bask in a concert atmosphere along with you. They'll be able to cash in on a whole lot more perks than they'd ever find working in a bar. Should your prospective bands play hard to get, point these facts out to them.

If you don't know of any area bands, contact your *local country music station, music store* or *local musician's union*. They, if anyone, will be able to steer you in the right direction.

"The Drummer Trick"

An effective compromise between using music tracks and a band is hiring a drummer to perform with you. While you're performing up front, a drummer fills the void on stage *visually*. The reasoning behind this is a drummer is often the most physical member on stage, and usually has the greatest amount of equipment. As you do your thing up front (and if you play an instrument, all the better), a drummer kickin' away in the background offers the illusion of having an entire band. Another thought: Having an additional person on stage to talk to and kid around with takes a lot of pressure off you and provides a more professional setting, as well.

Those of you old enough to remember might recall the "drums a go-go" clubs of the late 60's and early 70's, which featured "live" drummers playing to records.

Here again, it's important that you have an adequate sound system to give you a big concert effect. And it goes without saying, make sure the drummer has excellent timing. (You're going to sound pretty lousy if he can't keep a beat with your music tracks!)

Sound Systems

Fairs frequently provide their own "sound" (P.A. systems), though you may often find them inadequate for your particular needs. If this is the case -- or they don't provide one -- you must be prepared to bring your own. Carrying your own sound system and lights is referred to as being *self-contained.* If you don't own one, you will need to rent from a local music store.

Overall, it is a big plus to have your own system. Quite often you may find yourself in a situation where the fair is not only interested in hiring you, but *needs a system for some other activities* that may be held on the stage the day of your performance, as well. In other words, a good sound system can also be a *bargaining chip.* You may wind up with a longer and more lucrative engagement if you are willing to work something out for the use of your system, in addition to your performance. (I remember being booked for this reason on several occasions. It saves the fair a lot of money!)

Generally, an adequate sound system can be rented for $100 to $150 per day. Most likely you can negotiate for a *tech* (someone to run it) to be included in the package for a little extra. You might try bargaining with the store once they quote you a price -- agree to give them a big plug on stage if they, in turn, give you a "deal" on your rental.

Unless you are playing a large multi-thousand seating area, a basic two-way system will suffice. Go for one that includes a 15-inch (not 12-inch) speaker and high-frequency horn. (Of course, place a speaker cabinet on both sides of the stage.) Well-known brands include *Peavey, Yamaha, Electro Voice, Mackie* and *JBL*. If you want that "extra" in sound quality, consider renting a *three-way system* or additional *bass bins* which are usually loaded with dual 15" or 18" speakers. The difference is a wider frequency in overall sound, and you'll get that "chest-thumping" punch!

You might also consider renting a somewhat larger system -- say, a couple of extra speakers on each side -- because of their *cosmetic value.* This is a favorite trick of rock bands. In the music industry, *people often hear with their eyes.* If you have a very scantily-filled stage, even though your sound may be great, the overall professional look or image may be lacking. "More" means "better" to a lot of people. You might be well off spending an extra $25 or $50 to get a few more speakers (even if they're empties) to really look impressive.

Fairs, Festivals & Rodeos

If you are not sure what all your needs will be, any reputable music store or rental agency should be able to make suggestions. Make sure you don't forget *monitors*. These are the individual speakers (on stage) that you and your musicians hear yourselves through.

Lighting

If your performances are during the day, you don't need to worry about lighting. However, if you are booked for evening or night shows, lighting is an important element of the "hype" and production people want to see. Unless you are the *featured* grandstand performer (in which case the fair as a rule *contracts* sound and lights from a sound company), fairs generally don't offer any kind of fancy lighting for performances. The best you can hope for is bright, overhead flood lighting, but all of this will usually be just regular, boring white lights.

Depending on how fancy you want to go and what your budget constraints are, your options can range from using just a few colored lights on portable aluminum stands to more elaborate systems that include steel trusses with dozens of colored lights hanging on them. The big-name acts often use pyrotechnic effects (flash pots) and lasers, as well. It's amazing what today's sophisticated digital light systems are capable of. If you're limited dollar-wise, go with a few lights in the back of the bandstand or stage (*back-lighting*), a half-dozen *cans* hanging in the front and maybe a couple on either side of the stage (*side-lighting*), and that should be plenty. You could easily pull off your show with less than this, if need be. Most often the lights used in concert applications are called PAR-64's. They contain either 300, 500 or 1,000 watt bulbs resembling round automobile headlights or smaller halogen bulbs. The color comes from transparent *gels* affixed in front of the *PAR-64 "cans,"* as they are commonly referred to.

Be sure to inquire about the electrical *service* (power supply) that will be available on your stage. This is very important. If you will only have 110 (household) voltage, you'll be blowing fuses or popping circuit breakers like crazy. You need a 220 voltage source (or a very beefed-up 110 v. system) to handle the demands of multiple, high-wattage lights. Whatever you do, *don't fool around with electrical wiring or hook-ups* unless you really know what you're doing. That's what electricians are for! Most music stores or rental outfits that provide sound systems carry lights as well.

Again, it is to your advantage if you offer a good sound and light system as part of the "package deal." Your performance will be enhanced as well as creating an opportunity for the fair to "rent" from you.

Important suggestion: Do your best to acquire a spotlight. It generates that "big-time" concert image.

The "After-Market"

There are lots of big bucks in selling your CD's, T-shirts and anything else with *your name*, *likeness*, *music* or *logo* on it! This also includes baseball caps, pictures or posters, pop or beer can holders, anything that is a souvenir of you.

Remember, any kind of after-market sale is also a *gift that keeps on giving*. Not only is it a money-maker, it is also an advertising tool. Every time someone plays your CD or wears your T-shirt, there is a good chance you'll find a new fan (and customer)! After-market items remind the buyer of you and the good time had at your show -- that in itself is about the best advertising you could hope for.

The potential for making money in this area is enormous. You can often make far more than what you are actually being paid for your performance! For example, a CD with ten songs -- including the paper insert with your picture, printed matter and shrink-wrapping -- should only cost you around one dollar to manufacture. In turn, you can sell this item for at least $10 following your performance. *That means a 900% mark-up!!*

We're talking big bucks potential. A friend in Nashville told me about a duo that made $40,000 in CD sales at a Tennessee theme park in *one season alone*. That was *more than double the combination of their salaries* for the entire engagement. And they weren't even famous!

Performance Fees

As a safe bet, if you are a new and generally unknown artist performing with music tracks, a realistic minimum fee might be around $300 to $500 per day. Shows are usually 45 minutes to 1 hour in duration, and you may be asked to perform anywhere from 1 to 3 shows daily in your contract.

Should you have a band, or should you be hiring one for back-up, a realistic fee could range anywhere from $1,500 to $3,000. If you have *real* "credits" and name recognition (in other words, a *draw*), you could ask for substantially more. However, aside from the dollar figures, there are other factors to seriously consider when negotiating price.

- **What kind of *exposure* will your show provide?**

- **Will you be an *opening act* for a featured performer?**

- **Are there possibilities for a *multi-night package deal* engagement?**

- **Consider carefully the potential for *after-market sales*.**

- **Could it help bring in *future bookings* there or elsewhere?**

Once again, you may well earn more money with after-market sales (if you have anything to sell, that is) than the actual fee you are being paid. Money, although important, should never be your sole consideration.

Here's an important tip: Make sure that you do not accept any other engagements -- especially bar or club dates -- in the vicinity of the fair you are going to be booked at. The buyer will want you to be as much of an *exclusive feature act* as possible, not one that performed at a local lounge two weeks before! In fact, contracts frequently have *riders* or *clauses* which state that you cannot perform within a certain number of miles for a certain period of time before or after your engagement. For example, "No performances within 100 miles of Pueblo, 90 days prior to or following your Colorado State Fair date." (Sample performance/booking contract in Supplements to Part I.) You will find a listing of U.S. (state-by-state) and Canadian (province-by-province) fairs and festivals in Part II, Appendix B.

Chapter 16

MERCHANDISING YOURSELF

"Make the sale, son, just make the sale!"
Col. Parker

In the early stage of your career, you will undoubtedly be responsible for promoting yourself. The same holds true for merchandising -- selling CD's, T-shirts, pins, caps, etc. -- any product bearing your name, music, logo or likeness. Remember, the objective is to make money and advertise the fact that you exist!

If you have a record out on a major label, you have a huge advantage in that the company is set up to distribute and market your product through their own channels. Otherwise, if you are on a custom or independent label, you are largely responsible for creating and developing your own market. Your potential success will depend on *how hard you are willing to work* and *the size of your budget!* If you have the funding, you could even solicit the services of distribution companies and marketing agencies.

Basic Strategies For Self-Merchandising

1. **Sell direct to friends, relatives, etc.**

2. **Approach hometown stores about selling your product either as a favor or on a consignment basis. Local branches of big chains may not be interested because of the red tape involved. (Barnes & Noble and Borders are exceptions.)**

3. **Run ads in your local paper advertising availability of your product. Take out a 2x2 or 3x3 inch display ad. In a small local paper, this is relatively inexpensive. The ad could read something like: "Nashville recording artist Josh Rubino announces the release of his first album -- available at ..."**

4. **Advertise on radio** *using your own music* as the background for the ad. Rates for overnight (12 Midnight - 5 AM) 60-second ads are extremely inexpensive even in the largest markets. On average, the cost is $3 to $10 per spot. (And you can usually talk them down with a little effort.) This means that you could run five spots per night for a week for as little as $100 or so. Add to that another $100 for a newspaper ad, and you could reach hundreds of thousands -- perhaps even millions -- of potential buyers for only about $200 for an entire week!

5. **Advertise on cable TV.** Overnight rates here are low, also. (Often these programs advertise an 800-number to call for information.)

6. *Perform live.* Set up a small PA system and sing to tracks in parks or "touristy" areas. This is done in Nashville all the time, particularly along lower Broad's (downtown) souvenir shops and bars. (Check local laws and ordinances first!)

7. Set up a web-page and get a site on MySpace.com.

Remember, whenever you *perform live,* you have a *captive audience.* Capitalize on that. Be creative. Don't be afraid to help yourself even if it's in unconventional ways. You may feel silly singing and selling CD's on a street corner, but if it works -- hey, what the heck? *Better off you making the sale and getting the publicity instead of someone else!*

Other Things To Consider

- **Be certain there is an interest on the part of your audience to buy your merchandise!** Keep track of requests for different items before you spend a fortune manufacturing them. It is estimated that a major act sells to roughly 20% of their audience in after-market sales. Initially, you probably won't do even half that well. But let's say you play in front of a thousand people per week. You may want to stock a minimum of 50 T-shirts and 200 CD's to cover your potential sales. Do not invest too much in something that in the long run may not sell as well as you expect.

- **Make sure the overall quality of your merchandise is good and appealing.** No one wants to be represented by a cheap item -- material- or image-wise -- nor does the public want to invest in inferior quality.

Merchandising Yourself

- **Make sure your prices are realistic.** Sometimes circumstances dictate what your prices should be. Consider things like the local economy, unemployment, etc... Always remember the basic concept in sales pricing: *"When demand is high, jack up the price -- when demand is low, bring it down."*

- **Don't give too much of your merchandise away.** While it is good business to provide freebies for big-shots and other key people (*a little palm-greasing always does some good*), be careful not to be overly-generous with your hard-earned investment. You may want to consider offering a certain number of items for prizes or give-aways tied in with radio-sponsored events or other high-visibility affairs.

- **Advertise your merchandise.** If it is a well-kept secret, no one is going to know! Encourage friends and fans to wear your T-shirts and flaunt your items. This not only serves the purpose of making you bigger than life, it lets others know your merchandise is available. *An important tip:* Once your sales have grown brisk enough to require a concessions manager, make sure you hire an honest one! You don't need the headache of worrying about being ripped off by someone who works for you.

- **Acquire rights for merchandising** as part of your contract whenever you appear in concert. Sometimes the venue requires a percentage of sales. Check on this before you take anything for granted.

Here's an old trick when dealing with stores. Once you've convinced them (the owner or buyer) to carry your product – even if it's only on consignment – have a few friends buy some copies. This encourages the store to re-order, possibly even in large quantities. The same technique could work with distributors or wholesalers, as well.

Eventually -- if you're fortunate enough to really start making it -- you will need to consider other areas such as *licensing* of your product (the leasing of rights to your product), *mail order* (advertise your product on TV, radio and in magazines), along with manufacturing, distribution and promotions on a national level. By then you will most likely have a capable manager and record label taking care of these things for you.

A little advertising in *Amusement Business Magazine* or *Billboard* could prove effective to let the music world know you're around and on the way up.

Chapter 17

WHAT ABOUT BRANSON?

"A hillbilly town goes big-time!"
Pat Boyle

For several years now, Branson, Missouri, has become the "buzz-word" of the tourist and entertainment industry. There is no doubt from the way it's grown that it has become head-on competition for the other major entertainment meccas of Las Vegas and Atlantic City.

So how does a town of 6,500 people draw 7 million visitors annually? The five-mile stretch of motels, restaurants, theaters and gift shops that line Missouri Highway #76 actually got started about forty years ago with two establishments -- "Baldknobbers" and "Presley's Jubilee Theater" -- featuring old-fashioned comedy, gospel music and opry shows. Today, there's even a $420 million lake-front development in progress!

Although most folks think of Branson as a country music town, it has become a hodgepodge of just about every type of music and entertainment imaginable. Theaters range from Mickey Gilley's to comedian Yakov Smirnoff – all family-oriented (no gambling!). The busload after busload of tourists have a good choice -- about 100 shows a day in season.

So, one would almost think Branson is a great spot to get started or discovered, right? Not really.

"Name Act" Or "Lounge Act"

Las Vegas, Atlantic City and Branson offer basically the same possibilities for singers and entertainers looking for a break:

- **Show rooms for the "names" and headliners.**

- **The lounges for wanna-be's.**

To be a headliner, you must become a star first! Singers and musicians often don't seem to understand this concept. People *don't become stars* in Las Vegas, Atlantic City or Branson. You don't "graduate" from the lounges to the show rooms. It is cut and dry -- you're either a headliner or a wanna-be -- one or the other! Chances of getting signed to a record label as a result of performing in Branson aren't really better than if you were playing anywhere else, if that's what you're hoping for.

The Positive Side

A lounge is a lounge, but if you are going to play one it might as well be in an *area of high audience turn-over* and one *offering good publicity*. From this point of view, you're better off playing Branson than Elmer's Bar in North Nowhere, Minnesota. Besides a slim chance that a headliner takes an interest in you, there is a very good possibility of *finding a potential backer* in the audience. (Remember, one out of every two hundred people in the U.S. is a millionaire, at least on paper!)

If your goal is to "make it," one of your primary objectives in performing in high-visibility places like Branson should be to find a financial backer.

It works like this. Performing in Branson creates a "larger-than-life" illusion to the average person. People *like to believe* that even the lounge singers they see in places like Branson are going to be big stars some day. Then they can tell their buddies, "I remember so-and-so back when..." Learn how to make that reasoning work for you.

Practice the art of "mixing with the crowd" following performances and during breaks. It allows you to meet a continually changing supply of new fans and *potential backers*. Unlike local bars where the clientele is pretty much the same night after night, places like Branson, Las Vegas and Atlantic City offer the kind of audience turn-over that could dramatically increase your chances of finding someone.

Spend time with your "fans," but *be judicious about who you spend that time with*. If you let a slurping drunk dominate your free time, you're not a very good businessperson. Be gracious with everyone, but be selective. And remember, those people particularly impressed with your performance are obviously the ones who are going to be most interested in helping (backing) you. Learn to drop casual hints. When the conversation takes a turn to "What are you doing *here*, you ought to be in Nashville," don't be afraid to smile and say, "Well, I could be, but I need a little help!" As the Bible says, "Knock and the door shall be opened." -- but you need to knock first.

Make a point of always carrying business cards and getting contact numbers from people you meet, *especially* if they appear to be sincerely interested in you. **Once again, everyone is a potential backer.**

Another positive aspect about performing in Branson -- it bolsters your "credentials" and looks good in your promo pack! This could help your booking prospects.

Bear in mind, however, lots of "politics" dominate the entertainment agenda in Branson, as elsewhere. You might have to initially "brown-nose" the right booking agents. It's competitive, and this means you probably won't just waltz into an easy job.

So if you're really bent on playing Branson, that's fine, but it should be for all the *right* (business) reasons, and that's to:

- **Hone your craft in a competitive, high-visibility environment.**

- **Use it as a selling point for "credits."**

- **Find a backer.**

Chapter 18

THE OVERSEAS MARKET & CANADA

"Takin' it to the World"

American country music is certainly not unknown in other areas of the world. The country music explosion has spread widely, particularly in Europe, where it had already existed for years. In addition to England, country music has become extremely popular in Scandinavia, Germany, France, Switzerland, as well as a host of Eastern European countries. Proof of this are the dozens of country music festivals held in these locations every year. The "Nashville sound" is on an unprecedented rise in Australia, New Zealand and Japan, too!

Advantages Of Pursuing The Overseas Market

The overseas market is literally *wide open.* Unlike here, **the country music industry is not yet as *major label controlled* or *"saturated"* overseas**. There is a much stronger chance of getting airplay and into the charts -- actually high in the charts -- without a major label behind you. This is, for all intents and purposes, impossible here. It's possible for Americans who are "nobodies" at home to become stars in Europe without first needing a "hit" record under their belt. The potential of getting your career rolling overseas and making big bucks definitely exists. Look at the careers of Slim Whitman and Boxcar Willie. They became big stars in Europe first, then later, here as well.

Another advantage of breaking into the overseas market (Europe in particular) is that **European independent labels will as a rule pay all the costs to promote you once you have supplied them with "product**." In the United States, this is very seldom the case. In other words, once you provide the product (considering, of course, they are interested!), European independents will package, promote, market and distribute you at *their* expense. Or, they may even offer to lease your product, paying you cash up front!

Another plus in a situation like this is the strong possibility that a European label or booking agency might be interested in sponsoring a *support tour* for you. These tours can vary from actual concert performances to showcase dates in clubs. Generally, you can expect a minimum of $500 a week (possibly substantially more) plus expenses including round-trip airfare, land transportation, accommodations and meals. Although the pay itself wouldn't buy you a new Mercedes, the exposure, experience and publicity you can get from a deal like this could go a long ways in building your credibility and reputation!

European Radio

Although this is changing somewhat, European radio does not use the same *format system* as here in the United States. Instead of strictly "country," "rock" or "classical" stations as we know them, you have government-controlled radio stations that program *different formats at different hours of the day.*

European radio is not controlled by the same "politics" or *chart system* as in the United States. To begin with, European DJ's -- *show hosts* or *presenters* as they are called there -- are generally not employed by the radio station. **Most country DJ's do what they do as a love and a hobby.** Since they are seldom ever paid for their work, they are in it for the music. (Can you imagine a DJ here being asked to do it for a hobby??) Consequently, these DJ's *play whatever they want* -- and if they like *your* product, you're on! This holds true in part, too, because they have to provide their own records and CD's. Opportunities abound for new and unknown acts under these circumstances. Fortunately, an age of innocence still prevails with overseas radio that has yet to be spoiled by the pressures and big dollars of the "American way."

Radio personalities are also very active in sponsoring concerts and shows. I was invited to perform at the Fifth International Country Music Festival in Budapest, Hungary, in 1988 by a Hungarian concert organizer, who was a DJ and band leader for one of Europe's best-known country bands (*Bojtorján*) as well. The following year, I was invited back to represent the United States as part of the Sixth International Country Music Festival along with Emmylou Harris. These concerts also featured top names from six or seven other European countries. (Earlier in the spring of 1989, I was invited to Denmark to perform on a ticket with Skeeter Davis and Charlie McCoy.)

Opening The Right Doors

Make contacts with key overseas industry personnel as your first step. (Refer to the listing of overseas radio stations as found in Part II, Appendix A.)

Learn to recognize and take advantage of *any opportunities that come your way*! I remember how the door-opener for my tour in Denmark came about as a result of a chance encounter with a Danish producer whom I met at RCA Studios in Nashville. Once we were introduced and visited for a while, I was invited to submit a demo and promo pack. Fortunately, it was well-received and landed me a concert tour and CD release throughout Scandinavia. The tremendously successful tours of Hungary I was blessed with happened as a result of a little research on my part, then a few well-placed overseas phone calls!

Remember, *you can* make the necessary contacts and sell yourself *even before* you get signed to a record label here or have a big-name manager. (As I emphasize throughout this book, you make your own breaks!)

Some suggestions:

- **Contact *any* overseas radio promoters and other industry personnel you have access to.**

- **Provide them with a strong *Nashville-recorded* demo and a good promo pack.**

- **If you are able to put a high-quality CD album together and wish to sell it overseas, contact a reliable foreign distributor such as Dixi Raks of Nashville (DixiRaks@aol.com) who may (if interested) offer to sell it in Europe and *pay you a wholesale price at the same time!* To appear on a compilation CD, contact International Music Express at (615)944-2230.**

- **Attend the MIDEM Conferences, which are international conferences of labels, publishers and other music industry executives to further your windows of opportunity.**

Whereas the European market may offer the potential of ordering and selling lots of albums, smaller markets such as Australia and New Zealand seldom see sales move as briskly. Generally, the product is sold for anywhere between six and nine dollars apiece (U.S. funds).

You have two choices: If you've already manufactured product, you can sell it as is. Otherwise, because of new European Free Trade Agreements, a *lease deal* might be the way to go.

Typically, an artist is paid $1,000 *up front* for leasing their product in a particular country. Make sure your deal is a *non-exclusive, individual country* one. Assuming you get a ten country deal, that's $10,000 up front, and there well may be royalties, too. They'll provide promotions (at their cost) and probably tour support as well.

Remember, "hard country," not "cross-over" (styles), is generally what sells best overseas. The honky-tonk sounds are more appealing to these still more traditional-oriented markets as opposed to the cross-over and "new country" sounds that do well here in the United States.

Canada

While American country music is widely accepted in Canada, the converse is not true. Although scores of excellent musicians and singers can be found in every city, and even though their studios and recording technology is the same as ours, the "Canadian sound" as it is sometimes referred to, does not compete successfully in the U.S. Consequently, a lot of individuals who are hailed as big stars in Canada -- such as George Canyon, Ian Tyson and George Fox -- are vaguely, if at all, recognized by country fans here. This inequity, or lack of musical reciprocity, exists for probably a couple of reasons.

For one, many feel that the style of Canadian country is more traditional or "folksy" than what the average American listener prefers. Another reason may be that Canadian music reflects a lot of *regional* flavors and may lack the more "defined" or cohesive sound of mainstream American country. Whatever the case, the undeniable fact remains that the "Nashville sound" has become the standard of measure *worldwide* as far as country music is concerned. For this reason, many Canadian acts serious about the possibilities of breaking into the American market travel to Nashville to record. At least theoretically, "sound-wise" they then could have a better shot at making it in the U.S., too!

Not surprisingly, quite a few Canadian artists have made their way "south," and made it in a very big way! Amongst them most recently are Shania Twain, Terri Clark, Michelle Wright, k.d. lang, Paul Brandt and Carolyn Dawn Johnson.

Cancon

While opportunities abound music-wise within our neighbor to the north, Canadian artists have a marked advantage on their own turf. Due to government rulings, 35% of Canadian radio's format must be "Canadian content," or *Cancon*, as it is commonly referred to, for airplay eligibility. What this basically means is that while two-thirds of their programming is "up for grabs" (regardless of national origin), the remaining third is subject to Cancon scrutiny. This ruling is meant to insure that Canadian artists get a fair chance. In turn, that also means a "tightening" of airplay opportunities for non-Canadian acts.

The Overseas Market & Canada

The basis of Cancon is what is known as the "MAPL system" -- M standing for music, A for artist, P for production and L for lyrics. Canadian records and CD's "wear" a small emblem that is divided into *four* areas, each reflecting the Canadian content of that product. Each area represents 25%. If at least 50% -- or two of the MAPL system areas are met (marked) -- the record or CD fulfills Cancon criteria. In this way, Canadian recordings can be a mixture of joint Canadian, American (or whatever nationality) effort and still meet Cancon standards.

Here's another recent (and most Canadians would say long overdue) change concerning Cancon. Until not long ago, if a song was co-written by an American and a Canadian, though both would have shared in royalties, the Canadian writer did not receive Cancon "credit" for their share. Now, this has changed to a 50/50 arrangement which gives Canadian writers *full credit* point-wise towards fulfilling Cancon requirements. So, if a Canadian singer/writer collaborates on lyrics and music with an American, the musical and lyric portion would yield 12½% each, totalling 25%. That, together with 25% as artist, would add up to meet Cancon requirements even if the production was not done in Canada. Overall, a Canadian radio station's daily play list must include at least 35% Cancon material.

Cancon Requirements

A summary:

1. **Artist must be Canadian (25%).**

2. **Writer (lyrics) must be Canadian (25%).**

3. **Composer (music) must be Canadian (25%).**

4. **Production (recording) must be Canadian (25%).**

If at least 50% (or two) of the above criterion are met, it fulfills Cancon requirements.

Pursuing Airplay

Getting airplay in Canada for an American might be a bit tougher than breaking into the European market due to Cancon rulings. If you are a new act or are on an independent label, your best bet is to contact the music director of Canadian radio stations (listed in Part II of this book) and deal with them on a one-on-one basis. Briefly tell them about your product and ask them to give it a listen. If they like it, they might add it to their play list.

Secrets to Success in Country Music

I speak from experience, having had lots of airplay in Canada during the '80's. (A large portion of it was promoted by *myself*!) Another thing an American artist might want to take into consideration would be concentrating on radio stations not well-supplied with product by the labels. Most likely, these would be smaller market stations.

For Canadians wanting American airplay, simply follow the same techniques. A full state-by-state (as well as province-by-province) listing of country stations is found in Part II, Appendix A. In addition, consult the chapter entitled "Radio Airplay" for more detailed strategies.

Chapter 19

GENERATING PUBLICITY

*"My Dear, the bigger the humbug,
the better people will like it."*

Phineas T. Barnum

The dictionary defines *publicity* as "information with news value issued to gain public attention or support."

Good or bad, publicity is a constant reminder that you are alive and well! It is the substance that sustains gossip and the rag mags such as *The Enquirer* and *Globe*, as well as TV shows like *Entertainment Tonight* and *Inside Edition*. In short, publicity is the momentum that keeps you, the artist, going. Without this reminder in today's fast-paced world, people would quickly forget about you. So goes the adage "Out of sight, out of mind."

It's a fact that in today's competitive society, *attention* is one of the hardest commodities to get. You have to work extra hard to earn it.

Now, the chicken and the egg question -- how can you get publicity and attention if you have not done anything that warrants it? Answer: You must *generate* it! **If you have carefully planned events, you can get a spot in the public eye even before you become a celebrity.** Publicity should never be looked upon as just a *perk* or spin-off of success. *It must be generated at the start* to help you on the way up -- then continue to keep you there!

Public Relations Firms

If you have the money, one way to go is hire a professional PR (public relations) firm to represent you. But bear in mind, the service they provide is pricey.

To get your money's worth, however, it's important to remember that this type of professionally done, high-visibility publicity is only effective and worthwhile *if you have real "ammo"* to offer. Ideally, I'm talking about *first* getting a few legitimate credits under your belt such as a *nationally-released record* (and climbing in the charts!), a *video* for CMT, or getting signed to a record label -- even an independent label. You need *something* to publicize. Otherwise, the whole thing makes about as much sense as taking Voyageur II to McDonald's!

Typical Duties Of PR Firms:

• **Putting *press kits* (promo packs, artist packs) together**

• **Arranging *showcases***

• **Creating *blurbs* (announcements) for radio and TV**

• **Acting as *spokesperson* (making statements or quotes on your behalf)**

• **Providing *press releases* for newspapers and magazines (Sample press release on Pages 161 & 162 in Supplements to Part I.)**

Creating *Your Own* Publicity

As I indicated earlier, do whatever it takes (*as long as it's not illegal or immoral!*) to get attention. If you're too shy to *publicize yourself* to the world, you have no business being in the music business!

Let's take a look at some *key* door-opening, credibility-building avenues that are *realistically* accessible at ground-floor level. In other words, I mean where you're most likely at right now! (Listing of publicists can be found in Part II, Appendix C.)

Newspaper Write-Ups

The secret behind getting "good press" lies in being able to offer something interesting, unusual, or outstanding to write about. You are the one responsible for coming up with that. Whether it be talking about a recent recording you made in Nashville (everyone likes to read a "local boy or girl makes good" story) or sitting on top of a flagpole for two weeks, it needs to *arouse interest*. So if you are trying to make a big splash as a new, up-and-coming singer, you had better come up with something more interesting than winning a karaoke contest at a local bar!

Generating Publicity

Once you've managed to create interest or gotten involved with something worthwhile to write about, you or someone acting in a managerial capacity needs to contact the appropriate source. In the larger papers, speaking with the *regional, human interest, city* or *entertainment editor* is a good place to start. Briefly explain your "story." If the paper considers it newsworthy, you may make front page! Another nice thing about newspaper write-ups is the likelihood of their being left lying around and read by others in days and weeks to come. Make sure you save any articles on yourself for future press kits. (See Page 167 in Supplements to Part I.)

TV – Talk Shows And News

An appearance on a TV talk show is a tremendous credibility builder and shot in the arm. Of course, it's unlikely that the show will be Oprah initially (although you never know!), but *any* TV appearance, particularly when you are trying to get off the ground, is phenomenal publicity.

Virtually every TV station across our country has locally-produced shows. Whether the station is cable or a major network affiliate, talk shows abound these days. Here again, you must *generate* interest or be *involved* in something interesting for an invitation.

If you haven't done anything outstanding news-wise or musically as yet, *do something on the home front*. Throw a benefit for a good cause featuring yourself as the entertainment. This often brings a camera crew out to cover the story. As I suggest in the "Artist Pack" chapter, a great place to start might be the local humane society. Other options include volunteer fire departments, old folks homes, or individual families in dire need (such as victims of Hurricane Katrina).

If you do a little creative thinking, you could *invent or create a cause* (the "accident waiting to happen" concept) that needs attention. For example, every locality has it's own eyesore or "bad" section. Organize a "clean-up" day. Whatever you do, *make a big deal out of it*. That will further it's chances of success (and insure publicity for you!).

Radio Interviews

This venue is especially valuable if you can tie a *professionally-recorded* product, one that the station might be willing to play or "showcase," in with your interview. Bear in mind, as I stress so often in this book, *a recording must be Nashville-quality for any country radio station to take into serious consideration*.

The most effective approach is to directly contact the radio station's *program director* **or** *news director*. Submit your "news" (and recording, if you have one) to that individual. I have had many clients who have not only been called in for interviews but have received airplay, as well. Publicity of this kind is worth its weight in gold. Once you hit radio, in the ears and minds of listeners, you are the next potential Kenny Chesney or JoDee Messina!

Fan Clubs

A commonly-overlooked but excellent source of regional publicity is a fan club. I worked with a singer from Illinois who let some supportive and creative fans start one for him. The results were overwhelming! In fact, it had much to do with his move to Branson, where he now resides.

The objective in starting a fan club is always the same -- get attention for the artist! Usually the first step is recruiting friends, who in turn recruit others. Incentives to join can include providing gimmicks such as autographed pictures, free tickets to performances, buttons with names and pictures on them or other knickknacks -- whatever you can think of. Be cautious, however, about one important point. **Make sure your fans do not get carried away with calling radio stations to request your music** *until* **it has been played on a radio station in the area at least once.** Otherwise, the station will recognize the efforts as an obvious set-up.

Whatever your fans do, make certain they *don't lie* about what radio stations they've heard you on. Music directors and jocks know each other, and it is very easy to see through a ploy. Another thing -- see to it that your fans never get obnoxious! *Your name*, not theirs, will suffer if their actions turn people off. So, be careful with what your fan club takes upon itself to do. **Over-zealous fans can become a liability if they go overboard.**

Talent Contests

Theoretically, any and all exposure you can get is good. If a talent contest provides a cash prize, all the better. And if it presents nothing more than just *good local publicity*, win or lose, entering is probably worthwhile if you are a newcomer who needs the exposure and experience.

A major shortcoming of most talent contests, however, is the *criteria* **used in judging**. All too often, contestants are judged on how well they *imitate* other singers, or the popularity of the song! In reality, a contestant should strive for *originality* since that is the stuff that new stars are made of. Most frequently, these events don't amount to much more than a popularity contest or a go-nowhere, modern-day "Gong Show". (An obvious exception is Fox Network's "American Idol," which has been a viewer-ratings smash.) Another thing to watch out for in many so-called "talent contests" -- especially those *advertised in the paper* promising Nashville producers -- are scams. Be careful! (More on this in "Scams, Shams and Charlatans," Chapter 26.)

If you are working with a band as your accompaniment, *make sure that they are good,* or you will look bad. No matter whether you sing your tail off, if the band stinks, in the crowd's eyes so will you! (And you never know who might be in the audience.)

Whatever you do, don't put too much faith in these contest's outcomes. They have very little to do with predicting success. The few big-name country acts that got their start this way were Sawyer Brown (on the old "Star Search"), more recently, Buddy Jewell and Josh Gracin ("Nashville Star"), and Carrie Underwood ("American Idol"). Otherwise, the tons of singers who win these contests -- including those with mega-corporate sponsorships -- routinely go nowhere. Interestingly, lots of superstars (including Elvis in his early days) often lost talent contests. That should put things into perspective!

Oprys

If you check carefully, there's a good chance you'll find an opry -- a musical take-off of Nashville's Grand Ole Opry -- in your area. The Black Hills Opry, for example, is held in a little town outside of Rapid City, South Dakota. It is broadcast live during the summer on Sunday afternoons. The Opry is hosted by a popular local establishment, and guest stars are featured along with the house band. These regional Oprys provide wonderful opportunities to get recognition and experience working with a live band in front of an audience.

Jamborees

My former home area is definitely big on these. WYRK Radio, Buffalo and Western New York's leading country station, is constantly advertising local jamborees. Normally, a fire department or its ladies auxiliary sponsors these events, which are often held as benefits and fund-raisers for various causes. **A popular local band is usually asked to *host* the jamboree and provide equipment for guest singers and other bands**. It is non-stop entertainment and offers valuable publicity.

Other Avenues...

Another worthwhile venue to approach is the local *Chamber of Commerce.* They frequently sponsor events (often tourist-oriented) to increase the "visibility" of the town or region. These can include summer concerts in the park, exhibitions, circuses and a host of other activities. Don't forget the *American Legion*, *V.F.W.*, and service clubs such as the *Elks*, *Moose*, *Rotary* and *Lions*. Even *churches* have groups that are involved in fundraising activities. They sponsor such things as dances, lawn fetes and various festivals.

Be creative! With a little work and effort, you too can come up with some publicity-generating ideas that will make you stand out from the rest.

_____Chapter 20

JUKEBOXES

"Anywhere There's a Jukebox"
80's country song

An often overlooked and underestimated great source of publicity is the venerable jukebox. Jukeboxes are found in virtually every eating, drinking or entertainment establishment from national chains to locally-owned mom-and-pop hamburger stands. Since lots of jukeboxes are independently owned, their proprietors can easily add your CD if they wish to do so. If the business leases rather than owns the jukebox, all they need to do is contact the supplier and request that your product be added. It should not present any problem at all.

For starters, find out *where* and *how many* jukeboxes there are in your area -- or as large an area as you are willing to "work." Approach the owners individually with your product. Another option is to contact the jukebox suppliers directly. If the jukebox does not have a sticker identifying the supplier, the establishment's proprietor can tell you who it is, or look under "Amusements" in the yellow pages of your phone book, or go online.

"Perks" A Jukebox Offers

- As with radio, **it brings you to the eyes and ears of the public** giving you all-important *attention*. This translates into recognition, credibility and money-making opportunities.

- **You are creating the illusion of being bigger than life** and fostering the notion you are right up there amongst the other big names appearing on the jukebox.

- Should you generate a lot of cash and obvious interest for the jukebox owner, **they may be willing to help you expand your market,** creating a "grassroots" promotion of sorts.

Secrets to Success in Country Music

It must be remembered that even the jukebox business is *as competitive as anything else* in the music industry. There is only so much room available, and people who spend their money playing the jukebox generally relate to what is hot -- or their favorite oldies. It should be relatively easy to get on some locally-owned jukeboxes if the product is good. But as in everything else, the bigger you go, the more competitive it becomes. Incidentally, a few jukeboxes still use 45's (records), as well as CD's. (See pg. 71.)

Getting "Added" To The Jukebox

Several factors will influence a jukebox owner's interest:

1. **Do you have product out, and are you on a (record) label?**

2. **Are you getting any current airplay?**

3. Do you have any **current "hot" publicity** or recognition factor (appearances on talk shows, newspaper articles, etc.)?

4. **How good is your product** and how well does it fit into the operations format? (You won't sell a lot of country music to a jukebox owner who features primarily rap.)

5. **Does it realistically compete** quality-wise with what's on the market and on the jukebox (Nashville quality)?

6. How professionally and convincingly can you come across? In other words, **how well can you sell yourself?**

7. **How much will you charge?**

Jukebox suppliers and jobbers buy their CD's from distributors at wholesale, not retail, cost. Don't expect them to give you what you might ask in terms of sales to the public. How much money can you expect for your CD or record from a jukebox owner? Frankly, you should be thankful if they "add you" -- period! Should your product take off and create a demand, you can at that point easily charge at least a wholesale fee for it.

Overall, jukeboxes are very worthwhile for creating good publicity, so include them in your efforts.

Chapter 21

SPONSORSHIPS & ENDORSEMENTS

"Name recognition rules"
Dale Bohna

The concept of "name" (celebrities) advertising "brand name" has proven to be enormously successful in the mega-bucks world of corporate advertising. Sponsorships and endorsements reflect clever marketing strategies that offer the ultimate in the advertising world's "let's scratch each other's back" symbiotic relationship. All you have to do is turn on your TV, surf the web, page through a magazine or look at billboards along the highway and you'll see *someone promoting something* or vice versa.

Aside from the superstar ads -- you know, Michael Jordan with Nike and Bob Seger's "Like a Rock" for Chevy trucks -- you'd be surprised at the number of relatively unknown, up-and-coming singers, models and others involved in advertising/marketing campaigns. Of course, the more known you are, the better your chances of landing high-visibility, high-dollar deals. Nonetheless, there are lots of opportunities on a lesser scale. For every Cindy Crawford, there are hundreds more modeling for small regional retailers, while for every Toby Keith (or Alan Jackson) plugging Ford trucks and George Strait (Wrangler jeans), there are scores of virtual "unknowns" singing or doing promotions for local supermarkets, car dealerships, whatever. All you have to do is turn on the TV! The opportunities are out there, but, again, you must know how to find them.

Landing A Deal

Let's look at the difference between the two. **While a *sponsorship* uses a product or service to promote an act or event, an *endorsement* portrays an act or event using and benefiting from a particular product or service.** (*Act* refers to an individual, band or group of individuals.)

Suggested steps for pursuing a sponsorship or endorsement:

1. **Find a product you feel qualified to be associated with.** Remember, the main question in a potential sponsor's mind will be *what good will you do for them?*

2. **Approach the business office of the prospective "sponsor" yourself** if it's strictly local or regional. (There is much to be said for the "local boy or girl makes good" concept in promoting local and regional pride!)

3. **Research ad agencies** if it's a large or national company in order to find the public relations firm that represents them.

4. **Hire a music marketing specialist** from an advertising agency, or use your manager to approach the company.

5. **Consult an attorney** if you have no manager to do your bidding. The bottom line is to make contact with the appropriate people.

NOTE: It is extremely important to make sure "the fit" is appropriate -- in other words, a *suitable match* between the act and the product. In order to be beneficial to both parties, the sponsorship or endorsement must be *believable.* What I'm saying is while Richard Simmons was very appropriate in a TV diet or exercise ad, could you have seen him on horseback as the Marlboro Man?? On the same token, can you imagine Jessica Simpson advertising Polygrip denture adhesive?? **Also, avoid *controversial issues and situations* such as pushing a beer-drinking image to an under-age crowd.**

How "The Trade-Off" Works

The key bargaining chip in finding sponsorship and endorsement deals lies in a concept known as *borrowed equity.* It creates an equation which determines monetary value. The equity, or value, your name has generated over a period of time *is borrowed by the sponsor and applied to their product line* in the hope the public (like your fans) will follow in your footsteps! Remember, even if you have not yet achieved "celebrity status," you have time and money invested in your talent. It is potentially worth *something.* (In fact, its value may be more than you think!)

If you are successful in your approach, your deal will be based upon either an **image-driven** or **sales-driven** sponsorship. Here's the difference:

An image-driven sponsorship focuses on *good* product and image identification. Sales are generally not an issue. It is to the sponsor's benefit to be associated with the name and image of the individual or act. This is often the case with major beer companies in sponsoring well-known rock and country artists on national tours. Even though the acts might not want to actively advertise the beer, they allowed the beer to be associated with them in the form of high-powered TV commercials, instead. Image-driven sponsorships are particularly successful when the sponsor and the act are both well-known.

A sales-driven sponsorship, as the name implies, is intended to beef up sales of a product. This type of sponsorship is much more realistic and effective for new, up-and-coming acts. In situations like this, instead of dealing at the mega-corporate and superstar levels, local distributors sponsor these events, which are in turn funded by the head or main corporate office. Soft drink and beer companies such as Miller's, Budweiser, Coke and Pepsi do this a lot. Often this involves sponsoring merchandise give-aways, as well as contests. The arrangement may simply provide singers or bands with high-visibility items bearing the company logo, such as banners, posters and T-shirts. In return, the company stimulates sales by plugging itself (through the act!).

Benefits of Sponsorships

- **Pay cash.**

- **Provide services.**

- **Great source of publicity and exposure.**

- **Picking up the tab for your performances.**

- **Provide you with their product line (i.e. clothes, musical equipment, vehicles, etc.).**

When seeking sponsorships and endorsements, don't always think strictly in terms of *cash*. If a sponsor is willing to invest by promoting or advertising an *artist's name* or *tour*, it could be worth a lot more in the long run than just a sum of cash up front.

Endorsements

An endorsement indicates that you, the act, use a particular product or service. To be believable, it must show *how you benefit from it* or *how it helps you do what you do even better!* Endorsements serve three purposes:

- **Allows a company to increase sales through the credibility and popularity of the act or event.**

- **The act gets product line for personal use.**

- **Act or event is in public eye (through endorsement).**

Again, you need not be at the "superstar" or mega-corporate level to qualify. A local music store might give a singer or musician substantial breaks on equipment in exchange for conducting clinics, seminars or in-house performances to promote a particular brand or product line the store carries. Another good angle might lie in approaching a local *western clothing store* or *tack shop*, suggesting a trade-off for free jeans or boots in exchange for plugs during your performances.

As they say, necessity is the mother of invention. If you are resourceful enough, you may be able to create your own "demand" or "need" and land a sponsorship or endorsement of your own.

Chapter 22

SHOWCASING

"Here's your chance to strut your stuff!"

Peter Bäumler

A showcase is a performance in front of a select audience. Normally, this audience consists of music industry people which may include record company executives, booking agents, talent buyers, publicity reps, and record promoters. A good showcase can be a real credibility-builder and door-opener.

For our intents and purposes, we will concentrate on the two basic types of showcases most relevant to the career goals of an up-and-coming artist:

- **Showcases for record labels.**

- **Showcases for talent buyers (such as fairs) and booking agents.**

Basically, there are two approaches to a showcase, either *putting it together yourself* or *hiring a public relations firm* (if you have the money!) to do it for you.

The "Professional" (P.R. Firm) Approach

Most public relations firms can arrange a showcase. For a fee, they will take care of the entire event including rental of a location (with sound system and lights), designing and mailing invitations to industry personnel, putting a back-up band together, assembling press kits (promo packs) for distribution to guests, even catering hors d'oeuvres! Some agencies provide a "follow-up" by sending duplicate press kits out (or to those who didn't show up), as well as making calls to the labels' A&R departments for "feedback."

Secrets to Success in Country Music

A well-known company that provides this service in Nashville is *Aristo Media Associates*, headed up by Jeff Walker. Aside from dealing strictly with showcases, they offer several other services as well, including record and video promotions.

Although prices vary, a properly done showcase generally costs about $10,000 and up. If you're a good "visual" act, it could be money very well-spent! Other than having a real "in" at a record label, an impressive showcase is one of the best ways to bring yourself to their attention.

(Listing of publicists can be found in Part II, Appendix C.)

Setting Up Your Own Showcase

Look after the "logistics" properly! Find a centralized location, especially if you are expecting to draw individuals from more than just one particular area. If possible, rent a hall that specializes in this sort of thing. Try to find a venue that has an adequate sound system and lights (otherwise, it will be necessary to go out and rent them), as well as decent acoustics, plenty of seating and a good overall look or "feel."

Give yourself adequate time to publicize the event. However, don't wait too long between announcing it and the actual event, lest people forget.

Make sure that you have a good band backing you. Remember, you are the focal point and are only going to be as good as your accompaniment allows. Be rehearsed and tight. Should your showcase be scheduled shortly after your recording session, try to use the same crew (session musicians) for your back-up band. And if possible, hire the same (recording) engineer to run sound. The objective is to make your showcase sound as much like your recording as possible. Typically, musicians will charge master scale rate. (This fee should also include one rehearsal.)

It might be a good idea to conduct your showcase in a "By Invitation Only" manner. This would exclude the general public from just stopping in and possibly watering down the "select" atmosphere. Industry personnel recognize this, and it creates a much more professional setting. It may be wise, just the same, to station a trusted individual by the door in the event some unexpected industry people show up. (No need to turn anyone away who could do you some good!)

"Label" Showcases

If your showcase is an attempt to get a record deal, send personal invitations directly to the respective A&R individuals of the labels you are interested in. If you have a manager or booking agent, let them take care of this; otherwise, the burden falls upon you. Should you already be creating quite a "buzz" or sensation in town, chances are record company executives will hear about it through the grapevine. If you have ever walked the streets of Music Row in Nashville, you have undoubtedly seen all kinds of posters advertising showcases on phone poles, bus stop seats -- even trash cans!

Performance (Talent Buyer) Showcases

If your intention is to break into the lucrative area of bookings in fairs and such, your showcase will be aimed at *talent buyers*. Showcases are held during the annual *fair conventions* (found in every state), the majority of which run between the months of November and March. These conventions are normally two or three day affairs at which county and state fair officials get together to discuss everything from budgets to anything else of mutual interest. Topics include funding and planning attractions such as midways (rides), livestock exhibitions, rodeos, demolition derbies and musical entertainment. The showcases themselves are generally held following a dinner on one of these nights and are attended by the fair big-shots. Acts are often signed on the spot! Joining your home state's (or any other state's) fair association is a necessary first step. This usually involves paying a fee of about $50.

When approaching fair buyers, it's possible you may be referred to a booking agent, and your success at that point will depend on the agent's interest. If the agent has "favorites" (showcases can be political like anything else), you may have to sell yourself successfully to them first! Quite often, however, if you're able to interest the talent buyer enough, you can bypass the agent and book direct.

For starters, refer to "Fair Meetings" in Part II, or call your local fair. **Once you've contacted their secretary, find out how you can be included in their next showcase.** Ultimately, your success will depend on how impressed the fair board or buyers are with your artist pack and/or live performance (if they've already seen you!).

Two extremely helpful publications concerning this whole area are *The Guide to Fairs, Festivals & Expositions* and *Cavalcade of Acts & Attractions*. They are both available through *Amusement Business Magazine*, a subsidiary of *Billboard*. Their phone number is (615)321-4250, or you can write to them at 49 Music Square West, Nashville, TN 37203. The cost for either is about $80, but is worth its weight in gold if you're serious about *booking yourself*. You might also want to discuss doing some advertising in *Amusement Business Magazine*. It is a widely-read trade journal, and exposure of this kind can go a long way in promoting your credibility to those who have never heard of you. (List of state-by-state and province-by-province fair convention meetings is in Part II, Appendix B.)

Secrets to Success in Country Music

Chapter 23

MANAGERS

"Takin' Care of Business"
BTO

People who take care of an artist's business and personal affairs are referred to as managers. They represent the artist with booking agents, record company executives, publicity people and are the overall coordinators of the artist's team.

Managers earn their money by receiving a percentage of their artist's earnings. Although this figure may vary, a 15% share is generally the norm. Perhaps the ultimate example of an exaggerated split between artist and manager was that of Elvis and the Colonel. Over the years, many have criticized their reputed 50/50 deal -- that it was a bit short on Elvis' end. But who knows, without their deal, Elvis may still be driving a truck for Crown Electric in Memphis!

In the early stage of an artist's development -- before they become well-known -- it is difficult to acquire an effective manager. A manager does not make money unless you, the artist, does. Since he or she gets a percentage of your earnings, it follows that a capable manager won't have much interest in you until you've proven yourself to be a worthwhile, *money-making* commodity. Unless you find a *competent* individual who really believes in your talent and potential from the start, you are better off managing yourself for the time being.

Typical Duties Of A Manager

1. **Be a "mouthpiece" or liaison** between artist and outside world in general.

2. **Keep artist's personal affairs in order.**

3. **Find and deal with booking agents and promoters.**

4. **Pursue business interests** with record labels, publishers, endorsement deals, marketing, publicity firms and investments.

5. **Keep track of finances**, which includes accountability for *expenses* as well as *earnings* from all areas.

6. **Handle overall logistics**, like organizing tours, setting up recording sessions, arranging interviews.

7. **Delegate duties** for others to function in various capacities, such as road manager and band leader.

Maybe Another "Colonel Parker"?

Every singer has a dream of being picked up by a Colonel Parker-type manager who can make them a star. In reality, however, that scenario is very unlikely.

For one thing, the legendary Colonel was an extraordinarily capable and shrewd man, clever enough to latch on to a commodity as unique (and controversial) as Elvis. You could probably say he was a one-in-a-million kind of individual himself that had the vision necessary to pave Elvis' road to stardom and musical immortality.

Secondly, the '50's were very different times. The world in general was much more innocent and naive. Elvis and the Colonel came along at a perfect time. Rock 'n' Roll was just evolving, and the music scene was in its infancy with not nearly the competition there is today. There was much *more demand than supply* for the new craze called Rock 'n' Roll. In contrast, today there are ten bands for every job and 10,000 singers waiting to get signed to each major label!

The truth is, forget about all those "fairy tales" and come back down to earth! Get your act together and **prove you are a worthwhile commodity to someone who can do you some good**. That's a *realistic* approach to finding a competent manager.

Here's an important point you should consider before hiring someone (such as a friend) for a manager: Aside from being a **savvy business-person who understands the duties of a manager**, he or she should be **knowledgeable about and well-connected within the music industry**. Otherwise, how else will they be effective?

Bear in mind, too, your manager is your ambassador and representative. If you've really got the potential to make it, you need someone who has reached at least a certain plateau with their own success. The last thing you want is a well-meaning but useless "manager" who looks upon you for guidance.

Finding A Manager

1. **Talk to your local country music station's** program director or music director for suggestions.

2. **Consult a music attorney.**

3. **"Word-of-mouth" approach** from contacts in Nashville or your home area.

4. **Showcases.**

5. **Contact "big name" managers** and submit your artist pack, *but only* after you have developed your talent enough to truly have something worthwhile and *marketable* to offer.

6. **Go on the web, or check listings in yellow pages** of major cities under "Entertainment Management Companies."

7. **Run an ad in the classified section** of a music trade publication (the same concept we talked about under "Finding Investors").

8. **Consult Part II of this book.**

Create Your Own "Pre-Manager" Think-Tank

Henry Ford was once asked about the secret of his success. It's said he replied he always did his best to surround himself with people who knew more about their areas of expertise than he. That is the think-tank concept of the White House Cabinet and corporate boards -- to make suggestions and share ideas with the person in charge.

Put together your own team of "experts" -- people who can help you in areas of *their* strengths (bookings, recording, promotions, etc.) -- anything that will make you grow as an artist. **Concentrate your energies on *developing your talent*.** This is, by far, the best way to prepare yourself for interest from an effective manager.

If and when you do sign with a manager, make sure you understand what you are getting into -- the time frame, their obligations, your overall commitment, whatever. Remember, it's better for you to stay in charge for now than putting years of your future in the hands of a hapless or bungling manager. (A listing of some of country music's prominent managers can be found in Part II, Appendix C.)

_____Chapter 24

BOOKING AGENTS

"On the Road Again"
Willie Nelson

A booking agent by basic definition is an individual who procures employment for singers and entertainers through his or her efforts. These venues can be anything from bars to huge concerts.

As with managers, *a big-name booking agent* won't touch you until you have some sort of track record to go on. If you are just starting out, attracting an agent will mean having to prove yourself. And that can even mean bookings in cheap and dumpy places. The moral: If you are a total beginner, it is tough to be choosy! You go where they send you. *Where you're at* in your musical career will best determine the type of booking agent who can or will help you.

Finding The Right Agent

For the most part, there are two types of agents and agencies:

- **Ones that book clubs, lounges and honky-tonks.**

- **Others that book the *name* acts and concert venues.**

Agencies specializing in lounges and clubs can provide (that is, if they wish to work with you) fairly steady work but cannot do much more. The problem is if you are looking to launch your career as a singer, club jobs all tend to be at the same level. *Moving from one bar to another does nothing to advance your career!*

Agencies that book *name* acts generally won't touch you if you don't have any name recognition, which determines *draw factor*. If you are, however, an absolutely phenomenal act and/or have an extremely convincing promo pack -- *especially if you* *have ever independently released any records* -- this can paint a somewhat different picture. Under these circumstances, you may qualify for more "advanced" types of bookings, above and beyond the typical starter stuff others must endure. If this is the case, an agency of this type may slip you a date or two. Should you do well for them, they may be willing to use you on a more regular basis.

Overall, an agent's interest will be influenced by:

- **Name/Reputation**

- **Showcase or seeing a live performance**

- **Artist pack.**

Ideally, even if you are just starting out, try to find an agency that books not only clubs, but is involved in occasional *high-visibility* events such as festivals and concerts, as well. Exposure in concert situations goes a long way publicity and credibility-wise.

If your goal is "stardom," concentrate as much as possible on the non-club venues. The more career-launching type of opportunities you can create for yourself -- such as recording, getting airplay, publicity -- the more likely your chances for opening doors to high-powered agents.

Be Your Own Agent

Several years ago, an enterprising gentleman was employed as an agent by a well-known agency in Nashville. In a crafty way, he succeeded in using the facility and the contacts available to him for personal gain. This included an opportunity to book himself under an alias. Though the gentleman was quite successful for a while, in due time the "double agent" was discovered and fired -- not before, however, he successfully established himself as an act within the fair and theme park circuit!

Obviously, what the "double agent" did on someone else's time and money was not ethical, to say the least. However, it demonstrates a practical point: An individual can book and promote themselves successfully if they "learn the ropes" and have the *proper contacts*.

Booking yourself may be the only way to break into the types of jobs you want. For one thing, no one knows what's in your heart *goal-wise* as well as you, and for another, this avenue may become a necessity if you *know you are qualified* for certain levels of bookings but haven't been able to *convince an agent* of that yet!

Booking Agents

If you choose the booking yourself route, you must decide on *which approach* you will use:

1. **"Openly" acting as your own agent, or**

2. **Assuming the "Clark Kent/Superman" identity -- pretending you're someone else**.

Realistically, option #2 is much more effective because it presents *credibility through representation*. In other words, people put a lot more stock in hearing how great you are from someone *other than* yourself!

And here is where you have to make a "judgement" call. While some might say using a *pseudonym* (fake name) is dishonest, others argue it is not. Their opinion is as long as you deliver *what you promise to deliver*, what difference does it make in regards to who is making the calls or doing the booking? Everyone will agree misrepresenting or lying about what you have to offer is wrong. However, the art of helping yourself in creative or *unconventional* ways is subject to individual interpretation.

Making Your "Pitch"

A friend of mine who has become a master at booking herself offers these tips:

1. **Come up with a business name**, such as "XYZ Productions" or "XYZ Booking." To make it official, register it (with your county) as a *d.b.a.* -- doing business as.

2. **Get a P.O. Box address**, and if possible, **a separate telephone number** for the business.

3. **Create a web-site**, but be careful as to what you say. Don't make stuff up. (People *can* check things out.)

4. **Print up stationery, envelopes and business cards** with your company name. (Try to get a logo, too!)

5. **Make up a *believable* name** (if you are going the "Clark Kent/Superman" route) such as *Chuck Henderson* (of XYZ Promotions) or *Kathy White* (of XYZ Booking).

6. **Be extremely enthusiastic, but not phony!** Everyone relates to enthusiasm. A typical "pitch" might start something like, "*Mr. Smith? This is Kathy White of XYZ Promotions. I'd like a minute of your time to tell you about a phenomenal new singer I'm handling (or representing) by the name of _____ _____. He (or she) would be the perfect addition to top off your fair's entertainment calendar.*" If "the act" you are "representing" is just starting out, you might want to be quick to add, "*You probably haven't heard of him yet because he's new, but he's taking off like a rocket!*" Here's the time to substantiate *why* he's taking off "like a rocket" -- any kind of publicity, recording, airplay, other fair dates -- otherwise you must convince the buyer this act is definitely worth taking a chance on. Then add, "*Let me send you a promo pack. When can I call you back?*" Obviously, the more "goodies" in your promo pack, the better your chances. (This would be a good time to review the section on Booking Yourself -- A Practical Approach in the chapter "Fairs, Festivals and Rodeos.")

The "booking yourself" concept works great as long as you are willing to do your homework and get good at it. This means you must be ready to roll up your sleeves and do your share of work. Obviously, you will need time, practice and patience to develop your "selling" skills -- as well as your ability to handle personal rejection. Remember, if an *agent's band* is rejected, he pushes forward with another, and it's no big deal. However, if you are turned down *while you are "the agent,"* you may take it as a real blow to the ego. Don't! You'll get used to it, and, more importantly, find out what works best for you.

Six Key Points To Remember...

1. **Concentrate on getting "one-nighters"** -- they provide the most *visibility*. These can include everything from high school and college dances to performances at clubs like Rotary, Lions, Moose, etc. Spread your name around as much as possible. Avoid getting stagnant.

2. **Agencies don't make you a star, they just book you.**

3. **You are only a number amongst many others to an agent.** How many others depends on the size of the agency's roster. Think about it like this: If an agency has three agents hustling to book a total of 60 bands amongst themselves, how much attention -- especially *career-launching* or artist-development attention -- will that leave you?

4. **Agents make their money based on a percentage of what you earn** -- usually 15-20%. Their primary motivation is booking as much as possible -- never mind attending to individual career dreams.

5. **Don't become complacent -- make good use of your time and energies while in your prime.** Even though an agency may find you lots of work, be careful not to tie yourself down indefinitely thinking you've got it made forever. The clock keeps ticking. When you're 50, doing five hours a night six nights a week in a smoky bar isn't as easy (or as much fun!) as when you were 25. Not too many agents are interested in booking "oldsters" still trying to make it.

6. **Make sure your contract or agreement with an agency doesn't tie you up indefinitely.** Instead, propose a deal with options for renewal if an *exclusive* (contract) is necessary at all. On occasion, agencies have been known to hold acts back so as not to lose them to the "big times." If an agency doesn't benefit from or look upon the ascent of one of its acts into bigger and better things as a "feather in their cap," they'll have nothing to gain if that act moves out of their league bookings-wise. (Listing of talent agents can be found in Part II, Appendix C.)

Secrets to Success in Country Music

Chapter 25

ENTERTAINMENT ATTORNEYS

"The dealmakers"

A friend of mine who is currently head of A&R at a major label in Nashville told me some time ago that lawyers play a big part in getting acts signed. More often than not, they are the deal makers behind the scenes. Interestingly enough, most people are not aware of this and don't pursue this viable avenue.

Entertainment attorneys have key contacts at all the record labels, publishing houses and management companies. If you are able to interest one to represent you, your chances of getting a record deal could be greatly enhanced. Of course, it's up to you to *convince* the attorney that *you are worth their effort*!

Contacting An Entertainment Attorney

Check with your family lawyer for any recommendations. See if he or she would be willing to act as a "go between." Since this area of legal practice is quite specialized, it is unlikely that you will find many prospects in smaller towns or out-of-the-way places.

Your next best bet is looking through the yellow pages of a city phone book or on the web. Understandably, Nashville certainly has its share of attorneys specializing in this area, as would New York, Los Angeles, Chicago or any large metropolitan area. If you are pursuing the country market, looking for an attorney in Nashville obviously makes the most sense. Once you have contacted an attorney, it's up to you to "sell" yourself.

Finding influential individuals within your home area, such as the local country music station's program director or newspaper editor, is also a big plus. (Make sure, of course, that the individual you are planning to use as a referral *believes in your talent* and is willing to go to bat for you.) Here again, a good promo pack is definitely a must!

How An Entertainment Lawyer Can Help You

Lawyers can open doors that would otherwise almost certainly remain closed to you. These individuals have credibility and *can make the contacts that you can't*, particularly when approaching ultra-competitive, hard-to-access areas like record companies. And, if the attorney is well-known, a mere association with this individual's name *provides prestige* and can greatly enhance *your* credibility.

When submitting material to record labels and such, a lawyer's stationery in itself is often a door-opener. Publishing companies in particular feel more "protected" when receiving material submitted through an attorney. I'm talking about potential *infringement* lawsuits regarding songs. People have a tendency (somtimes rightfully, but seldom so) to say, "Hey, that sounds like my song on the radio -- the one I sent to that publisher a few months ago!"

Once you reach a certain plateau, a good lawyer is vital in safeguarding your interests and helping you plan your career moves properly. This area includes everything from artist development efforts to advising you on contracts regarding record deals, publishers, endorsements -- *virtually anything that involves you, your talent and the exchange of money.* It is a good move, in general, not to sign anything in the entertainment industry without first checking with your lawyer.

What's In It For The Attorney?

Money, obviously! It is the main motivating force for anyone in business -- attorney or otherwise. Sure, some individuals may enjoy the "star status" of their practice and "perks" associated with it, but **the dollar is always the common denominator.** Although attorneys occasionally work on "spec" deals (contingent upon getting "signed"), most charge an hourly rate. This fee is generally hefty, somewhere in the area of $100 to $300 an hour. In addition, it's quite possible the attorney will want a percentage of advances or bonuses upon signing as well!

Remember that when you're dealing with a lawyer you are putting your life (at least professionally) in their hands. Make sure that you end up with one that you can trust and who will genuinely look out *for your own best interest* as well as theirs!

Chapter 26

SCAMS, SHAMS & CHARLATANS
(Nashville's Sucker Business)

"Son, there are more liars in Nashville than anywhere else in the world!"

Terry Rosco

As in any walk of life, the music industry has its share of "rip-off's" and otherwise unethical characters. It can arguably be said, *probably more* than its share.

Con men find it easy to prey on people in search of a dream. To a certain extent, you can blame it on vanity. Let's face it, one of man's greatest weaknesses is the tendency to believe what one wants to believe. It stands to reason that it is a lot easier to bilk someone out of their money when they are told what they want to hear -- especially if it is done convincingly!

Although it is often difficult to recognize cleverly-concealed schemes, there are telltale signs you can look for. The best way to protect yourself, of course, is to do your "homework." *Becoming informed* is the best way to make yourself scam-proof!

The "Sin Of Omission"

Most of the scams that you run into are not necessarily illegal. And interestingly, those who do get scammed aren't always done so because they have been lied to. More often, it is a matter of *what they haven't been told,* or the "sin of omission," that is the culprit.

Think about it like this. If you are buying real estate, a smart salesman isn't going to open a can of worms by saying anything like "The heat is unbearable here in July," or "The mosquitoes are murder near this beautiful property." In business transactions, most "sellers" aren't going to be *unnecessarily* honest. A lot of facts that should be known are often (and conveniently) not brought up *unless* by the customer. Hence the saying *caveat emptor* -- buyer beware.

Within the music industry, the biggest problem is people all too often *assume* things "just happen" when, in fact, they don't! For example, doing a recording session doesn't automatically mean getting signed to a record label (as some hustler may want you to believe), nor does just sending out your CD's mean anyone is going to even bother to listen!

Certain judgement calls don't require much more than *common sense*. I mean, anyone short of being an idiot should know that there is something smelly if you are expected to pay $500 *to enter* a talent contest! Unfortunately, a lot of people actually do just this -- spend hundreds for alleged "networking fees" to enter a contest. This spells U-N-B-E-L-I-E-V-A-B-L-E S-T-U-P-I-D-I-T-Y.

Overall, "Three Rules of Thumb" can save you a lot of heartache -- and money, too!

1. **Deal with ethical, reputable people. (Check 'em out!)**

2. **Educate yourself about the business (like reading this book!)**

3. **Learn to ask the right kind of questions, then listen carefully!**

Bad reputations travel quickly in Nashville. The "insiders" of the music industry certainly know who the shamsters are. What makes it difficult to put these people out of business, however, is the fact that a great part of Nashville's recording industry is dependent upon what are called "vanity" or "independent" recording projects. More money is generated through these independent sessions than by what the major labels spend recording the stars!

You Do Have To Pay Your Own Way!

Don't automatically assume that everyone who asks for money is a crook. Not so. With the exception of less than a handful of today's stars, all invested money (theirs or someone else's) to get off the ground. **The old saying "If they really believe in you, they will foot the bill" is, in fact, a fairy tale!**

The truth is, initially **you and you alone are responsible for being able to prove what you have to offer -- and that means paying for your own recordings**. Or, as they say in legal jargon, the *burden of proof* is upon your shoulders! Once a record label signs you, then and only then is the tab picked up by someone else. Interestingly enough, though, even at that point, *recording costs* are deducted or *recouped* from your artist royalties. (Hey, but who cares about a measly $100,000 when you're making millions, right?!)

A good avenue to explore in determining the legitimacy of prospective individuals you're considering working with is to contact the **Musician's Union in Nashville**. Additional sources might include the **CMA** (Country Music Association), **AFTRA** (American Federation of Television and Radio Artists), **ASCAP** (American Society of Composers, Authors, and Publishers), **BMI** (Broadcast Music, Inc.) or **SESAC**.

If you are contemplating what looks like a real high-dollar project, it might not be a bad idea to retain the services of a lawyer to check it out. Better to spend a few hundred dollars to protect yourself than to take the chance of being bilked out of tens or hundreds of thousands! (This, of course, is assuming *your* lawyer is a straight shooter, too.)

Here's a look at some of the more "popular" scams floating around Nashville, and a few quite likely making their way to your (yes, *your*) own hometown, too!

"Talent Contest" Or "Audition" Sham

Typically, people are sucked into this one by an ad in their *local paper's classified section*. **The ad indicates singers are wanted or auditions will be held in your area at a motel in town**. There may be a number for you to call, or you are simply instructed to show up at a certain time and place. Be careful not to misinterpret the contest's name. Charlatans sometimes cleverly mislead people by creating names or titles that *closely resemble* well-known, legitimate programs on TV. Unfortunately, everyone from kids to grandparents fall for this one because it all sounds so much like a dream come true -- real producers from Nashville who might discover you. The truth is that *they are not real producers* and *no one is going to get discovered like this*!

And it continues (with different variations):

You are told that if you do well in the talent contest, **you will have the opportunity to go to Nashville to participate in a much larger and prestigious talent search that will be televised, or have a chance to perform at a well-known country music landmark or popular club in town**. Often, however, the catch is you are required to *sell tickets* to your friends, family, neighbors, or whomever to qualify. The price of these tickets is generally $10-$20. **The truth is, selling tickets has absolutely nothing to do with entering a legitimate talent contest or advancing your career.** And at this point, rather than worry about ticket sales, most "suckers" just *buy the tickets themselves*! (Another angle of this sham requires contestants to shell out hundreds of dollars for "entry fees.")

Following the "audition" or "talent contest," you will be informed whether you made it or not. (As you might suspect, virtually *everyone* does!) Of course, the individual must still pay for his or her own transportation to Nashville. What you see when you finally get to your destination will probably surprise and disappoint you -- lots and lots of people -- standing in line! Any feeling of "being special" or being "one of a select few" evaporates quickly when you find out you are number 56 -- take a seat and wait your turn!

Supposedly, as the deal goes, there are "big" producers and VIP's in the audience waiting to listen to you. Aside from performing one or two songs (which you are planning on), you may have the option of performing an "extra" song or two -- however, *it will cost more*. This extra cost is to compensate the producers for "staying longer," which is *total* nonsense!

Once your performance is concluded, you will be interviewed or *counseled* by one of the so-called "producers" who will do their best to convince you that you have potential but *need to invest* in a recording session or video. While what they are saying -- that you need a good recording to get started -- may be true, their particular angle is a rip-off.

Here's how these "producer/counselors" operate. **It's the same concept as salesmen on a used car lot**. Following the contest, each one is assigned to certain contestants -- Joe gets #1-10, Sam gets #11-20, and so on. The "counselors" then go to work on the starry-eyed contestants, cleverly trying to sell them on (big-dollar) recording/video/promotional projects. If they are successful, each "producer/ counselor" gets a percentage of what they rake in, while the rest of the loot goes to the head honcho who organized the shameless event!

Another thing to watch out for with talent contests is the practice of frequently advertising deceptively huge prizes -- such as a recording session *valued at* $50,000 or $100,000 - as a come-on. (*Valued at* is usually a tip-off!) People are led to believe that the recording session itself, along with promotions, distribution, etc., will be worth this sum of money if they win. If you are signed to a major label, yes, this would be valid because they spend hundreds of thousands, even millions, in developing and promoting new acts. However, the *true* amount that a contest like this spends on a winner is at best a joke!

"Video" Sham

Another ploy very similar to the "talent contest" is the *video sham*. Here's how this one works: You are once again suckered into a talent contest, but **instead of just singing, someone shoots a video during your performance**. This video is then allegedly forwarded to "big producers" in Nashville who will determine if you "have what it takes." If you are selected (and again, almost *everyone* is), you are required to go back to Nashville where a "professional" video will be shot. Rest assured, the quality of this so-called professional video won't be much (if at all) better than what a friend or neighbor could shoot on their home camcorder, *but will cost you thousands of dollars*!

One of the give-aways to watch for in this sham (as in others) is the typical "hype" that goes along with it. **More than likely, you will be told that your performance is going to be televised, and millions of people in Tennessee -- or perhaps around the whole country -- are going to get a look at you**. This also is nonsense. If in fact your performance is televised at all, *it will be on a remote channel that is available strictly on satellite dishes*! Very few people watch these locally-originating programs, and the chances of being discovered in this way are, in reality, non-existent.

Be that as it may, the shamsters will convince you that the studio switchboard "lit up like a Christmas tree" with calls from interested producers and other big-shots after your performance. If you are naive enough to believe this, they have an easy "kill." Once you have been duly convinced you are a "hit," all you have to do is to wire for money or go back home to get it! Regardless of whether you have to mortgage your house or take out a huge loan, *you are convinced that they can make you a star*. (A lot of these charlatans have no mercy, they'll hustle your last penny, even if you're on social security benefits!)

"Consultation" Or "Evaluation" Sham

Another real sucker game is one that presents itself as providing an "expert" evaluation of your talent. This deal normally involves your putting up a few hundred dollars to be *listened to*. At best, the most you can expect for your money is a letter with some general comments telling you pretty much what you already know! The "experts" will, however, almost certainly "counsel" you into doing recordings that you (of course) will be responsible for funding.

The selling point of these "consultation-evaluation" shams is the (in reality, very remote) possibility of your demo being heard by a major producer. The truth is, calling this a "long-shot" would be an understatement. It's a virtual guarantee, of the hundreds of people paying their fee to be "evaluated" and later recorded at their own expense, the likelihood of anyone going anywhere is zip!

This sham has become quite successful due to the fact that a couple of the people involved were very well-known and successful producers several years ago. Though a former mega-producer's name is often used as a selling point, it is questionable as to how much this individual is actually part of the program. Reportedly, prospective clients seldom meet with him, only his "associates." With this one, you're better off spending that money on lotto tickets because your odds are about the same!

"We'll Pay Half" Sham

This one may sound good but is as phony as a three-dollar bill. Here is the general idea:

You are told by the independent label they "really believe in you!" Of course, by now you are probably smart enough to know that there are no free rides. With that in mind, the label proposes a project in which they will pick up *half the cost.* They may shoot a figure of $14,000 to $15,000 at you with the understanding that since they will cover half, it will *only* cost you $7,000 or $8,000. Although this may sound very inviting, the truth is the "share" you are paying for is probably the *whole cost* -- they haven't put up a cent! How can this be? Figures and costs can be blown up easily and presented to you in any way the shamsters want. **As long as you know what legitimate recording, CD manufacturing and promotional costs are, you will realize it is *impossible* to deliver what they propose.**

In a case like this, something has to be drastically compromised. To get *everything* you are being promised, the best you can hope for is a very watered-down and substandard-quality effort which will get you nowhere!

"Trade Magazine" Sham

Beware of independent labels that *print their own publications or charts.* These can be incredibly misleading, if not downright false. Here is a typical scenario:

You, the client, are investing $10,000 to record with an independent label. To make sure you are satisfied, (and hopefully *invest* even more) once your record has been out for a couple of weeks, you are presented with a "chart" -- and not surprisingly, one from an unknown or rather "vague" publication (which is most likely their own!).

As part of the ploy, the bogus chart may show Lonestar's current song as number one, Sara Evans' as number two, Alan Jackson's as number three, YOURS as number four, Dierks Bentley's as five, and so on and so on. *How can you help but feel pumped* when they look at you and say -- "Didn't we tell you it was a hit??" Unless you know better, at this point, you're ready to sell your house to do it again!

"Radio Station Talent Scout" Sham

You are approached by an individual who presents his business card and tells you he represents some radio stations and can get you airplay if the station's music director likes your product. You submit it and are later told that the station is willing to play your product at least once a day for a full month *at a cost of only $500*. This definitely smells and is not at all the way *real* radio works. Stay away from this one!

"Publisher" Sham

This one may sound a bit more legitimate but, in fact, is not. In a nutshell, you are asked to pay anywhere from $500 to $1,000 to record *cover* material (stuff that has already been out) or make a video *to pitch to publishers* who have original material and are looking for new singers. **The fact is, publishers are not interested in what you sound like singing covers.** Since publishing-house "demo" singers are a dime a dozen in Nashville, the only legitimate interest a publishing company might have in your voice would go along with the *strength of your own song-writing*!

"Paying A Fee To Enter Talent Contests" Sham

We've already touched on this earlier, but aside from perhaps a nominal filing fee of $10 or $20, you should *never* be asked or expected to pay hundreds of dollars to enter a talent contest, no matter what the reasoning. And the concept of paying hundreds of dollars because of "networking fees" is absurd.

CD Manufacturer "Mail Direct To Radio" Sham

This is another "sounds good, but goes nowhere" scheme! It's become common for some manufacturers of CD's to advertise, as an "optional" part of their service, direct mailings of *your* CD to radio stations. They may even pump you more by boasting that your product will be sent to *Billboard, Music Row Magazine* or *R&R (Radio & Records)* stations, the "hottest" (reporters) of all. What they neglect to tell you (once again, the "sin of omission") is that the music directors of these high-profile radio stations will routinely pitch CD's like yours into the trash can! Why? Because of *no label recognition* (credibility factor), *unknown artist*, and *no direct promotions* on the part of your product. All of these spell "zip" to a music director. Another thing these CD manufacturers don't bother to tell you is that the "hot" stations your CD is being sent to (*if* you're being sent at all!) are the *least likely* to play your product as an unknown. In other words, the mailing option you're paying the CD maker for is a total waste of money! Your only *realistic* shot at getting airplay is on *secondary, starter stations* until you're established.

"Win a Recording in Nashville" Sham

This dandy sounds great, but almost always turns out to be a nasty surprise to the starry-eyed winner(s). First of all, winning a recording session in Nashville means *only studio time* 99% of the time. So, let's say (once the *real* details are disclosed!) the prize is six hours of *free* time. Big deal! At $50 per hour (typical "off peak" studio rate), that's worth about $300. Figure your trip to Nashville will cost *at least* three to four times that, so "collecting" your prize will be a losing proposition from the get-go!

Secondly, without using *real* studio musicians (who almost guaranteed *won't* be included), you're defeating the whole purpose of recording in Nashville. To get the prize you *thought* (and hoped!) you had won will in reality cost several thousand dollars more, a fact you probably won't discover until you're already there. Unless your prize *includes* session players and back-up singers *as well as* studio time, you're better off giving this one to the runner-up!

"Internet CD Promo" Sham

Here's another beauty, a "high-tech" one at that! Naive wanna-be's are sold on the idea that their CD will be advertised and promoted to labels on the internet. The objective, of course, is to find a major label or publishing deal. The fact is neither major labels nor publishers "surf" the net in search of new acts! There is so much "junk" and rip-off potential on the internet, you're smart not to get your music or name involved in stuff like this.

"Talent Contest on the Internet" Sham

Sounds sweet, but it is a zero! You get suckered into submitting a demo and are told there will be a panel of "industry professionals" judging you – or – you'll just receive votes "on line." Here again, there will most likely be a catch before *or after* you enter, which will involve shelling out some cash. Of course, you'll probably be required to come to Nashville (you finish the story!).

"Showcase" Sham

Most often you'll find this in the classifieds of a newspaper or magazine. It's a dandy. People are asked to sing over the phone (or sometimes submit a demo), whereupon 99% of the respondees are told they have great potential. At that point they are asked to pay a fee (normally around $300) to reserve themselves a place in an upcoming "showcase." Rather than being a legit showcase for *real* industry record reps or talent buyers, the attendees are a group of nobodies parading as producers and ready to bilk you out of a lot of money.

"Seminar" Sham

This one *almost* seems legit. Wanna-be's are sucked into a one- or two-day "seminar" in Nashville (once again, generally through a classified ad). The fee is usually $150-$300 and must be paid in advance. Of course, it is non-refundable! The "seminar" itself is just a ploy to further hit on hapless singers for big dollar schemes that are virtually always worthless!

"Scholarship" Sham

This one is for real dummies only! Following initial contact (usually responding to a classified ad), you are told that if you are under 30 you may qualify for a "scholarship." After presenting a demo (or singing on the phone), interested individuals are told that if they qualify (and again, virtually everyone does), the scholarship pays for all the recording costs. Aside from being asked to sign worthless "scholarship" contracts, your only cost (you are led to believe) is for *licensing of songs*, or some other technical nonsense. This smells from the get-go! In reality, you are paying for the recording no matter how you cut it.

Other Things To Look Out For

Probably the most flagrant and convincing lie ever spoken in Nashville is the phrase "It's a hit!" A typical scenario takes place as follows: You, your "producer" and one of his cronies are in their office listening intently to your demo. Once it's over, they look at each other and, with the enthusiasm of winning the lottery, proclaim, "It's a hit!" This phrase has proven to be real sucker bait, so watch out and don't be overly-impressed when you hear it -- lest your ego becomes your wallet's undoing.

Watch out for scams that are outright frauds from the word go. You'd be surprised as to how brazen some can get. A good example: A person approaches you at a club (or karaoke contest), then hands you their card which indicates they are affiliated with a record label or management company. Although you may be very impressed, don't take the information or the card for granted. *Anyone* can have *anything* printed on a business card! And very seldom do "talent scouts" of a record label travel the countryside looking for acts. A&R Department personnel (the *real* talent scouts), listen to demos of promising new acts in their meetings or see them at *legitimate* showcases.

Remember, the best way to become "scam-, sham- and charlatan-proof" is by doing your homework and learning how the music industry really works.

A PERSONAL END-NOTE

I want to sincerely thank you for buying my book. I am very proud of it, and I believe the many years of experience and knowledge I've shared within its pages will greatly increase your chances for success. As I look back, I have one regret — I wish *Secrets to Success in Country Music* would have been available when I got started. It would've saved me lots of headaches, disappointments, wasted time... and money, I guarantee it!

My friends, I am excited about what the future holds for you. The possibilities are endless. Even though I may never get to meet each and every one of you, knowing that I might be a little part of your success because of this book, is a real rush to me.

Remember this, though. Your talent is a Gift. It's up to *you* to bear fruit with it. If you don't, that talent becomes meaningless — like a check that's never cashed.

So what are you waiting for? You were created for success!

Good luck, and may the Lord bless and prosper you—

PS. Please visit my website at http://www.gabrielmusicgroup.com. Anyone interested in contacting me may do so by calling (615) 944-2230 or emailing me at gf@gabrielmusicgroup.com.

GLOSSARY OF NAMES & TERMS

A & R Department -- A & R stands for "Artist and Repertoire"; the department of a record label that picks new artists and material (songs).

A.F. of M. -- American Federation of Musicians, commonly referred to as the musicians union.

AFTRA -- American Federation of Television and Radio Artists (singers and back-up singers union).

ASCAP -- American Society of Composers, Authors and Publishers, a performance rights society. (See *Performance Rights Societies*.)

act(s) -- referring to an artist, band or group.

"adds" -- additions of new songs, usually weekly, to a radio station playlist. (See also *playlist*.)

airplay -- the "airing" or playing of a record on a radio station.

American Society of Composers, Authors and Publishers -- See *ASCAP*.

artist -- music industry term for singer.

artist pack -- a packet of promotional items, usually including a demo, pictures, write-ups, posters or videos.

autotune – electronic/digital pitch correction software made by Antares.

Glossary of Names & Terms

BMI -- Broadcast Music Incorporated, a performance rights society. (See *Performance Rights Societies*.)

backer -- a financial investor, benefactor.

bail-out option -- a release clause in a contract.

ballad -- usually referring to a slow song.

bar code -- a series of tiny lines and numbers found on the back corner of commercially sold products which offer data on pricing, acquisition sources and other relevant information.

Billboard -- popular music trade magazine.

bio -- abbreviation for biography, a brief narrative or story about an artist.

"blocks" of time -- referring to specific time frames Nashville recording sessions are booked, usually scheduled at 10 AM, 2 PM, 6 PM, 10 PM.

"book" – front picture and printed matter in a CD (jewel case).

CMA – Country Music Association

Canadian content – term used to refer to the amount of actual Canadian "contribution" or involvement in a recording. Four areas of criterion include: music (origin), artist (nationality), production (location) and lyrics (origin).

Cancon -- industry abbreviation for Canadian content.

cartage -- pick-up and delivery of musical equipment to recording studios or other locations.

CashBox – former popular music trade magazine (discontinued).

catalog -- a collection or assortment of songs belonging to a (music) publisher.

charts -- referring to playlist charts such as the top 10 or top 40. Chart position reflects amount of airplay, sales and overall popularity. Radio stations each have their own charts, as do the music trade magazines. (See also *music charts*.)

"code" -- a password of sorts worn on demos sent to record labels and publishers. The "code" is a word, number or drawing somewhere on the front of the envelope (packet).

Glossary of Names & Terms

compilation CD -- an assortment of (generally six to twelve) songs by various artists on a single CD.

contractor -- "session leader" for back-up singers (equivalent to musician's union session leader).

"copy" songs -- songs that have been previously recorded.

copyright management agency -- an agency, such as Harry Fox, responsible for collecting (mechanical) royalties for publishers.

"cover" (songs, material) -- see *copy* songs.

custom label -- generally a "one artist only" record label most often owned and operated by the artist or their backer.

DAT -- Digital Audio Tape.

DAW – see *digital audio workstation*.

"deal" (record) -- record contract.

demo -- two meanings: either a basic (not totally perfected) recording; or, in a loose context, any recording (ready to market or otherwise) presented to record labels, publishers, talent buyers or booking agents.

digital audio workstation (DAW) – all functions (recording, mixing, editing) are computer-based (i.e. ProTools, Sonar, Nuendo, Digital Performer).

Digital Performer – recording format, digital audio workstation software.

double scale -- double the amount of standard union "scale," or fee, as paid to session leaders.

"drop" (radio) -- referring to a song deleted from a radio station playlist (airplay).

DVD – digital video disc (taking place of VHS tapes).

endorsement -- a testimony as to how an individual (often a celebrity) benefits from the use of a particular service or product; or, sometimes used in the same context as a sponsorship. (See *sponsorship*.)

engineer (sound) -- individual in charge of the technical aspects of a recording session (running the recording console, mixing, etc.)

final mix -- the finished blending of instruments and voices after a recording session.

Glossary of Names & Terms

Gavin – former popular music trade magazine (discontinued).

hard drive – stores digital information, replaces tape in digital recording.

independent label -- a privately-owned and typically small record label not affiliated with parent corporations or other record companies.

"indie" -- industry expression for independent label.

J-card -- paper insert (cover) of a cassette.

jewel box – plastic CD case.

label -- referring to record company.

label roster -- line-up of artists on a record label.

licensing -- procedure by which the rights to a song (such as in a record release) are officially granted.

limited scale session/pressing -- an alternative to the (higher priced) master session which technically allows for a limited number of records (CD's) to be manufactured.

MAPL system -- basis for Canadian content (Cancon) requirements.

major label -- the large, mega-corporate record labels.

manager -- individual who handles business affairs of an artist.

master session -- premium union recording session.

mastering -- process during which a finished recording is prepared for production and manufacture.

mechanical royalty -- a percentage, or "royalty," paid to writer and publisher based on record sales.

mix, mixing -- combining of various tracks, or channels, containing the individual instruments and voices during and after a recording session. (Sometimes this term is applied to "live" mixing sessions such as during a concert.)

multi-track -- reference to the large tape (i.e. 24-track 2", 32-track 1" (digital), 48-track ½" (digital)) or hard-drive audio files which contain recorded music in an "unmixed," channel-by-channel (track-by-track) mode.

Glossary of Names & Terms

music calls -- promotional calls made to radio stations.

music charts -- scores or lead sheets individual musicians use in recording sessions. (Nashville uses a method called "number system.")

Music City -- reference to Nashville, Tennessee.

music director -- individual in charge of picking material for a radio station's playlist.

Music Row -- the section of Nashville that the major labels, publishers, most recording studios and other music industry offices are located in.

Music Row Magazine -- music trade magazine ("replaced" Gavin).

"name" -- an individual or artist of some repute within the music industry.

non-reporter -- a radio station not aligned with or "reporting" to a music trade magazine, usually located in a secondary market.

one-nighter -- a single night performance in a concert or club.

open-mike -- a popular affair in clubs hosting performances by people from the audience.

over-dub -- referring to additional recording of voices or music once a session is completed.

PAR-64 -- steel canister holding high-wattage bulbs; the basic lighting source in professional lighting systems.

paper ads -- non-existent, bogus "reports" of airplay by radio stations to music trade magazines.

per inquiry -- reference to the ordering and shipping arrangements (between manufacturer and supplier of products) as advertised on TV.

performance rights societies -- organizations responsible for keeping track of "musical performances" (such as radio airplay) and collection of those royalties. They include ASCAP, BMI and SESAC.

"picker" -- popular Nashville expression for a musician, commonly referred to studio musicians.

play list -- songs currently being played in rotation on a radio station.

Glossary of Names & Terms

presenter -- British term for radio DJ.

press kit -- another term for promo pack, or artist pack, which contains promotional items such as a demo, printed articles and pictures.

producer -- an individual providing artistic development for artists including procurement of material (songs) to record, the actual production of recording sessions and often liason between artist and record label.

"product" -- generally a reference to finished CD's, albums, DVD's, etc.

program director -- individual in charge of overall musical programming and other related (non-sales) areas of a radio station.

promo pack -- see *press kit*.

ProTools -- extremely popular DAW hardware and software.

publishing company -- an organization that represents songs and writers.

RADAR -- Random Access Digital Audio Recorder, a popular stand-alone digital recording/editing format (not a DAW system).

"record" -- frequently used to refer to an artist's song or CD (actual *vinyl* records are seldom manufactured these days).

record promoter -- an individual who promotes artists and records to radio stations.

Record World – former popular trade magazine (discontinued).

"reporter" -- a radio station of industry significance aligned with a major music trade publication such as *Billboard, Music Row Magazine,* or *R & R* (*Radio & Records*).

reversion clause -- refers to that area in a publisher/writer contract whereby the publishing rights (ownership) of a song go back to the writer after a certain amount of time.

"rider" -- any addendum or clause in a contract involving conditions not set forth under the normal provisions of the contract. (eg. Artist wants a cooler full of Dr. Pepper at concert location.)

"road" musician -- referring to professional musicians that "go on the road" or tour with the artists.

Glossary of Names & Terms

royalties -- money earned from the sales and performance (such as radio airplay) of songs.

SESAC -- performance rights society, initials originally standing for Society of European Stage Authors and Composers. ("Full" title not used anymore.)

satellite broadcasting -- pre-programmed ("canned") radio. Subscribing stations simultaneously broadcast (except for local news and advertisements) the exact same thing.

scale -- the (union) fee musicians charge for recording.

secondary stations -- non-reporting radio stations, seldom aligned with trade publications.

self-contained -- referring to artists or bands who supply their own sound and lighting systems.

session leader -- individual acting as musical leader of a recording session.

session musician -- studio musician.

show host -- British term for radio DJ.

showcase -- musical performance by a band or artist for a select audience such as record company execs.

"side" -- means a (single) song in music industry and recording terminology.

solicited material -- referring to songs (demo) *requested* or expected by a record company (or publisher, etc.)

SONAR -- DAW software.

"split" publishing -- an arrangement of sharing royalties between publishers.

sponsorship -- an arrangement between a company and an artist whereby the *sponsor* (e.g. beverage company) uses a product or service to promote an act or event.

starter stations -- refers to secondary (less-competitive), non-reporter radio stations that give new, unknown acts airplay opportunities.

"tracks" -- in a recording context, meaning the individual channels of a studio console (board); or, a relatively new meaning, referring to musical accompaniment CD's such as karaoke.

Glossary of Names & Terms

trade magazine -- a publication that offers general information on the music industry as well as its own "charts," which are made up based on chart "action" (play lists) from the various radio stations with which it is aligned.

tray card – back paper insert in CD case.

union scale -- see *scale*.

unsolicited material -- songs or demos not expected by previous arrangement with record company, publisher, agencies, etc. (These items are generally sent back or discarded.)

up-tempo -- meaning a fast song.

vibrato -- the amount or intensity of tremolo (controlled "shaking") in one's voice.

vinyl -- "plastic" records, formerly manufactured 45's and albums.

SUPPLEMENTS TO PART I

80TH STATE FAIR OF OKLAHOMA
City Culture - Country Charm
September 19 through 28, 1986
Oklahoma City, Oklahoma

OFFICERS AND DIRECTORS
Maj. Gen. E.L. "Mike" Massad (A.U.S./Ret.)
Chairman of the Board
Donald J. Hotz
President/General Manager
Kenneth J. Griggy
First Vice Chairman
Edward C. Joullian, III
Second Vice Chairman
C.A. Vose, Sr.
Treasurer
Edward H. Cook
Executive Committee
Edward L. Gaylord
Executive Committee
John R. Parsons
Executive Committee
Paul B. Strasbaugh
Executive Committee
Bill Swisher
Executive Committee
Frances R. Young
Secretary

Ray T. Anthony
Dr. L.L. Boger
M.O. "Bud" Breeding
Robert F. Browne
Maj. Gen. Richard A. Burpee
William V. Carey, Jr.
L. Thomas Dulaney, Jr.
Maj. Gen. J.T. Edwards (U.S.A.F./Ret.)
Richard L. Gaugler
Fred J. Hall
James G. Harlow, Jr.
R.D. Harrison
Dan Hogan, III
Dr. Frank E. Horton
John Kilpatrick, Jr.
Max L. Knotts
Joseph G. Rucks
Dr. Kenneth E. Smith
James E. Stewart
Stanton L. Young

EX-OFFICIO MEMBERS
The Honorable George Nigh
The Honorable Andy Coats
Scott Johnson
Dr. Arthur W. Steller

LIFETIME MEMBERS
Ralph L. Bolen
E.J. Braun
Roy V. Edwards
Dan W. James
Dr. Robert B. Kamm
Donald S. Kennedy
John E. Kirkpatrick
James R. McEldowney
D.A. McGee
O.O. "Sandy" Saunders
Ben C. Wileman

ADVISORY BOARD
Irvin K. Bollenbach
John N. "Happy" Camp
W.D. "Jim" Finney
H.C. "Ladd" Hitch, Jr.
Lee Allan Smith

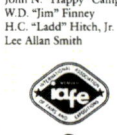

October 7, 1986

To: All Talent Buyers

Our Fairgoers enjoyed every minute of it - all 29 performances.

When we hired Gabriel and his band, we knew he was good because other Fairs told us so. We found this group to be even better than we had been told.

Gabriel played our outdoor stage for the eleven days of our Fair. His warm and friendly personality along with his exceptional talent made him a real crowd pleaser. All of us on our Fair Staff found Gabriel and his band members very cooperative and a pleasure to work with.

Each year on the last Friday of our Fair, we have a "Gold Medal Day." Gold State Fair medallions are awarded to exhibitors and entertainers in several categories. This year the committee awarded the "Outdoor Entertainment of the Year" gold medallion to Gabriel.

Given the right "breaks", Gabriel can become a superstar. We highly recommend him for any situation, be it a Fair, concert or wherever there is a need for good entertainment.

Sincerely,

Rex Ochs
State Fair Consultant

RO:yc

500 N. LAND RUSH STREET • P.O. BOX 74943 • OKLAHOMA CITY, OKLAHOMA 73147 • (405) 942-5511

GABRIEL

"The stadium was jammed as recording stars from six different nations gave their best at the IV International Country Music Festival in Budapest, on August 13, 1988. Gabriel came on...and proceeded to steal the show!"
- Hungarian T.V. commentary

T.V. CREDITS

Nashville Network
CNN • MTV (Europe)
Joe Franklin Show
PM Magazine

CONCERTS & SHOWS with..

David Frizell
Lakeview, OR - radio sponsor KQIK

Earl Thomas Conley
Great Falls, MT - Montana State Fair

Tom Wopat
Lake Charles, LA - radio sponsor KYKZ

Jim Glaser & Younger Brothers
Waco, TX - H.O.T. Fair and Rodeo

Gary Morris
E. Grand Fords, MN - radio sponsor KRRK

Southern Pacific & Osmond Brothers
Pueblo, Co - Colorado State Fair

Tammy Wynette
Hibbing, MN - radio sponsor WKKQ

Ronnie McDowell
Altoona, PA - radio sponsor WVAM

Gerry Ford Ampitheater
Vail, CO

Clear Lake P.R.C.A. Rodeo
Clear Lake, SD

GABRIEL

FAIR PERFORMANCES

Montana State Fair
Alabama State Fair
Arkansas State Fair
State Fair of Oklahoma
Iowa State Fair
Colorado State Fair
Wyoming State Fair
Mobile Greater Gulf State Fair

Heart O' Texas Fair & Rodeo
All-Indian Crow Fair (MT)
Gila County Fair (AZ)
S.W. Louisiana Trade Fair & Expo
Lake County Fair (OR)
Wheatland Communities Fair (WA)
Ventura County Fair (CA)
Erie County Fair (NY)

RECORDS & REVIEWS

Five nationally-charted "Country Top 100" singles to date:

"New Orleans Ladies"
Billboard (Recommended Pick) • Cash Box (Feature Pick)

"I Think I Could Love You"
Billboard (Pick Hit of the Week) • Cash Box (Feature Pick)

"Friends Before Lovers"
Billboard (Pick Hit of the Week) • Cash Box (Feature Pick)

"My Kind of Woman"
Cash Box (Feature Pick)

"Ghost of Another Man"
Cash Box (Feature Pick)

*"It's not a question of is Gabriel going to be a big star . . .
. . . it's a question of what day of what month!"*
- John Curb, *national record promoter, Brea, CA*

For more information contact:

Gabriel

Gabriel

with his sizzlin' new single...

"Little Somethin' On the Side"

...former COUNTRY TOP 100s

"New Orleans Ladies"
"Ghost of Another Man"
"My Kind of Woman"
"I Think I Could Love You"
"Friends Before Lovers"

**—ON TOUR—
AMERICA'S HOTTEST
NEW COUNTRY STAR!**

T.V. CREDITS	SHOWS	CONCERTS with
"Nashville Network" MTV (Europe) CNN "Joe Franklin Show" "PM Magazine"	Heart O' Texas Fair & Rodeo V International Country Music Festival (Budapest, Hungary) Scandinavian Country Music Festival (Aalborg, Denmark) State Fair of Oklahoma Iowa State Fair "Samstown" (Las Vegas)	Emmylou Harris Earl Thomas Conley Willie Nelson Southern Pacific Lee Greenwood Gary Morris Tammy Wynette

Appearing at: _____

Date & Time: _____

Card 1

NASHVILLE RECORDING ARTIST
SONNY RUIZ

- ON TOUR -
AMERICA'S HOTTEST NEW COUNTRY STAR!

DON'T MISS THE NEW-COMER EVERYONE'S TALKING ABOUT!

Appearing at: _____
Time / Date: _____

Card 2

- ON TOUR -
AMERICA'S HOTTEST NEW COUNTRY STAR!

DON'T MISS THE NEW-COMER EVERYONE'S TALKING ABOUT!

Nashville Recording Artist
ELISE

Appearing at: _____
Time / Date: _____

Card 3

- ON TOUR -
AMERICA'S HOTTEST NEW DUET

DON'T MISS THIS!

Nashville Recording Artists
Nathan & Polly

Appearing at: _____
Time / Date: _____

Card 4

Nashville Recording Artist
SONNY RUIZ

- ON TOUR -
AMERICA'S HOTTEST NEW COUNTRY STAR!

DON'T MISS THE NEW-COMER EVERYONE'S TALKING ABOUT!

Appearing at: _____
Time / Date: _____

Greg Spivy is the real deal.

Be it from his 'outlaw eyes' (to hear the ladies tell it!) to his snakeskin boots, he is all Country.

Born in Morenci, Arizona, a copper mining town, the rugged thirty-four year old singer always knew he was born to be in the spotlight. "The first gig I ever got paid for was when I was eight singing with my uncle's band," Spivy recalls. "In fact, I was on stage with my dad (a bass player) when I was only five!"

In high school Greg was a jock but was talked into joining chorus when he realized he needed four more credits to graduate. "That chorus teacher was pretty persistent," he says with a grin. "She must have seen something in my voice." Little did he realize that that something would yield a great harvest in the years to come.

After graduation, Spivey played Triple A league ball for a while, then moved to Texas to be with his dad. Touring around Ft. Worth and Galveston, he quickly gained attention perfecting the Chris LeDoux thing: "singing country but putting on a rock show."

Following gut feelings, he returned to Tuscon and joined the band Wild Ride. With a style somewhere between a Garth Brooks and a George Strait, Spivy quickly became the focal point and built a large area following. In 2005 he clinched the coveted Budweiser True Music title and won a $2,500 Gibson guitar.

By the spring of 2006, Greg made a connection with a Nashville producer who recorded his first five-song project. The mini-album proved to be so successful that local bars and clubs began to play songs from the CD even before it had been officially released! With plenty of interest building in the talented Arizonian, a summer concert tour and radio promotions are in the works.

Spivy remains humble about his new found success. He says that no matter what, he'll always be a regular Joe at heart. "Sure it would be nice to be a big star, but more than anything I just want to make my living playing country music," he says.

We can bet on this, if talent and charm have anything to do with it, Greg Spivy is destined to become America's next household name.

Sarah Huston was swinging when she made her singing debut. "She was only two and the words didn't make sense," her mom recalls. "But you should have heard her. She was something else!"

Born in Weiser, Idaho, the twenty year old aspiring songstress has always had an undeniable air of self-assurance about her. It comes as no surprise that Huston has several beauty pageant successes behind her including two Miss Western Idaho competitions..

In school Sarah played basketball and soccer, and even became a state golf champ! Horseback riding and the "cowgirl thing" were a natural passion, too. But there was no denying it, deep down inside Sarah Huston knew her spotlight would someday shine on her music.

LeeAnn Rimes and Martina McBride soon became her biggest influences. "I remember I was only twelve when I heard Martina McBride do a song that brought tears to my eyes. It did something to me I'll never forget," Sarah says. Though her dad was into rock, Sarah jokes, "In Weiser everybody listened to country on the radio. That's all there was!"

Tying sports and music together proved to be a door opener for the pretty Idahoan. She quickly became a "first call" to sing the National Anthem at local games and events. She also became a regular performing at the "Old Time Fiddlers Festival," a major annual event held in Weiser.

When she graduated high school, Sarah finally had an opportunity to go to Nashville, where through friends she met a producer involved with Rascal Flatts. The meeting yeilded serious interest and encouragement to record a demo, which is in the works at the time of this writing. It will be pitched to several major labels.

"Right now I'm finishing nursing school," Sarah says, "So I can support myself when I move to Tennessee. I've read too many stories about all those starving waitresses."

Those who know Sarah Huston don't think it's likely she'll have to fall back on nursing for a living. "I believe God will bless me with whatever He has planned," Sarah says with a smile. "He knows how much I want to touch people's hearts with a song like Martina McBride touched mine a long time ago."

Sarah Huston photos courtesy of Fenton Photography.

Humane act brings reunion; M

There was a reunion at the Humane Society in Sioux Falls last week.

Gabriel Farago of Gowanda, N.Y., was passing through Sioux Falls 10 years ago and stopped to visit. On his layover, he adopted a Doberman at the Humane Society.

Ten years later, Farago and his dog, Hobbie, shown in the photo at left, returned to visit Nila Sando, the director of the Humane Society.

"I wanted to come back and say thank you and let people know how important it is that such a place is there and that there are animals who need a good home," Farago said.

■ **FISTICUFFS ON THE FARM:** When Gov. Walter D. Miller visited the Arden Shields farm near Harrisburg to view damaged crops on Monday, he was greeted by political foe, state Sen. Roger McKellips of Alcester, majority leader for Democrats.

"Who's that guy over there?" Miller, a Republican, said after arriving.

"Why'd you take your coat off? You wanna fight?" McKellips replied as he put up his dukes.

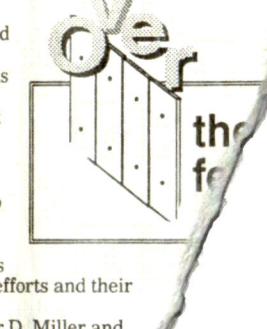

Miller had just shed his suit coat because of the heat — from the sun, not politics.

■ **BALD IS BEAUTIFUL:** Several South Dakotan's were proud to see a front-page story in the *Los Angeles Times*, featuring South Dakota's economic development efforts and their successes.

A photo of Gov. Walter D. Miller and Dave O'Hara, the new commissioner of the Governor's Office of Economic Development, accompanied the story. The ex was good for the state and even mea few business leads, O'Hara said.

But perception is everything a are enough untruths about our s

Argus Leader photo by LEW SHERMAN

GABRIEL

Rising country star's earliest days 'daring and desperate' as Hungarian refugee.

American Press, Lake Charles Louisiana

Seems most singers with a dream come to Nashville from the bayous or the badlands, but not Gabriel Ernest Miklos Farago. He's traveled a lot farther than that. Now on the verge of national success, and better known simply as Gabriel, he was born in Hungary and came to the U.S. as a refugee.

Gabriel didn't stay long in his native land. A few month after his birth, his parents decided to flee because of the advancing Russian army, and fears of Nazi reprisals following a last minute German takeover. Gabriel's father, a physician, had risked his life by providing Jewish friends with phony medical documents to help them escape the concentration camps.

They left one night during an artillery barrage, going on to brave months of hunger, merciless bombing raids and eventual separation. Miraculously, as the war ended, they were reunited by the International Red Cross in Austria. Gabriel's earliest memories are of the mountains around Innsbruck.

Hello America

When he was for the family sailed to America

Gathering momentum with each record, Gabriel was well on his way to national success. "The head of a major label met with me... he loved my singing," Gabriel remembers. "We all thought this was it." The label tentatively proposed a $300,000 artist development deal, then a week later it was a no go. But, as his backer says, "If it was easy, everyone'd be doing it!"

Then Secord, hard-hit by the souring economy, had to withdraw his financial support. But by now Gabriel began to augment his club dates by working shows with the likes of Gary Morris, Ronnie McDowell, Little Jimmy Dickens, Leon Everett and Tammy Wynette.

The Best Tight-Fittin' Jeans

Along the way, he's even lent his club performances as benefit shows via a promotional idea he came up with to help some needy volunteer firemen in South Dakota. It's a beauty contest called the **Foxy Lady Festival**, which includes a competition for the ***best tight-fittin' jeans***.

"I was watching a late show about firefighters," re Gabriel, "and I was really impressed with how on the line. Well, the very next

Debbie Davis is a cutie but the door and dresser make this a **composition disaster** and "home photo" give-away

Chad Cunningham is blessed with Mr. Hollywood chiseled good looks but the **background and graininess** make this too "snapshotty."

Canadian artist Suzanne Palmer is all about looking good in this picture but her **hand competes for attention.**

Cody Stewart has 'the look', but **staring off yonder makes this full body shot way too impersonal** for a new artist promo photo.

Elise lets her youth and natural charm work for her in this **well framed shot.**

Good photo of Buddy Baker at his piano, but the picture is way **too cluttered and his face and hands need a little color correction.**

A **fun photo** of the author, Gabriel Farago, in his sky diving outfit during a photo shoot for his Christian album *Holy Ghost Power*.

168

REASONS TO REQUEST INVESTMENT MONEY
("Backer Prospectus")

1) **To make money selling your own CD.** Typically, once you record you can get a 10 song CD album manufactured for about one dollar each. Figure you will sell that album for about $10.00 (or substantially more) on stage after a show, in a store, or to all your friends. Your profit margin should be about 900 percent per album sold. Even if you pay royalties (.09 cents per song) that's only another .90 cents per album cost to you! Profits on CD sales are extraordinary! (Many stores, including Barnes & Noble and Borders, carry "local" artists.)

2) **To help you get signed to a record label**, a major milestone towards stardom.

3) **To get radio airplay.** Radio stations will be far more likely to play your recording if they know you have "product" (an album) available. It legitimizes you in their eyes. Why should they play something that is unavailable?? It's a handy reason for stations to blow off unknown artists' recordings. Also, anyone who knows the industry will figure you have at least $30,000 wrapped up in your product and must be pretty good (you'd have to be to spend that kind of money!!) An album offers real credibility.

4) **To create booking/performance opportunities.** Talent buyers - the people on fair boards who book entertainment - will see you as a "gonna-be" rather than just another "wanna-be." Your recording is the backbone of your artist/promo pack, and having competitive Nashville product is a must. Remember, venues like fairs, rodeos, theme parks, festivals and conventions are willing to pay upwards of $1,000 to $2,000 (per show!) for a brand new artist who impresses them even though they might not be famous yet!

5) **To find sponsorship/endorsements deals,** local or national, with car dealerships, supermarkets, clothing stores - any other high visibility business. Great cash and publicity potential.

6) **To generate publicity.** Getting a nice write-up or review in a local paper or magazine is going to be a lot easier if you're able to send them your new album.

7) **To break into the "world-wide" market.** The international market, especially Europe and Australia, offers lots of opportunities for new, up and coming artists like yourself. These include airplay, product sale and support tours. A number of American artists even got started overseas. David Hasselhoff (Knight Rider, Baywatch) and several others, although unknown as singers here, sell millions of CDs in Europe.

8) **To collect publishing/writer's royalties.** If you're a talented writer, big dollar potential exists.

Contract and Agreement

    Let it be known that this contract, and agreement between _____ (herein and hereafter referred to as "**Artist**") and _____(herein and hereafter referred to as "**Backer**"), has come about because of **Backer's** financial investment in **Artist**.

    Whereas, it is understood that **Backer** has invested in **Artist** for the purpose of furthering **Artist's** efforts and opportunities as a country singer.

    Whereas, **Artist** agrees to the following terms and conditions as repayment/return to **Backer** for said investment:

1) **Artist** shall pay **Backer** <u>15%</u> of any and all **Artist** royalties received from record company in the event of a major label signing, for the period of one year from date of this signing.

2) **Artist** shall pay **Backer** <u>25%</u> of any and all revenues generated from sales of "independently manufactured" CDs and Cassettes, (other than major label product) for the period of one year from date of this signing.

3) **Artist** shall pay **Backer** <u>10%</u> of any and all revenues generated by **Artist's** "live" performances (concerts, shows) for the period of one year from date of this signing.

4) **Artist** shall pay **Backer** <u>10%</u> of any and all royalties earned from publishing for a period of one year from date of this signing.

5) **Artist** shall pay **Backer** <u>10%</u> of any and all monies received from sponsorships and/or endorsements for period of one year from date of this signing.

And whereas, **Artist** and **Backer** agree as per stated above terms and conditions, this contract and agreement is signed _____day of _____ , 20 _____.

_____ **Artist**

_____ **Backer**

_____ **Witnessed (Notary Public)**

PERFORMANCE CONTRACT

THIS CONTRACT for the personal services of artist or band on the engagement described below is made this _____ day of _____, _____, between the undersigned purchaser of music (herein called "Purchaser") and the undersigned artist or band.

1. Name and Address of Place of Engagement: _____

   Name of Artist or Band: _____

   Number of Musicians (optional): _____

2. Date (s) of Engagement; daily or weekly schedule and daily clock hours: _____

3. Type of Engagement (specify whether dance, concert, banquet, etc.): _____

4. Compensation Agreed Upon: $ _____

5. Purchaser Will Make Payment As Follows: _____

IN WITNESS WHEREOF, the parties hereto have hereunto set their names and seals on the day and year first above written.

Print Purchaser's Full and Correct Name (If Purchaser is Corporation, Full and Correct Corporate Name)	Print Name of Band Leader or Artist
X _____ Signature of Purchaser (or Agent thereof)	**X** _____ Signature of above Artist
Street Address	Artist's Home Address
City State Zip Code	City State Zip Code
e-mail address Telephone	e-mail address Telephone

PART II
(Appendix)

*Appendix A*

U.S. COUNTRY STATIONS
(State-By-State Listing)

* Notates Reporter (Primary) Station

Appendix A

Appendix A

Alabama

Andalusia	WAAO	(334) 222-1166		Hamilton	WERH	(205) 921-3481
Anniston	WCKS	(256) 237-0810		Hartselle	WQAH	(256) 773-4114
Arab	WRAB	(256) 586-4123		Huntsville	*WDRM	(256) 353-1750
Ardmore, TN	WSLV	(931) 427-2178		Jacksons Gap	WKGA	(256) 825-4222
Ashland	WZZX	(256) 354-4600		Jackson	WBMH	(251) 246-4431
Athens	WUSX	(256) 830-8300		Jasper	WIXI	(205) 384-3461
Birmingham	WNBC	(205) 916-1100		Loretto, TN	WJOR	(931) 845-4172
Birmingham	*WDXB	(205) 439-9600		Luverne	WAOQ	(334) 335-2877
Birmingham	*WZZK	(205) 916-1100		Milton	*WXBM	(850) 994-5357
Brewton	WKNU	(251) 867-4824		Mobile	*WKSJ	(251) 450-0100
Centre	WRHY	(256) 523-1059		Montgomery	*WBAM	(334) 244-1170
Centre	WEIS	(256) 927-5152		Montgomery	*WLWI	(334) 240-9274
Clanton	WEZZ	(205) 755-0980		Muscle Shoals	WLAY	(256) 383-2525
Columbus, GA	WSTH	(706) 576-3000		Oneonta	WKLD	(205) 625-3333
Cullman	WFMH	(256) 734-3271		Opelika	WKKR	(334) 745-4656
Cullman	WKUL	(256) 734-0183		Opp	WAMI	(334) 493-3588
Demopolis	WINL	(334) 289-9850		Opp	WOPP	(334) 493-4545
Donalsonville, GA	WBBK	(229) 524-5124		Pell City	WFHK	(205) 338-1430
Dothan	WTVY	(334) 792-0047		Roanoke	WELR	(334) 863-4139
Dothan	*WDJR	(334) 721-9233		Russellville	WGOL	(256) 332-0214
Elba	WELB	(334) 897-2216		Scottsboro	WKEA	(256) 259-2341
Elba	WZTZ	(334) 897-2216		Scottsboro	WWIC	(256) 259-1050
Evergreen	WPGG	(251) 578-2780		Selma	WDXX	(334) 875-3350
Fayette	WLDX	(205) 932-3318		Tallassee	WQSI	(334) 2836888
Florence	*WXFL	(256) 764-8121		Talladega	WTDR	(256) 362-8890
Ft. Payne	WZOB	(256) 845-2810		Thomasville	WJDB	(334) 636-4438
Gadson	WCKS	(256) 435-8172		Tuscaloosa	WFFN	(205) 345-7200
Geneva	WGEA	(334) 684-7079		Tuscaloosa	WNPT	(205) 758-5523
Greenville	WQZX	(334) 382-6633		Tuscaloosa	WTXT	(205) 344-4589
Guntersville	WTWX	(256) 582-8131		Winfield	WKXM	(205) 487-3261
Haleyville	WJBB	(205) 486-2277				

Alaska

Anchorage	KASH	(907) 522-1515		Juneau	KTKU	(907) 586-3630
Anchorage	KBRJ	(907) 344-9622		Kenai	KWHQ	(907) 283-5821
Fairbanks	KSWD	(907) 455-9890		Ketchikan	KGTW	(907) 225-2193
Fairbanks	KAIK	(907) 450-1000		Kodiak	KVOK	(907) 486-5159
Homer	KPEN	(907) 235-6000		Valdez	KVAK	(907) 835-5825

Arizona

Bullhead City	KFLG	(928) 763-5586		Flagstaff	*KAFF	(928) 774-5231
Cottonwood	KVRD	(928) 634-2286		Gallup, NM	KFXR	(505) 863-9391
Douglas	KDAP	(520) 364-3484		Globe	KRDE	(928) 402-9222
Flagstaff	KSED	(928) 779-1177		Kingman	KGMN	(928) 753-9100

Appendix A

Lake Havasu City	KJJJ	(928) 855-9336	Show Low	KZUA	(928) 532-3232
Miami	KQSS	(928) 425-7186	Sierra Vista	KWCD	(520) 458-4313
Page	KPGE	(928) 645-8181	Tempe	*KNIX	(480) 966-6236
Parker	KLPZ	(928) 669-9274	Tucson	KAVV	(520) 586-9797
Payson	KMOG	(928) 474-5214	Tucson	*KIIM	(520) 887-1000
Phoenix	*KMLE	(602) 258-8181	Wickenburg	KBSZ	(928) 668-1250
Prescott	KNOT	(928) 445-6880	Wickenburg	KSWG	(602) 254-6644
Prescott Valley	KFPB	(928) 775-2530	Willcox	KHIL	(520) 384-4626
Safford	KCUZ	(928) 428-0916	Window Rock	KTNN	(928) 871-2582
Safford	KFMM	(928) 428-0916	Winslow	KINO	(928) 289-3364
Safford	KXKQ	(928) 428-1230	Yuma	KTTI	(928) 344-4980
Show Low	KTHQ	(928) 532-1010			

Arkansas

Arkadelphia	KYXK	(870) 246-9272	Little Rock	*KSSN	(501) 217-5000
Batesville	KWOZ	(870) 793-4196	Magnolia	KVMA	(870) 234-5862
Benton	KEWI	(501) 778-6677	Magnolia	KWDO	(870) 234-5862
Berryville	KTHS	(870) 423-2147	Malvern	KBOK	(501) 332-6981
Blytheville	KHLS	(870) 762-2093	Malvern	KCDI	(501) 332-6981
Blytheville	KLCN	(870) 762-2093	McGehee	KVSA	(870) 222-4200
Blytheville	KOSE	(870) 762-2093	Mena	KENA	(479) 394-1450
Camden	KCXY	(870) 836-9567	Monticello	KXSA	(870) 367-6854
Clarksville	KLYR	(479) 754-3092	Morrilton	KVOM	(501) 354-2484
Clarksville	KXIO	(479) 705-1069	Mountain Home	KPFM	(870) 492-5100
Clinton	KHPQ	(501) 745-4474	Mountain Home	KTLO	(870) 425-3101
De Queen	KDQN	(870) 642-2446	Nashville	KMTB	(870) 845-3601
El Dorado	KIXB	(870) 863-6126	Newport	KOKR	(870) 523-5891
Fayetteville	KQSM	(479) 521-5566	Ozark	KDYN	(479) 667-4567
Fayetteville	KAMO	(479) 521-5566	Pine Bluff	KPBQ	(870) 534-8978
Fayetteville	*KKIX	(479) 521-0104	Pine Bluff	KOTN	(870) 534-8978
Fordyce	KQEW	(870) 352-7137	Pocahontas	KRLW	(870) 892-5234
Forrest City	KBFC	(870) 633-1252	Russellville	KCJC	(479) 968-6816
Ft. Smith	KMAG	(479) 782-8888	Russellville	KYEL	(479) 968-1184
Ft. Smith	KOMS	(479) 474-3422	Searcy	KBGR	(501) 305-1015
Ft. Smith	KTCS	(479) 646-6151	Searcy	KWCK	(501) 268-7123
Harrison	KBCN	(870) 743-1157	Siloam Springs	KUOA	(479) 524-6572
Helena	KFFA	(870) 338-8361	Stuttgart	KAFN	(870) 673-1596
Hope	KHPA	(870) 777-8868	Stuttgart	KDEW	(870) 673-1595
Hot Springs Nt'l Park	KBHS	(501) 525-4600	Stuttgart	KXFE	(870) 673-1595
Jonesboro	KWHF	(870) 932-1079	Thayer, MO	KAMS	(417) 264-7211
Jonesboro	KDXY	(870) 239-8588	West Plains, MO	KHOM	(417) 255-0427
Jonesboro	KFIN	(870) 932-1079	Warren	KWRF	(870) 226-2653
Little Rock	KHKN	(501) 217-5000	Wynne	KWYN	(870) 238-8141

California

Alturas	KCNO	(530) 233-3570	Bakersfield	KBKO	(661) 3229929
Bakersfield	KCWR	(661) 326-1011	Bakersfield	*KUZZ	(661) 326-1011

Appendix A

Barstow	KIXF	(760) 256-0326		**Palm Springs**	*KPLM	(760) 320-4550
Barstow	KIXW	(760) 256-0326		**Point Arena**	KYOE	(707) 682-2323
Bishop	KIBS	(760) 873-6324		**Redding**	KNCQ	(530) 244-9700
Brawley	KROP	(760) 344-1300		**Ridgecrest**	KLOA	(760) 375-8888
Burbank	*KZLA	(818) 525-5000		**Ridgecrest**	KWDJ	(760) 384-4937
Chico	KALF	(530) 899-3600		**Ridgecrest**	KZIQ	(760) 384-4937
Chico	KHSL	(530) 345-0021		**Riverside**	KTDD	(909) 684-1991
Chico	KKCY	(530) 673-2200		**Rohnert Park**	KRPQ	(707) 584-1058
Colton	KELT	(909) 825-9525		**Sacramento**	*KNCI	(916) 338-9200
Colton	KVFG	(909) 825-9525		**Salinas**	*KTOM	(831) 755-8181
Colton	KXFG	(909) 825-9525		**San Diego**	KSOQ	(619) 297-3698
Colton	*KFRG	(909) 825-9525		**San Diego**	*KUSS	(858) 292-2000
Crescent City	KPOD	(707) 464-3183		**San Diego**	*KSON	(619) 297-3698
Crescent City	KURY	(541) 469-2111		**San Jose**	*KZBR	(415) 957-0957
El Centro	KWST	(760) 352-2277		**San Jose**	*KRTY	(408) 293-8030
Escondido	KSOQ	(619) 297-3698		**San Luis Obispo**	KKAL	(805) 781-2750
Eureka	KEKA	(707) 442-5744		**San Luis Obispo**	KSLY	(805) 545-0101
Eureka	KRED	(707) 442-2000		**San Luis Obispo**	*KKJG	(805) 781-2750
Fresno	KHGE	(559) 230-4300		**Santa Maria**	*KSNI	(805) 925-2582
Fresno	KUUS	(559) 230-0104		**Santa Rosa**	KFGY	(707) 543-0100
Kernville	KCNQ	(760) 379-5636		**Solvang**	*KRAZ	(805) 688-8386
King City	KRKC	(831) 385-5421		**Sonora**	KKBN	(209) 533-1450
Lakeport	KQPM	(707) 263-6113		**Susanville**	KJDX	(530) 257-2121
Los Angeles	KTIM	(310) 478-5540		**Tulare**	*KJUG	(559) 686-2866
Merced	KUBB	(209) 383-7900		**Ukiah**	KUKI	(707) 466-5868
Modesto	*KATM	(209) 523-7756		**Ventura**	*KHAY	(805) 642-8595
Moreno Valley	KCAA	(909) 247-6199		**Yreka**	KSYC	(530) 842-4158

Colorado

Alamosa	KALQ	(719) 589-6645		**Gunnison**	KPKE	(970) 641-4000
Avon	KSKE	(970) 949-0140		**Julesburg**	KJBL	(970) 474-0953
Burlington	KNAB	(719) 346-8600		**La Junta**	KTHN	(719) 384-5456
Colorado Springs	KLIM	no number		**Lamar**	KLMR	(719) 336-2206
Colorado Springs	*KKCS	(719) 633-9200		**Lamar**	KVAY	(719) 336-8734
Craig	KRAI	(970) 824-6574		**Monte Vista**	KSLV	(719) 852-3581
Denver/Boulder	KXDC	(719) 633-9200		**Montrose**	KKXK	(970) 249-4546
Denver	KCKK	(303) 321-0950		**Montrose**	KRYD	(970) 249-8989
Denver	*KYGO	(303) 321-0950		**Pagosa Springs**	KWUF	(970) 264-1400
Denver	KWLI	(303) 832-5665		**Pueblo**	*KCCY	(719) 545-2080
Dillon	KRKY	(970) 468-2353		**Salida**	KBVC	(719) 539-2575
Durango	KRSJ	(970) 259-4444		**Strasburg**	KAGM	(303) 622-4888
Ft. Collins/Greeley	KXDC	(719) 633-9200		**Steamboat Springs**	KBCR	(970) 879-2270
Glenwood Springs	KMTS	(970) 945-9124		**Sterling**	KNNG	(970) 522-1607
Grand Junction	KUBC	(970) 249-4546		**Trinidad**	KBKZ	(719) 846-3355
Grand Junction	KAYW	(970) 241-6460		**Trinidad**	KCRT	(719) 846-3355
Grand Junction	KEKB	(970) 242-7788		**Walsenburg**	KSPK	(719) 738-3636
Grand Junction	KMOZ	(970) 241-9230		**Windsor**	*KUAD	(970) 686-2791
Grand Junction	KZKS	(970) 241-6460		**Wray**	KATR	(970) 332-4171

Appendix A

Connecticut

Hartford	*WWYZ	(860) 723-6000	**Norwich**	*WCTY	(860) 887-3511
Hope Valley, RI	WJJF	(401) 539-1180			

Delaware

Dover	WDSD	(302) 674-1410	**Havre de Grace, MD**	WXCY	(410) 939-1100

District of Columbia

Rockville, MD	*WMZQ	(301) 255-4300

Florida

Bartow	WBAR	(863) 533-2658	**Marianna**	WJAQ	(850) 482-3046
Belle Glade	WBGF	(561) 996-2063	**Marianna**	WTYS	(850) 482-2131
Blountstown	WPHK	(850) 674-5101	**Melbourne**	WHKR	(321) 984-1000
Clearwater	WDCF	(727) 726-8247	**Miami**	*WKIS	(305) 654-1700
Clewiston	WAFC	(863) 902-0995	**Milton**	*WXBM	(850) 994-5357
Crestview	WAAZ	(850) 682-4623	**Naples**	WBGY	(239) 404-9849
Crestview	WJSB	(850) 682-4623	**Ocala**	*WOGK	(352) 622-5600
Daytona Beach	WKRO	(386) 255-9300	**Okeechobee**	WOKC	(863) 467-1570
De Funiak Springs	WZEP	(850) 892-3158	**Orlando**	*WWKA	(407) 299-9595
Eastpoint	WOCY	(850) 670-8450	**Palatka**	WIYD	(386) 625-4556
Ft. Myers	WUSV	(239) 337-2346	**Palatka**	WPLK	(386) 325-5800
Ft. Myers	*WCKT	(239) 225-4300	**Panama City**	WAKT	(850) 234-8858
Ft. Myers	*WWGR	(239) 936-2599	**Panama City**	*WPAP	(850) 769-1408
Ft. Pierce	WAVW	(772) 335-9300	**Panama City Beach**	WMXP	(850) 234-8858
Ft. Walton Beach	*WYZB	(850) 243-7676	**Pensacola**	WNRP	(850) 494-2800
Gainesville-Ocala	WDVH	(352) 372-2528	**Pensacola**	WYCT	(850) 494-2800
Gainesville-Ocala	WCFI	(845) 561-2131	**Punta Gorda**	WIKX	(941) 639-1188
Gainesville-Ocala	WDVH	(352) 498-0304	**Quincy**	*WTNT	(850) 422-3107
Gainesville	WYGC	(352) 375-1317	**Sebring**	WWOJ	(863) 382-9999
Homestead	WCTH	(305) 245-8150	**St. Augustine**	WAOC	(904) 797-4444
Jacksonville	*WQIK	(904) 642-3030	**Summerland Key**	WPIK	(305) 745-9988
Jacksonville	*WROO	(904) 642-3030	**Tallahassee**	WAIB	(850) 386-8004
Kingsland, GA	WKBX	(912) 729-6106	**Tampa**	*WQYK	(813) 287-0995
Lake City	WNFK	(386) 752-0960	**Tampa**	WFUS	(813) 839-9393
Lake City	WQLC	(386) 752-0960	**Trenton**	WDFL	(352) 498-0304
Lakeland-Winter Haven	WQXM	(863) 533-9227	**Trenton**	WDJY	(352) 498-0304
Lakeland	*WPCV	(863) 682-8184	**Venice**	*WCTQ	(941) 484-2636
Live Oak	WQHL	(386) 362-1250	**West Palm Beach**	*WIRK	(561) 686-9505
Madison	WMAF	(850) 973-3233	**Zolfo Springs**	WZZS	(863) 494-4111

Appendix A

Georgia

City	Call	Phone
Albany	WKAK	(229) 888-5000
Albany	WOBB	(229) 439-9704
Alma	WAJQ	(912) 632-1000
Atlanta	*WKHX	(404) 521-1015
Atlanta	*WYAY	(404) 521-1067
Augusta	WPCH	(706) 396-6010
Barnesville	WBAF	(770) 358-1090
Baxley	WBYZ	(912) 367-3000
Blackshear	WKUB	(912) 449-3391
Blue Ridge	WPPL	(706) 632-9775
Brunswick	WRJY	(912) 261-1000
Brunswick	WYNR	(912) 267-1025
Calhoun	WJTH	(706) 629-6397
Canton	WCHK	(770) 479-2101
Carrollton	WBTR	(770) 832-9685
Cleveland	WRWH	(706) 865-3181
Columbus	*WKCN	(706) 327-1217
Columbus	*WSTH	(706) 576-3000
Commerce	WJJC	(706) 335-3155
Cordele	WKKN	(229) 271-3500
Cuthbert	WCUG	(229) 732-3725
Copperhill	WYHG	(423) 496-3311
Dalton	WQMT	(706) 278-9950
Donalsonville	WBBK	(229) 524-5124
Donalsonville	WSEM	(229) 524-5124
Douglas	WOKA	(912) 384-8153
Dublin	WMCG	(478) 272-4422
Dublin	WXLI	(478) 272-9270
Dublin	WQZY	(478) 272-4422
Eastman	WUFF	(478) 374-3437
Elberton	WSGC	(706) 283-1400
Ellijay	WLJA	(706) 276-2016
Ellijay	WPGY	(706) 276-2016
Folkston	WATY	(912) 261-1484
Griffin	WEKS	(770) 412-8700
Griffin	WHIE	(770) 227-9451
Hartwell	WKLY	(706) 376-2233
Hazelhurst	WVOH	(912) 375-4511
Jasper	WYYZ	(706) 692-4100
Jesup	WIFO	(912) 427-3711
Kingsland	WKBX	(912) 729-6106
La Fayette	WQCH	(706) 638-3276
Louisville	WPEH	(478) 625-7248
Lyons	WLYU	(912) 526-8122
Milledgeville	WKZR	(478) 452-0586
Monroe	WMOQ	(770) 267-0923
Montezuma	WMNZ	(478) 472-8386
Macon	WEBL	(478) 781-1063
Mountain City	WALH	(706) 746-2256
Newnan	WCOH	(770) 253-4636
North Augusta, SC	*WKXC	(803) 279-2099
Rome	WTSH	(706) 291-9742
Rome	WGJK	(706) 232-3160
Sandersville	WSNT	(478) 552-5182
Savannah	*WJCL	(912) 961-9000
Statesboro	WHKN	(912) 764-1029
Statesboro	WSYL	(912) 764-5446
Statesboro	WZBX	(912) 764-5446
Swainsboro	WXRS	(478) 273-1590
Tallapoosa	WKNG	(770) 574-1060
Thomaston	WTGA	(706) 647-7121
Thomasville	WTUF	(229) 225-1063
Thomson	WTHO	(706) 595-1561
Tifton	WTIF	(229) 382-1340
Trenton	WYMR	(706) 495-9999
Valdosta	WKAA	(229) 244-8642
Valdosta	WAAC	(229) 242-4513
Vidalia	WYUM	(912) 537-9202
Washington	WXKT	(706) 678-0100
West Point	WCJM	(706) 645-2991
Winder	WIMO	(770) 867-1300

Hawaii

City	Call	Phone
Honolulu	KHCM	(808) 533-0065
Kahului	KDLX	(808) 244-9145
Kailua	KKOA	(808) 934-8866

Idaho

City	Call	Phone
Boise	KFXD	(208) 344-6363
Boise	KSRV	(208) 658-9807
Boise	*KIZN	(208) 336-3670
Boise	*KQFC	(208) 336-3670

Appendix A

Boise	KMHI	(208) 658-9807
Boise	KLTB	(208) 344-6363
Boise	KDZY	(208) 377-3790
Driggs	KCHQ	(208) 354-3387
Grangeville	KORT	(208) 983-1230
Idaho Falls	KID	(208) 524-5900
Idaho Falls	KUPI	(208) 522-1101
Idaho Falls	KTHK	(208) 785-1400
Idaho Falls	KUPI	(208) 522-1101
Jerome	KART	(208) 324-8181
Lewiston	KMOK	(208) 743-1551
Lewiston	KRLC	(208) 743-1551
Montpelier	KVSI	(208) 847-1450
Nampa	KGZH	(208) 463-2900
Oldtown	KMJY	(208) 437-5700
Orofino	KLER	(208) 476-5702
Osburn	KWAL	(208) 752-1141
Pocatello	KTHK	(208) 785-1400
Pocatello	KOUU	(208) 234-1290
Pocatello	KBRV	(208) 232-7177
Pocatello	KZBQ	(208) 234-1290
Rupert	KKMV	(208) 678-2244
Salmon	KSRA	(208) 756-2218
Sandpoint	KIBR	(208) 263-2179
Sandpoint	KICR	(208) 263-2179
Soda Springs	KITT	(208) 547-4012
Twin Falls	KEZJ	(208) 733-1310
Twin Falls	KAYN	(208) 735-8300
Twin Falls	KTFI	(208) 735-8300

Illinois

Aledo	WRMJ	(309) 582-5666
Anna	WIBH	(618) 883-9424
Atlanta	WMNW	(217) 648-5510
Beardstown	WRMS	(217) 323-1790
Bloomington	*WBWN	(309) 829-1221
Bourbonnais	WIVR	(815) 933-9287
Cairo	WKRO	(618) 734-1490
Cape Girardeau, MO	KEZS	(573) 335-8291
Carmi	WRUL	(618) 382-4161
Carterville	WOOZ	(618) 985-4843
Champaign	*WIXY	(217) 352-4141
Chicago	*WUSN	(312) 649-0099
Crest Hill	WCCQ	(815) 729-4400
Danville	WKZS	(765) 793-4823
Decatur	WDZQ	(217) 429-9595
Decatur	WZUS	(217) 428-4487
Dixon	WRCV	(815) 288-3341
Du Quion	WDQN	(618) 542-3894
East Peoria	WFYR	(309) 694-7578
Effingham	WCRC	(217) 342-4141
Effingham	WKJT	(217) 347-5518
Evansville	WYNG	(812) 425-4226
Evansville	*WKDQ	(812) 422-5995
Fairfield	WOKZ	(618) 842-2159
Freeport	WFPS	(815) 235-7191
Galesburg	WAAG	(309) 342-5131
Greenville	WGEL	(618) 664-3300
Harrisburg	WEBQ	(618) 252-6307
Havana	WDUK	(309) 543-3331
Hoopeston	WHPO	(217) 283-7744
Jacksonville	WJVO	(217) 245-5119
Janesville, WI	WJVL	(608) 752-7895
Jeffersonville	WAVG	(812) 283-3577
Litchfield	WSMI	(217) 324-5921
Loves Park	WLUV	(815) 877-9588
Macomb	WLMD	(309) 833-5561
Marion	WDDD	(618) 997-8123
Mattoon	WMCI	(217) 235-5624
McLeansboro	WMCL	(618) 643-2311
Mendota	WGLC	(815) 539-6751
Monmouth	WRAM	(309) 734-9452
Mt. Vernon	WMIX	(618) 242-3500
Paris	WACF	(217) 465-6336
Peoria	WIRL	(309) 637-3700
Peoria	*WXCL	(309) 686-0101
Perryville, MO	KSGM	(573) 547-8005
Peru	WALS	(815) 224-2100
Pittsfield	WBBA	(217) 285-2157
Princeton	WRVY	(815) 875-8014
Quincy	KICK	(573) 221-3450
Quincy	WCOY	(217) 224-4102
Rockford	*WXXQ	(815) 399-2233
Salem	WJBD	(618) 548-2000
Savanna	WCCI	(815) 273-7757
Scottsburg	WMPI	(812) 752-5612
Springfield	*WFMB	(217) 528-3033
Taylorville	WMKR	(217) 824-3395

Appendix A

Indiana

Aurora	WSCH	(812) 438-2777		Lagrange	WTHD	(260) 463-8500
Aurora	WXCH	(812) 438-2777		Logansport	WHZR	(574) 732-1037
Batesville	WRBI	(812) 934-5111		Marion	WCJC	(765) 664-6239
Benton Harbor, MI	WHFB	(269) 925-9300		Martinsville	WCBK	(765) 342-3394
Bloomington	WHCC	(812) 336-8000		Mishawaka	*WBYT	(574) 258-5483
Bourbonnais, IL	WIVR	(815) 933-9287		Mt. Vernon	WRCY	(812) 838-4484
Carmi, IL	WRUL	(618) 382-4161		Mt. Vernon	WYFX	(812) 838-4484
Columbus	WKKG	(812) 372-4448		New Castle	WMDH	(765) 526-2600
Connersville	WCNB	(765) 825-6411		North Vernon	WIKI	(812) 273-2879
Connersville	WIFE	(765) 825-6411		North Vernon	WJCP	(812) 346-1927
Evansville	WYNG	(812) 425-4226		Owensboro, KY	WBKR	(270) 683-1558
Evansville	WLFW	(812) 424-8284		Paoli	WKLO	(812) 723-4484
Evansville	*WKDQ	(812) 422-5995		Paris	WACF	(217) 465-6336
French Lick	WFLQ	(812) 936-9100		Portland	WPGW	(260) 726-8780
Ft. Wayne	WBTU	(260) 482-9288		Princeton	WRAY	(812) 386-1250
Ft. Wayne	*WQHK	(260) 447-5511		Richmond	WQLK	(765) 962-1595
Greencastle	WREB	(765) 653-9717		Rushville	WKWH	(765) 932-3983
Greensburg	WTRE	(812) 663-3000		Salem	WSLM	(812) 883-5750
Huntingburg	WBDC	(812) 683-4144		Seymour	WQKC	(812) 522-1390
Indianapolis	WIRE	(317) 870-8400		Sullivan	WNDI	(812) 268-6322
Indianapolis	WLHK	(317) 266-9700		Terre Haute	*WTHI	(812) 232-9481
Jasper	WQKZ	(812) 482-2131		Terre Haute	WSDM	(812) 234-9770
Knightstown	WKPW	(765) 345-9070		Valparaiso	WLJE	(219) 462-6111
Kokomo	WWKI	(800) 456-1106		Vevay	WKID	(812) 427-9590
Lafayette	WLAS	(765) 474-1410		Vincennes	WFML	(812) 888-4950
Lafayette	WLFF	(765) 474-1410		Wabash	WKUZ	(260) 563-4111
Lafayette	*WKOA	(765) 447-2186		Washington	WWBL	(812) 254-4300

Iowa

Algona	KLGA	(515) 295-2475		Ft. Dodge	KIAQ	(515) 573-5748
Atlantic	KSOM	(712) 243-6885		Ft. Dodge	KWMT	(515) 576-7333
Austin, MN	KAUS	(507) 437-7666		Galesburg, IL	WAAG	(309) 342-5131
Burlington	KBKB	(319) 752-2701		Jefferson	KGRA	(515) 386-2222
Burlington	KDMG	(319) 752-5402		Knoxville	KNIA	(641) 842-3161
Carroll	KIKD	(712) 792-4321		Lancaster, WI	WGLR	(608) 723-7671
Cedar Rapids	*KHAK	(319) 365-9431		Maquoketa	KMAQ	(563) 652-2426
Centerville	KMGO	(641) 856-3996		Marshalltown	KXIA	(641) 753-3361
Charles City	KCZE	(641) 228-1000		Mason City	*KIAI	(641) 423-1300
Creston	KSIB	(641) 782-2155		Mason City	KYTC	(641) 423-8634
Dakota Dunes, SD	KKYY	(712) 258-5655		Mt. Pleasant	KILJ	(319) 385-8728
Davenport	KBOB	(563) 326-2541		Newton	KCOB	(641) 792-5262
Davenport	*WLLR	(563) 344-7000		Osceola	KIIC	(641) 342-6536
Denison	KDSN	(712) 263-3141		Oskaloosa	KBOE	(641) 673-3493
Dubuque	WVRE	(563) 690-0800		Ottumwa	KRKN	(641) 684-5563
Dubuque	WJOD	(563) 557-1040		Perry	KDLS	(515) 465-5357
Dyersville	KDST	(563) 875-8193		Quad Cities	WKBF	(563) 344-9487
Elkader	KCTN	(563) 245-1400		Red Oak	KCSI	(712) 623-2584
Estherville	KILR	(712) 362-2644		Red Oak	KOAK	(721) 623-2584

183

Appendix A

Sheldon	KIWA	(712) 324-2597	**Urbandale**	KJJY	(515) 331-9200
Shellsburg	KRQN	(319) 436-2676	**Urbandale**	*KHKI	(515) 331-9200
Sioux Center	KIHK	(712) 722-1090	**Waterloo**	KOEL	(319) 833-4800
Sioux City	*KSUX	(712) 239-2100	**Waterloo**	KXEL	(319) 234-2200
Spencer	KICD	(712) 262-1240	**Waukon**	KNEI	(563) 568-3476
Storm Lake	KKIA	(712) 732-3520	**Waverly**	KWAY	(319) 352-3550
Storm Lake	KKIA	(712) 732-9200	**Yankton, SD**	WNAX	(605) 665-7442
Stuart	KKRF	(515) 523-1107			

Kansas

Arkansas City	KSOK	(620) 442-5400	**Liberal**	KLDG	(620) 624-3891
Atchison	KAIR	(913) 367-1470	**Liberal**	KSLS	(620) 624-8156
Belleville	KREP	(785) 527-2266	**Manhattan**	KXBZ	(785) 776-1350
Coffeyville	KUSN	(620) 251-3800	**Marysville**	KNDY	(785) 562-2361
Colby	KXXX	(785) 462-3305	**Oberlin**	KFNF	(785) 475-2225
Emporia	KVOE	(620) 342-1400	**Ottawa**	KOFO	(785) 242-1220
Eureka	KOTE	(620) 583-7414	**Pittsburg**	KKOW	(620) 231-7200
Garden City	KKJQ	(620) 276-2366	**Pittsburg**	KKOW	(620) 231-7200
Garden City	KULY	(620) 276-2366	**Salina**	KSKG	(785) 825-4631
Glen Elder	KDNS	(785) 545-3220	**Salina**	KYEZ	(785) 823-1111
Goodland	KWGB	(785) 899-2309	**Stockton**	KRWP	(417) 276-5253
Great Bend	KHOK	(620) 792-3647	**Topeka**	KQTP	(785) 272-2122
Hays	KHAZ	(785) 625-2578	**Topeka**	KTPK	(785) 273-1069
Hays	KKQY	(785) 625-2578	**Topeka**	*WIBW	(785) 272-3456
Hiawatha	KMZA	(785) 547-3461	**Westwood**	*WDAF	(913) 677-8998
Hiawatha	KNZA	(785) 547-3461	**Wichita**	KFDI	(316) 838-9141
Hutchinson	KHUT	(620) 662-4486	**Wichita**	KFTI	(316) 838-9141
Hutchinson	KXKU	(620) 665-5758	**Wichita**	*KZSN	(316) 832-9600

Kentucky

Albany	WANY	(606) 387-5186	**Cynthiana**	WYCN	(859) 253-5900
Bardstown	WBRT	(502) 348-3943	**Cynthiana**	WCYN	(859) 234-1400
Bardstown	WYSB	(502) 348-3943	**Danville**	WHBN	(859) 236-2711
Benton	WCBL	(270) 527-7716	**Dry Ridge**	WNKR	(859) 824-9106
Bowling Green	WLYE	(270) 651-5290	**Elizabeth Town**	WULF	(270) 351-0943
Bowling Green	WBVR	(270) 843-3333	**Elizabethtown**	WAKY	(270) 763-0800
Bowling Green	WGGC	(270) 782-9595	**Elizabethtown**	WKMO	(270) 763-0800
Brandenburg	WMMG	(270) 422-4440	**Elizabethtown**	WLVK	(270) 766-1035
Burkesville	WKYR	(270) 433-7191	**Evansville, IN**	*WKDQ	(812) 422-5995
Cadiz	WKDZ	(270) 522-3232	**Evansville, IN**	WYNG	(812) 425-4226
Calvert City	WCCK	(270) 395-5133	**Flemingsburg**	WFLE	(606) 849-4433
Campbellsville	WAKY	(270) 789-1464	**Franklin**	WFKN	(270) 586-4481
Campbellsville	WGRK	(270) 789-2401	**Fulton**	WFUL	(270) 472-0405
Campbellsville	WVLC	(270) 789-0099	**Hardinsburg**	WXBC	(270) 756-1043
Columbia	WAIN	(270) 384-2134	**Harlan**	WTUK	(606) 573-1470
Corbin	WKDP	(606) 528-6617	**Hazard**	WSGS	(606) 436-2121
Cumberland	WCPM	(606) 589-4623	**Hodgenville**	WXAM	(270) 358-4707

Appendix A

Horse Cave	WLOC	(270) 786-1000	**Owensboro**	WKCM	(270) 683-5200
Horse Cave	WHSX	(270) 786-1000	**Owingsville**	WKCA	(606) 674-2266
Irvine	WCYO	(859) 623-1386	**Paducah**	WLIE	(270) 443-1000
Jackson	WJSN	(606) 666-7531	**Paducah**	WLLE	(270) 443-1000
Jamestown	WJRS	(270) 343-4444	**Paducah**	WMOK	(270) 538-5251
Jeffersonville, IN	WAVG	(812) 283-3577	**Paducah**	*WKYQ	(270) 554-8255
Lexington	*WBUL	(859) 422-1000	**Pikeville**	WDHR	(606) 437-4051
Lexington-Fayette	*WLXX	(859) 253-5900	**Pikeville**	WLSI	(606) 432-9805
Liberty	WKDO	(606) 787-7331	**Pineville**	WRIL	(606) 337-5200
London	WWEL	(606) 864-2148	**Renfro Valley**	WRVK	(606) 256-2146
Louisville	WPTI	(502) 589-4800	**Russell Springs**	WJKY	(270) 343-4444
Louisville	WIBL	(502) 479-2222	**Salyersville**	WRLV	(606) 349-6125
Louisville	*WAMZ	(502) 479-2222	**Scottsburg, IN**	WMPI	(812) 752-5612
Madisonville	WFMW	(270) 821-4096	**Scottsville**	WVLE	(270) 237-3148
Manchester	WKLB	(606) 598-2445	**Somerset**	WSEK	(606) 678-5151
Martin	WMDJ	(606) 874-8005	**Stanton**	WSKV	(606) 663-2811
Mayking	WXKQ	(606) 633-2711	**Tompkinsville**	WTKY	(270) 487-6119
Metropois, IL	WTHQ	(618) 564-2171	**Tompkinsville**	WKWY	(270) 487-6119
Monticello	WMKZ	(606) 348-3393	**Tompkinsville**	WVFB	(270) 487-6119
Morganfield	WMSK	(270) 389-1550	**Tyner**	WWAG	(606) 287-9924
Morgantown	WLBQ	(270) 526-3321	**Vanceburg**	WKKS	(606) 796-3031
Murray	WFGE	(270) 753-2400	**West Liberty**	WLKS	(606) 784-4141
North Vernon, IN	WIKI	(812) 273-2879	**West Liberty**	WMOR	(606) 784-4141
Owensboro	WBIO	(270) 683-5200	**Wickliffe**	WGKY	(270) 335-3696
Owensboro	WBKR	(270) 683-1558	**Williamsburg**	WEZJ	(606) 549-2285

Louisiana

Alexandria	*KRRV	(318) 443-7454	**Many**	KWLV	(318) 256-5177
Baton Rouge	*WTGE	(225) 388-9898	**Marksville**	KAPB	(318) 253-5272
Baton Rouge	*WYPY	(225) 388-9898	**Monroe**	KMYY	(318) 387-3922
Baton Rouge	*WYNK	(225) 231-1860	**Monroe**	*KJLO	(318) 388-2323
Bogalusa	WBOX	(985) 732-4288	**Morgan City**	KQKI	(985) 395-2853
Hammond	KHMD	(985) 345-0060	**Natchitoches**	KSBH	(318) 354-4000
Hammond	WFPR	(985) 345-0060	**Natchitoches**	KDBH	(318) 352-9696
Houma	KCIL	(985) 851-1020	**New Iberia**	*KXKC	(337) 365-6651
Jena	KJNA	(318) 992-4155	**New Orleans**	*WNOE	(504) 679-7300
Lafayette	KEUN	(337) 457-3041	**New Orleans**	KKND	(504) 581-7002
Lafayette	WYPY	(225) 388-9898	**Opelousas**	KSLO	(337) 942-2633
Lafayette	*KMDL	(337) 233-6000	**Pineville**	KLAA	(318) 487-1035
Lake Charles	KJEF	(337) 433-1641	**Pineville**	KBKK	(318) 487-1035
Lake Charles	KLCL	(337) 433-1641	**Ruston**	KXKZ	(318) 255-5000
Lake Charles	KYKZ	(337) 439-3300	**Shreveport**	KYLA	(318) 222-3122
Lake Charles	KNGT	(337) 433-1641	**Shreveport**	KWKH	(318) 688-1130
Leesville	KJAE	(337) 239-3402	**Shreveport**	*KRMD	(318) 865-5173
Leesville	KVVP	(337) 537-5887	**Shreveport**	*KXKS	(318) 688-1130
Logansport	KORI	(318) 697-4000	**Vivian**	KNCB	(318) 375-3278
Logansport	KJVC	(318) 697-4000	**Ville Platte**		(337) 363-2124
Mandeville	WOMN	(985) 624-9452	**Winnfield**	KVCL	(318) 628-5822
Mandeville	WUUU	(985) 624-9452	**Winnsboro**	KMAR	(318) 435-5141

Appendix A

Maine

Augusta	WEBB	(207) 623-4735	**Norway**	WOXO	(207) 743-5911
Bangor	WBFB	(207) 942-3311	**Norway**	WTBM	(207) 743-5911
Brewer	WQCB	(207) 989-5631	**Portland**	WTHT	(207) 797-0780
Dover, NH	WPKQ	(603) 749-9750	**Presque Isle**	WBPW	(207) 769-6600
Ellsworth	WLKE	(207) 667-7573	**Rockland**	WMCM	(207) 594-9400
Millinocket	WSYY	(207) 723-9657	**South Portland**	*WPOR	(207) 774-4561

Maryland

Annapolis	WINX	(410) 626-0103	**Mountain Lake Park**	WWHC	(301) 334-3800
Baltimore	*WPOC	(410) 366-3693	**Parksley, VA**	WVES	(757) 665-6500
Cambridge	WAAI	(410) 228-4800	**Pocomoke City**	WBEY	(410) 957-1904
Cumberland	WROG	(301) 777-5400	**Rockville**	*WMZQ	(301) 255-4300
Frederick	*WFRE	(301) 663-4337	**Salisbury**	WWFG	(410) 742-1923
Frostburg	WFRB	(301) 689-8871	**Salisbury**	WXJN	(410) 219-3500
Greencastle, PA	*WAYZ	(717) 597-9200	**Salisbury**	*WICO	(410) 219-3500
Havre de Grace	WXCY	(410) 939-1100			
La Plata	WKIK	(301) 870-5550			

Massachusetts

Dorchester	*WKLB	(617) 822-9600	**Southbridge**	WESO	(508) 764-4381
Newton	WBNW	(617) 964-1817	**Springfield**	*WPKX	(413) 781-1011
Northampton	WPVQ	(413) 585-9555	**Worcester**	WGFP	(508) 791-2111
Providence, RI	*WCTK	(401) 467-4366			

Michigan

Adrian	WQTE	(517) 265-9500	**Gladwin**	WGDN	(989) 426-1031
Alpena	WATZ	(989) 354-8400	**Grand Rapids**	WTNR	(616) 774-8461
Alpena	WWTH	(989) 354-4611	**Grand Rapids**	*WBCT	(616) 459-1919
Alpena	WHAK	(989) 354-4611	**Grand Rapids**	WCXT	(616) 774-8461
Ann Arbor	*WWWW	(734) 302-8100	**Grayling**	WGRY	(989) 348-6171
Bad Axe	WLEW	(989) 269-9931	**Greenville**	WSCG	(616) 754-3656
Baraga	WCUP	(906) 353-9287	**Hastings**	WBCH	(269) 945-3414
Battle Creek	*WNWN	(269) 968-1991	**Houghton**	WHKB	(906) 482-7700
Benton Harbor	WHFB	(269) 925-9300	**Iron Mountain**	WJNR	(906) 774-5731
Caro	WKYO	(989) 672-1360	**Ironwood**	WJMS	(906) 932-2411
Cheboygan	WAVC	(231) 627-2341	**Lansing**	WITL	(517) 394-7272
Cheboygan	WMKC	(231) 627-2341	**Ludington**	WKZC	(231) 843-3438
Escanaba	WCMM	(906) 789-9700	**Marinette, WI**	WHYB	(715) 735-6631
Escanaba	WYKX	(906) 786-3800	**Marquette**	WFXD	(906) 228-6800

Appendix A

Marquette	WJPD	(906) 225-1313	**Southfield**	*WYCD	(248) 799-0600
Muskegon	WTNR	(616) 774-8461	**St. Joseph**	WYTZ	(269) 925-1111
Muskegon	*WMUS	(231) 733-2600	**St. Louis**	WMLM	(989) 463-4013
Newberry	WNBY	(906) 293-3221	**Swartz Creek**	*WFBE	(810) 720-9510
Ontonagon	WUPY	(906) 884-9668	**Tawas City**	WKJC	(989) 362-3417
Port Huron	WSAQ	(810) 982-9000	**Traverse City**	WBCM	(231) 947-7675
Saginaw	WCEN	(989) 752-3456	**Three Rivers**	WLKM	(269) 278-1815
Saginaw	WKCQ	(989) 752-8161	**Traverse City**	WBYB	(231) 947-0003
Sandusky	WBGV	(810) 648-2700	**Traverse City**	WBYC	(231) 947-0003
Sandusky	WMIC	(810) 648-2700	**Traverse City**	WOUF	(231) 947-3220
Southfield	WCXI	(248) 557-3500	**Traverse City**	*WTCM	(231) 947-7675

Minnesota

Ada	KRJB	(218) 784-2844	**Morris**	KKOK	(320) 589-3131
Aitkin	KKIN	(218) 927-2344	**New Prague**	KCHK	(952) 758-2571
Albany	KASM	(320) 845-2184	**New Ulm**	KNUJ	(507) 359-2921
Albert Lea	KATE	(507) 373-2338	**North Mankato**	KYSM	(507) 388-2900
Alexandria	KIKV	(320) 762-2154	**Owatonna**	KRFO	(507) 451-2250
Austin	KAUS	(507) 437-7666	**Park Rapids**	KPRM	(218) 732-3306
Bemidji	KBHP	(218) 444-1500	**Park Rapids**	KXKK	(218) 732-3306
Bemidji	WBJI	(218) 751-7777	**Pine City**	WCMP	(320) 629-7575
Blue Earth	KBEW	(507) 526-2181	**Pipestone**	KJOE	(507) 825-4282
Brainerd	KBLB	(218) 828-1244	**Pipestone**	KLOH	(507) 825-4282
Brainerd	KFGI	(218) 829-2853	**Preston**	KFIL	(507) 765-3856
Detroit Lakes	KBOT	(218) 847-5624	**Princeton**	KLCI	(763) 389-1300
Detroit Lakes	KRCQ	(218) 847-2001	**Redwood Falls**	KLGR	(507) 637-2989
Duluth	KTCO	(218) 722-4321	**Rochester**	KMFX	(507) 288-3888
Duluth	*KKCB	(218) 727-4500	**Rochester**	KWWK	(507) 288-1971
Fairmont	KSUM	(507) 235-5595	**Sauk Rapids**	WVAL	(320) 252-6200
Faribault	KDHL	(507) 334-0061	**St. Cloud**	KZPK	(320) 251-1450
Fergus Falls	KBRF	(218) 736-7596	**St. Cloud**	WWJO	(320) 251-4422
Fergus Falls	KJJK	(218) 736-7596	**St. James**	KRRW	(507) 375-3386
Fosston	KKCQ	(218) 435-1919	**St. Peter**	KRBI	(507) 931-3220
Hibbing	WUSZ	(218) 263-7531	**Thief River Falls**	KKAQ	(218) 681-4900
Hutchinson	KARP	(320) 587-2140	**Thief River Falls**	KKDQ	(218) 681-4900
Hutchinson	KDUZ	(320) 587-2140	**Thief River Falls**	KSRQ	(218) 681-0770
International Falls	KSDM	(218) 283-3481	**Wadena**	KKWS	(218) 631-1803
Jackson	KKOJ	(507) 847-5400	**Wadena**	KNSP	(218) 631-1803
La Crosse, WI	KQYB	(608) 782-1230	**Wadena**	KVKK	(218) 631-3441
Little Falls	WYRQ	(320) 632-5414	**Wadena**	KWAD	(218) 631-1803
Long Prairie	KEYL	(320) 732-2164	**Wahpeton, ND**	KBMW	(701) 642-8747
Madison	KLQP	(320) 598-7301	**Warroad**	KKWQ	(218) 386-3024
Mankato	KQYK	(507) 345-4646	**Willmar**	KDJS	(320) 231-1600
Marshall	KARL	(507) 532-2282	**Willmar**	KOLV	(320) 523-1017
Marshall	KMHL	(507) 532-2282	**Windom**	KDOM	(507) 831-3908
Milbank, SD	KDIO	(605) 432-5516	**Winona**	KAGE	(507) 452-4000
Minneapolis	WIXK	(651) 642-4107	**Winona**	KWNO	(507) 452-4000
Minneapolis	*KEEY	(952) 820-4200			
Montevideo	KDMA	(320) 269-8815			

Appendix A

Mississippi

Batesville	WBLE	(662) 563-4664	Laurel	WBBN	(601) 649-0095
Batesville	WJBI	(662) 563-4664	Lexington	WAGR	(662) 834-1666
Bay Springs	WIZK	(601) 764-9888	Louisville	WLSM	(662) 773-3481
Biloxi	*WKNN	(228) 388-2323	Lucedale	WRBE	(601) 947-8151
Brookhaven	WBKN	(601) 833-9210	McComb	WAKH	(601) 684-4116
Bruce	WCMR	(662) 983-6940	Meridian	WYYW	(601) 693-2381
Clarksdale	WKDJ	(662) 843-4091	Meridian	*WOKK	(601) 693-2661
Cleveland	WMJW	(662) 843-4091	Meridian	WQST	(601) 469-1960
Cleveland	WDTL	(662) 846-0929	Meridian	WZQK	(601) 469-1960
Columbia	WFFF	(601) 736-1360	Mobile, AL	WBUB	(251) 450-0100
Columbus	WKOR	(662) 327-1183	Monticello	WRQO	(601) 587-9363
Columbus	WQLB	(662) 324-6000	Natchez	WQNZ	(601) 442-4895
Forest	WQST	(601) 469-1960	Picayune	WRJW	(601) 798-4835
Greenville	WDMS	(662) 334-4559	Prentiss	WJDR	(601) 792-2056
Greenville	WDMS	(662) 334-4559	Quitman	WYKK	(601) 776-2931
Grenada	WQXB	(662) 226-1400	Ridgeland	*WUSJ	(601) 956-0102
Grenada	WYKC	(662) 226-1400	Ripley	WKZU	(662) 837-1023
Gulfport	WGCM	(228) 896-5500	Tupelo	WWMS	(662) 842-7658
Gulfport	WZKX	(228) 896-5500	Tupelo	WBIP	(662) 728-0200
Gulfport	WUJM	(228) 388-2001	Tupelo	*WWZD	(662) 842-1067
Hattiesburg	WUSW	(601) 296-9800	Tylertown	WTYL	(601) 876-2105
Houston	WCPC	(662) 456-3071	Vicksburg	WBBV	(601) 636-2340
Iuka	WADI	(662) 423-9533	Waynesboro	WABO	(601) 735-4331
Iuku	WFXO	(662) 423-2369	Wiggins	WIGG	(601) 928-7281
Jackson	WMSI	(601) 982-1062	Yazoo City	WBYP	(662) 746-7676
Laurel-Hattiesburg	WHER	(601) 296-9800			

Missouri

Aurora	KTRI	(417) 678-0416	Dexter	KDEX	(573) 624-3545
Ava	KKOZ	(417) 683-4191	Doniphan	KOEA	(573) 996-3124
Bethany	KAAN	(660) 425-6380	El Dorado Spgs	KESM	(417) 876-2741
Bolivar	KYOO	(417) 326-5257	Farmington	KTJJ	(573) 756-6476
Boonville	KWRT	(660) 882-6686	Farmington	KYLS	(573) 701-9590
Branson	KRZK	(417) 334-6003	Florissant	KKAC	(314) 921-9330
Brookfield	KCSX	(660) 258-3383	Florissant	KESY	(314) 921-9330
Brookfield	KLTI	(660) 258-3383	Fulton	KFAL	(573) 642-3341
Butler	KMAM	(660) 679-4191	Harrison	KHOZ	(870) 741-2301
Butler	KMOE	(660) 679-4191	Houston	KBTC	(417) 967-3353
California	KREL	(573) 796-3139	Houston	KUNQ	(417) 967-3353
Cape Girardeau	KEZS	(573) 335-8291	Jefferson City	KATI	(573) 893-5696
Cape Girardeau	KRHW	(573) 339-7000	Jefferson City	KRLL	(573) 796-3139
Cape Girardeau	WKZ	(573) 334-7800	Jefferson City	KLIK	(573) 893-5100
Carrollton	KMZU	(660) 542-0404	Joplin	KBTN	(417) 781-1313
Carrollton	KAOL	(660) 542-0404	Joplin	*KIXQ	(417) 624-1025
Charleston	KCHR	(573) 683-6044	Kansas City	*KBEQ	(816) 753-4000
Clinton	KDKD	(660) 885-6141	Kansas City	*KFKF	(816) 753-4000
Columbia	KCLR	(573) 875-1099	Kennett	KCLQ	(573) 888-4616

Appendix A

Kennett	KCRV	(573) 888-4616	**Salem, AR**	KSAR	(870) 895-2665
Kennett	KOTC	(573) 888-8881	**Sedalia**	KDRO	(660) 826-5005
Kennett	KTMO	(573) 888-4616	**Sedalia**	KXKX	(660) 826-1050
Kirksville	KTUF	(660) 665-9828	**Sikeston**	KBXB	(573) 332-1071
Lebanon	KCLQ	(417) 532-2962	**Springfield**	*KTTS	(417) 865-6614
Lebanon	KJEL	(417) 532-9111	**Springfield**	KOMG	(417) 886-5677
Louisiana	KJFM	(573) 754-5102	**Springfield**	KSWF	(417) 890-5555
Marshall	KMMO	(660) 886-7422	**St. Joseph**	KSJQ	(816) 233-8881
Memphis	KMEM	(660) 465-7225	**St. Louis**	*KSD	(314) 436-9370
Memphis, TN	KPPL	(901) 375-9324	**St. Louis**	*WIL	(314) 983-6000
Mexico	KWWR	(573) 581-5500	**Stockton**	KRLK	(417) 276-5253
Moberly	KRES	(660) 263-6999	**Sullivan**	KTUI	(573) 468-5101
Monett	KRMO	(417) 235-6041	**Thayer**	KAMS	(417) 264-7211
Mountain Grove	KELE	(417) 926-4650	**Trenton**	KGOZ	(660) 359-2727
Neosho	KBTN	(417) 451-1420	**Trenton**	KTTN	(660) 359-2261
Nevada	KNEM	(417) 667-3113	**Versailles**	KTKS	(573) 378-5669
Nevada	KNMO	(417) 667-3113	**Warrenton**	KFAV	(636) 456-3311
Perryville	KBDZ	(573) 547-8005	**Warrenton**	KWRE	(636) 456-3311
Perryville	KSGM	(573) 547-8005	**Warsaw**	KAYQ	(660) 438-7343
Pittsburg, KS	KKOW	(620) 231-7200	**Washington**	KLPW	(636) 583-5155
Pittsburg, KS	KWXD	(620) 232-5993	**Washington**	KWMO	(636) 239-6800
Poplar Bluff	KKLR	(573) 785-0881	**West Plains**	KHOM	(417) 255-0427
Potosi	KYRO	(573) 438-2136	**West Plains**	KKDY	(417) 256-3131
Rolla	KZNN	(573) 364-2525	**Westwood, KS**	*WDAF	(913) 677-8998
Salem	KSMO	(573) 729-6117			

Montana

Anaconda	KBCK	(406) 563-8011	**Helena**	KBLL	(406) 442-6620
Baker	KFLN	(406) 778-3371	**Helena**	KHKR	(406) 442-4490
Billings	KCTR	(406) 248-7827	**Kalispell**	KDBR	(406) 755-8700
Billings	KGHL	(406) 238-1000	**Kalispell**	KHNK	(406) 755-8700
Bozeman	KBOZ	(406) 587-9999	**Lewistown**	KXLO	(406) 538-3441
Bozeman	KXLB	(406) 586-2343	**Libby**	KLCB	(406) 293-6234
Butte	KAAR	(406) 494-1030	**Malta**	KMMR	(406) 654-2472
Butte	KBOW	(406) 494-7777	**Miles City**	KKRY	(406) 232-5626
Deer Lodge	KQRV	(406) 846-1100	**Missoula**	KGGL	(406) 721-9300
Dillon	KDBM	(406) 683-2800	**Missoula**	KYSS	(406) 728-9300
Forsyth	KIKC	(406) 346-2711	**Plentywood**	KATQ	(406) 765-1480
Glasgow	KLTZ	(406) 228-9336	**Polson**	KERR	(406) 883-5255
Glendive	KDZN	(406) 377-3377	**Scobey**	KCGM	(406) 487-2293
Great Falls	KIKF	(406) 727-7211	**Shelby**	KZIN	(406) 434-5241
Great Falls	KMON	(406) 761-7600	**Wolf Point**	KVCK	(406) 653-1900
Havre	KPQX	(406) 265-7841			

Appendix A

Nebraska

Ainsworth	KBRB	(402) 387-1400	McCook	KIOD	(308) 345-1100
Alliance	KAAQ	(308) 762-1400	Nebraska City	KNCY	(402) 873-3348
Alliance	KQSK	(308) 762-1400	Norfolk	KUSO	(402) 371-0100
Bellevue	KKSC	(402) 827-1020	North Platte	KXNP	(308) 532-3344
Broken Bow	KCNI	(308) 872-5881	Ogallala	KMCX	(308) 284-3633
Chadron	KCSR	(308) 432-5545	Omaha-Council Bluffs	KHUS	(402) 561-2000
Columbus	KZEN	(402) 564-2866	Omaha	*KXKT	(402) 561-2000
Fairbury	KUTT	(402) 729-3382	O'Neill	KBRX	(402) 336-1612
Gordon	KSDZ	(308) 282-2500	Scottsbluff	KNEB	(308) 632-7121
Grand Island	KRGI	(308) 381-1430	Scottsbluff	KOLT	(308) 635-1320
Kearney	KRNY	(308) 237-2131	Sidney	KSID	(308) 254-5803
Lexington	KRVN	(308) 324-2371	Superior	KRFS	(402) 879-4741
Lincoln	KFGE	(402) 475-4567	Wayne	KTCH	(402) 375-3700
Lincoln	*KZKX	(402) 484-8000	West Point	KTIC	(402) 372-5423

Nevada

Carson City	KCMY	(775) 884-8000	Las Vegas	KCYE	(702) 730-0300
Elko	KRJC	(775) 738-9895	Pioche	KBZB	(775) 329-9261
Ely	KDSS	(775) 289-6474	Reno	KUUB	(775) 962-5681
Fallon	KVLV	(775) 423-2243	Reno	*KBUL	(775) 789-6700
Fallon	KHWG	(775) 428-1764	Winnemucca	KWNA	(775) 623-5203
Las Vegas	*KWNR	(702) 732-7753			

New Hampshire

Dorchester, MA	*WKLB	(617) 822-9600	Portsmouth	WUBB	(603) 436-7300
Dover	WPKQ	(603) 749-9750	Wells River, VT	WYKR	(802) 757-2773
Dover	*WOKQ	(603) 749-9750	West Lebanon	WZLF	(603) 298-5106
Franklin	WSCY	(603) 934-2500	Winchester	WYRY	(603) 239-8200
Hooksett	WNHW	(603) 225-1160			
Lebanon	WXXK	(603) 448-1400			

New Jersey

Newton	WNNJ	(973) 383-3400	Ocean	WADB	(732) 897-8282
Northfield	*WPUR	(609) 645-9797	Stirling	WKMB	(908) 647-4400

Appendix A

New Mexico

Alamogordo	KRSY	(505) 437-1505	Grants	KQNM	(505) 285-5598
Alamogordo	KZZX	(505) 434-1414	Hobbs	KIXN	(505) 397-4969
Albuquerque	KKRG	(505) 262-1142	Hobbs	KPER	(505) 393-1551
Albuquerque	*KBQI	(505) 830-6400	Las Cruces	KGRT	(505) 525-9298
Albuquerque	*KRST	(505) 767-6700	Las Vegas	KFUN	(505) 984-1029
Artesia	KTZA	(505) 746-2751	Portales	KSEL	(505) 359-1759
Belen	KARS	(505) 864-3024	Reserve	KNMA	(505) 533-6100
Carlsbad	KATK	(505) 885-2151	Roswell	KMOU	(505) 622-6450
Clayton	KLMX	(505) 374-2555	Ruidoso Downs	KNMB	(505) 258-9922
Clovis	KCLV	(505) 763-4401	Ruidoso Downs	KWNW	(505) 258-9922
Clovis	KKYC	(505) 762-6200	Ruidoso	KWES	(505) 258-2222
Clovis	KMUL	(505) 762-6200	Santa Fe	KKRG	(505) 262-1142
Deming	KOTS	(505) 546-9011	Santa Fe	KQBA	(505) 473-5722
Durango, CO	KRSJ	(970) 259-4444	Silver City	KNFT	(505) 388-1958
Farmington	KISZ	(505) 325-3541	Silver City	KWNM	(505) 534-1055
Farmington	KNDN	(505) 325-1996	Socorro	KMXQ	(505) 835-1286
Farmington	KTRA	(505) 325-1716	Taos	KKTC	(505) 758-4491
Gallup	KFXR	(505) 863-9391	Trinidad, CO	KBKZ	(719) 846-3355
Gallup	KGLX	(505) 863-9391	Truth or Consequences	KCHS	(505) 894-2400
Gallup	KYVA	(505) 863-6851	Tucumcari	KTNM	(505) 461-0522

New York

Albany-Schenectady	WEGQ	(518) 456-6101	Newark	WUUF	(585) 482-9667
Albany-Schenectady	WZMR	(518) 786-6600	Newburgh-Middleton	WRWD	(845) 471-2300
Binghamton	WHWK	(607) 772-8400	Ogdensburg	WNCQ	(315) 393-1220
Buffalo	*WYRK	(716) 852-9292	Olean	WPIG	(716) 372-0161
Buffalo	WECK	(716) 856-3550	Oneonta	WBKT	(607) 432-1030
Dundee	WFLR	(607) 243-7158	Oneonta	WDLA	(607) 432-1030
Elmira	WYTX	(607) 732-4400	Oneonta	WDOS	(607) 432-1500
Elmira	WOKN	(607) 733-5626	Poughkeepsie	WRWD	(845) 471-2300
Elmira	WPGI	(607) 732-4400	Poughkeepsie	WRWD	(845) 454-2800
Fulton	WAMF	(315) 593-1300	Pulaski	WSCP	(315) 298-3185
Geneva	WFLK	(315) 781-1101	Queensbury	WFFG	(518) 793-7733
Glen Falls	WEGQ	(518) 456-6101	Rochester	*WBEE	(585) 423-2900
Hornell	WCKR	(607) 324-4141	Syracuse	*WBBS	(315) 472-9797
Ithaca	WQNY	(607) 257-6400	Utica	WBGK	(315) 734-9245
Jamestown	WHUG	(716) 664-2313	Utica	WBUG	(315) 734-9245
Lancaster	WXRL	(716) 681-1313	Vestal	WBBI	(607) 584-5800
Latham	*WGNA	(518) 785-9800	Warsaw	WCJW	(585) 786-8131
Liberty	WVOS	(845) 292-5533	Watertown	WBDR	(315) 782-1240
Liberty	WDNB	(845) 292-7535	Watertown	*WFRY	(315) 788-0790
Lowville	WBRV	(315) 376-7500	Wellsville	WLSV	(585) 593-6070
Lowville	WLLG	(315) 376-7500	Wellsville	WZKZ	(585) 593-9553
Malone	WVNV	(518) 483-1100	Whitesboro	*WFRG	(315) 768-9500

Appendix A

North Carolina

Ahoskie	WQDK	(252) 332-7993		Mocksville	WDSL	(336) 751-1520
Asheboro	WKXR	(336) 625-2187		Monroe	WIXE	(704) 289-2525
Asheville	*WKSF	(828) 257-2700		Morehead City	WNBR	(252) 247-2002
Benson	WPYB	(919) 894-1130		Morehead City	WZBR	(252) 247-2002
Black Mountain	WWRN	(828) 669-3880		Morehead	WZBR	(252) 247-2002
Burlington	WKXU	(336) 584-0126		Morganton	WMNC	(828) 437-0521
Burnsville	WKYK	(828) 682-3798		Mount Airy	WSYD	(336) 786-2147
Canton	WPTL	(828) 648-3576		Murphy	WCVP	(828) 837-2151
Charlotte	*WKKT	(704) 714-9444		Murphy	WKRK	(828) 837-4332
Charlotte	*WSOC	(704) 342-2644		Nags Head	*WRSF	(252) 449-8331
Clinton	WRRZ	(910) 592-2165		New Bern	WSME	(252) 633-1490
Deep Gap	WMMY	(336) 877-1060		New Bern	WWNK	(252) 672-5900
Fayetteville	*WKML	(910) 483-9565		New Bern	WWHA	(252) 672-5900
Fayetteville	WFVL	(910) 864-5222		Newland	WECR	(828) 733-0188
Florence, SC	WEGX	(843) 665-0970		No. Wilkesboro	WKBC	(336) 667-2221
Forest City	WAGY	(828) 245-9887		Powells Point	WWOC	(252) 491-9295
Franklin	WNCC	(828) 524-4418		Raleigh	*WQDR	(919) 790-6961
Galax, VA	WBRF	(276) 236-9273		Raleigh	WCMC	(919) 890-6101
Goldsboro	WKIX	(919) 736-1699		Roanoke Rapids	WPTM	(252) 536-3115
Greensboro	*WTQR	(336) 822-2000		Rocky Mount	WDWG	(252) 442-8092
Greenville	WWEA	(252) 672-5900		Roxboro	WKRX	(336) 599-0266
Greenville	WWGL	(252) 442-8092		Rutherfordton	WCAB	(828) 287-3356
Greenville	WNBB	(252) 638-8500		Sanford	WWGP	(919) 775-3525
Henderson	WIZS	(252) 492-3001		Shallotte	WCCA	(910) 754-9840
High Point	WGOS	(336) 434-5024		Shelby	WADA	(704) 482-1390
High Point	WAAA	(336) 887-0983		Smithfield	WMPM	(919) 934-2434
High Point	WIST	(336) 887-0983		Sparta	WCOK	(336) 372-8231
Kill Devil Hills	WCMS	(252) 480-4655		Statesville	WBRF	(704) 872-6348
Kings Mountain	WKMT	(704) 739-1220		Statesville	WFMX	(704) 872-6348
Kinston	*WRNS	(252) 522-4141		Taylorsville	WACB	(828) 632-4621
Lenoir	WKGX	(828) 754-4180		Wanchese	WNHW	(252) 475-1888
Louisburg	WYRN	(919) 496-3105		West Jefferson	WKSK	(336) 246-6001
Marion	WBRM	(828) 652-9500		Wilmington	*WWQQ	(910) 763-9977

North Dakota

Belcourt	KEYA	(701) 477-5686		Fargo	KVMI	
Bismarck	KBMR	(701) 255-1234		Grafton	KAOC	(701) 352-0431
Bismarck	KQDY	(701) 255-1234		Grafton	KXPO	(701) 352-0431
Bottineau	KBTO	(701) 228-5151		Grand Forks	KNOX	(701) 775-4611
Bowman	KPOK	(701) 523-3883		Grand Forks	KYCK	(701) 775-4611
Carrington	KDAK	(701) 652-3151		Grand Forks	KSNR	(701) 746-1417
Detroit Lakes, MN	KBOT	(218) 847-5624		Hettinger	KNDC	(701) 567-2421
Devils Lake	KDLR	(701) 662-2162		Jamestown	KSJB	(701) 252-3570
Devils Lake	KZZY	(701) 662-7563		Jamestown	KYNU	(701) 252-1400
Dickinson	KCAD	(701) 227-1876		Langdon	KNDK	(701) 256-1080
Fargo	KFAB	(701) 237-5346		Lisbon	KQLX	(701) 683-5287
Fargo	*KVOX	(701) 237-4500		Minot	KCJB	(701) 852-0361
Fargo	KDAM	(701) 237-5346		Minot	KYYX	(701) 852-0361

Appendix A

New Town	KMHA	(701) 627-3333	Valley City	KOVC	(701) 845-1490
Oakes	KDDR	(701) 742-2187	Wahpeton	KBMW	(701) 642-8747
Plentywood, MT	KATQ	(406) 765-1480	Williston	KDSR	(701) 572-4478
Rugby	KZZJ	(701) 776-5254	Williston	KEYZ	(701) 572-5371
Tioga	KTGO	(701) 664-3322	Williston	KYYZ	(701) 572-5371

Ohio

Akron	*WQMX	(330) 869-9800	Lima	WIMT	(419) 223-2060
Ashland	WNCO	(419) 289-2605	Logan	WLGN	(740) 385-2151
Ashtabula	WYBL	(440) 993-2126	Marion	WMRN	(740) 383-1131
Brookfield	WICT	(330) 448-5050	Middletown	WPFB	(513) 422-3625
Cambridge	WWKC	(740) 432-5605	Milan	WKFM	(419) 609-5961
Chillicothe	WKKJ	(740) 773-3000	Montpelier	WLZZ	(419) 485-5530
Cincinnati	*WUBE	(513) 721-1050	Nelsonville	WAIS	(740) 753-4094
Cincinnati	*WYGY	(513) 241-9898	Nelsonville	WSEO	(740) 753-4094
Columbus	*WCOL	(614) 486-6101	New Philadelphia	WTUZ	(330) 339-2222
Columbus	*WHOK	(614) 225-9465	Newark	WCLT	(740) 345-4004
Coshocton	WTNS	(740) 622-1560	Oberlin	WOBL	(440) 774-1320
Dayton	WEDI	(937) 372-3531	Richmond, IN	WQLK	(765) 962-1595
Dayton	WHKO	(937) 259-2111	Springfield	WKSW	(937) 399-5300
Dayton	WKFI	(937) 372-3531	Steubenville	WOGH	(740) 283-4747
Defiance	WZOM	(419) 784-1059	Toledo	WTOD	(419) 725-5700
East Liverpool	WOGF	(330) 385-1490	Toledo	*WKKO	(419) 725-5700
Findlay	WCKY	(419) 425-1077	Washington Court House	WCHO	(740) 335-0941
Fremont	WFRO	(419) 332-8218	Waverly	WXIZ	(740) 947-2166
Geneva	WKKY	(440) 466-9559	West Union	WRAC	(937) 544-9722
Georgetown	WAOL	(937) 378-6151	Wheeling, WV	*WOVK	(304) 232-1170
Greenville	WTGR	(937) 548-5085	Wooster	WQKT	(330) 264-5122
Hillsboro	WSRW	(937) 393-1590	Xenia	WBZI	(937) 372-3531
Independence	*WGAR	(216) 520-2600	Youngstown	*WQXK	(330) 783-1000
Jackson	WCJO	(740) 286-1330	Youngstown-Warren	WWGY	(724) 654-5501
Lima	WFGF	(419) 331-1600			

Oklahoma

Ada	KKFC	(580) 332-2211	Enid	KNID	(580) 237-1390
Ada	KYKC	(580) 436-1616	Enid	KOFM	(580) 234-6371
Altus	KEYB	(580) 482-1555	Eufaula	KTNT	(918) 689-3663
Altus	KWHW	(580) 482-1450	Frederick	KYBE	(580) 335-5923
Ardmore	KKAJ	(580) 226-0421	Grove	KGVE	(918) 786-2211
Atoka	KHKC	(580) 889-3392	Guymon	KGYN	(580) 338-1210
Bartlesville	KRIG	(918) 336-1001	Hobart	KTJS	(580) 726-5656
Bristow	KREK	(918) 367-5501	Hugo	KIHN	(580) 326-6411
Broken Bow	KKBI	(580) 584-3388	Hugo	KITX	(580) 326-2555
Duncan	KKEN	(580) 255-1350	Idabel	KBEL	(580) 286-6642
Duncan	KRPT	(580) 255-1350	Lawton	KLAW	(580) 581-3600
Durant	KLBC	(580) 924-3100	Lindsay	KBLP	(580) 286-6642
Elk City	KECO	(580) 225-9696	Marlow	KFXI	(580) 658-9292

Appendix A

Marlow	KIXO	(580) 622-6000
McAlester	KMCO	(918) 426-1050
McAlester	KNED	(918) 426-1050
Muskogee	KMMY	(918) 682-2488
Muskogee	KTFX	(918) 684-1022
Oklahoma City	*KTST	(405) 840-5271
Oklahoma City	KKNG	(405) 616-5500
Oklahoma City	KMMZ	(405) 848-0100
Oklahoma City	*KXXY	(405) 840-5271
Okmulgee	KOKL	(918) 756-3646
Ponca City	KPNC	(580) 765-2485
Poteau	KPRV	(918) 647-3221
Shawnee	KIRC	(405) 382-0105
Shawnee	KWSH	(405) 382-0105
Stillwater	KGFY	(405) 372-7800
Tahlequah	KEOK	(918) 456-2511
Tulsa	KMUR	(918) 496-7700
Tulsa	KWEN	(918) 743-3434
Tulsa	KXBL	(918) 743-7814
Tulsa	*KVOO	(918) 743-7814
Weatherford	KWEY	(580) 772-5939
Woodward	KWFX	(580) 256-0935
Woodward	KWOX	(580) 256-4101

Oregon

Albany	KXPC	(541) 928-1926
Astoria	KCYS	(503) 717-9643
Astoria	KVAS	(503) 325-2911
Bend	KMTK	(541) 389-9500
Bend	KRCO	(541) 383-3825
Bend	KSJJ	(541) 388-3300
Burns	KZZR	(541) 573-2055
Clackamas	KGUY	(503) 222-1150
Coquille	KSHR	(541) 396-2141
Cottage Grove	KNND	(541) 942-2468
Enterprise	KWVR	(541) 426-4577
Eugene	*KKNU	(541) 484-9400
Grants Pass	KRRM	(541) 479-6497
Hermiston	KOHU	(541) 567-6500
Hood River	KIHR	(541) 386-1511
John Day	KJDY	(541) 575-1185
Klamath Falls	KFLS	(541) 882-4656
Klamath Falls	KLAD	(541) 882-8833
La Grande	KCMB	(541) 963-3405
Medford	KAKT	(541) 779-1550
Medford	*KRWQ	(541) 857-0340
Milton Freewater	KTEL	(541) 938-6688
Newport	KNCU	(541) 265-2266
Newport	KSHL	(541) 265-6477
Pendleton	KWHT	(541) 278-2500
Portland	*KWJJ	(503) 228-4393
Reedsport	KDUN	(541) 271-5558
Roseburg	KRNR	(541) 673-5551
Roseburg	KRSB	(541) 672-6641
St. Helens	KOHI	(503) 397-1600
Sweet Home	KFIR	(541) 367-5115
The Dalles	KYYT	(541) 296-9102
Tillamook	KIXT	(503) 842-3888
Woodburn	KCKX	(503) 769-1460

Pennsylvania

Avis	WQBR	(570) 769-2327
Bala Cynwyd	*WXTU	(610) 667-9000
Brownsville	WFGI	(724) 938-2000
Brownsville	WOGG	(724) 938-2000
Carlisle	WIOO	(717) 243-1200
Clarion	WWCH	(814) 226-4500
Corry	WEYZ	(814) 664-8694
Coudersport	WFRM	(814) 274-8600
Du Bois	WOWQ	(814) 371-6100
Elizabethtown	*WCAT	(717) 367-7700
Emporium	WLEM	(814) 486-3712
Ephrata	*WIOV	(717) 738-1191
Erie	WUSE	(814) 461-1000
Erie	*WXTA	(814) 868-5355
Everett	WSKE	(814) 652-2600
Frostburg, MD	WFRB	(301) 689-8871
Gettysburg	*WGTY	(717) 334-3101
Greencastle	*WAYZ	(717) 597-9200
Harrisburg	*WRBT	(717) 540-8800
Hollidaysburg	WFGY	(814) 941-9800
Johnstown	*WMTZ	(814) 535-8554
Johnstown	WFGI	(814) 255-4186
Kane	WLMI	(814) 837-9711
Lebanon	WWSM	(717) 272-1510
Lehigh Valley	*WCTO	(610) 266-7600
Lewistown	WVNW	(717) 242-1493
Mansfield	WDKC	(570) 662-9000
Meadville	WGYI	(814) 724-1111

Appendix A

Meadville	WGYY	(814) 724-1111	**Shenandoah**	WMBT	(570) 462-2759
Mexico	WJUN	(717) 436-2135	**Steubenville**	WOGH	(740) 283-4747
Philipsburg	WPHB	(814) 342-2300	**Troy**	WHGL	(570) 297-0100
Pittsburgh	*WDSY	(412) 920-9400	**Warren**	WKNB	(814) 723-1310
Pittsburgh	*WOGI	(412) 279-5400	**Washington**	WKZV	(724) 228-6678
Pittston	WGGI	(570) 883-9800	**Wilkes Barre-Scranton**	WBZR	(570) 928-7200
Pittston	*WGGY	(570) 883-9800	**Wilkes Barre-Scranton**	WCDL	(570) 735-0730
Ridgway	WDDH	(814) 772-9700	**Wilkes Barre-Scranton**	WSJR	(570) 824-9000
Roaring Spring	WKMC	(814) 224-7501	**Williamsport**	WBLJ	(570) 327-1400
Selinsgrove	WLGL	(570) 374-8819	**Williamsport**	WBYL	(570) 327-1400
Selinsgrove	WWBE	(570) 374-8819	**Williamsport**	WILQ	(570) 323-8200
Selinsgrove	WYGL	(570) 374-8819	**York**	WHVR	(717) 637-3831

Rhode Island

Hope Valley	WJJF	(401) 539-1180	**Providence**	*WCTK	(401) 467-4366

South Carolina

Allendale	WDOG	(803) 584-3500	**Loris**	WLSC	(843) 756-1183
Bishopville	WAGS	(803) 484-5415	**Mount Pleasant**	*WEZL	(843) 884-2534
Bishopville	WJDJ	(803) 484-5415	**Murrells Inlet**	WYAK	(843) 651-7869
Columbia	WWNQ	(803) 447-1283	**North Augusta**	*WKXC	(803) 279-2099
Columbia	WWNU	(803) 447-1283	**North Charleston**	*WNKT	(843) 277-1200
Columbia	WCOS	(803) 771-0105	**Rock Hill**	WRHM	(803) 324-1071
Florence	WEGX	(843) 665-0970	**Rock Hill**	WVSZ	(803) 324-1071
Florence	WHLZ	(843) 661-5000	**Spartanburg**	WKDY	(864) 573-1400
Gaffney	WAGI	(864) 489-9066	**Sumter**	WKHT	(803) 775-2321
Gaffney	WEAC	(864) 489-9066	**Surfside Bch**	*WGTR	(843) 293-0107
Greenville	*WESC	(864) 242-4660	**Tabor City, NC**	WTAB	(910) 653-2131
Greenville	*WSSL	(864) 242-4660	**Union**	WBCU	(864) 427-2411
Greenville	WGVC	(864) 271-3200	**Walhalla**	WGOG	(864) 638-3616
Hilton Head Island	WGZR	(843) 785-9569	**Walterboro**	WALI	(843) 549-1543
Lancaster	WAGL	(803) 283-8431			

South Dakota

Aberdeen	KKAA	(605) 225-1560	**Lemmon**	KBJM	(605) 374-5747
Belle Fourche	KBFS	(605) 892-2571	**Luverne, MN**	KLQL	(507) 283-4444
Brookings	KKQQ	(605) 692-9125	**Madison**	KJAM	(605) 256-4515
Dakota Dunes	KKYY	(712) 258-5655	**Milbank**	KDIO	(605) 432-5516
Hot Springs	KZMX	(605) 745-3637	**Mitchell**	KMIT	(605) 996-9667
Huron	KOKK	(605) 352-1933	**Mobridge**	KMLO	(605) 845-3654
Huron	KZNC	(605) 352-8621	**Pierre**	KGFX	(605) 224-8686
Pierre	KPLO	(605) 224-8686	**Rapid City**	KIQK	(605) 343-0888
Rapid City	KIMM	(605) 348-1100	**Rapid City**	*KOUT	(605) 348-1100

Appendix A

Sioux Falls	KIKN	(605) 361-0300		**Sturgis**	KBHB	(605) 347-4455
Sioux Falls	KKHG	(605) 335-6896		**Watertown**	KDLO	(605) 886-8444
Sioux Falls	KTWB	(605) 331-5350		**Watertown**	KSDR	(605) 886-5747
Sioux Falls	KXRB	(605) 361-0300		**Winner**	KWYR	(605) 842-3333
Sioux Falls	KWSF	(605) 335-6896		**Yankton**	KKYA	(605) 665-7892
Sisseton	KBWS	(605) 698-3471		**Yankton**	WNAX	(605) 665-7442
Spearfish	KZZI	(605) 642-5747				

Tennessee

Ardmore	WSLV	(931) 427-2178		**Hohenwald**	WMLR	(931) 796-5967
Ashland City	WQSV	(615) 792-6789		**Huntingdon**	WDAP	(731) 986-9746
Athens	WJSQ	(423) 745-1000		**Huntingdon**	WVHR	(731) 986-0242
Athens	WLAR	(423) 745-1000		**Huntingdon**	WWON	(731) 986-9746
Bolivar	WMOD	(731) 658-4320		**Jackson**	WTNE	(731) 855-0098
Bristol, VA	*WXBQ	(276) 669-8112		**Jackson**	WTNV	(731) 427-3316
Brownsville	WTBG	(731) 772-3700		**Jackson**	WWYN	(731) 427-9616
Byrdstown	WSBI	(606) 387-6625		**Jamestown**	WDEB	(931) 879-8164
Camden	WFWL	(731) 584-7570		**Jefferson City**	WJFC	(865) 475-3825
Carthage	WUCZ	(615) 735-1350		**Kingsport**	WHHG	(423) 543-6875
Centerville	WNKX	(931) 729-5191		**Knoxville**	WKZX	(865) 981-9636
Chattanooga	*WUSY	(423) 892-3333		**Knoxville**	*WIVK	(865) 588-6511
Chattanooga	WNGA	(423) 892-3333		**La Fayette, GA**	WQCH	(706) 638-3276
Chattanooga	WOGT	(423) 756-6141		**La Follete**	WQLA	(423) 566-1000
Clarksville	WVVR	(931) 431-4984		**Lafayette**	WLCT	(615) 666-2189
Cleveland	WAYA	(423) 242-7656		**Lawrenceburg**	WDXE	(931) 762-4411
Clinton	WYSH	(865) 457-1380		**Lawrenceburg**	WLLX	(931) 762-6200
Columbia	WMCP	(931) 388-3241		**Lawrenceburg**	WWLX	(931) 762-6200
Cookeville	WTZK	(931) 836-1055		**Lebanon**	WANT	(615) 449-3699
Cookeville	WHUB	(931) 526-2131		**Lebanon**	WCKD	(615) 449-3699
Cookeville	*WGSQ	(931) 526-2131		**Lenoir City**	WLIL	(865) 986-7536
Copperhill	WLSB	(423) 496-3311		**Lewisburg**	WAXO	(913) 359-6641
Covington	WKBL	(901) 476-7129		**Livingston**	WLIV	(931) 823-1226
Crossville	WWSR	(931) 484-1057		**Loretto**	WJOR	(931) 845-4172
Crossville	WOWF	(931) 707-1102		**Marion, VA**	WMEV	(276) 783-3151
Dalton, GA	WTUN	(706) 278-5511		**McMinnville**	WBMC	(615) 473-9253
Dickson	WDKN	(615) 446-4000		**McMinnville**	WTRZ	(931) 473-9253
Elizabethton	WBEJ	(423) 542-2184		**Memphis**	KPPL	(901) 375-9324
Erwin	WEMB	(423) 743-6123		**Memphis**	*WGKX	(901) 682-1106
Fairview	WPFD	(615) 799-8585		**Memphis**	WMC	(901) 726-0555
Fayetteville	WEKR	(931) 433-3545		**Mountain City**	WMCT	(423) 727-6701
Fayetteville	WYTM	(931) 433-1531		**Nashville**	*WKDF	(615) 244-9533
Florence	WLVS	(256) 764-8121		**Nashville**	*WSIX	(615) 664-2400
Franklin	WAKM	(615) 794-1594		**Nashville**	*WSM	(615) 889-6595
Gallatin	WHIN	(615) 451-0450		**Newport**	WNPC	(423) 623-8743
Gate City, VA	WGAT	(276) 386-7025		**Paris**	WMUF	(731) 644-9455
Gray	WGOC	(423) 477-1000		**Parsons**	WKJQ	(731) 847-3011
Greeneville	WGRV	(423) 638-4147		**Pikeville**	WUAT	(423) 447-2906
Greenville	WIKQ	(423) 639-1831		**Pulaski**	WKSR	(931) 363-2505
Harrogate	WXJB	(423) 869-2266		**Ripley**	WTRB	(731) 635-1570
Hartsville	WTNK	(615) 374-2111		**Rockwood**	WOFE	(865) 354-0580
Hendersonville	WYXE	(615) 822-9942		**Rogersville**	WRGS	(423) 272-2628

Appendix A

Savannah	WKWX	(731) 925-9600	Tazewell	WCTU	(423) 626-7145
Savannah	WORM	(731) 925-4981	Tazewell	WNTT	(423) 626-4203
Savannah	WXOQ	(731) 925-4981	Tompkinsville, KY	WVFB	(270) 487-6119
Shelbyville	WLIJ	(931) 684-1514	Union City	WYVY	(731) 885-0051
Smithville	WJLE	(615) 597-4265	Wartburg	WECO	(423) 346-3900
South Pittsburg	WEPG	(423) 837-0747	Winchester	WCDT	(913) 967-2201
South Pittsburg	WSDQ	(423) 837-0747	Woodbury	WBRY	(615) 563-2313
Springfield	WSGI	(615) 384-9744			

Texas

Abilene	KBCY	(915) 793-9700	Columbus	KULM	(979) 732-5766
Abilene	KYYW	(325) 676-7711	Conroe	KUST	(936) 788-1035
Abilene	*KEAN	(915) 676-7711	Conroe	KVST	(936) 788-1035
Alpine	KALP	(915) 837-2144	Corpus Christi	KFTX	(361) 883-5987
Amarillo	KATP	(806) 355-9777	Corpus Christi	KOUL	(361) 883-1600
Amarillo	KMML	(806) 355-9777	Corpus Christi	*KRYS	(361) 289-0111
Amarillo	*KGNC	(806) 355-9801	Corsicana	KAND	(903) 874-7421
Andrews	KACT	(915) 523-2845	Crockett	KIVY	(936) 544-2171
Ardmore, OK	KICM	(580) 226-9393	Dalhart	KXIT	(806) 249-4747
Arlington	*KSCS	(817) 640-1963	Dalhart	KXDJ	(806) 249-4747
Austin	KVET	(512) 684-7300	Dallas-Ft. Worth	KCLE	(817) 645-1140
Austin	*KASE	(512) 684-7300	Dallas-Ft. Worth	KHYI	(972) 396-1640
Austin	KEMA	(512) 383-1112	Dallas-Ft. Worth	*KTYS	(817) 695-3500
Ballinger	KRUN	(915) 365-5500	Dallas	*KPLX	(214) 526-2400
Bay City	KMKS	(979) 244-4242	Del Rio	KDLK	(830) 775-9583
Beaumont	KAYD	(409) 833-9421	Denison	KMKT	(903) 463-6800
Beaumont	KSTB	(409) 833-9421	Dimmitt	KDHN	(806) 647-4161
Beaumont	KYKR	(409) 896-5555	Dumas	KDDD	(806) 935-4141
Beeville	KTKO	(361) 358-1490	Eastland	KATX	(254) 629-2621
Big Spring	KBST	(915) 267-6391	Eastland	KEAS	(254) 629-2621
Bonham	KFYN	(903) 583-3151	El Campo	KULP	(979) 543-3303
Bonham	KFYZ	(903) 583-3151	El Paso	KHEY	(915) 351-5400
Borger	KQTY	(806) 273-7533	Fairfield	KNES	(903) 389-5637
Brady	KNEL	(915) 597-2119	Falfurrias	KPSO	(361) 325-2112
Breckenridge	KLXK	(254) 559-6543	Floresville	KWCB	(830) 393-6116
Brenham	KTTX	(979) 836-3655	Floydada	KFLP	(806) 983-5704
Brenham	KWHI	(979) 836-3655	Fredericksburg	KNAF	(830) 997-2197
Brownwood	KSTA	(915) 646-3535	Ft. Stockton	KFST	(915) 336-2226
Brownwood	KOXE	(915) 646-3505	Ft. Worth	KRVA	(817) 332-0959
Bryan	KORA	(979) 776-1240	Ft. Worth	KRVF	(817) 332-0959
Bryan	*KAGG	(979) 846-5597	Gainesville	KGAF	(940) 665-5546
Bryan-College Station	KHTZ	(979) 836-9411	Gonzales	KCTI	(830) 672-3631
Cameron	KMIL	(254) 697-6633	Graham	KSWA	(940) 549-1330
Carrizo Springs	KBEN	(830) 876-2210	Granbury	KPIR	(817) 579-7850
Carthage	KGAS	(903) 693-6668	Grapeland	KBHT	(936) 544-9350
Center	KDET	(936) 598-3304	Greenville	KIKT	(903) 450-1400
Center	KQBB	(936) 598-3304	Greenville	KGVL	(903) 450-1400
Center	KQSI	(936) 598-3304	Hallettsville	KGUL	(361) 798-4333
Childress	KCTX	(940) 937-6316	Hallettsville	KHLT	(361) 798-4333
Colorado City	KAUM	(915) 728-5224	Hallettsville	KTXM	(361) 798-4333
Colorado City	KVMC	(915) 728-5224	Hallettsville	KYKM	(361) 798-4333

Appendix A

Hamilton	KCLW	(254) 386-8804	Nacogdoches	KJCS	(936) 559-8800
Haskell	KVRP	(940) 864-8505	Odessa-Midland	KWTR	(325) 884-3451
Hereford	KPAN	(806) 364-1880	Orange	KOGT	(409) 883-4381
Hillsboro	KHBR	(254) 582-3431	Palestine	KYYK	(903) 729-6077
Hondo	KCWM	(830) 741-5296	Pampa	KOMX	(806) 669-6809
Horseshoe Bay	KBEY	(830) 598-2840	Paris	KOYN	(903) 785-1068
Houston	KTHT	(713) 622-5533	Pearsall	KVWG	(830) 334-8900
Houston	*KILT	(713) 881-5100	Pecos	KIUN	(915) 445-2497
Houston	*KKBQ	(713) 961-0093	Perryton	KEYE	(806) 435-5458
Huntsville	KSAM	(936) 295-2651	Plainview	KKYN	(806) 296-2771
Jacksonville	KEBE	(903) 939-1065	Rockdale	KRXT	(512) 446-6985
Jasper	KCOX	(409) 384-6801	San Angelo	KDCD	(915) 947-0899
Jasper	KTXJ	(409) 384-6801	San Angelo	KKCN	(915) 658-2966
Kennedy	KAML	(830) 583-2990	San Antonio	KKYX	(210) 615-5400
Kerrville	KRNH	(830) 896-4990	San Antonio	*KAJA	(210) 736-9700
Kerrville	KRVL	(830) 896-1230	San Antonio	KUZN	(936) 348-6344
Kerrville	KBRN	(830) 896-1230	San Antonio	KRPT	(210) 736-9700
Killeen-Temple	KTON	(254) 939-9377	San Antonio	*KCYY	(210) 615-5400
LaGrange	KVLG	(979) 968-3173	San Saba	KBAL	(915) 372-5225
Lake Charles, LA	KYKZ	(337) 439-3300	Seguin	KWED	(830) 379-2234
Lamesa	KPET	(806) 872-6511	Seminole	KIKZ	(915) 758-5878
Lampasas	KACQ	(512) 556-6193	Seminole	KSEM	(915) 758-5878
Lampasas	KCYL	(512) 556-6193	Seymour	KSEY	(940) 889-2637
Laredo	KLNT	(956) 725-1000	Snyder	KSNY	(915) 573-9322
Levelland	KLVT	(806) 894-3134	Sonora	KHOS	(915) 387-3553
Littlefield	KZZN	(806) 385-4474	Sonora	KYXX	(915) 387-3553
Livingston	KLSN	(936) 327-8916	Stephenville	KCUB	(254) 968-5282
Livingston	KETX	(936) 327-8916	Stephenville	KSTV	(254) 968-2141
Longview	KIXK	(903) 759-1061	Stephenville	KYOX	(254) 968-2141
Longview	KFRO	(903) 663-9800	Sweetwater	KXOX	(915) 236-6655
Longview	KYKX	(903) 663-3700	Temple	KUSJ	(254) 773-5252
Lubbock	KQBR	(806) 789-7078	Texarkana	KCAR	(903) 793-1109
Lubbock	KRBL	(806) 749-1057	Texarkana	KPGG	(903) 793-1109
Lubbock	*KLLL	(806) 762-3000	Texarkana	KKYR	(870) 772-3771
Lufkin	KYKS	(936) 639-4455	Tyler	KKUS	(903) 534-5133
Madisonville	KMVL	(936) 348-9200	Tyler	KMHT	(903) 593-1744
Magnolia	KZHE	(870) 234-7790	Tyler	KWRD	(903) 593-1744
Malakoff	KCKL	(903) 489-1238	Tyler	KCUL	(903) 581-9966
Many, LA	KTHP	(318) 256-5177	Tyler	*KNUE	(903) 581-0606
Marble Falls	KHBL	(830) 693-5551	Tyler-Longview	KDVE	(903) 939-1065
Marble Falls	KRHC	(830) 693-5551	Tyler-Longview	KLBL	(903) 759-1061
Marshall	KZEY	(903) 923-8000	Uvalde	KVOU	(830) 278-2555
McAllen	KBUC	(956) 383-2777	Vernon	KVWC	(940) 552-6221
McAllen	KVJY	(956) 383-2777	Victoria	KROY	(361) 572-0105
McAllen	KBMI	(956) 383-2777	Victoria	KIXS	(361) 573-0777
Memphis	KLSR	(806) 839-1183	Victoria	KZAM	(361) 572-0105
Mexia	KRQX	(254) 562-5328	Waco	KBCT	(254) 388-5945
Mexia	KWGW	(254) 562-5328	Waco	KTON	(254) 939-9377
Midland	KHKX	(915) 520-9912	Waco	KQRL	(254) 772-0930
Midland	KKJW	(915) 620-8282	Waco	*WACO	(254) 776-3900
Midland	*KNFM	(915) 563-5636	Waxahachie	KBEC	(972) 923-1390
Mineola	KMOO	(903) 569-3823	Weslaco	*KTEX	(866) 973-1041
Mineral Wells	KFWR	(817) 594-9509	Wichita Falls	KOLI	(940) 691-2311
Mineral Wells	KREL	(940) 325-1140	Wichita Falls	KWFS	(940) 763-1111
Mt. Pleasant	KSCH	(903) 572-8726	Wichita Falls	*KLUR	(940) 691-2311
Mt. Pleasant	KSCN	(903) 572-8726	Woodville	KWUD	(409) 283-2777

Appendix A

Utah

Heber City	KTMP	(435) 654-3244	**Roosevelt**	KNEU	(435) 789-5101
Logan	KKEX	(435) 752-1390	**Salt Lake City**	*KKAT	(801) 908-1300
Logan	KYLZ	(435) 752-5141	**Salt Lake City**	*KSOP	(801) 972-1043
Manti	KMTI	(435) 835-7301	**Salt Lake City**	*KUBL	(801) 485-6700
Moab	KCYN	(435) 259-1035	**Salt Lake City**	KEGA	(801) 524-2600
Price	KSLL	(435) 637-1080	**St. George**	KONY	(435) 673-3579
Price	KARB	(435) 637-1167	**Vernal**	KLCY	(435) 789-0920
Richfield	KCYQ	(435) 896-4456			

Vermont

Barre	WWFY	(802) 476-4168	**St. Albans**	WLFE	(802) 524-2133
Burlington	*WOKO	(802) 658-1230	**St. Albans**	WTWK	(802) 524-2133
Morrisville	WLVB	(802) 888-4294	**St. Johnsbury**	WKXH	(802) 748-2362
Newport	WIKE	(802) 766-9236	**Wells River**	WYKR	(802) 757-2773
Northampton, NH	WPVQ	(413) 585-9555	**West Lebanon**	WZLF	(603) 298-5106
Randolph Center	WCVR	(802) 728-4411	**Winchester, MA**	WYRY	(603) 239-8200
Rutland	WJAN	(802) 775-7500	**Winooski**	WVAA	(802) 655-6754
Rutland	WJEN	(802) 775-7500			

Virginia

Altavista	WKDE	(434) 369-5588	**Harrisonburg**	WSIG	(540) 432-1063
Big Stone Gap	WAXM	(276) 679-1901	**Harrisonburg**	WKCY	(540) 434-1777
Blackstone	WBBC	(434) 292-4146	**Jonesville**	WJNA	(276) 346-2000
Charlottesville	WCYK	(434) 978-4408	**Lebanon**	WLRV	(276) 889-1380
Chilhowie	WXMY	(276) 496-7402	**Lebanon**	WXLZ	(276) 889-1073
Clifton Forge	WXCE	(540) 862-5751	**Lexington**	WREL	(540) 463-2161
Clintwood	WDIC	(276) 835-8626	**Louisa**	WLSA	(540) 967-1142
Covington	WIQO	(540) 962-1133	**Luray**	WRAA	(540) 801-1057
Crewe	WSVS	(434) 645-7734	**Lynchburg**	*WYYD	(434) 385-8298
Danville	WAKG	(434) 797-4290	**Lynchburg**	*WYYD	(434) 385-8298
Dillwyn	WBNN	(434) 983-6621	**Lynchburg**	WWZW	(540) 463-2161
Dunmore, WV	WCHG	(304) 799-6004	**Marion**	WMEV	(276) 783-3151
Dunmore, WV	WVLS	(304) 799-6004	**Norton**	WNVA	(276) 328-2244
Farmville	WFLO	(434) 392-4195	**Onley**	WESR	(757) 787-3200
Farmville	WVHL	(434) 392-9393	**Orange**	WJMA	(540) 672-1000
Franklin	WLQM	(757) 562-3135	**Oxford**	WLUS	(919) 693-7900
Fredericksburg	WGRX	(540) 891-9696	**Parksley**	WVES	(757) 665-6500
Fredericksburg	*WFLS	(540) 373-1500	**Pennington Gap**	WSWV	(276) 546-2520
Galax	WBRF	(276) 236-9273	**Pound**	WDXC	(276) 796-5411
Gate City	WGAT	(276) 386-7025	**Radford**	WWBU	(540) 633-5330
Gretna	WMNA	(434) 656-1234	**Radford**	*WPSK	(540) 633-5330
Grundy	WMJD	(276) 935-7227	**Richmond**	WCLM	(804) 233-1847
Hampton	WBYM	(757) 766-9262	**Richmond**	WJZV	(804) 327-9902
Hampton	WLRT	(757) 766-9262	**Richmond**	WKHK	(804) 330-5700

Appendix A

Rocky Mount	WYTI	(540) 483-9955	Virginia Beach	*WGH	(757) 671-1000
Rocky Mount	WZBB	(276) 629-7999	Warsaw	WNNT	(804) 333-4900
South Hill	WKSK	(434) 447-4007	Winchester	WFTR	(540) 635-4121
Staunton	WKDW	(540) 886-2376	Winchester	WSIG	(540) 432-1063
Stuart	WHEO	(276) 694-3114	Winchester	WUSQ	(540) 662-5101
Virginia Beach	*WCMS	(757) 671-1000	Wytheville	WYVE	(276) 228-3185

Washington

Aberdeen	KXXK	(360) 533-1320	Olympia	KGY	(360) 943-1240
Astoria, OR	KVAS	(503) 325-2911	Omak	KNCW	(509) 826-0100
Centralia	KMNT	(360) 736-3321	Pasco	KORD	(509) 547-9791
Centralia	KMNT	(360) 736-3321	Pendleton, OR	KWHT	(541) 278-2500
Centralia	KNBQ	(360) 736-3321	Sandpoint	KICR	(208) 263-2179
Colfax	KCLX	(509) 397-3441	Seattle	*KMPS	(206) 805-0941
Colfax	KZZL	(509) 397-3441	Seattle	KKWF	(206) 285-7625
Colville	KCVL	(509) 684-5032	Spokane	*KIXZ	(509) 459-9800
Ellensburg	KXLE	(509) 925-1488	The Dalles, OR	KYYT	(541) 296-9102
Ephrata	KULE	(509) 754-4661	Twisp	KVLR	(509) 997-5857
Forks	KBIS	(360) 374-6233	Wenatchee	KKRV	(509) 663-5186
Grand Coulee	KEYG	(509) 633-2020	Wenatchee	KWIQ	(509) 663-5186
Kelso	KUKN	(360) 636-0110	Wenatche	KWNC	(509) 787-4461
Kennewick	KIOK	(509) 783-0783	Wenatchee	KYSN	(509) 665-6565
Lewiston, ID	KCLK	(208) 743-6564	Yakima	KDBL	(509) 972-3461
Longview	KBAM	(360) 425-1500	Yakima	KUTI	(509) 972-3461
Milton Freewater, OR	KTEL	(541) 938-6688	Yakima	*KXDD	(509) 248-2900
Mt. Vernon	KAPS	(360) 424-4278			

West Virginia

Ashland, KY	WLGC	(606) 920-9565	Grayson, KY	WGOH	(606) 474-5144
Beckley	WTNJ	(304) 253-7000	Huntington	WDGG	(304) 523-8401
Beckley	*WJLS	(304) 253-7311	Huntington	*WTCR	(304) 525-7788
Berkeley Springs	WDHC	(304) 258-1010	Kingwood	WKMM	(304) 329-0967
Berkeley Springs	WCST	(304) 258-1010	Marion	WMEV	(276) 783-3151
Bluefield	WHQX	(304) 327-7114	Matewan	WHJC	(606) 427-7261
Bluefield	*WHKX	(304) 327-7114	Matewan	WVKM	(606) 427-7261
Buckhannon	WBRB	(304) 472-1460	Morgantown	WKKW	(304) 296-0029
Buckhannon	WVUC	(304) 472-1460	Morgantown	WZST	(304) 292-1101
Buckhannon	WVUC	(304) 472-1460	New Martinsville	WETZ	(304) 455-1111
Charleston	WKWS	(304) 342-8131	Paintsville, KY	WSIP	(606) 789-5311
Charleston	*WQBE	(304) 744-7020	Parkersburg	WHNK	(304) 295-6070
Clarksburg	WPDX	(304) 624-6425	Parkersburg	WGGE	(304) 485-4565
Danville	WZAC	(304) 369-3976	Point Pleasant	WBYG	(304) 675-2763
Dunmore	WVMR	(304) 799-6004	Portsmouth, OH	WPAY	(740) 353-5176
Elkins	WDNE	(304) 636-1300	Ravenswood	WLWF	(304) 273-2544
Fairmont	WGIE	(304) 363-8888	Ravenswood	WMOV	(304) 273-2544
Fairmont	WGYE	(304) 363-8888	Ripley	WCEF	(304) 372-9800
Fisher	WELD	(304) 538-6062	Romney	WVSB	(304) 822-4838

Appendix A

Rupert	WYKM	(304) 392-6003
Spencer	WVRC	(304) 927-3760
Steubenville, OH	WOGH	(740) 283-4747
Sutton	WDBS	(304) 765-7373
Vienna	WNUS	(304) 295-6070
Webster Springs	WVAR	(304) 847-5144
Wheeling	*WOVK	(304) 232-1107
White Sulphur Springs	WKCJ	(304) 536-1310
Williamson	WXCC	(304) 235-3600

Wisconsin

Antigo	WATK	(715) 623-4124
Ashland	WBSZ	(715) 682-2727
Beaver Dam	WXRO	(920) 885-4442
Berlin	WISS	(920) 361-3551
Cleveland	WKTT	(920) 693-3103
Clintonville	WJMQ	(715) 823-5128
Dodgeville	WDMP	(608) 935-2302
Eau Claire	WATQ	(715) 830-4000
Eau Claire	WQRB	(715) 830-4000
Eau Claire	WAXX	(715) 832-1530
Green Bay	*WNCY	(920) 435-3771
Janesville	WJVL	(608) 752-7895
La Crosse	KQYB	(608) 782-1230
La Crosse	WQCC	(608) 782-8335
Ladysmith	WLDY	(715) 532-5588
Lancaster	WGLR	(608) 723-7671
Madison	WWQM	(608) 273-1000
Madison	WMAD	(608) 274-5450
Manitowoc	WCUB	(920) 683-6800
Milwaukee	WMIL	(414) 545-8900
Monroe	WEKZ	(608) 325-2161
Oconto	WOCO	(920) 834-3540
Oshkosh	WPCK	(920) 236-4242
Oshkosh	WPKR	(920) 236-4242
Park Falls	WCQM	(715) 762-3221
Portage	WDDC	(608) 742-8833
Poynette	WBKY	(608) 635-7341
Prairie Du Chien	WQPC	(608) 326-2411
Reedsburg	WNFM	(608) 524-1400
Rhinelander	WHDG	(715) 362-1975
Rice Lake	WAQE	(715) 234-2131
Rice Lake	WJMC	(715) 234-2131
Richland Center	WRCO	(608) 647-2111
Ripon	WBJZ	(920) 748-9205
Shawano	WTCH	(715) 524-2194
Sheboygan	WBFM	(920) 458-2107
Shell Lake	WPLT	(715) 231-9500
Shell Lake	WDMO	(715) 231-9500
Shell Lake	WQOQ	(715) 231-9500
Sparta	WCOW	(608) 269-3307
Stevens Point	WYTE	(715) 341-8838
Sturgeon Bay	WAUN	(920) 743-6677
Sturgeon Bay	WRUL	(920) 746-9430
Tomah	WTMB	(608) 372-9600
Viroqua	WVRQ	(608) 637-7200
Waupaca	WDUX	(715) 258-5528
Wausau	*WDEZ	(715) 842-1672
Wausau	WJMT	(715) 536-6262
West Bend	WBKV	(262) 334-2344
West Bend	WBWI	(262) 334-2344
Whitewater	WSLD	(608) 883-6677

Wyoming

Afton	KRSV	(307) 885-5778
Belle Fourche, SD	KYDT	(605) 892-2571
Buffalo	KLGT	(307) 684-7070
Casper	KQLT	(307) 265-1984
Casper	KWYY	(307) 266-5252
Cheyenne	KRAE	(307) 638-8921
Cheyenne	KOLZ	(307) 632-4400
Cody	KZMQ	(307) 578-5000
Douglas	KKTY	(307) 358-3636
Evanston	KEVA	(307) 789-9101
Gillette	KGWY	(307) 686-2242
Green River	KFRZ	(307) 875-6666
Jackson	KJAX	(307) 733-4500
Kemmerer	KDWY	(307) 877-4422
Lander	KOVE	(307) 332-5683
Laramie	KCGY	(307) 745-4888
Newcastle	KASL	(307) 746-4433
Pinedale	KPIN	(307) 367-2000
Riverton	KTAK	(307) 856-2251
Rock Springs	KQSW	(307) 382-5619
Sheridan	KYTI	(307) 672-7421
Thermopolis	KDNO	(307) 864-2119
Torrington	KGOS	(307) 532-2158
Wheatland	KYCN	(307) 322-5926

Appendix A

Appendix A

CANADIAN COUNTRY STATIONS
(Province-By-Province)

Appendix A

Appendix A

Alberta

Athabasca	CKBA	(780) 675-5301	**High Prairie**	CKVH	(780) 523-5111
Brooks	CIBQ	(403) 362-3418	**Lethbridge**	CHLB	(403) 329-0955
Calgary	CKRY	(403) 716-2105	**Lloydminister**	CKSA	(780) 875-3321
Calgary	CKMX	(403) 240-5800	**Medicine Hat**	CHAT	(403) 529-1270
Camrose	CFCW	(780) 672-9822	**Reed Deer**	CKGY	(403) 343-1303
DraytonValley	CIBW	(780) 542-9290	**Slave Lake**	CKWA	(780) 849-2577
Drumheller	CKDQ	(403) 823-3384	**St. Paul**	CHLW	(780) 645-4425
Edmonton	CFCW	(780) 437-4996	**Stettler**	CKSQ	(403) 742-2930
Edmonton	CISN	(780) 428-1104	**Wainwright**	CKKY	(780) 842-4311
Edmonton	CKRA	(780) 437-4996	**Westlock**	CFOK	(780) 349-4421
Fort McMurray	CJOH	(780) 743-2246	**Westlock**	CKKY	(780) 842-4321
High Prairie	CJXX	(780) 532-0840	**Westaskiwin**	CKJR	(780) 352-0144

British Columbia

100 Mile House	CKBX	(250) 395-3848	**Powell River**	CHQB	(604) 485-4207
Abbotsford	CKQC	(604) 853-4756	**Prince George**	CJCI	(250) 564-2524
Campbell	CFWB	(250) 287-7106	**Quesnel**	CKCQ	(250) 992-7046
Crankbrook	CHBZ	(250) 426-2224	**Terrace**	CJFW	(250) 635-6816
Dawson Creek	CJDC	(250) 782-3341	**Vancouver**	CJJR	(250) 731-7772
Fort Nelson	CKRX	(250) 774-2525	**Vanderhoof**	CIVH	(250) 567-4914
Penticton	CIGV	(250) 493-6767	**Williams Lake**	CKWL	(250) 392-6551
Port Alberni	CJAV	(250) 723-2455			

Manitoba

Brandon	CKLQ	(204) 726-8888	**Portage La Prairie**	CFRY	(204) 239-5111
Dauphin	CKDM	(204) 638-3230	**Winkler**	CKMW	(204) 325-9506
FlinFlon	CFAR	(204) 687-3469	**Winnipeg**	CINC	(204) 772-8255
Portage La Prairie	CFAR	(204) 239-5111			

New Brunswick

Moncton	CJXL	(506) 858-5525	**Sussex**	CJCW	(506) 432-2529
Saint John	CHSJ	(506) 432-2529			

Appendix A

Newfoundland

Carbonear	CHVO	(709) 596-7144	**Marystown**	CHCM	(709) 279-2560

Northwest Territories

Yellowknife	CKLB	(867) 920-2277

Nova Scotia

Digby	CKDY	(902) 245-2111	**Middleton**	CKAD	(902) 825-3429
Halifax	CFDR	(902) 453-2524	**Sydney**	CJCB	(902) 564-5596
Halifax	CHFX	(902) 422-1651	**Truro**	CKTY	(902) 893-6060
Kentville	CKEN	(902) 678-2111	**Windsor**	CFAB	(902) 798-2111

Ontario

Ajax	CJKX	(905) 428-9600	**Ottawa**	CKBY	(613) 736-2001
Belleville	CJBQ	(613) 969-5555	**Owen Sound**	CKYC	(519) 376-2030
Cornwall	CJSS	(613) 932-5180	**Pembroke**	CHVR	(613) 735-9670
Hamilton	CHAM	(905) 526-8200	**Peterborough**	CJQM	(705) 759-8844
Hamilton	CING	(905) 521-9900	**Sault Ste. Marie**	CJQM	(705) 759-8844
Kingston	CFMK	(613) 549-1911	**Sudbury**	CIGM	(705) 566-4480
London	CJBX	(519) 686-2525	**Tilsonburg**	CKOT	(518) 842-4281
Midland	CICZ	(705) 526-2268	**Waterloo**	CIKZ	(519) 746-3331
Moosonee	CHMO	(705) 336-2466	**Wingham**	CKNX	(519) 357-1310
NorthBay	CKAT	(705) 474-2000			

Prince Edward Island

Charlottetown	CFCY	(902) 892-1066	**Summerside**	CJRW	(902) 436-2201

Quebec

St. Constant	CJMS	(450) 632-5224	**Verdun**	CKVL	(514) 766-2311

Appendix A

Saskatchewan

Estevan	CJSL	(306) 236-6494	**Saskatoon**	CFQC	(306) 244-1975
Meadow Lake	CJNS	(306) 236-6494	**Shaunavon**	CJSN	(306) 297-2671
Melfort	CJVR	(306) 752-2587	**Swift Current**	CKSW	(306) 773-4605
Moose Jaw	CILG	(306) 694-0800	**Weyburn**	CFSL	(306) 848-1190
North Batteford	CJNB	(306) 445-2477	**Yorktown**	CJGX	(306) 782-2256
Regina	CKRM	(306) 566-9800			

Appendix A

Appendix A

INTERNATIONAL RADIO STATIONS PROGRAMMING COUNTRY MUSIC
(Nation-By-Nation)

Appendix A

Appendix A

Argentina

Capital Federal Buenos Aires Country Music
Lorena Favario
Tacuari 1609
Capital Federal, Buenos Aires 1139
Ph#: 54011-3001002

San Pedro La Radio
Gustav Laurino
Av. J.F.Kennedy 289
San Pedro, Buenos Aires B29301RJ
Ph#: 54-3329-427862

Australia

Adelaide 5CST
Chris Hill
25 Naldera Street
Adelaide, South Australia 5037
Ph#: 08-8371-5887

Alice Springs 8KIN-FM CAAMA Radio
Stan Coombe
PO Box 2068
Alice Springs, North Territory 0871

Bentley Curtain Radio FM 100.1
Brendon T Moylan
Bldg. 004, Curtin Uni Kent St.
Bentley, Western Australia 6162
Ph#: 618-926-62121

Bordertown 5TCB FM
Bev Coad
PO Box 526
Bordertown, South Australia 5268
Ph#: 618-8752-2777

Box Hill 3WBC
Daniel Anderson
PO Box 159
Box Hill, Victoria 3128
Ph#: 61 38 61 17 936

Bundaberg KIX FM
Larry Cann
38 Crofton St.
Bundaberg, Queensland 4670
Ph#: 617-4153-0800

Canberra QBN FM
Parko
4 McMahon Ct
Canberra, Capital Territory 2902
Ph#: 61 41 20 44 940

Canberra ABC Radio
Jordie Kilby
GPO Box 9994
Canberra, New South Wales 2601

The Entrance Cool Country 94.1 FM
PO Box 2
The Entrance, New South Wales 2261
Ph#: 61 26 67 60 283
2261

Heidelberg 3INR inner FM
Bill Corrie
PO Box 410
Heidelberg, Victoria 3084
Ph#: 61 39 45 71 718

Hobart 7HH0 - FM
Paul Shirley
GPO Box H0-FM
Hobart, Tasmania 7001

Inverloch 3M FM
Alan Clement
10B William Street
Inverloch, Victoria 3996
Ph#: 61 35 67 41 900

Kalgoorlie GGF/GEB Kalgoorlie
Irene Monttefiori
GPO Box 125
Kalgoorlie, Western Australia 6430
Ph#: 618-9021-2666

Launceton City Park Radio
Alan W. Lawson
GPO Box 1400
Launceton, Tasmania 7250

Lakes Entrance 3REG FM Radio East Gippsland, Inc.
Charles Sicura
P.O. Box 603
Lakes Entrance, Victoria 3909
Ph#: 61 35 15 51 011

Lake Munmorah Hawksbury Radio 89.9
Phil Magee
PO Box 6166
Lake Munmorah, New Sth Wales 2259

Appendix A

Mount Gambier	5MG Spence Denny GPO Box 1448 Mount Gambier, Sth Australia 5290	**St. Clair**	2GLF FM Doug Weedon 50 Explorers Way St. Clair, New South Wales 2760 Ph#: 61 29 82 28 893
Mudgee	2MG Ted Guinea 15 Putta Bucca Rd Mudgee, New South Wales 2850 Ph#: 61 26 37 21 777	**Thornlands**	4BAY FM P.O. Box 1003 various 95 Cleveland Redland Bay Rd. Thornlands, Queensland 4164 Ph#: 61 73 82 10 022
North Geelong	Country FM 89.3 Ron Cockell 43 Separation Street North Geelong, Victoria 3215 Ph#: 61 35 27 21 234	**Townsville**	Australian Broadcasting Corporation PO Box 694 John Nutting Townsville, Queensland 4810 Ph#: 61 74 72 23 060
Northcote	Nu Country FM Paul Hicks PO Box 625 Northcote, Victoria 3070 Ph#: 61 39 88 94 546	**Werribee**	WYN-FM Rod Browne Victoria University Hoppers Lane Werribee, Victoria 3030 Ph#: 61 39 21 68 089
Orange	FM 107.5 The Local Station (2OCB) Jim Black & Doug Spicer 77 Kite St. Orange, New South Wales 2800 Ph#: 61 26 36 18 877	**Windsor**	Hawkesbury Radio Annie Zee 11 Fitzgerald St. P.O. Box 248 Windsor, New South Wales 2756 Ph#: 61 24 58 79 899
Perth	Curtain Radio 927GNR Brendon Moylan GPO Box U1987 Perth, Western Australia 68	**Woori Yallock**	Yarra Valley FM 99.1 Graele Godlin PO Box 991 Victoria 3139 Ph#: 61 35 96 15 991
Queenstown	7XS West Coast Steve Adermann 89 Conlan Street Queenstown, Tasmania 7467 Ph#: 613-6471-1711		

Austria

Lienz	Radio Austtirol Hans Mair Amlacher St. 2 Lienz A-9900	**Rum**	Radio Arabella/Tirol Lilly Staudigl Mielestr .2 Rum 6063 Ph#: 43 51 22 02 498
Linz	Jimmy Hirsch Freistadtter Str 55 Linz A-4020		

Appendix A

Belgium

Aalst	Radio Katanga Patrick Laureys Nieuwbeekstraat 149 Aalst B-9300	**Liege**	Equinoxe Joseph Bonfond Rue Montange Sainte Walburge 261 Liege Ph#: 32 43 26 11 11
Antwerp	Radio Zuiderlicht Steve Brandon Graaf Van Egmont Straat 14 Antwerp 2000 Ph#: 32 32 37 70 58	**Lobbes**	Radio ZCI Wallonie Paulet Francine 16 Rue Gromet Lobbes B-6540
Antwerp	Arta FM 107 Mario Aarden Weeltjens 18-C Antwerp B-2040	**Merelbeke**	Radio USA Patrick Lee Hundelgemsesteenweg 469a Szajyessky Merelbeke 9820 Ph#: 32 92 31 17 92
Berlaar	Lokale Radio Bevel Leo Van Camp Daalstraat 7 Berlaar 2590	**Mol**	Radio Mol Eric Van De Mert St Picterstraat 342 Mol, Antwerpen B-2400 Ph#: 32 14 31 85 71
Brussels	VRT-Radio 2 Erik Baeyens Gentsestenweg 229 Brussels B-9300 AALST Ph#: 32 27 41 31 11	**Oostkamp**	Radio Zenith Jesse W. James Bareelstraat 21 Oostkamp 8020 Ph#: 324-8644-1841
Herenthout	Radio RL Sonja Mertens Wiekevorstse Stwg 3 Herenthout B2270 Ph#: 32-1451-6000	**Seraing**	Ciel FM Network 17 Rue des Areines Various Seraing 4100 Ph#: 32 43 36 62 45
Herstal	Radio Charlemagnrie Herstal Tim Gonzales 11 Rue H. Nottet Herstal 4040 Ph#: 32 42 64 46 46	**Vottem**	Radio Rouby Marylou LeCoq Allee Des Arondes 18 Vottem 4041 Ph#: 32 42 27 34 70
Kapellen	Radio Contact GuyWeyers Hoevensebaan, 92 Kapellen 2950 Ph#: 32 36 05 77 05	**Wellen**	Radio V.R.W. Lucien Boes Nutstraat 18 Wellen 3830 Ph#: 32 22 74 36 66

Brazil

Porto Alegre	Unisinos Paulo Torino RS Porto Alegre

Appendix A

Bulgaria

Shoumen Radio Shumen
Dragomir Simeonov
7 D Voynikov St.
Shoumen 9700

Croatia

Velika Gorica Radio Velika Gorica
Nenad Matic
Zagrebacka 37
Velika Gorica 10410
Ph#: 385 16 22 37 00

Czech Republic

Benesov Radio Presston
Jan M. Hula
NAM TGM 100
Benesov 256 27

Karlovy Vary Radio Diana
Antonin Foglar
Fibichova 770
Karlovy Vary 360 17

Pilsen Czech Radio Pilsen
Petr Vacek
Namesti Miru 10
Pilsen 320 70
Ph#: 42-1927-3240

Pizen Radio Karolina
Ondrej Lane
P.O. Box 31
Z Wintra 21
Pizen 20 320 81
Ph#: 421-9742-1291

Prague 2 Czech Radio 2
Jan Spaleny
Vinohradska 12
Prague 2 120 99
Ph#: 422-2155 2417

Denmark

Aalborg DNR
Michale Hollaender
Petersborgvej 27
Aalborg DK9000

Bronderslev BNR Veronica
Michael Hollaender
Algade 32
Bronderslev 9700
Ph#: 45 98 80 15 55

Copenhagen Norrebro Radio
Otto Waldoft
SCAWC
P.O. Box 1278
Copenhagen 2300
Ph#: 45 32 95 05 71

Fakse Radio Oestjaelland
Hans-Henrik Thamdrup
Vinkaeldertorvet 2
P.O. Box 34
Fakse 4640
Ph#: 45 56 71 30 03

Appendix A

Hjoerring Radio Sindal
Bjarne Christensen
Ugiltvej 900 Loerslev
Hjoerring 9800

Langeskov Radio Midt Imellem
Finn Bruun
P.O. Box 58
Langeskov 5550
Ph#: 45 65 38 38 70

Nordborg Radio Als
Mikael Jorgensen
Peblingestien 1
Nordborg 6430
Ph#: 45 74 45 10 10

Ringsted Radio Toesen Town and Country
Sven Seehusen
Anlaegsvej 26
Ringsted 4100
Ph#: 45 57 67 30 23

Rodovri Radio Rodovr
Solveig Pedersen Clark
Valhojs Alle 91 7 TV
Rodovri DK-2610

Roedovre Karlsro Naerradio
Rosa & John Frid
Tarnvej 233-7
Roedore 2610
Ph#: 45-3672-1122

Roende Radio Roende
Peder Thomsen
Engblommevej 40
Roende 8410

Roskilde Roskilde Dampradio
Dann Hansen
Helligkorsvej 5 1th
Roskilde 4000
Ph#: 45 46 36 36 37

Skanderborg Radio Hinnerup
Poul Stokholm
Ustrupvej 4
Skanderborg 8660

Skjern Radio Aadalen
Holger Petersen
Finderupsvej 26
Skjern 6900
Ph#: 45 97 19 84 42

Vejle Radio Adalen
Leif Berg
Boulevarden 8
Vejle 7100

Viborg Radio Viborg PL
Kirsten Petersen
SCT Mogensgade 23-C
Viborg DK8800

England
-see United Kingdom-

Estonia

Voru Voru Radio 103.2
Toomas Hoole & Ann Roy
Vee Str 6-1
Voru EE-2710

Faroe Islands

Torshaven Utvarp Foroya
Jogvan Jeppersen
Nordra Ringvegi
Torshaven 110
Ph#: 29 83 11 182

Appendix A

Finland

Helsinki
Radio Suomi
Teppo Nattila
Radiokatu 5 Yleisradio
Helsinki 00024
Ph#: 358 91 48 01

Kuopio
Oikea Asema
Mikko Vesa
PO Box 967
Kupio SF-70101

Mantsala
Radio 103.4
Timo Mikkonen
PO Box 6
Mantsala SF-04601

France

Brest
Frequece Mutine
Dominique Guiard
4 rue Alain Fergent
Brest F-29200

Carcassonne
Radio Marseillette
Dominique Costanoga
33 rue Des Hauts De Serres
Carcassonne F-11000

Chigny Les Roses
Radio Primitive
Jean-Claude Francoi
18 Rue Georges Legros Mame
Chigny Les Roses 51500
Ph#: 33 3 26 03 46 94

Dijon
C.I.N.Q.-PV Productions
C. Aimel
10 rue Heudelet
Dijon 21000
Ph#: 333-8074-3088

Dunkerque
Radio Rencontre
Jolly Jean-Pierre
2, rue Vauban
Dunkerque 59140
Ph#: 33 3 28 61 25 00

Le Vesinet
Country Music USA
Gerard Meffre
34 Ave Les Pages
Le Vesinet 78110

Lyon
Radio Lyon 1
Jacques DuFour
BP9 Rillieux Cedex
Lyon 69144
Ph#: 33 4 78 88 25 25

Manosque
Mistral Radio
Vincent Vachet
7 rue Saunerie
Manosque 04100
Ph#: 334-9272-4645

Marmoutier
Radio Frequence Verte
Jean Castro
91 rue du General Leclerc
Marmoutier 67440

Marseille
Radio Galere
J.E. Prato
41 rue Jobin
Marseille 13003
Ph#: 33 4 91 62 66 55

Metz
RPL
Christophe Von Gouvvin
30 Sente A MY
Metz 5700

Orleans
RCF Orleans
51 Blvd. Aristide Briand
Orleans 45000
Ph#: 332-3824-0024

Paris
Music Box
Jean Agostini
BP 7 Guerville
Paris 78930
Ph#: 33 1 30 93 93 93

Paris
NSEO FM (Radio Ici & Maintenant)
Mathias Andrieu
8, rue Violet
Paris 75015

Appendix A

Perpignan	Sky Rock Phil Edwards 16 bis Cours Lazare Escarguel Perpignan 66000 Ph#: 33 4 68 34 66 11	**Strasbourg Cedex**	Radio Arc En Ciel Marion Lacroix 65 rue de la Canardiere Strasbourg Cedex F-67100 Ph#: 333-8879-0901
Pont de Beauvoisin	ISA Radio Mike Penard rue des Etrets Pont de Beauvoisin 73330 Ph#: 33 47 850 51 30	**Toulon Cedex**	RCF Mediterranee Paulin Pascal BP 523 Toulon Cedex 83060 Ph#: 33 4 94 20 02 20
Rennes Cedex 3	Radio Rennes Gabriel Aubert 130 Blvd Jacquest Cartier Rennes Cedex 3 F-35000	**Wiwersheim**	Radio Frequence Verte Jean Castro 1 Rte de Saverne Wiwersheim 67370 Ph#: 33 3 88 69 73 22
Ruel Cedex	Radio Waves International Philippe Bertrand BP 130 Ruel Cedex 92504	**Yssingeaux**	Radio FM 43 Georges Pumain 18 Ave. de la Marne Yessingeaux 43200 Ph#: 334-7159-0565
Saint-Priest Cedex	Radio Pluriel Patrice Berger BP 106 Saint-Priest Cedex F69801		

Germany

Berlin	SFB Rolf Larry Schuba Stadt Radio Masuren Allee 8-14 Berlin 14057 Ph#: 49 30 30 310	**Essen**	Country Friends Koetz Thomas Van Ryn Diemel Str 57 Essen 45136
Berlin	Country Special Radio Berlin Birgit Walter Hildburghauser Str 35 Berlin D-12279	**Frankfurt**	Hessischer Rundfunk Dieter Vulpus Bertramstrasse 8 Frankfurt 60320 Ph#: 49 69 15 51
Bremen	Radio Bremen Hasso Henke Bgm. Spitta Allee 45 Bremen 28353 Ph#: 4942 1246 13 38	**Hamburg**	NDR 2 Volker Schultz Rothenbaumchaussee Hamburg 22761 Ph#: 4940 4156 23 86
Cologne	Deutschland Radio Rolf Larry Schuba Hans Rosentalplatz 1 Cologne 50968 Ph#: 4922-1345-1612	**Henstedt-Ulzburg**	OK Hamburg E.L.B.E. media Neuer Weg 24 Schleswig-Holstein Henstedt-Ulzburg D-24558 Ph#: 4941-9399-7818
Dresden	Radio Dresden Media BU Mario Wildner Kaitzer Str 60 Dresden O-01187	**Hof**	Radio Eurohertz "Doc" Schultz Aussere Bayreuther Str 89 Hof D-95032 Ph#: 49-9281-8800

Appendix A

Ichenhausen	Radio KO/BPC Richard Roth Gunzburger Str. 39 Ichenhausen D-89335 Ph#: 4982 2340 92 99	**Munich**	Country Jukebox Max. W. Achatz Th. Dombart Str. 5 Munich 80805 Ph#: 4989 5526 76 69
Ingolstadt	Gata Enterprises Walter Vogelstein Post Fach 211011 Ingolstadt W-85025	**Neumunster**	Radio NORA Jorg-Peter Triebel Schneiderweg 41 Neumunster 24537 Ph#: 49 69 15 51
Ingolstadt	Radio Riverside Ernst Erb Umterer Graesweg 50 Ingolstadt W-85055 Ph#: 49-8413-0090	**Obermarchtal**	Radio Free FM Friedrich Hog Fuerst-Albert Str. 5 Obermarchtal D-89611
Kiel	Radio NORA Jorg-Peter Triebel Wittland 3 Kiel D-24145 Ph#: 49 43 17 18 00	**Wiesbaden**	Radio Rhein Wella 92.5 "Rye" Henderson Post Fach 4920 Wiesbaden W-65039
Koln	WDR 4 Horst vom Hofe Appellhofplatz 1 NRW Koln D-50600 Ph#: 4922 1220 42 41	**Tuebingen**	Wueste Welle Freies Radio Tuebingen Rainer Zellner Saarstrasse 8 Tuebingen , Baden-Wuerttemberg 72070 Ph#: 49-7073-2250
Ludwigshafen	RPR Zwei Walter Fuchs Turmstrasse 8 Rheinlan-Pfalz Ludwigshafen D-67059 Ph#: 4962159 000148		

Greece

Athens	Love Radio 99 FM Nikos Garavelas 31, Dimitros Str. 17778 Tavros Athens Ph#: 30 1 34 12 607	**Athens**	WWCM Radio Yiannis Iridos 2 Ahtens

Holland
-see Netherlands -

Hungary

Budapest	Radio Saturnus Victor Kemeny Hegedus Gyula u. 30 Budapest H-1136

Appendix A

Iceland

Skagastrond Country Radio of Iceland
Hallbjorn J. Hjartarssen
Brimnes 545
Skagstrond

Ireland

Clonmel Tipp
John O'Connell
Davis Rd.
Clonmel, Co. Tipperary
Ph#: 35-3522-5299

Dublin Tallaght FM
Dave Byrne
The Square, Tallaght
Dublin, Co Dublin 24
Ph#: 353 1 462 33 33

Dublin Near FM
Noel Clinton
Northside Civic Center
Bunratty Rd.
Dublin 17

Kerry Radio Kerry
John Buckley
103 Meadowlands Oak Park
Kerry, Co. Tralee

Kilkenny Radio Kilkenny
Kay Brennan
Hebron Rd.
Kilkenny

Leinster Shannonside/Northern Sound Radio
Joe Finnegan
Minard House
Sligo Road
Leinster, Co. Longford
Ph#: 353-4347-777

Mayo Mid West Radio FM
Tommy Murphy
33 Lord Edward St.
Mayo, Co. Ballina

Portadown Radio Star Country
Tom Lambert
P.O. Box 981
Portadown, Co. Armagh
Ph#: 353 478 79 88

Waterford JRRI-The Pirate
Joe Cashin
PO Box 39
Waterford

Italy

Biella Radio Biella
Alfonso Pella
Regione Setterio 35
Biella, 13900

Borca Di Cadore Radio Cortina
Gianni Milani
Via Antelao 16
Borca Di Cadore, 32040

Galatina CMN Country Music Network
Daniele Masciullo
P.O. Box 227
Lecoe
Galantina, 73013
Ph#: 39 32 9975 94 99

Lecco Radio Cristal
Andrea Aglio
Corso Martiri della
Liberta 55
Lecco, 23900
Ph#: 39 34 12 82 454

Pesaro Radio Encontro
Maurizio Benvenuti
Via Meucci No. 13
Pesaro, 61100
Ph#: 39-7213-4200

Piotello Milano Radio Europe Z-94
Alessio Bertini
Via Roma 1
Piotello Milano, 20096

Appendix A

Japan

Kawasaki-City FM K-City
Mayu Inagaki
Tower Place 5F
1-403 Kosugi-cho
Nkahara-ku, Kawasaki City,
Kanagawa 211-0063
Ph#: 81 44 71 21 791

Kobe AM Kobe
Kazunori Ane
1-5-7 Higasikawasaki
Chuo-ku, Kobe, Hyougo 650-8580
Ph#: 81 783 62 73 73

Sendai TBC Radio
Shuichi Motoki
5-2-11 Yakata,
Izumi-Ku, Sendai, Miyagi 981-3214
Ph#: 81 22 37 92 063

Shibuya NHK-FM
Takehisa Matsuda
2-2-1 Jinnan
Shibuya, Tokyo 150-8001
Ph#: 813 5 455 4144

Suginami-ku Shonan Beach
Miya Ishida
Onozuka-ura
3-22-2 Nishiogikita
Suginami-ku, Tokyo 167-0042
Ph#: 8103-8382-8382

Kenya

Nairobi "Gems of Truth"
Job Gathemia
PO Box 49256
Nairobi-Kenya

Latvia

Riga Radio Latvai
Ivars Erdmanis
8 Dome Square
Riga LV-1505

Lithuania

Jonava Radio Kauno Fonas
Arunas Gruseckas
Erutes 29
Jonava LT-5000

Kaunas Radio Kaumo Fonas Radio Stotis
Ted Slavskis
Radastu 2
Kaunas LT-3000

Vilnius Radio Laisvoji Banga
Algirdis Klova
Arkliy 20-11
Vilnius

Appendix A

Luxembourg

Chauthem Radio F
Joe Herrmann
No. 7 rue Metzler
Chauthem L-3328

Hesperange Radio WAKY
Claude Wassenich
300 D, route de Thionville
P.O. Box 2503
Hesperange L-1025
Ph#: 352 44 75 74

Malta

Marsa Super 1 Radio
Vince Laus
Industrial Estate
Marsa HMR 15
Ph#: 356 24 49 05

Mexico

Chihuahua D95 FM
Armando Velazquez
Rio Candameno 7102
Chihuahua 31120
Ph#: 14-418-9595

Namibia

Windhoek Radio Kudu
Norman Kotze
16 Diaz Street
Windhoek, Namibia
Ph#: 264-6124-3042

Netherlands

Aalten Radio Lindeboom
Bert te Beest
Ludgerstraat 47 A
Aalten 7121 EG
Ph#: 31 54 34 77 886

Beverwyk Radio Beverwyk
Raimond Bos
P.O. Box 90
Beverwyk, Noord Holland 1940 AB
Ph#: 312-5125-4958

Appendix A

Den Haag	Country FM Otto D. Lusink P.O. Box 617 Den Haag 2501 CP Ph#: 31 70 375 00 88	**Oosterhout**	ORTS Ton Hogewoning Slotjesveld 3 Noord Brabant Oosterhout 4902 AD Ph#: 31 16 24 60 024
Drachten	R.T.S. (Radio & T.V. Smallingerland) Joris Smits P.O. Box 102 Brachten, Friesland 9200 AC Ph#: 31 51 25 25 278	**Oudewater**	Radio Midland FM Cor Berkouwer Gasthuissteeg 1 Oudewater 3421-SR
Geldermalsen	Logo Radio Peter Van Houwelingen P.O. Box 208 Geldermalsen, Gelderland 4190 CE Ph#: 31 34 55 73 040	**Rotterdam**	Radio DVN Aad Huigen Beverwaardseweg 118 Rotterdam 3077-GB
Heerenveen	HOS Houwelingen P.O. Box 367 Heerenveen, Friesland 8440 AJ Ph#: 31 5 13 62 88 88	**Rucphen**	Radio Rucphen Ad van Loon P.O. Box 55 Rucphen 4715 ZH Ph#: 311-6534-2480
Hilversum	Vara Radio 1 & 2 Paul Van Gelder P.O. Box 175 Hilversum 1200 AD Ph#: 31 35 67 11 911	**Ryswyk**	Radio Ryswyk Wilm Reparon Spinetstraat 2 Ryswky 2287 BP Ph#: 317-0396-0808
Leeuwarden	Omrop Fryslan Gurbe Douwstra P.O. Box 7600 Leeuwarden, Fryslan 8903 JP Ph#: 315-8299-7799	**Spijkenisse**	Lokale Omroep Spijkenisse Herman Willemshoevelaan 2 Burgemeester P.O. Box 554 Spijkenisse 3200 AM Ph#: 431 1816 22 028
Katwyk	VLOK Radio Bart van der Pol Mr. E.N. Rahusenstraat 2A Katwyk ZH 2225 TW Ph#: 317-1401-3551	**Zwijndrecht**	ATOS Radio Leo den Hartog P.O. Box 428 Zwijndrecht 3330 AH Ph#: 31 78 61 94 900
Nieuwegein	Nieuwegein Radio Ab Plant P.O. Box 7033 Nieuwegein 3430 JA Ph#: 31 30 60 43 863		

New Zealand

Dargaville	Big River FM Phil Godfrey PO Box 199 Dargaville	**Invercargill**	Country Radio Bryan Scott 145 Islington St. Invercargill 9501 Ph#: 64 32 17 04 26
Hastings	KCA Radio Herbert Burkin 1022 Southland Rd. Hastmgs 1022	**Lower Hutt**	Town & Country Radio Eddie O'Strange Belmont 21 Redvers Drive Lower Hutt, Wellington 6009 Ph#: 64 45 65 31 64

Appendix A

Dunedin	Radio Dunedin Shirley Sneton 47 Carlyle Rd. Dunedin	**Wellington**	Wellington Access Radio Mary Moylan Unit 4/75 Ellice St. Mount Victoria Wellington
Timaru	3ZC "Radio Caroline" Ron D. Heney 22-A Otipua Rd. Timaru	**Woodville**	Radio Woodville Dianna Watson 79 Vogel St. Woodville 80240

Northern Ireland

Armagh	Thunder Country George Patton 27 Ashley Gardens Armagh, No. Ireland BT60 1HF Ph#: 44028-37-20151	**Eglinton**	Tyrone Community Radio Connie Cooper 61 Brisland Rd. Eglinton, Co. Derry BT47 3EA
Belfast	Radio Star Country Colly Graham 14-D Bredahouse Drumart Dr. Belfast BT8 4EW		

Norway

Akrehavn	Radio Vestland Kjell Egeland P.O. Box 262 Akrehavn 4270 Ph#: 47 52 83 65 11	**Kongsvinger**	Radio Kongsvinger Stian Berg P.O. Box 530 Hedmark Kongsvinger N-2203 Ph#: 47 62 88 24 00
Amot	Radio R-35 Thormod R. Hansen Post Boks 25 Amot N-3340 Ph#: 47-3278-4640	**Kopervik**	Radio 102 Kjell Egeland P.O. Box 102 Kopervik 4251 Ph#: 47 52 85 51 02
Andalsnes	Radio Rauma Per G. Berg Post Boks 141 Andalsnes 6301	**Oslo**	NRK Jan Thoresen Bjoernstjerne Bjoernsons Pl. 1 Oslo N-0340 Ph#: 47 23 04 84 38
Fredrikstad	Radio Fredrikstad Vidar Thomt P.O. Box 435 Fredrikstad 1601 Ph#: 47 69 38 80 88	**Oslo**	Radio Follo FM 99 Rodny Kaasta Post Boks 9 Mortensrud Oslo 1215
Hol	Radio Hallingdal Knut Medhus Post Boks 156 Hol N-3576 Ph#: 47-3208-9111	**Risor**	Radio Risor Alte Sorensen Gronningvn 31 Risor Risor 4951 Ph#: 47 37 15 30 53

Appendix A

Royken	Raio Hutum &Royken Jan Aurholm Post Boks 191 Royken N-3340	**Strommen**	Radio I North Bjorn Knudsen P.O. Box 104.5 Strommen Ph#: 47 63 89 20 30
Skytta	Radio Extra Agnar Bakke P.O. Box 18 Skytta 1483 Ph#: 47 67 07 01 05	**Telemark**	Radio Midt-Telemark A/S Torstein Borte P.O. Box 163 Telemark N-3800 BO Ph#: 4735 95 43 43
Straume	Radio Sotra John Bjoersvik P.O. Box 128 Straume 5342 Ph#: 47 56 31 36 60	**Trondheim**	Radio Midt-Norge FM Per A. Hansen Post Boks 1023 Trondheim N-7002

Poland

Teresin	Radio Niepokalanow Mikolaj Kruczynski o. Maksymiliana Teresin Ph#: 48 46 461 34 88	**Krakow**	Polskie Radio Krakow Waclaw L. Nowotarski Witosa 31/3 Krakow 30-612
Warsaw	Polskie Radio Korneliusz Pacuda Warszawa 3 ul. Lazienkowska Warsaw 3/5/7 Ph#: 48 22 645 56 43	**Bydgoszcz**	El Radio FM 68.3/FM 96.2 Andrzej Fabis Ulatowski Sobieskiego 1 Bydgoszcz 85-959

Portugal

Seixal	Radio Baia Nelson Fernando Apartado 33 Seixal 2840

Romania

Cluj-Napoca	S.C. Irsiando Exposery Ltd. Dorin Marincas O.P. 12CP835 Cluj-Napoca 3400

Appendix A

Russia

Krasnodar Krasnodar 103.3 FM
Marina Lubushkina Vladimirovna
Ulbrativaegnatobih 46-A
Krasnodar 35-000

Scotland

Edinburgh Lothian Scot FM
Dave Johanssen
1F1 11 Comiston Gardens
Edingurgh Lothian EH10 5QW

Galashiels CMR Radio
Stuart Cameron
PO Box 13243
Galashiels TD1 2YL

Glasgow Neon Productions-Radio Scotland
Marine Crescent
Studio One 19
Glasgow G51 1HO

Inverness Moray Firth Community Radio
Helen MacPherson
PO Box 271
Scorguie Pl
Inverness IV3 6SF

Paisley Radio Clyde
Bill Black
111 Greenhill Rd
Paisley PA3 1RD

Slovakia, Slovak Republic

Bratislava Fun Radio Bratislava 94.3
Ing Ziman Patriz
Leskova 5
PO Box 525
Bratislava 81104

Martin Radio Zilina
Miro Stanek
V.P. Totha 16
Martin 036 01
Ph#: 42 18 962 49 21

Presov Radio Vychod
Miro Stanek
Moyzesova 45
Presov 08 001
Ph#: 4219 177 24 333

Slovenia

Ljubljana National Radio Slovenia
Jane Weber
P.O. Box 3822
Ljubljana 1001
Ph#: 386-1475-2406

Appendix A

South Africa

Benmore Gauteng   Cani Community Radio
David Batzofin
PO Box 652252
Benmore Gauteng 2010

Spain

Barcelona   Spanish Nt'l Radio Network, Radio 3
Tony Videl
Passeig de Gracia 1
Barcelona 08007
Ph#: 349-3304-8165

Madrid   Onda Verde
Monserrat Moreno
Plaza de Luca de Terra 13
Madrid 28045
Ph#: 34-1530-5767

Betera (Valencia)   Radio Turia
Juan Carlos Martinez Hernandez
PO Box 99
Betera 46117

Palafrugell   Radio Palafrugell FM
Rafel Corbi
Botines 26 Costa Brava
Palafrugell 17200
Ph#: 34 630 15 02 11

Calldentenes   Radio Taradell
Ramon Anfruns Prat
C/Gran 15,2 Catalonia
Calldentenes 08506
Ph#: 34 38 86 39 17

Palma de Mallorca   Tramonstana Radio
Frank Montenegro
Apartat Correos 1786
Palma de Mallorca 07080

Sri Lanka

Colombo   Garco (Private) Ltd.
Godwin A.R. Peruma
146, New Chetty St.
Colombo 13

Sweden

Borlange   Radio Borlange
Kent Sundgren
PO Box 10016
Borlange S-781 10

Kumla   Radio 94.3
Thomas Hyden
Box 123
Kumla SE-69222
Ph#: 46 19 58 37 74

Falun   Radio Dalarna
Lars Kjellberg
Slattavagen 2
Falun S-791 75

Marieholm   Radio CMR FM 105.5
Goran Hank Svensson
PO Box 95
Marieholm S-240 30

Helsingborg   Hit FM 94.5
Thomas Hyden
S Stenbocksgatan 128
Helsingborg S-252 45

Skarholmen   Country Music Sweden
Janne Lindgren
Frostrabacken 10
Stockholm
Skarholmen S-127 37

Appendix A

Solleron	Mora Narradio Janne Sundqvist Gullgravsvagen 31 Solleron S-792 90	**Vasteras**	Sveriges Radio Vast Stefan Lanehed Bystammogatan 4 Vasteras S-725 91
Spanga	Radio Viking Spanga Peter Ahlm Lattingebacken 40 Spanga S-163 62		

Switzerland

Schaffhausen	Radio Munot David Bolli Bachstrasse 29A Schaffhausen 8201 Ph#: 41 52 62 47 690	**Staefa**	Radio Eviea Rene Hofmann Im Riet 10 Staefa 8712
Luzern	Radio Pilatus FM 104.9 R. Tschuppert Post Fach 4140 Luzern CH-6001	**Crissier**	Radio Framboise P. Zumbrunn Vaudoise 23-25 Route De Prilly Crissier
Sirnach	Radio Top Oliver Marklowski Fischingerstr 21 Sirnach CH-8370	**Zurich**	Radio Eviva Irene Schmidt Kreuzstrasse 26 Zurich CH-6402 Ph#: 41 1 262 36 36
Birsfelden	Radio Edelweiss Peter R. Gisin Hofstrasse 17 Birsfelden CH-4127		

United Arab Emirates

Abu Dhabi	Emirates Radio 2 Lee Moulsdale P.O. 63 Abu Dhabi Ph#: 971-2445-0406

United Kingdom

Bristol	BBC South Kelvin Henderson P.O. Box 194 Bristol B599 7QT Ph#: 44 117 974 1111	**Basingstoke Hants**	Wey Valley Radio John Matthews 19 Princes Crescent South Basingstoke Hants RG22 6DP

Appendix A

Brighton East Sussex   Radio Sole
Jim Marshall
3 Chester Terrace
Brighton East Sussex BN1 6GB

Cambridge
BBC Radio Cambridgeshire
Helen West
104 Hills Road
Broadcasting House
Cambridge CB2 1LD
Ph#: 44 1223 259696

Cheshire
Silk FM 106.9
Fran D. Bradshaw
37 Compass Close Runcorn
Cheshire WA7 6DL

Dundee
Radio Tay
Ken Macleod
P.O. Box 123
Dundee, Tayside   DD1 9UF
Ph#: 44 1382 200800

Edinburgh
Scot FM
David Johanssen
No. 1 Shed Albert Quay
Edinburgh, Midlothian EH6 7DN
Ph#: 44 131 554 6777

Folkestone
BBC Radio Kent
Trevor Claringbold
40 Hollands Avenue
Folkestone, Kent CT19 6PN

Glasgow
BBC Radio Scotland
Brian Burnett
Queen Margaret Dr.
Broadcasting House
Glasgow G12 8DG
Ph#: 44 141 339 8844

Kinston-Upon-Hull - Kingstown Radio Ctry Music
Tom Robinson
219 Summergangs Road
Kinston-Upon-Hull, Yorkshire
HU8 8LD

Leicester
BBC Radio Nottingham
Mick Smith
6 The Green Syston
Leicester, Leicestershire LE7 1HQ

Liverpool
Radio Broadgreen
Alan Foulkes
35 Crofton Crescent Old Swan
Liverpool, Mercyside Ll3 5HL

London
Radio Caroline
Graham Hall
426 Archway Rd.
London, Highgate N6 4JH
Ph#: 44 181 340 3831

Manchester
BBC GMR-Greater Manchester Radio
David Spencer
P.O. Box 951
Oxford Rd.
Manchester M60 1SD
Ph#: 44 161 200 2000

Norwich
BBC Radio Norfolk
David Clayton
Norfolk Tower
Surrey St.
Norwich NR1 3PA
Ph#: 4416-0361-7411

Peterborough
Lite FM
Peter Tee
43 Wyndham Park
Orton Wistow
Peterborough PE1 1XB
Ph#: 44 1733 898106

Sheffield
BBC Radio Sheffield
Bob Preedy
54 Shoreham St.
Sheffield S1 4RS
Ph#: 44 114 273 1177

Southport
Dune FM
Phil Roberts
"Rose Cottage"
2 Bentham St.
Southport, Mercyside PR8 1RR
Ph#: 4417-0452-0500

Stone
BBC Radio Stoke
Les Scott
29 St. Michael's Mount
Stone, Straffordshire ST15 8PZ

Warrington
Wire FM
Peter Fairhead
Warrington Bus. Park Long Lane
Warrington WA2 6TX
Ph#: 4419-2544-5545

York
BBC Radio York
Bob Preedy Bootham Row
York Y03 7BR
Ph#: 44 1904 641 351

Appendix A

Uruguay

Montevideo
La Costa FM 88
Julio Cavallaro
Jose Serrato 2668
Montevideo 112000
Ph#: 598 25 06 75 69

Montevideo
Cabildo Mas FM
Paul Tejeiro
Jose Ellauri 1010/401
Montevideo 113000
Ph#: 598 25 06 16 51

Appendix A

Appendix B

U.S. FAIR LISTINGS
(State-by-State)

Appendix B

Appendix B

Alabama

Andalusia - Kiwanis Covington Co. Fair - (334) 222-4250
Anniston - Calhoun Co. Fair - (256) 238-1554
Attalla – Etowah Co. Fair
Birmingham - The Greater Alabama Fall Fair & Festival - (205) 786-8100
Boaz - Marshall Co. Fair - (256) 593-2494
Cullman - Cullman Co. Fair - (256) 734-0463
Decatur - Tennessee Valley Expo. (Morgan Co. Fair) - (256) 353-3976
Dothan - National Peanut Festival & Fair - (334) 793-4323
Fayette - Fayette Co. Fair - (205) 932-4293
Fort Payne - DeKalb Co. Fair - (256) 845-4752
Gadsden - Etowah Co. Fair - (256) 538-2815
Greenville – Butler Co. Fair – (334) 382-3057
Huntsville - NE Alabama State Fair - (256) 883-5252
Jacksonville – Calhoun Co. Fair – (256) 435-6188

Jasper - Jaycee's NW Alabama Fair - (205) 387-8950
Luverne - Crenshaw Co. Fair - (334) 335-3270
Mobile - Greater Gulf State Fair - (251) 344-4573
Monroeville - Monroe Co. Fair - (251) 575-4782
Montgomery - Alabama National Fair & Agricultural Expo.,Inc. – (334) 272-6831
Moulton - Lawrence Co. Fair - (256) 974-6056
Muscle Shoals - No. Alabama State Fair, Inc. - (256) 383-3247
Oneonta - Blount Co. Fair - (205) 274-8839
Opelika - Lee Co. Fair - (334) 749-9680
Prattville - Autauga Co. Fair - (334) 365-8944
Scottsboro - Jackson Co. Fair - (256) 574-1869
Troy - Pike Co. Fair - (334) 566-6572
Tulia - Etowah Co. Fair (256) 538-2815
Tuscaloosa - West Alabama State Fair - (205) 556-1285

Alaska

Delta Junction - Deltana Fair - (907) 895-3247
Fairbanks - Tanana Valley State Fair - (907) 452-3750
Haines - SE Alaska State Fair/Alaskan Bald Eagle Music Festival - (907) 766-2476

Kodiak - Kodiak Rodeo & State Fair (907) 487-4440
Ninilchik - Kenai Peninsula State Fair - (907) 567-3670
Palmer - Alaska State Fair - (907) 745-4827

Arizona

Casa Grande - Pinal Co. Fair - (520) 723-5242
Cottonwood - Verde Valley Fair - (928) 634-3290
Douglas - Cochise Co. Fair - (520) 364-3819
Duncan - Greenlee Co. Fair - (928) 359-9037
Flagstaff - Coconino Co. Fair - (928) 774-5139
Fredonia - No. Arizona Fair - (928) 643-7431
Globe - Gila Co. Fair - (928) 425-0602
Holbrook - Navajo Co Fair - (928) 524-6407
Kingman - Mohave Co Fair - (928) 753-2636
Parker - La Paz Co Fair - (928) 669-8100
Peoria – San Gennaro Feast – (623) 487-7774
Phoenix - Arizona National Livestock Show - (602) 258-8568

Phoenix - Arizona State Fair - (602) 252-6771
Phoenix - Maricopa Co. Fair - (602) 252-0717
Prescott - Prescott Frontier Days "World's Oldest Rodeo" - (928) 445-3103
Prescott Valley - Yavapai Co. Fair - (928) 775-8000
Safford - Graham Co. Fair - (928) 428-6240
Sonoita - Santa Cruz Co. Fair - (520) 455-5553
Tucson - Pima Co. Fair - (520) 762-9100
Whiteriver - White Mountain Apache Tribal Fair & Rodeo - (928) 338-4346
Window Rock - Navajo Nation Fair - (928) 871-6478
Yuma - Yuma Co. Fair - (928) 726-4420

Appendix B

Arkansas

Arkadelphia - Clark Co. Fair & Livestock Show - (870) 246-4825
Ash Flat - Sharp Co. Fair - (870) 994-7914
Augusta - Three Co. Fair - (870) 347-5622
Batesville - Independence Co. Fair - (870) 793-6006
Bentonville - Benton Co. Fair - (479) 273-9266
Berryville - Carroll Co. Fair - (870) 438-6143
Blytheville - Mississippi Co. Fair-Fall - (870) 763-1293
Blytheville - Spring Carnival - (870) 763-1293
Booneville - So. Logan Co. Fair & Livestock Show - (479) 996-2070
Bryant - Saline Fair - (501) 847-3649
Camden - Ouachita Co. Livestock & Fair - (870) 231-6120
Charleston - So. Franklin Co. Fair - (479) 965-2269
Clarksville - Johnson Co. Fair - (479) 754-6425
Clinton - Van Buren Co. Livestock Show & Fair - (501) 745-8100
Conway - Faulkner Co. Fair - (501) 450-4712
Crossett - Ashley Co. Fair - (870 364-6032
Danville - Yell Co. Fair - (479) 495-2216
DeQueen - Sevier Co. Fair - (870) 642-7352
Des Arc - Prairie Co. Fair - (870) 854-3809
DeWitt - Arkansas Co. Fair - (870) 946-2087
Dumas - Desha Co. Fair & Livestock Show - (870) 382-6972
El Dorado - Union Co. Fair - (870) 863-8719
Elaine - Tri-Co. Fair - (870) 827-6265
Fayetteville - Washington Co. Fair - (479) 643-2113
Fordyce - Dallas Co. Fair - (870) 352-2566
Foreman - Little River Co. Fair & Rodeo - (870) 542-7311
Forrest City - St. Francis Fair - (870) 633-8479
Ft. Smith - Arkansas-Oklahoma State Fair - (479) 783-6176
Fouke - Miller Co. Fair - (870) 653-4327
Glenwood - Pike Co. Fair & Livestock Show - (870) 356-4355
Greenwood - Sebastian Co. Fair - (479) 996-4142
Hampton - Calhoun Co. Fair - (870) 798-2207
Harrisburg - Poinsett Co. Fair - (870) 578-2314
Harrison - NW Arkansas Dist. Fair - (870) 743-3713
Heber Springs - Cleburne Co. Fair - (501) 362-2524
Hindsville - Madison Co. Fair - (479) 789-2384
Hope - SW Arkansas Dist. Fair - (870) 777-5111
Hot Springs - Garland Co. Fair - (501) 525-0196

Imboden - Lawrence Co. Fair - (870) 869-2953
Jasper - Newton Co. Fair - (870) 434-5376
Jonesboro - NE Arkansas Dist. Fair - (870) 935-4331
Lewisville - Lafayette Co. Fair - (870) 921-5393
Little Rock - Arkansas State Fair - (501) 372-8341
Lonoke - Lonoke Co. Fair - (501) 676-3106
Magnolia - Colombia Co. Fair & Livestock Show - (870) 901-6517
Malvern - Hot Springs Co. Fair - (501) 337-5125
Marshall - Searcy Co. Fair - (870) 448-3884
Melbourne - Izard Co. Fair - (870) 368-4311
Melbourne - No. Ctrl. Arkansas Dist. Fair - (870) 346-5794
Mena - Polk Co. Fair - (479) 394-1110
Monticello - Drew Co. Livestock Show & Fair - (870) 367-9283
Morrilton - Conway Co. Fair - (501) 354-2551
Mount Ida - Montgomery Co. Fair - (870) 334-2660
Mountain Home - Baxter Co. Fair - (870) 425-5726
Mountain View - Stone Co. Fair - (870) 591-6629
Nashville - Howard Co. Fair - (870) 845-4315
Ozark - No. Franklin Co. Fair - (479) 667-4384
Paragould - Greene Co. Fair - (870) 236-3187
Paris - No. Logan Co. Fair - (479) 934-4057
Perryville - Perry Co. Fair - (501) 432-5210
Piggott - Clay Co. - (870) 598-2813
Pine Bluff - SE Arkansas Dist Livestock Show & Rodeo - (870) 535-2900
Pocahontas - Randolph Co. Fair & Livestock Show - (870) 892-0086
Portland - Chicot Co. Fair - (870) 265-3215
Prescott - Nevada Co. Fair - (870) 887-5598
Rison - Cleveland Co. Fair & Livestock Show - (870) 357-2246
Russellville - Pope Co. Fair - (479) 968-5640
Salem - Fulton Co. Fair - (870) 895-2491
Searcy - White Co. Fair - (501) 882-2757
Sheridan - Grant Co. Fair - (870) 942-4245
Star City - Lincoln Co. Fair - (870) 628-4509
Summit - Marion Co. Fair - (870) 449-5303
Texarkana - Four States Fair - (870) 773-2941
Waldron - Scott Co. Fair - (479) 637-4819
Warren - Bradley Co. Fair - (870 226-2143
Winthrop – Little River Co. Fair & Rodeo - (870) 542-7311

Appendix B

California

Anderson - Shasta Dist Fair - (530) 378-6789

Angels Camp - Calaveras Co. Fair & Jumping Frog Jubilee - (209) 736-2561

Antioch - Contra Costa Co. Fair - (925) 757-4400

Auburn - Gold Country Fair - (530) 823-4533

Bakersfield - Kern Co. Fair - (661) 833-4900

Bishop - Eastern Sierra Tri-Co. Fair - (760) 873-3588

Blythe - Colorado River Country Fair - (760) 922-3247

Boonville - Mendocino Co. Fair & Apple Show - (707) 895-3011

Calistoga - Napa Co. Fair - (707) 942-5111

Cedarville - Modoc Dist. Fair - (530) 279-2315

Chico - Silver Dollar Fair - (530) 895-4666

Chowchilla - Chowchilla-Madera Co. Fair - (559) 665-3728

Cloverdale - Cloverdale Citrus Fair - (707) 894-3992

Costa Mesa - Orange Co Fair - (714) 708-3247

Crescent City - Del Norte Co. Fair - (707) 464-9556

Daly City - Grand National Rodeo, Horse & Stock Show - (415) 404-4100

Del Mar - San Diego Co. Fair - (858) 793-5555

Dixon - Dixon May Fair - (707) 678-5520

Eureka - Redwood Acres Fair - (707) 445-3037

Ferndale - Humboldt Co. Fair - (707) 786-9511

Fresno - The Big Fresno Fair - (559) 650-3247

Grass Valley - Draft Horse Classic & Harvest Faire - (530) 273-6217

Grass Valley - Nevada Co. Fair - (530) 273-6217

Gridley - Butte Co. Fair - (530) 846-3626

Hanford - Kings Fair - (559) 584-3318

Hayfork - Trinity Co. Fair - (530) 628-5223

Imperial - California Mid-Winter Fair & Fiesta - (760) 355-1181

Indio - Riverside Co. Fair/National Date Festival - (760) 863-8247

King City - Salinas Valley Fair - (831) 385-3243

Lake Perris - So. California Fair - (909) 657-4221

Lakeport - Lake Co. Fair - (707) 263-6181

Lakeview Terrace - San Fernando "Valley Fair" - (818) 557-1600

Lancaster - Antelope Valley Fair & Alfalfa Festival - (661) 948-6060

Lodi - Lodi Grape Festival & Harvest Fair - (209) 369-2771

Los Banos - Merced Co. Spring Fair - (209) 826-5166

Madera - Madera Dist Fair - (559) 674-8511

Mariposa - Mariposa Dist Fair & Homecoming - (209) 966-3686

McArthur - Inter-Mountain Fair of Shasta Co. - (530) 336-5695

Merced - Merced Co. Fair - (209) 722-1507

Monterey - Monterey Co. Fair - (831) 372-5863

Napa - Napa Town & Country Fair - (707) 253-4900

Orland - Glenn Co. Fair - (530) 865-1168

Paso Robles - California Mid-State Fair - (805) 239-0655

Perris - Farmers Fair & Festival - (909) 657-4221

Petaluma - Sonoma-Marin Fair - (707) 283-3247

Placerville - El Dora Co. Fair - (530) 621-5860

Pleasanton - Alameda Co. - (925) 426-7600

Plymouth - Amador Co. Fair - (209) 245-6921

Pomona - L.A. Co. Fair - (909) 865-4050

Quincy - Plumas-Sierra Co. Fair - (530) 283- 6272

Red Bluff - Tehama Dist. Fair - (530) 527-5920

Ridgecrest - Desert Empire Fair-Fall - (760) 375-8000

Roseville - Placer Co. Fair - (916) 786-2023

Sacramento - California State Fair - (916) 263-FAIR

Sacramento - Sacramento Co. Fair - (916) 263-2975

San Bernardino - National Orange Show - (909) 888-6788

San Jose - Santa Clara Co. Fair - (408) 494-3247

San Mateo - San Mateo Co Fair - (650) 574-3247

San Rafael - Marin Co. Fair - (415) 499-6400

Santa Barbara - Santa Barbara Fair & Expo - (805) 687-0766

Santa Rosa - Sonoma Co. Fair & Expo, Inc. - (707) 545-4200

Santa Rosa - Sonoma Co. Harvest Fair - (707) 545-4203

Sonora - Mother Lode Fair - (209) 532-7428

Stockton - San Joaquin Fair - (209) 466-5041

Tres Pinos - San Benito Co. Rodeo, Saddle Horse Show & Fair - (831) 628-3545

Tres Pinos - San Benito Co. Fair - (831) 628-3421

Tulare - Tulare Co. Fair - (559) 686-4707

Tulelake - Tulelake-Butte Valley Fair - (530) 667-5312

Turlock - Stanislaus Co. Fair - (209) 668-1333

Ukiah - Redwood Empire Fair - (707) 462-3247

Vallejo - Solano Co. Fair - (707) 551-2000

Ventura - Ventura Co. Fair - (805) 648-3376

Victorville - San Bernardino Co. Fair - (760) 951-2200

Watsonville - Santa Cruz Co. Fair - (831) 724-5671

Woodland - Yolo Co. Fair & 40th Dist. Agricultural Fair - (530) 662-5393

Yreka - Siskiyou Golden Fair - (530) 842-2767

Yuba City - Yuba Sutter Fair - (530) 674-1280

Appendix B

Colorado

Akron - Washington Co. Fair - (970) 345-2701

Black Hawk - Gilpin Co. Fair - (303) 582-5214

Brighton - Adams Co. Fair & Rodeo - (303) 637-8007

Burlington - Kit Carson Co. Fair & Rodeo
  - (719) 346-0111

Calhan - El Paso Co. Fair - (719) 520-7880

Canon City - Fremont Co. Fair - (719) 275-6722

Castle Rock - Douglas Co. Fair & Rodeo
  - (303) 660-7314

Cheyenne Wells - Cheyenne Co. Fair & Rodeo
  - (719) 767-5716

Colorado Springs - El Paso Co. Fair - (719) 520-7880

Cortez - Montezuma Co. Fair - (970) 565-3123

Craig - Moffat Co. Fair - (970) 824-3476

Cripple Creek - Teller Co. Fair - (719) 889-2295

Denver - National Western Stock Show, Rodeo
  & Horse Show - (303) 297-1166

Dove Creek - Dolores Co. Fair - (970) 677-2283

Durango - La Plata Co. Fair - (970) 563-3000

Eads - Kiowa Co. Fair - (719) 438-5321

Eagle - Eagle Co. Fair & Rodeo - (970) 328-3646

Estes Park - Rooftop Rodeo - (970) 586-6104

Ft. Morgan - Morgan Co. Fair - (970) 542-3526

Golden - Gilpin Co. Fair - (303) 582-5214

Golden - Jefferson Co. Jeffco Fair - (303) 271-6620

Grand Junction - Mesa Co. Fair - (970) 256-1531

Greeley - Greeley Independence Stampede
  - (970) 356-2855

Greeley - Weld Co. Fair - (970) 356-4000

Hayden - Routt Co. Fair - (970) 879-0825

Henderson - Adams Co. Fair & Rodeo - (303) 637-8007

Holly - Holly Gateway Fair (Prowers) - (719) 537-6215

Holyoke - Phillips Co. Fair - (970) 854-3616

Hotchkiss - Delta Co. Fair - (970) 874-2195

Hugo - Lincoln Co. Fair & Rodeo - (719) 743-2606

Julesburg - Sedgwick Co. Fair - (970) 474-2448

Kiowa - Elbert Co. Fair - (303) 621-3152

Kremmling - (Grand) Middle Park Fair
  - (970) 724-3436

La Veta - Huerfano Co. 4-H Fair & Rodeo
  - (719) 738-3329

Las Animas - Bent Co. Fair & Rodeo - (719) 456-0764

Longmont - Boulder Co. Fair & Rodeo
  - (303) 772-7170

Loveland - Larimer Co. Fair & Rodeo - (970) 669-6760

Meeker - Rio Blanco Co. Fair/Rodeo - (970) 878-4093

Monte Vista - San Luis Valley Fair - (719) 274-4204

Montrose - Montrose Co. Fair - (970) 249-3935

Montrose - Ouray Co. Fair - (970) 249-3935

Norwood - San Miguel Basin Fair & Rodeo
  - (970) 327-4341

Pagosa Springs - Archuleta Co. Fair - (970) 264-593

Pueblo - Colorado State Fair - (719) 561-8484

Pueblo - Pueblo Co. Fair - (719) 583-6566

Ridgway - Ouray Co. Fair - (970) 249-3935

Rifle - Garfield Co. Fair - (970) 625-2514

Rocky Ford - Arkansas Valley Fair & Expo
  - (719) 254-7723

Salida - The New, Old Fashion Chaffee Co. Fair
  - (719) 539-6151

Silverthorne - (Summit) Mountain Community Fair
  - (970) 513-8081

Simia - Elbert Co. Fair - (303) 621-3162

Springfield - Baca Co. Fair - (719) 523-6971

Sterling - Logan Co. Fair - (970) 522-0888

Walden - (Jackson) North Park Fair - (970) 723-4298

Westcliffe - Custer Co. Fair - (719) 783-2514

Yuma - Yuma Co. Fair - (970) 848-2291

Connecticut

Berlin - Berlin Fair - (860) 828-1389

Bethlehem - Bethlehem Fair - (203) 266-5350

Bridgewater - Bridgewater Country Fair - (860) 354-1509

Brooklyn - Brooklyn Fair - (860) 779-0012

Brooklyn - Windham Co. 4-H Fair - (860) 774-9600

Cheshire Grange - Cheshire Grange Community Fair
  - (203) 272-4620

Chester - Chester Fair - (860) 526-5947

Durham - Durham Agricultural Fair - (860) 349-9495

Goshen - Connecticut Agricultural Fair - (860) 564-7614

Goshen - Goshen Fair - (860) 491-3655

Guilford - Guilford Fair - (203) 453-3543

Haddam Neck - Haddam Neck Fair - (860) 267-4671

Appendix B

Harwinton - Harwinton Fair - (860) 485-9369
Hebron - Hebron Harvest Fair - (860) 228-0892
Lebanon - Lebanon Country Fair - (860) 642-7410
Ledyard - Ledyard Fair - (860) 886-0329
Lyme - Hamburg Fair - Manchester - (860) 434-1459
Manchester - Wapping Fair - (860) 290-9588
Middle Haddam - Haddam Neck Fair - (860) 267-4671
North Haven - North Haven Fair - (203) 239-3700
North Stonington - North Stonington Agricultural Fair - (860) 535-3956
Orange - Orange Country Fair - (203) 795-6489
Plymouth - Terryville Country Fair - (860) 283-9300

Portland - Portland Agricultural Fair - (860) 342-3550
Riverton - Riverton Fair - (203) 738-4227
Somers - Four Town Fair - (860) 749-6527
Somers - Hartford Co. 4-H Fair - (860) 668-9345
South Windsor - (860) 643-1877
South Woodstock - (860) 928-4626
Terryville - Terryville Country Fair - (860) 283-9300
Uncasville - Montville Fair - (860) 848-9671
Vernon - Tolland Co. 4-H Fair - (860) 749-3193
Wolcott - Wolcott Country Fair - (203) 879-4842
Woodstock - Woodstock Fair - (860 928-3246

Delaware

Harrington - Delaware State Fair - (302) 398-3269

Florida

Arcadia - DeSoto Co. Fair - (863) 494-5678
Bonifay - Holmes Co. Fair - (850) 547-3394
Brooksville - Hernando Co. Fair & Youth Livestock - (352) 796-4552
Bunnell - Flagler Co. Fair & Youth Show - (386) 437-3240
Bushnell - Sumter Co. Fair - (352) 793-2750
Callahan - Northeastern Florida Fair - No Phone
Clewiston - Hendry Co. Fair & Livestock Show - (863) 983-9282
Dade City - Pasco Co. Fair - (352) 567-6678
De Funiak Springs - Walton Co. Fair - (850) 892-3972
Deland - Volusia Co. Fair & Youth Show, Inc. - (386) 734-9515
East Palatka - Putnam Co. Fair - (386) 329-0318
Elkton - The Great St. Johns Co. Fair - (904) 829-6476
Eustis - Lake Co. Fair - (352) 357-7111
Ft. Myers - SW Florida & Lee Co. Fair - (239) 543-8368
Ft. Pierce - St. Lucie Co. Fair - (772) 464-2910
Ft. Walton Beach - NW Florida Fair - (850) 862-0211
Gainesville - Alachua Co. Fair - (352) 372-1537
Green Cove Springs - Clay Co. Agricultural Fair - (904) 284-1615
Homestead - Country Fair of So. Dade - (305) 247-2016
Inverness - Citrus Co. Fair - (352) 726-2993

Jacksonville - Greater Jacksonville Agricultural Fair - (904) 353-0535
Kissimmee - Osceola Co. Fair & Livestock Show - (407) 846-6046
Lake City - Columbia Co. Fair - (386) 752-8822
Live Oak - Suwannee Co. Fair & Youth Livestock Show - (386) 362-7366
Macclenny - Baker Co. Fair - (904) 259-7314
Marianna - Jackson Co. Agricultural Fair - (850) 482-3744
Miami - Miami-Dade Co. Fair & Exposition - (305) 223-7060
Milton - Santa Rosa Co. Fair - (850) 623-5055
Naples - Collier Co. Fair - (239) 455-1444
Okeechobee - American Legion Free Fair - (863) 763-2950
Orlando - Central Florida Fair - (407) 295-3247
Palm Bay - Brevard Co. Fair - (321) 633-4028
Palmetto - Manatee Co. Fair - (941) 722-1639
Panama City - Bay Co. Fair - (850) 769-2645
Pensacola - Pensacola Interstate Fair - (850) 944-4500
Plant City - Florida Strawberry Festival & Fair - (813) 752-9194
Pompano Beach - Broward Co. Fair - (954) 450-1234
Port Charlotte - Charlotte Co. Fair - (941) 629-4252
Sarasota - Sarasota Co. Agricultural Fair - (941) 365-0818
Sebring - Bradford Co. Fair - (863) 382-2255

Appendix B

Starke - Bradford Co. Fair - (904) 964-5252
Stuart - Martin Co. Fair - (772) 220-FAIR
Tallahassee - North Florida Fair - (850) 878-3247
Tampa - Florida State Fair - (813) 621-7821
Tampa - Greater Hillsborough Co. Fair
- (813) 737-3247
Vero Beach - Firefighters Indian River Co. Fair
- (772) 562-2974

Wauchula - Hardee Co. Fair - (863) 773-2418
West Palm Beach - South Florida Fair - (561) 793-0333
Winter Haven - Florida Citrus Festival & Polk Co. Fair
- (863) 292-9810
Ybor City, Tampa - Spring FunFair & Expo
- (813) 621-7121

Georgia

Adel - Cook Co. Exchange Club Fair - (229) 896-2504
Albany - Exchange Club Fair of SW Georgia
- (229) 436-8827
Americus - Sumter Civic Fair - (229) 924-5696
Augusta - Georgia-Carolina State Fair - (760) 860-8718
Baxley - Tri-Co. Fair - (912) 366-1010
Brunswick - Brunswick Exchange Club Fair
- (912) 265-3464
Calhoun - Cherokee Capital Fair-Spring - (706) 625-496
Calhoun - Cherokee Capital Fair-Fall - (706) 625-4964
Carrollton - West Georgia Fair - (770) 836-0227
Cedartown - Polk Co. Fair - (770) 748-4882
Clarkesville - Chattahoochee Mtn. Fair - (706) 778-4434
Columbus - Greater Columbus Fair - (706) 653-4482
Comer - Madison Co. Fair - (706) 795-2096
Cordele - Ctrl. Georgia Fair - (229) 273-3713
Cumming - Cumming Country Fair & Festival
- (770) 781-3491
Dalton - No. Georgia Agricultural Fair - (706) 278-1712
Douglas - SE Georgia Fair - (912) 383-8187
Elberton - Elberton 12-County Fair - (706) 283-3401
Fayetteville - Fayette Co. Fair - (770) 461-5519
Gray - Jones Co. Lions Club Fair - (478) 746-3997
Griffin - Spalding Co. Fair - (770) 227-9187
Grovetown - Columbia Co. Fair - (706) 863-0785
Hazlehurst - Jeff Davis Fair - (912) 375-5838

Hiawassee - Georgia Mtn. Fair - (706) 896-4191
Jonesboro - Clayton Co. Kiwanis Fair - (770) 473-0709
Lawrenceville - Gwinnett Co. Fair - (770) 963-6522
Louisville - Louisville Lions Club Fair - (478) 625-7929
Macon - Georgia State Fair - (478) 746-7184
Marietta - No. Georgia State Fair - (770) 423-1330
Newnan - Coweta Co. Fair - (770) 253-3649
Perry - Georgia National Fair - (478) 987-3247
Rome - Coosa Valley Fair - (706) 291-9951
Sandersville - Washington Co. Fair - (478) 552-3491
Savannah - Coastal Empire Fair - (912) 354-3542
Springfield - Effingham Co. Fair - (912) 728-3368
Statesboro - Kiwanis Ogeechee Fair - (912) 786-4716
Swainsboro - SE Georgia Jaycee Fair - (478) 237-3986
Tennille - Washington Co. Fair - (478) 552-3491
Thomasville - Deep South Agricultural Fair
- (229) 226-6331
Thomson - Thomson Co. Lions Club Fair - (706) 595-9705
Tifton - Coastal Plains Agricultural Fair
- (229) 382-4795
Vidalia - Kiwanis Fall Fair - (912) 538-888
Warner Robins - Houston Co. Fair - (478) 923-4904
Washington - Lions Club Agricultural Fair - (706) 678-7790
Waycross - Okefenokee Fair - (912) 283-7617
Waynesboro - Waynesboro Exchange Club Fair
- (706) 554-9176

Hawaii

Honolulu - Hawaii State Farm Fair - (808) 848-2074

Appendix B

Idaho

Blackfoot - Eastern Idaho State Fair - (208) 785-2480

Boise - Western Idaho Fair - (208) 376-3247

Bonners Ferry - Boundary Co. Fair - (208) 267-7041

Burley - Cassia Co. Fair & Rodeo - (208) 678-9150

Caldwell - Canyon Co. Fair & Festival - (208) 455-8500

Cascade - Valley Co. Fair & Rodeo - (208) 382-4371

Challis - Custer Co. Fair & Rodeo - (208) 879-2344

Coeur d'Alene - North Idaho Fair & Rodeo
 - (208) 765-4969

Downey - So. Bannock Co. Fair - (208) 237-1340

Emmett - Gem-Boise Co. Fair & Rodeo - (208) 365-0932

Fairfield - Camas Co. Fair - (208) 764-2230

Filer - Twin Falls Co. Fair / Magic Valley Stampede
 - (208) 326-4396

Glenns Ferry - Elmore Co. Fair & Rodeo
 - (208) 587-2136

Gooding - Gooding Co. Fair & Rodeo - (208) 934-4529

Grace - Caribou Co. Fair & Rodeo - (208) 574-2244

Homedale - Owyhee Co. Fair & Rodeo - (208) 337-3888

Jerome - Jerome Co. Fair & Rodeo - (208) 324-7209

Lewiston - Nez Perce Co. Fair - (208) 743-3302

Malad City - Oneida Co. Fair - (208) 766-2552

Montpelier - Bear Lake Co. Fair - (208) 847-3135

Nampa - Snake River Stampede - (208) 466-8497

New Plymouth - Payette Co. Fair - (208) 278-3150

Orofino - Orofino Clearwater Co. Fair & Lumberjack Days
 - (208) 476-3412

Pocatello - No. Bannock Co. Fair - (208) 237-1340

Pocatello - So. Bannock Co. Fair - (208) 237-1340

Pocatello - Spring Fair - (208) 232-2232

Preston - Franklin Co. Fair - (208) 852-1139

Rexburg - Madison Co. Fair - (208) 356-4271

Rupert - Minidoka Co. Fair & Rodeo - (208) 436-9748

Salmon - Lemhi Co. Fair - (208) 756-3032

Sandpoint - Bonner Co. Fair - (208) 263-8414

Shoshone - Lincoln Co. Fair & Rodeo - (208) 886-2406

Terreton - Mud Lake Fair & Rodeo - (208) 663-4981

Wayan - Caribou Co. Fair - (208) 574-2244

Illinois

Albion - Edwards Co. Fair - (618) 445-2842

Aledo - Mercer Co. Fair - (309) 582-5659

Altamont - Effingham Co. Fair - (888) 854-3247

Amboy - Lee Co. 4H Fair & Jr. Show - (815) 453-2200

Anna - Union Co. Fair - (618) 833-2406

Arthur - Moultrie-Douglas Co. - (217) 543-2664

Athena - Menard Co. Fair - (217) 636-8124

Augusta - Hancock Co. Fair - (217) 842-5804

Belleville - St. Clair Co. Fair - (618) 235-0666

Belvidere - Boone Co. Fair - (815) 544-4522

Benton - Franklin Co. 4H Fair - (618) 439-3178

Bloomington - McLean Co. Fair - (309) 829-3976

Brownstown - Fayette Co. Fair - (618) 245-6221

Butler - Montgomery Co. Fair - (217) 272-4489

Cambridge - Henry Co. Fair - (309) 944-4321

Carlinville - Macoupin Co. Fair - (217) 854-2172

Carlyle - Clinton Co. Fair - (618) 594-3669

Carmi - White Co. Fair - (618) 382-8592

Carrollton - Greene Co. Agricultural Fair
 - (217) 942-3094

Cerro Gordo - Platt Co. Jr. Fair - (217) 763-6017

Charleston - Coles Co. Fair - (217) 345-6212

Crescent City - Iroquois Co. Fair - (815) 698-2270

Cullom - Cullom Jr. Fair - (815) 689-2146

Danville - Vermillion Co. Fair & Expo. - (217) 442-1309

Decatur - Decatur-Macon Co. Fair - (217) 877-8941

DuQuoin - DuQuoin State Fair - (618) 542-1515

East Moline - Rock Island Co. Fair - (309) 796-1620

Fairbury - Fairbury Fair - (815) 692-3222

Fairfield - Wayne Co. Fair - (618) 897-2497

Farmer City - Farmer City/DeWitt Co. Fair
 - (309) 928-3312

Fisher - Fisher Community Fair & Horse Show
 - (217) 897-6299

Freeport - Stephenson Co. Fair - (815) 235-2918

Georgetown - Georgetown Fair - (217) 662-8865

Gladstone - Henderson Co. Fair - (309) 924-1177

Grayslake - Lake Co. Fair - (847) 223-2204

Green Valley - Tazewell Co. Veteran's Memorial Fair
 - (309) 348-2345

Appendix B

Greenup - Greenup-Cumberland Co. Fair - (217) 923-3034
Greenville - Bond Co. Fair - (618) 664-1412
Greenville - Butler Co. Fair - (334) 382-3057
Griggsville -Western Illinois Fair - (217) 833-2116
Hardin - Calhoun Co. Fair - (618) 576-2215
Harrisburg - Saline Co. Fair - (618) 252-3473
Havana - Mason Co. Jr. Show & 4H Fair - (309) 543-3308
Henry - Marshall-Putnam Co. Fair - (309) 364-2814
Highland - Madison Co. Fair - (618) 644-5441
Jacksonville - Morgan Co. Agricultural Fair
 - (217) 245-6800
Ina - Jefferson Co. Youth Fair - 9618) 246-2430
Jerseyville - Jersey Co. Fair - (618) 498-5848
Kankakee - Kankakee Co. Fair - (815) 932-6714
Knoxville - Knox Co. Fair - (309) 289-2714
Lewistown - Fulton Co. Fair - (309) 547-2532
Lincoln - Logan Co. Fair - (217) 732-3311
Macomb - McDonough Co. Jr. Fair - (309) 837-3939
Macomb - Warren Co. Agricultural Fair - (309) 837-0610
Marion - Williamson Co. Fair - (618) 993-3513
Marshall - Clark Co. Fair - (217) 826-6477
Martinsville - Martinsville Agricultural Fair
 - (217) 382-4121
McLeansboro - Hamilton Co. Fair - (618) 773-4625
Melvin - Ford Co. Fair - (217) 388-2398
Mendon - Adams Co. Fair - (217) 936-2230
Mendota - Mendota Tri-Co. Fair - (815) 539-7974
Metropolis - Massac Co. Fair - (618) 524-7320
Milledgeville - Carroll Co. Fair - (815) 493-2498
Morris - Grundy Co. Fair - (815) 448-5473
Morrison - Whiteside Co. Fair - (815) 336-2046
Mount Carmel - Wabash Co. Youth Exhibition
 - (618) 262-5264
Mount Sterling - Brown Co. Fair - (217) 894-6269
Nashville - Nashville-Washington Co. Fair - (618) 327-4401
New Berlin - Sangamon Co. Fair - (217) 488-2685
Newton - Jasper Co. Fair - (618) 783-3901
Oblong - Crawford Co. Fair - (618) 592-3517
Okawville - Okawville Agricultural Fair - (618) 243-6285

Olney - Richland Co. Fair - (618) 863-2606
Oregon - Ogle Co. Fair - (815) 734-4320
Ottawa - LaSalle Co. Jr. Fair - (815) 433-0371
Paris - Edgar Co. Fair - (217) 466-0905
Pecatonica - Winnebago Co. Fair - (815) 239-1641
Pekin - Tazewell Co. Veteran's Memorial Fair
 - (309) 348-2345
Pena - Pena Tri-Co. Fair - (217) 539-4263
Peoria - Heart of Illinois Fair - (309) 691-6332
Peotone - Will Co. Fair - (708) 258-9359
Petersburg - Menard Co. Fair - (217) 636-8123
Pickneyville - Perry Co. Fair - (618) 357-2787
Pleasant Hill - Pike Co. Fair - (217) 335-2279
Pontiac - Livingston Co. Fair - (815) 842-1776
Princeton - Bureau Co. Fair - (815) 875-2905
Pulaski - Pulaski Co. Fair - (618) 342-6212
Ridgway - Gallatin Co. Fair - (618) 272 8971
Roseville - Warren Co. Agricultural Fair - (309) 837-2230
Rushville - Schuyler Co. Fair - (217) 322-4318
St. Charles - Kane Co. Fair - (630) 584-6926
Salem - Marion Co. Fair - (618) 548-1251
Sandwich - The Sandwich Fair - (815) 786-2389
Shelbyville - Shelby Co. Fair - (217) 774-9546
Sparta - Randolph Co. Fair - (618) 443-6279
Springfield - Illinois State Fair - (217) 782-0771
Sumner - Lawrence Co. Fair - (618) 936-2439
Taylorville - Christian Co. Agricultural Fair
 - (217) 824-2623
Urbana - Champaign Co. Fair - (217) 367-8461
Virginia - Cass Co. Fair - (217) 452-3541
Walshville - Montgomery Co. Fair - (217) 272-4489
Waltonville - Jeffersonville Co. Youth Fair
 - (618) 279-3330
Warren - Jo Daviess Co. Fair - (815) 745-2200
Waterloo - Monroe Co. Fair - (618) 939-4695
Wheaton - DuPage Co. Fair - (630) 668-6636
Woodstock - McHenry Co. Fair - (815) 338-5315
Yorkville - Kendall Co. Fair - (630) 553-2860

Indiana

Anderson - Anderson Free Fair - (765) 649-7156
Angola - Steuben Co. 4H Fair - (260) 668-1000
Argos - Marshall Co. 4H Fair - (574) 935-8545

Auburn - DeKalb Co. Free Fall Fair - (260) 925-1834
Bedford - Lawrence Co. 4H Fair - (812) 275-2339
Bloomfield - Greene Co. 4H Fair - (812) 659-2122

Appendix B

Bloomington - Monroe Co. Fair - (812) 332-4894
Bluffton - Bluffton Free Street Fair - (260) 824-4351
Bluffton - Wells Co. 4H Fair - (260) 824-6412
Boswell - Benton Co. Fair - (765) 742-1334
Brazil - Clay Co. 4H Fair - (812) 448-9041
Brookville - Franklin Co. 4H Fair - (765) 647-3511
Brownstown - Jackson Co. Fair - (812) 522-2313
Charlestown - Clark Co. 4H Fair - (812) 256-4591
Columbus - Bartholomew Co. 4H Fair - (812) 372-6133
Connersville - Fayette Co. Free Fair - (765) 825-1351
Converse - Converse Fair - (765) 395-3256
Corydon - Harrison Co. Fair - (812) 738-4968
Crawfordsville - Montgomery Co. 4H Fair - (765) 364-6363
Crown Point - Lake Co. Fair - (219) 663-3617
Danville - Hendricks Co. 4H Fair - (317) 745-4212
Elnora - Daviess Co. Fair, Inc. - (812) 254-1135
Evansville - Vanderburgh Co. Fair - (812) 426-1323
Flora - Carroll Co. 4H Fair - (574) 967-4692
Ft. Wayne - Allen Co. Fair - (260) 449-4444
Frankfort - Clinton Co. 4H Fair - (765) 659-6380
Franklin - Johnson Co. 4H & Agricultural Fair
  - (317) 736-3724
Goshen - Elkhart Co. 4H Fair & Agricultural Expo.
  - (574) 533-3247
Greencastle - Putnam Co. 4H Club Fair - (765) 653-8411
Greenfield - Hancock Co. 4H Fair - (317) 462-1469
Greensburg - Decatur Co. Agricultural Fair - (812) 663-8388
Greentown - Howard Co. 4H Fair - (765) 628-3247
Hamlet - Starke Co. Fair - (574) 772-9141
Hartford City - Blackford Co. 4H & Open Fair
  - (765) 348-3213
Huntingburg - Dubois Co. 4H Fair - (812) 482-1782
Indianapolis - Indiana State Fair - (317) 927-7500
Indianapolis - Marion Co. Agricultural & 4H Club Fair
  - (317) 353-2444
Kendallville - Noble Co. Community Fair
  - (260) 318-2127
Kentland - Newton Co. "Pun' kin Vine" Fair - (219) 474-5745
La Porte - La Porte Co. Fair - (219) 362-2647

Lafayette - Tippecanoe Co. 4H Fair - (765) 474-0793
LaGrange - LaGrange Co. 4H Fair - (260) 768-4165
Lawrenceburg - Dearborn Co. 4H & Community Fair
  - (812) 537-1040
Logansport - Cass Co. 4H Fair - (574) 753-7750
Loogootee - Martin Co. 4H Fair - (812) 247-3041
Madison - Jefferson Co. 4H Fair - (812) 265-8919
Marion - Grant Co. 4H Fair - (765) 668-8871
Martinsville - Morgan Co. Fair & 4H Club Assoc.
  - (765) 342-9905
Muncie - Delaware Co. Fair - (765) 288-1854
New Albany - Floyd Co. Fair - (812) 949-8119
New Harmony - Posey Co. Fair - (812) 682-3297
North Vernon - Jennings Co. 4H Fair - (812) 346-8721
Osgood - Ripley Co.4H Fair - (812) 689-6511
Peru - Miami Co. 4H Fair - (765) 427-1921
Petersburg - Pike Co. 4H Fair - (812) 354-6838
Portland - Jay Co. Fair - (260) 726-8176
Princeton - Gibson Co. Fair - (812) 385-3445
Rensselaer - Jasper Co. Fair - (219) 866-8100
Reynolds - White Co. 4H Fair - (219) 984-5115
Richmond - Wayne Co. 4H Fair - (765) 855-2369
Rising Sun - Ohio Co. 4H Fair - (812) 438-3656
Rochester - Fulton Co. 4H Fair - (574) 223-3397
Rushville - Rush Co. Agricultural Fair - (765) 932-3211
Scottsburg - Scott Co. Fair - (812) 752-3895
Shelbyville - Shelby Co. Fair - (812) 587-2521
South Blend - St. Joseph Co. 4H Fair - (574) 291-4870
Terre Haute - Vigo Co. Fair - (812) 462-3371
Valparaiso - Porter Co. Fair - (219) 464-2783
Veedersburg - Fountain Co. 4H Fair - (765) 793-2297
Vevay - Switzerland Co. 4H Fair - (812) 427-3152
Wabash - Wabash Co. 4H Fair - (260) 563-0661
Warsaw - Kosciusko Co. 4H & Community Fair
  - (574) 269-1823
Williamsport - Warren Co. 4H Fair - (765) 762-3231
Winamac - Pulaski Co. 4H & Community Fair
  - (574) 946-3412

Iowa

Adel - Dallas Co. Fair - (515) 993-3728
Afton - Union Co. Fair - (641) 347-5272
Albia - Monroe Co. 4H-FFA Fair - (641) 932-7681
Algona - Kossuth Co. Fair - (515) 295-3913

Allison - Butler Co. Fair - (319) 267-2775
Alta - Buena Vista Co. Fair - (712) 284-2561
Arthur - Ida Co. Fair - (712) 364-2500
Atlantic - Cass Co. Fair - (712) 243-1132

Appendix B

Audubon - Audubon Co. Fair - (712) 563-2250
Avoca - Pottawattamie Co. Fair - (712) 343-2377
Beckford - Taylor Co. Fair - (712) 523-2326
Bloomfield - Davis Co. Fair - (641) 664-3713
Boone - Boone Co. Fair - (515) 432-5899
Bouton - Dallas Co. Fair - (515) 992-3222
Buffalo Center - Winnebago Co. Fair - (641) 584-2011
Calamus - Clinton Co. 4H Fair - (563) 659-5300
Cedar Rapids - The Hawkeye Downs Fair - (319) 365-8656
Centerville - Appanoose Co. Fair - (641) 658-2469
Central City - Linn Co. Fair - (319) 438-6842
Chariton - Lucas Co. 4-H Achvmt Show - (641) 774-2016
Charles City - Floyd Co. Ag & Ind Days - (641) 228-1300
Cherokee - Cherokee Co. Fair - (712) 225-5843
Clarinda - Page Co. Fair - (712) 583-3390
Clation - Wright Co. District Jr. Fair - (515) 825-3312
Coin - Page Co. Fair - (712) 583-3390
Colfax - Jasper Co. Fair - (515) 674-4382
Columbus Junction - Louisa Co. Fair - (319) 728-2527
Coon Rapids - Carroll Co. Fair - (712) 999-7447
Corning - Adams Co. 4H & FFA Youth Fair - (641) 322-3184
Corydon - Wayne Co. Fair - (641) 872-1611
Council Bluffs - Westfair - (712) 322-3400
Cresco - Mighty Howard Co. Fair - (563) 547 3400
Curlew - Palo Alto Co. Fair - (712) 852-2562
Davenport - Mississippi Valley Fair - (563) 326-5338
Decorah - Winneshiek Co. Fair - (563) 382-8514
Denison - Crawford Co. Fair - (712) 263-5306
Des Moines - Iowa State Fair - (319) 642-3465
Des Moines - Polk Co. 4H & FFA Fair - (515) 274-0275
Dewitt - Clinton Co. 4-H Fair - (563) 659-5300
Donnellson - Lee Co. Fair - (319) 835-2323
Dubuque - Dubuque Co. Fair - (563) 588-1406
Eagle Grove - Wright Co. Dist. Jr. Fair - (515) 448-3351
Earlville - Delaware Co. 4H & FFA Fair - (563) 927-6449
Eldon - Wapello Co. Regional Fair - (641) 652-7521
Eldora - Hardin Co. Fair - (641) 642-3926
Emmetsburg - Palo Alto Co. Fair - (717) 852-3343
Estherville - Emmet Co. Agricultural Fair - (712) 362-7163
Fairfield - Jefferson Co. Fair - (641) 472-4166
Floyd - Floyd Co. Agriculture & Industry Days - (641) 398-2889
Ft. Dodge - Webster Co. Fair - (515) 955-3764
Garnavillo - Clayton Co. Fair - (563) 964-2671
Gladbrook - Tama Co. Fair - (641) 473-3225

Greenfield - Adair Co. Fair - (641) 343-7056
Grinnell - Poweshiek Co. Fair - (641) 236-7959
Grundy Center - Grundy Co. Fair - (319) 824-2311
Guthrie Center - Guthrie Co. Fair - (641) 747-3478
Hampton - Franklin Co. Fair - (641) 456-2049
Harlan - Shelby Co. Fair - (712) 755-3335
Humboldt - Humboldt Co. Fair - (515) 332-5154
Ida Grove - Ida Co. Fair - (712) 364-2500
Independence - Buchanan Co. Fair - (319) 334-6656
Indianola - Warren Co. Agricultural Fair - (515) 961-5861
Iowa City - Johnson Co. 4H & FFA Fair - (319) 337-5865
Jefferson - Greene Co. Fair - (712) 386-4317
Keosauqua - Van Buren Co. Fair - (319) 293-3745
Kingsley - Woodbury Co. Fair - (712) 873-3202
Knoxville - Marion Co. Fair - (641) 842-5431
Le Mars - Plymouth Co. Fair - (712) 546-4525
Leon - Decatur Co. Fair - (641) 446-4648
Lucas - Lucas Co. 4H Achievement Show - (641) 774-2016
Malvern - Mills Co. Fair - (712) 624-8995
Manchester - Delaware Co. Fair - (563) 927-6449
Maquoketa - Jackson Co. Fair - (563) 652-4282
Marcus - Marcus Community Fair - (712) 376-2316
Marengo - Iowa Co. Fair - (319) 642-5504
Marshalltown - Central Iowa Fair - (641) 753-3671
Mason City - No. Iowa Fair - (641) 423-3811
Missouri Valley - Harrison Co. Fair - (712) 642-3466
Molville - Woodbury Co. Fair - (712) 873-3202
Monticello - Great Jones Co. Fair - (319) 465-3275
Mount Ayr - Ringgold Co. Fair - (641) 464-2638
Mount Pleasant - Henry Co. Fair - (319) 385-4533
Nashua - Chickasaw Big Four Fair - (641) 435-4849
National - Clayton Co. Fair - (563) 964-2671
Nemoha - Sac Co. Fair - (712) 662-7188
Nevada - Story Co. Fair - (515) 382-6551
Northwood - Worth Co. Fair - (641) 324-1783
Onawa - Monona Co. Fair - (712) 423-2214
Osage - Mitchell Co. Fair - (641) 710-2190
Osceola - Clarke Co. 4H Fair - (641) 342-4554
Oskaloosa - Southern Iowa Fair - (641) 673-7004
Palmer - Pocahontas Co. Fair - (712) 335-4176
Pocahontas - Pocahontas Co. Fair - (712) 335-4176
Postville - Big Four Fair - (563) 864-3316
Pottawattamie - Westfair - (712) 322-3400
Primghar - O'Brien Co. Fair - (712) 757-0016
Red Oak - Montgomery Co. Fair - (712) 623-6849
Rock Rapids - Lyon Co. Fair - (712) 472-2067

Appendix B

Rockwell City - Calhoun Co. Expo - (712) 297-5526

Sac City - Sac Co. Fair - (712) 664-2967

Sibley - Osceola Co. Livestock Show - (712) 754-3407

Sidney - Fremont Co. Fair - (712) 374-2715

Sioux Center - Sioux Co. Youth Fair - (712) 722-2249

Spencer - Clay Co. Fair - (712) 262-4740

Spirit Lake - Dickinson Co. 4H & FFA Fair - (712) 336-0479

Tama - Central Iowa Fair - (641) 753-3671

Thompson - Winnebago Co. Jr. Show & Fair
 - (641) 584-2011

Tipton - Cedar Co. Fair - (563) 886-6170

Traer - Tama Co. Fair - (641) 473-3225

Vinton - Benton Co. Fair - (319) 472-5358

Washington - Washington Co. Fair - (319) 653-6510

Waterloo - National Cattle Congress - (319) 234-7515

Waukon - Allamakee Co. Fair - (563) 568-2667

Waverly - Bremer Co. Fair - (319) 352-5326

Webster City - Grundy Co. Fair - (515) 832-1443

Webster City - Hamilton Co. Expo. - (515) 9832-1443

West Burlington - Des Moines Co. Fair
 - (319) 758-0370

West Liberty - Muscatine Co. Fair - (319) 627-2414

West Point - Lee Co. Fair - (319) 835-5323

West Union - Fayette Co. Fair - (563) 422-5202

What Cheer - Keokuk Co. Fair - (641) 634-2201

Winterset - Madison Co. Fair - (515) 462-1295

Kansas

Abilene - Central Kansas Free Fair - (785) 263-4570

Alma - Wabaunsee Co. Fair - (785) 765-3821

Ashland - Clark Co. Fair - (620) 635-2811

Atwood - Rawlins Co. Fair - (785) 626-9058

Belleville - No. Central Kansas Free Fair - (785) 527-5084

Beloit - Mitchell Co. Fair - (785) 738-9702

Belpre - Pawnee Co. Fair - (620) 995-3665

Blue Rapids - Marshall Co. Fair - (785) 363-7306

Burlington - Coffey Co. Free Fair - (620) 256-6621

Caldwell - Sumner Co. Fair - (620) 863-2466

Canton - McPherson Co. Fair - (620) 628-4466

Cheney - Sedgwick Co. Fair - (316) 542-3142

Cimarron - Gray Co. Fair - (620) 855-3821

Clay Center - Clay Co. Fair - (785) 632-5335

Coffeyville - Coffeyville Interstate Fair & Rodeo
 - (620) 251-2550

Colby - Thomas Co. Free Fair - (785) 462-4593

Coldwater - Comanche Co. Fair - (620) 582-2411

Columbus - Cherokee Co. American Legion Fair
 (620) 783-5154

Concordia - Cloud Co. Fair - (785) 439-6518

Cottonwood Falls - Chase Co. Fair - (620) 297-4545

Council Grove - Morris Co. Fair - (620) 767-5136

Dighton - Lane Co. Free Fair - (620) 397-5356

Dodge City - Ford Co. Fair - (620) 227-4542

Effingham - Atchison Co. Fair - (913) 847-4701

El Dorado - Butler Co. Fair - (316) 775-6779

Elkhart - Morton Co. Fair - (620) 697-2558

Ellsworth - Ellsworth Co. Fair - (785) 472-4442

Emmett - Pottawatomie Co. Fair - (785) 457-3319

Emporia - Lyon Co. Fair - (620) 341-3220

Eureka - Greenwood Co. Fair - (620) 583-7455

Fort Scott - Bourbon Co. Fair - (620) 223-3720

Fredonia - Wilson Co. Fair - (620) 378-2191

Garden City - Finney Co. Fair - (620) 272-3844

Gardner - Johnson Co. Fair - (913) 256-8860

Garnett - Anderson Co. Fair - (785) 448-6826

Girard - Crawford Co. Fair - (620) 724-8233

Goodland - Northwest Kansas District Fair
 - (785) 899-5868

Great Bend - Barton Co. Fair - (620) 797-3247

Greensburg - Kiowa Co. 4H & Free Fair
 - (620) 723-2156

Hardtner - Barber Co. Fair - (620) 672-3706

Harper - Harper Co. Agricultural & Co.4H Club Fair
 - (620) 842-5445

Hays - Ellis Co. Fair - (785) 628-9430

Herington - Tri Co. Free Fair - (785) 258-3359

Hiawatha - Brown Co. Free Fair - (785) 742-7871

Hill City - Graham Co. Fair - (785) 421-3411

Hillsboro - Marion Co. Fair - (620) 947-2585

Holton - Jackson Co. Fair - (785) 364-2006

Horton - Brown Co. Free Fair - (785) 486-3811

Howard - Elk Co. Fair - (620) 374-2174

Hoxie - Sheridan Co. Fair - (785) 675-3268

Houghton - Stevens Co. Fair - (620) 544-4359

Hutchinson - Kansas State Fair - (620) 669-3600

Hutchinson - Reno Co. Fair - (620) 538-2233

Appendix B

Iola - Allen Co. Fair - (620) 365-6513
Jetmore - Hodgeman Co. Fair - (620) 357-8321
Johnson - Stanton Co. 4H Fair - (620) 492-2240
Junction City - Geary Co. Free Fair - (785) 238-4161
Kansas City - Wyandotte Co. Fair - (913) 788-7898
Kingman - Kingman Co. Fair - (620) 532-5131
Kinsley - Edwards Co. Fair - (620) 659-2149
LaCrosse - Rush Co. Fair - (785) 222-2710
Lakin - Kearny Co. Fair - (620) 355-6551
Lane - Lane-Franklin Co. Fair - (785) 867-3298
Larned - Pawnee Co. Fair - (620) 285-6901
Lawrence - Douglas Co. Fair - (785) 842-7058
Leoti - Wichita Co. Fair - (620) 375-2724
Liberal - Five State Free Fair - (620) 624-3712
Lyons - Rice Co. 4H Fair - (620) 257-5131
Manhattan - Riley Co. Fair - (785) 537-6350
Mankako - Jewell Co. Fair - (785) 378-3174
McPherson - McPherson Co. 4H Fair - (620) 241-1532
Meade - Meade Co Fair - (620) 873-8790
Minneapolis - Ottawa Co. Fair - (785) 392-2103
Mound City - Linn Co. Fair - (913) 795-2591
Ness City - Ness Co. Fair - (785) 731-2951
Newton - Harvey Co. Free Fair - (316) 284-6930
Norton - Norton Co. Free Fair - (785) 877-5755
Oakley - Logan Co. Fair - (785) 672-3245
Oberlin - Decatur Co. Fair - (785) 475-8121
Olathe - Johnson Co. Fair - (913) 764-6300
Onaga - Pottawatomie Co. Fair - (785) 457-3319
Osage City - Osage Co. Fair - (785) 528-3963
Osborne - Osborne Co. Fair - (785) 346-2521

Oswego - Labette Co. Fair - (620) 784-5337
Overbrook - Overbrook-Osage Co. Fair - (785) 665-7532
Paola - Miami Co. Fair & Rodeo - (913) 294-4306
Phillipsburg - Phillips Co. Fair - (785) 543-6845
Pratt - Pratt Co. Fair - (620) 672-6121
Russell - Russell Co. Free Fair - (785) 658-2296
St. Francis - Cheyenne Co. Fair - (785) 332-3171
St. John - Stafford Co. Fair - (620) 549-3502
Salina - Tri-Rivers Fair & Rodeo - (785) 827-4425
Scammon - Cherokee Co. Free Fair - (620) 783-5154
Scott City - Scott Co. Free Fair - (620) 276-3333
Sedan - Chautauqua Co. Fair - (620) 725-3280
Seneca - Nemaha Co. Free Fair - (785) 336-2184
Sharon Springs - Wallace Co. Free Fair - (785) 852-4285
Smith Center - Smith Co. Fair - (785) 282-6823
Stafford - Stafford Co. Fair - (620) 549-6109
Stockton - Rooks Co. Free Fair - (785) 839-4470
Sylvan Grove - Lincoln Co. Fair - (785) 524-4432
Syracuse - Hamilton Co. Fair - (620) 384-5225
Tonganoxie - Leavenworth Co. Fair - (913) 250-2300
Topeka - Shawnee Co. Fair - (785) 862-2010
Tribune - Greeley Co. Fair - (620) 376-4284
Ulysses - Grant Co. Fair - (620) 356-1808
Valley Falls - Jefferson Co. 4H Fair - (785) 863-2212
Wakeeney - (785) 462-3354
Washington - Washington Co. Fair - (785) 325-2121
Wellington - Sumner Co. Fair - (620) 326-7477
Winfield - Cowley Co. Fair - (620) 221-1088
Yates Center - Woodson Co. Fair - (620) 625-3113

Kentucky

Albany - Clinton Co. Fair - (606) 387-7290
Alexandria - Alexandria Fair & Horse Show
    - (859) 635-7919
Argillite - Greenup Co. Fair - (606) 473-5904
Ashland - Boyd Co. Fair - (606) 928-4134
Bardstown - Nelson Co. Fair - (502) 348-4167
Bardwell - Carlisle Co. Fair - (270) 628-3761
Beaver Dam - Ohio Co. Fair - (250) 274-0441
Bedford - Trimble Co. Fair - (502) 255-3067
Benton - Marshall Co. A&I Fair - (270) 527-5659
Bowling Green - So. Kentucky Fair - (270) 842-9427
Brandenburg - Meade Co. Fair - (270) 422-2450

Burkesville - Cumberland Co. Fair - (270) 864-5391
Burlington - Boone Co. 4H & Utopia Fair
    - (859) 586-7441
Calhoun - McLean Co. Fair - (270) 736-2627
Campbellsville - Taylor Co. Fair - (270) 789-2964
Carrollton - Carroll Co. Fair - (502) 732-5177
Clinton - Hickman Co. Fair - (270) 653-4301
Columbia - Adair Co. Fair - (270) 384-4524
Cox Creek - Shelby Co. Fair & Horse Show - (502) 647-0064
Crittenden - Grant Co. Fair & Horse Show - (859) 824-5943
Cynthiana - Harrison Co. Fair - (253) 234-4331
Danville - Boyle Co. Fair - (859) 236-5152

Appendix B

Dover - Germantown Fair - (606) 763-6631
Edmonton - Metcalfe Co. Fair & Horse Show - (270) 432-5168
Ewing - Ewing-Fleming Co. Fair - (606) 267-2516
Falmouth - Pendleton Co. Youth Fair - (859) 654-3395
Frankfort - Franklin Co. Fair & Horse Show - (502) 875-3020
Franklin - Franklin/Simpson Co. Fair - (270) 586-9557
Georgetown - Scott Co. Fair - (502) 863-2512
Glendale - Hardin Co. Community Fair & Horse Show -(270) 369-6098
Grayson - Carter Co. Fair - (606) 414-6670
Greensburg - Green Co. Fair & Horse Show - (270) 932-4034
Hardyville - Hart Co. Fair - (270) 528-3641
Harrodsburg - Mercer Co. Fair & Horse Show (859) 734-2216
Hartford - Ohio Co. Fair - (270) 298-3762
Hawesville - Hancock Co. Fair - (270) 927-8021
Henderson - Henderson Co. Fair - (270) 826-9825
Hodgenville - Larue Co. Fair - (270) 358-3379
Hopkinsville - Western Kentucky State Fair - (270) 886-7426
Independence - Kenton Co. Fair - (859) 356-1259
Inez - Martin Co. Fair - (606) 298-3022
Irvine - Estill Co. Fair - (606) 723-8166
Jeffersonville - Montgomery Co. Fair - (859) 498-2589
La Grange - Oldham Co. Fair - (502) 222-5634
LaCenter - Ballard Co. Fair - (270) 665-5012
Lancaster - Garrard Co. Fair - (859) 792-2256
Lawrenceburg - Lawrenceburg Fair & Horse Show - (502) 839-5523
Lebanon - Marion Co. Fair - (270) 692-6426
Leitchfield - Grayson Co. Fair - (270) 259-5653
Lexington - Lexington Lions Club Bluegrass Fair - (321) 633-4028
London - Laurel - Co. Fair - (606) 878-2262
Louisville - Kentucky State Fair - (502) 362-5000
Louisville - No. American Int'l Livestock Expo -(502) 595-3166
Madisonville - Hopkins Co. Fair - (270) 821-0950
Marion - Crittenden Co. Fair - (270) 965-3327
Mayfield - Purchase District Fair - (270) 247-5376
McKee - Jackson Co. Fair - (606) 287-0606

Miracle - Bell Co. Fair - (606) 337-1235
Monticello - Wayne Co. Fair & Horse Show - (606) 348-9557
Morehead - Morehead-Rowan Co. Fair - (606) 784-1289
Mount Herman - Monroe Co. Fair - (270) 427-2564
Mount Olivet - Robertson Co. Fair - (606) 724-5647
Munfordville - Hart Co. Fair - (270) 528-3641
Murray - Murray-Calloway Co. Fair - (270) 753-5940
New Castle - Henry Co. Fair - (502) 743-9404
Nicholasville - Jessamine Co. Fair - (859) 885-5542
Owenton - Owen Co. 4H Fair & Horse Show - (502) 463-2353
Paducah - McCracken Co. Fair - (270) 444-6413
Paris - Bourbon Co. Fair & Horse Show - (859) 987-4809
Philpot - Daviess Co. Lions Fair - (270) 729-4594
Powderly - Muhlenberg Co. Fair - (270) 338-2581
Richmond - Madison Co. Fair & Horse Show - 859) 623-7542
Runsey - McLean Co. Fair - (270) 273-9110
Russell Springs - Russell Co. Jaycee Fair - (270) 866-1251
Russellville - Legion Logan Co. Fair - (270) 726-6686
Scottsville - Allen Co. Fair - (270) 622-6223
Shelbyville - Shelby Co. Fair & Horse Show - (502) 633-5077
Shepherdsville - Bullitt Co. Fair - (502) 543-4855
Smithfield - Henry Co. Fair - (502) 845-4734
Somerset - Pulaski Co. Jaycee Fair - (859) 679-7175
Stanford - Lincoln Co. Fair - (606) 365-2347
Stanton - Powell Co. Fair - (606) 663-6405
Sturgis - Union Co. Fair - (270) 333-4107
Taylorsville - Spencer Co. Fair - (502) 477-2508
Tompkinsville - Monroe Co. Fair - (270) 427-2564
Vanceburg - Lewis Co. School & Agriculture Fair - (606) 796-2653
Versailles - Woodford Co. Fair & Horse Show - (859) 983-3253
Wallingford - Morehead-Rowan - (606) 845-2252
Warsaw - Gallatin Co. Fair - (859) 567-6331
West Liberty - Morgan Co. Agricultural Fair - (606) 743-3195
Winchester - Clark Co. Fair & Horse Show - (859) 744-8608

Louisana

Alexandria - Rapides Parish Fair - (318) 473-6605
Amite - Tangipahoa Parish Fair - (985) 748-6800

Bastrop - No. Louisiana Cotton Fair & Festival - (318) 283-6185

Appendix B

Baton Rouge - Greater Baton Rouge State Fair - (225) 755-3247

Coushatta - Red River Parish Fair & Rodeo - (318) 932-5105

Covington - St. Tammy Parish Fair - (85) 892-5410

Cut Off - Cut Off Youth Center Fair - (985) 632-7616

DeRidder - Beauregard Parish Fair - (337) 462-3135

Franklinton - Washington Parish Free Fair (985) 839-7840

Houma - Terrebonne Livestock & Agriculture Fair - (985) 868-4178

Jena - LaSalle Parish Fair - (318) 992-5481

Lafayette - Cajun Heartland State Fair - (337) 265-2100

Livingston - Livingston Parish Fair - (225) 686-1333

Many - Sabine Parish Fair - (318) 586-7853

Monroe - Ark-La-Miss Fair - (318) 329-2225

Oberlin - Allen Parish Fair - (337) 639-4475

Shreveport - State Fair of Louisiana - (318) 635-1361

Sulphur - Calcasieu Cameron Fair - (337) 528-2693

Thibodaux - Thibodaux Fireman's Fair - (985) 446-5995

Maine

Acton - Acton Fair - (207) 636-2026

Athens - Athens Fair - (207) 654-2028

Bangor - State Fair - (207) 947-5555

Blue Hill - Blue Hill Fair - (207) 374-3701

Clinton - Clinton Lion's Club Agricultural Fair - (207) 426-8013

Cumberland - Cumberland Co. Fair - (207) 829-553

Dover-Foxcroft - Piscataquis Valley Fair - (207) 564-7738

Embden - New Portland Lions Fair - (207) 566-5722

Farmington - Farmington Fair - (207) 778-6083

Fryeburg - Fryeburg Fair - (207) 935-3268

Harmony - Harmony Free Fair - (207) 683-587

Hiram - Ossipee Valley Fair - (207) 793-8434

Houlton - Houlton Agricultural Fair - (207) 532-4315

Kingfield - New Portland Lions Fair - (207) 678-2151

Litchfield - Litchfield Fair - (207) 683-2487

Monmouth - Monmouth Fair - (207) 933-2752

Oxford - Oxford Co. Fair - (207) 674-2694

Pittston - Pittston Fair - (207) 582-0037

Presque Isle - No. Maine Fair - (207) 764-8082

Skowhegan - Skowhegan State Fair - (207) 474-2947

South Hiram - Ossipee Valley Fair - (207) 793-8434

Springfield - Springfield Fair - (207) 738-2165

Topsham - Topsham Fair - (207) 725-2735

Union - Union Fair - (207) 236-8009

Unity - Common Ground Country Fair - (207) 568-4142

Windsor - Windsor - (207) 549-7121

Maryland

Barstow – Calvert Co. Fair – (410) 535-0026

Bel Air – Harford Co. Farm Fair – (410) 838-8663

Bel Air - John Carroll Country Fair - (410) 838-8333

Chestertown – Kent Co. Fair – (410) 778-1661

Childs - Cecil Co. Fair - (410) 392-3440

Crownsville – Anne Arundel Co. Fair – (410) 923-3400

Cumberland – Allegany Co. Fair – (301) 729-1200

Denton – Caroline Co. Fair – (410) 479-0565

Easton – Talbot Co. Fair – (410) 819-8000

Forest Hill – Eastern Nat'l Livestock Show - (410) 838-1193

Frederick - Great Frederick Fair - (301) 663-5895

Gaithersburg - Montgomery Co. Ag. Fair - (410) 228-8800

Hurlock - Dorchester Co. 4-H Fair - (301) 926-3100

La Plata - Charles Co. Fair - (301) 934-6221

Leonardtown - (301) 475-2256

Pocomoke City - The great Pocomoke Fair - (410) 957-1919

Salisbury - Wicomico Farm & Home Show - (410) 883-2343

Snow Hill - Worcester Co. 4-H & FFA Fair - (410) 632-1972

Timonium - Baltimore Co. 4-H Fair - (410) 665-0042

Timonium - Maryland State Fair - (410) 252-0200

Appendix B

Upper Marlboro - Prince George's Co. Fair - (301) 579-2598

West Friendship - Howard Co. Fair - (410) 442-1022

Westminster - Carroll Co. 4H/FFA Fair - (410) 848-3247

Massachusetts

Adams - Adams Agricultural Fair - (413) 743-5594

Belchertown - Belchertown Fair - (413) 323-9710

Blandford - Blandford Fair - (413) 848-2888

Bolton - Bolton Fair - (978) 779-6253

Brockton - Brockton Fair - (508) 586-8000

Chester _ Littleville Fair - (413) 667-3987

Chicopee - Hampden Co. 4H/Youth Fair - (413) 592-1792

Cummington - Cummington Fair - (413) 238-7724

East Falmouth - Barnstable Co. Fair - (508) 563-3200

Foxboro - Spring Fair at Foxboro Stadium - (603) 474-5424

Greenfield - Franklin Co. Fair - (413) 774-4282

Hardwick Community Fair - (413) 477-0213

Heath - Heath Agricultural Fair - (413) 337-5716

Lancaster - Bolton Fair - (978) 779-6253

Marshfield - Marshfield Fair - (781) 834-6629

Middlefield - Middlefield Fair - (413) 568-2226

Northampton - Hampshire Co. 4H Fair - (413) 549-8800

Pittsfield - Berkshire Co. 4H Youth Fair - (413) 448-8285

Spencer - Spencer Fair - (508) 885-5814

Sterling - The Sterling Fair - (978) 422-6741

Topsfield - Topsfield Fair - (978) 887-5000

West Springfield - Ea. States Expo - The Big E - (413) 737-2443

West Tisbury - Martha's Vineyard Agricultural Fair - (508) 693-4343

Westfield - Westfield Fair - (413) 562-9555

Westford - Middlesex Co. 4H Fair - (978) 256-4623

Westport - Westport Fair - (508) 636-8949

Wrentham - Crackerbarrel Fair - (508) 384-1635

Michigan

Adrian - Lenawee Co. Fair - (517) 263-3007

Allegan - Allegan Co. Fair - (269) 673-6501

Alma - Gratiot Co. Fair for Youth - (989) 875-5292

Alpena - Alpena Co. Fair - (989) 356-1174

Ann Arbor - Washtenaw Co. 4H Fair - (734) 429-3145

Armada - Armada Fair - (586) 784-5488

Bad Axe - Huron Community Fair - (989) 883-3997

Bay City - Bay Co. Fair & Youth Expo. - (989) 895-3744

Belleville - Wayne Co. Fair - (734) 697-7002

Berrien Springs - Berrien Co. Youth Fair - (269) 473-4251

Big Rapids - Mecoast Co. Agriculture Fair - (231) 796-5378

Cadillad - Northwestern Michigan Fair - (231) 943-4150

Caro - Tuscola Co. Fair - (989) 673-2161

Cassopolis - Cass Co. Fair - (269) 445-8265

Centreville - St. Joseph Co. Grange Fair - (269) 467-8935

Charlotte - Eaton Co. 4H Fair - (517) 649-8580

Chatham - Alger Co. Fair - (906) 439-5114

Cheboygan - Cheboygan Co. Fair - (231) 627-6353

Chelsea - Chelsea Community Fair - (734) 475-1270

Chesaning - Saginaw Co. Fair (9 89) 845-2143

Coldwater - Branch Co. 4H Fair - (517) 278-5367

Corunna - Shiawassee Co. Fair - (989) 743-3611

Croswell - Croswell Agricultural Society Fair - (810) 679-4456

Croswell - Sanilac Co. 4H Fair - (810) 378-5588

Davisburg - Oakland Co. 4H Fair - (248) 634-8830

Detroit - Michigan State Fair - (313) 369-8250

Escanaba - Upper Peninsula State Fair - (906) 786-4011

Evart - Osceola 4H & FFA Fair - (231) 734-5481

Fair Haven - St. Clair Co. 4H & Youth Fair - (586) 725-3787

Fowlerville - Fowlerville Fair - (517) 223-8166

Fremont - Newaygo Co. Fair - (231) 924-4450

Gaylord - Otsego Co. Fair - (989) 732-3811

Gladwin - Gladwin Co. Fair - (989) 426-2311

Appendix B

Grayling - Crawford Co. Fair - (989) 348-8094
Greenland - Ontonagon Co. Fair - (906) 883-3447
Greenville - Montcalm Co. 4H Fair - (616) 754-7884
Hale - Iosco County Fair - (989) 728-3566
Hancock - Houghton Co. Fair - (906) 482-6200
Harrison - Clare Co. Fair - (989) 539-9011
Hart - Oceana Co. Fair - (231) 873-2955
Hartford - Van Buren Co. Youth Fair - (269) 621-2038
Hastings - Barry Co. Fair - (269) 945-2224
Hillsdale - Hillsdale Co. Agricultural Society Fair - (517) 437-3622
Holland - Ottawa Co. Fair - (616) 399-2605
Hudson - Hudson Area Fair - (517) 448-8595
Hudsonville - Hudsonville Community Fair - (616) 669-1630
Imlay City - Ea. Michigan Fair - (810) 724-4246
Ionia - Greater Ionia Fair - (616) 527-1310
Iron River - Iron Co. Fair - (906) 265-3857
Ironwood - Gogebic Co. Fair - (906) 932-1420
Ithaca - Gratiot Agriculture Expo. - (989) 875-4878
Jackson - Jackson Co. Fair - (517) 788-4405
Kalamazoo - Kalamazoo Co. Fair - (269) 349-9791
Kalkaska - Kalkaska Co. Fair - (231) 258-4362
Kinross - Chippewa Co. Fair - (906) 495-5778
Lake Odessa - Lake Odessa Fair - (616) 374-8055
Lincoln - Alcona Co. Fair - (989) 736-9550
Lowell - Kent Co. Youth Fair - (616) 897-6050
Ludington - Western Michigan Fair - (231) 757-3450
Manchester - Manchester Community Fair - (734) 428-8474
Manistique - Schoolcraft Co. Fair - (906) 341-3688
Marion - Marion Fair - (231) 743-6415

Marne - Berlin Fair - (616) 899-2634
Marquette - Marquette Co. Fair - (906) 249-4111
Marshall - Calhoun Co. Fair - (269) 781-8161
Mason - Ingham Co. Fair - (517) 676-2428
Midland - Midland Co. Fair - (989) 835-7901
Millersburg - Presque Isle Co. Fair - (989) 733-2584
Monroe - Monroe Co. Fair - (734) 241-5775
Mount Morris - Genesee Co. Fair - (810) 687-0953
Mount Pleasant - Isabella Co. Youth & Farm Fair - (989) 773-9070
Muskegon - Muskegon Co. Youth Fair - (231) 788-4568
Newberry - Luce-West Mackinac Co. Fair - (906) 293-8785
Norway - Dickinson Co. Fair - (906) 774-8021
Ocqueoc - Presque Isle Co. Fair - (989) 733-8340
Onekama - Manistee Co. Fair - (231) 889-5566
Ossineke - Alpena Co. Fair - (989) 356-1174
Pelkie - Baraga Co. Fair - (906) 524-6300
Petoskey - Emmet/Charlevoix Co. Fair - (231) 347-1010
Roscommon - Roscommon Co. Fair - (989) 275-5056
Saginaw - Saginaw Co. Fair - (989) 737-1845
Saint John - Clinton Co. 4H & Youth Fair - (989) 224-5240
Saline - Saline Community Fair - (734) 429-1131
Sandusky - Sanilac Co. 4-H Fair - (810) 679-2487
Sebewang - Huron Community Fair - (989) 883-3997
Skandia - Marquette Co. Fair - (906) 249-4111
Sparta - Sparta Town & Country Fair - (616) 887-1224
Stephenson - Menominee Co. Fair - (906) 753-2209
Traverse City - N.W. Michigan Fair - (586) 573-7800
Warren - Warren City Fair - (586) 573-7800
West Branch - Ogemaw Co. Fair - (989) 345-4845

Minnesota

Ada - Norman Co. Fair - (218) 784-3391
Aitkin - Aitkin Co. Fair - (218) 927-7331
Albert Lea - Freeborn Co. Agricultural Society Fair - (507) 373-6965
Alexandria - Douglas Co. Fair - (320) 834-4796
Arlington - Sibley Co. Fair - (320) 289-2066
Anoka - Anoka Co. Fair - (763) 427-4070
Appleton - Swift Co. Fair - (320) 289-2066
Arlington - Sibley Co. Fair - (320) 864-5252
Austin - Mower Co. Fair - (507) 433-1868
Badger - Roseau Co. Fair - (218) 469-1009

Bagley - Clearwater Co. Fair - (218) 785-2368
Barnesville - Clay Co. Fair - (218) 354-7279
Barnum - Carlton Co. Fair - (218) 389-6737
Baudette - Lake of the Woods Co. Fair - (218) 634-1034
Baxter - Crow Wing Co. Fair - (218) 829-5128
Bemidji - Beltrami Co. Fair - (218) 759-1425
Bird Island - Renville Co. Fair - (320) 365-3242
Blue Earth - Faribault Co. Fair - (507) 526-5380
Brainerd - Crow Wing Co. Fair - (218) 829-6680
Breckenridge - Wilkin Co. Fair - (218) 643-6561

Appendix B

Caledonia - Houston Co. Fair - (507) 542-4677
Cambridge - Isanti Co. Fair - (763) 689-3143
Canby - Yellow Medicine Co. Fair - (507) 223-7814
Cannon Falls - Cannon Valley Fair - (507) 263-3548
Chisholm - St. Louis Co. Fair - (218) 263-4256
Clinton - Big Stone Co. Fair - (320) 325-5963
Corcoran - Hennepin Co. Oldetyme Fair - (763) 420-4546
Detroit Lakes - Becker Co. Fair - (218) 334-2321
Eagle Bend - Todd Co. Fair - (218) 738-4421
Elk River - Sherburne Co. Fair - (763) 441-8542
Fairmont - Martin Co. Fair - (507) 235-9576
Faribault - Rice Co. Fair - (507) 685-4342
Farmington - Dakota Co. Fair - (651) 463-8818
Fergus Falls - West Ottertail Co. Fair - (218) 736-0272
Fertile - Polk Co. Fair - (218) 945-6885
Floodwood - S.W. St. Louis Co. Fair - (218) 476-2641
Fountain - Fillmore Co. Fair - (507) 352-6191
Frazee - Becker Co. Fair - (218) 334-2321
Glenwood - Pope Co. Fair - (320) 268-3304
Grand Marais - Cook Co. Fair - (218) 387-1667
Grand Rapids - Itasca Co. Fair - (218) 326-1997
Hallock - Kittson Co. Fair - (218) 843-2645
Herman - Grant Co. Fair - (320) 284-2146
Hibbing - St. Louis Co. Fair - (218) 263-4256
Howard Lake - Wright Co. Fair - (763) 972-2880
Jackson - Jackson Co. Fair - (507) 847-4700
Jordan - Scott Co. Fair - (952) 492-2436
Kasson - Dodge Co. Fair - (507) 635-5571
Lake Elmo - Washington Co. Fair - (651) 459-3377
LeCenter - LeSuer Co. Fair - (507) 357-4033
Litchfield - Meeker Co. Fair - (320) 275-4049
Little Falls - Morrison Co. Fair - (320) 632-9432
Littlefork - No. Minnesota District Fair
  - (218) 278-6749
Long Prairie - Todd Co. Fair - (320) 732-6657
Luverne - Rock Co. Fair - (570) 283-9813
Madison - Lac Qui Parle Co. Fair - (320) 598-3989
Mahnomen - Mahnomen Co. Fair - (218) 935-9015
Maplewood - Ramsey Co. Fair - (651) 777-6514
Marshall - Lyon Co. Fair - (507) 532-2038
Montevideo - Chippewa Co. Fair - (320) 269-9404
Mora - Kanabec Co. Fair - (320) 679-1358

Morris - Stevens Co. Fair - (320) 589-1062
Motley - Morrison Co. Fair-Motley - (218) 352-6545
New Ulm - Brown Co. Fair - (507) 354-2223
Norcross - Grant Co. Fair - (320) 284-2146
Northome - Kooch Co. Agriculture Assoc. Fair
  - (218) 897-5748
Oklee - Red Lake Co. Fair - (218) 465-4359
Owatonna - Steele Co. Free Fair - (507) 451-5305
Park Rapids - Shell Prairie Fair - (218) 732-1216
Perham - East Ottertail Fair - (218) 346-4591
Pillager - Cass Co. Fair - (218) 568-4971
Pine City - Pine Co. Fair - (320) 629-2465
Pine River - Cass Co. Agricultural Fair - (218) 568-4971
Pipestone - Pipestone Co. Fair - (507) 825-3931
Preston - Fillmore Co. Fair - (507) 867-3304
Princeton - Mille Lacs Co. Fair - (763) 389-2979
Proctor - So. St. Louis Co. Fair - (218) 729-7080
Redwood Falls - Redwood Co. Fair - (507) 644-5090
Rochester - Olmsted Co. Free Fair - (507) 282-9862
Roseau - Roseau Co. Fair - (218) 463-1555
Rush City - Chisago Co. Fair - (320) 358-4965
St. Charles - Winona Co. Fair - (507) 932-3059
St. James - Wantowan Co. Fair - (507) 375-5515
St. Paul - Minnesota State Fair (651) 642-2200
St. Peter - Nicollet Co. Fair - (507) 931-3108
Sauk Centre - Stearns Co. Fair - (320) 352-2482
Sauk Rapids - Benton Co. Fair - (320) 251-3154
Sedan - Pope Co. Fair - (320) 268-3304
Slayton - Murray Co. Fair - (507) 836-8266
Theif River Falls - Pennington Co. Fair - (218) 681-2457
Two Harbors - Lake Co. Fair - (218) 834-6174
Tyler - Lincoln Co. Fair - (507) 247-5675
Wabasha - Wabasha Co. Fair - (507) 534-2912
Waconia - Carver Co. Fair - (952) 442-2333
Wadena - Wadena Co. Fair - (218) 631-4412
Waseca - Waseca Co. Free Fair - (507) 835-1538
Watertown - Carver Co. Fair - (952) 955-1772
Wheaton - Traverse Co. Fair - (320) 563-8758
Willmar - Kandiyohi Co. Fair - (320) 235-7315
Windom - Cottonwood Co. Fair - (507) 831-4684
Worthington - Nobles Co. Fair - (507) 376-6139
Zumbrota - Goodhue Co. Fair - (507) 732-7132

Appendix B

Mississippi

Biloxi - Summer Fair & Expo - (228) 594-3700
Bude - Franklin Co. Fair & Livestock Show - (601) 384-5112
Canton - Canton Fair - (601) 859-4358
Choctaw - Choctaw Indian Fair - (601) 650-7450
Eastabuchie - Great South Fair-Summer - (601) 582-4653
Luka - Tishomingo Co. Fair - (662) 423-7016
Jackson - Dixie National Livestock show & Rodeo - (601) 961-4000
Jackson - Mississippi State Fair - (601) 961-4000
Kosciusko - Ctrl. Mississippi Fair - (662) 289-2981
Laural - South Mississippi Fair - (601) 649-9010
Lucedale - George Co. Fair - (601) 947-4223

New Albany - Union Co. Fair & Livestock Show - (662) 534-1916
Pascagoula - Jackson Co. Fair - (228) 762-6043
Petal - Great South Fair-Spring - (601) 582-4653
Philadelphia - Choctaw Indian Fair - (601) 650-7450
Philadelphia - Neshoba Co. Fair - 656-8480
Poplarville - Pearl River Co. Fair & Livestock Shows - (601) 795-4224
Ripley - Tippah Co. Fair - (662) 837-8184
Verona - No. Mississippi Fair - (662) 566-5605
Waynesboro - Wayne Co. Fair - (601) 735-2243
Wiggins - Tishomingo Co. Fair - (662) 423-7016
Yazoo City - Yazoo Co. Fair - (662) 746-2528

Missouri

Ava - Douglas Co. Fair - (417) 683-4147
Bethany - NW Missouri State Fair - (660) 425-2294
Bolivar - Polk Co. Jr. Livestock Show & Youth Fair - (417) 326-4916
Boonville - Cooper Co. Youth Fair - (660) 882-2156
Bowling Green - Pike Co. Fair - (573) 324-5257
Brookfield - Linn Co. 4H & FFA Fair - (660) 695-3658
Burlington Junction - Nodaway Co. Fair - (660) 725-4617
Butler - Bates Co. Fair - (660) 679-6272
Cape Girardeau - SE Missouri District Fair - (573) 334-9250
Carthage - Jasper Co. Youth Fair - (417) 358-8475
Center - Ralls Co. Jr. Fair - (573) 985-3911
Centerview - Johnson Co. Fair - (660) 747-3193
Centerville - Reynolds Co. Fair - (314) 846-2721
Chesterfield - St. Louis Co. Fair & Air Show - (636) 530-9386
Chillicothe - No. Ctrl. Missouri Fair - (660) 636-5277
Clarksville - Pike Co. Fair - (573) 242-3714
Clinton - Henry Co. Fair - (660) 885-2319
Cole Camp - Cole Camp Fair - (660) 668-3033
Columbia - Boone Co. Fair & Horse Show - (573) 474-9435
Cuba - Crawford Co. Fair - (573) 885-9910
Dexter - Stoddard Co. Fair - (573) 624-6734
Edina - Knox Co. 4H/FFA Fair - (660) 397-2179

El Dorado Springs - Land-O'-Lakes Youth Fair - (417) 876-4969
Eldon - Miller Co. Fair - (573) 392-1006
Farmington - St. Francois Co. Fair - (573) 756-8497
Fayette - Howard Co. Fair - (660) 248-3920
Forsyth - Taney Co. Fair - (417) 546-3870
Fulton - Kingdom of Callaway Co. Fair - (573) 642-4224
Gilman City - Gilman City Fair & Horse Show - (660) 876-5221
Hannibal - Marion Co. Fair/Palmyra Fall Festival - (573) 769-4470
Higginsville - Higginsville Country Fair - (660) 584-3030
Hillsboro - Jefferson Co. Fair - (636) 789-2600
Houston - Texas Co. Fair & Old Settler's Reunion - (417) 967-2220
Jefferson City - Jefferson City Jaycee Cole Co. Fair - (573) 897-4045
Kahokia - Clark Co. Fair - (660) 727-3366
Kansas City - American Royal Livestock, Horse Show & Rodeo - (816) 221-9800
Kennett - Delta Fair - (573) 888-6421
Kirksville - NE Missouri Fair - (660) 665-8800
Lamar - Lamar Free Fair - (417) 667-2124
Laurie - Hillbilly Fair - (573) 374-4871
Leeton - Leeton Fair - (660) 653-4805
Lewiston - Lewis Co. Agricultural Fair - (573) 497-2770

Appendix B

Linn - Osage Co. Fair - (573) 897-2889

Macon - Macon Co. Town & Country Fair - (660) 385-2173

Marshall - Saline Co. Fair - (660) 886-6908

Marshfield - Webster Co. Fair - (417) 859-4172

Maryville - Nodaway Co. Fair - (660) 752-4617

Memphis - Scotland Co. Fair - (660) 465-8948

Mexico - Audrain Co. 4H & Youth Fair - (573) 581-3231

Milan - Sullivan Co. Fair - (660) 265-4541

Moberly - Randolph Co. Fair - 4H & FFA Ag. Show - (660) 263-2898

Montgomery City - Montgomery Co. Fair - (573) 564-3526

Neosho - Newton Co. Fair - (417) 624-0415

Nevada - Vernon Co. Youth Fair - (417) 944-2972

Owensville - Gasconade Co. Fair - (573) 437-3262

Ozark - Christian Co. Fair - (417) 581-3558

Palmyra - Marion Co. Fair - (573) 769-4470

Paris - Monroe Co. Fair - (660) 327-4158

Platte City - Platte Co. Fair - (816) 431-FAIR

Pleasant Hill - Cass County Fair - (816) 540-3135

Poplar Bluff - Butler Co. Fair - (573) 686-4989

Potosi - Washington Co. Fair - (573) 438-2193

Princeton - Mercer Co. 4H & FFA Fair - (660) 748-3340

Redford - Reynolds Co. Fair - (314) 846-2721

Richland - Tri-Co. Fair - (573) 165-2711

Richmond - Ray Co. Fair - (816) 776-6141

Rock Port - Atchison Co. Fair - (660) 744-6231

Rolla - Ctrl. Missouri Regional Fair - (573) 341-6265

Savannah - Andrew Co. Community Fair - (816) 324-3147

Sedalia - Missouri State Fair - (660) 530-5600

Shelbina - Shelby Co. Fair - (573) 588-4115

Sikeston - Jaycee Bootheel Rodeo - (573) 471-7196

Smithton - Smithton Town & Country Fair - (660) 343-5656

Springfield - Ozark Empire Fair - (417) 833-2660

St. Charles - St. Charles Co. Fair - (636) 327-6949

Stover - Stover Fair - (573) 377-2356

Sullivan - Meramec Community Fair - (573) 860-2861

Tracy - Platte Co. Fair - (816) 431-FAIR

Trenton - No. Ctrl. Missouri State Fair - (660) 359-6819

Troy - Lincoln Co. Fair - (636) 528-2402

Unionville - Putnam Co. Fair - (660) 947-2676

Vienna - Maries Co. Fair - (573) 744-5882

Warrensburg - Johnson Co. Fair - (660) 747-1811

Warrenton - Warren Co. Fair - (636) 456-4627

Washington - Washington Town & Country Fair - (636) 239-2715

Wellington - Wellington Community Fair - (816) 240-2325

Wentzville - St. Charles Co. Fair - (636) 327-6949

West Plains - Heart of the Ozarks Fair (Howell Co. Fair) - (417) 256-2198

Montana

Baker - Fallon Co. Fair - (406) 778-2451

Billings - Montana Fair - (406) 256-2400

Billings - No. Int'l Livestock Expo. - (406) 256-2495

Bozeman - The Gallatin Co. Fair - (406) 582-3270

Butte - Butte Silver Bow Co. Fair - (406) 497-6221

Chinook - Blaine Co. Fair - (406) 357-3205

Choteau - Teton Co. Fair - (406) 466-2491

Circle - McCone Co. Fair - (406) 485-2605

Culbertson - Roosevelt Co. Fair - (406) 787-5312

Deer Lodge - Tri-Co. Fair - (406) 846-2854

Dillon - Beaverhead Co. Fair - (406) 683-2743

Dodson - Phillips Co. Fair - (406) 654-4013

Ekalaka - Carter Co. Fair - (406) 775-6268

Eureka - Lincoln Co. Fair - (406) 296-3471

Forsyth - Rosebud-Treasure Co. Fair - (406) 356-2144

Fort Benton - Chouteau Co. Fair - (406) 622-5282

Glasgow - NE Montana Fair - (406) 228-8221

Glendive - Dawson Co. Fair - (406) 377-6781

Great Falls - Montana State Fair - (406) 727-8900

Hamilton - Ravalli Co. Fair - (406) 363-3411

Havre - The Great Northern Fair - (406) 265-7121

Helena - Last Chance Stampede & Fair - (406) 442-1098

Kalispell - NW Montana Fair - (406) 758-5810

Lewiston - Ctrl Montana Fair - (406) 538-8841

Livingston - Park Co. Fair - (406) 222-4185

Miles City - Ea. Montana Fair - (406) 232-9554

Missoula - Western Montana Fair - (406) 721-3247

Plains - Sanders Co. Fair - (406) 826-3202

Plentywood - Sheridan Co. Fair - (406) 765-3407

Appendix B

Ronan - Lake Co. Fair - (406) 676-8660
Scobey - Daniels Co. Fair - (406) 783-5660
Shelby - Marias Fair - (406) 434-2692
Sidney - Richland Co. Fair - (406) 433-2801
Superior - Mineral Co. Fair - (406) 822-4052

Terry - Prairie Co. Fair - (406) 635-2121
Townsend - Broadwater Co. Fair - (406) 266-4261
Twin Bridges - Madison Co. Fair & Rodeo - (406) 684-5824
Wibaux - Wibaux Co. Fair - (406) 796-2486

Nebraska

Albion - Boone Co. Fair - (402) 395-6579
Aurora - Hamilton Co. Fair - (402) 694-3936
Bartlett - Wheeler Co. Fair - (402) 843-2384
Bassett - Rock Co. Fair - (402) 684-3472
Bayard - Morrill Co. Fair - (308) 586-2927
Beatrice - Gage Co. Fair & Expo. - (402) 223-3247
Beaver City - Furnas Co. Fair - (308) 268-4018
Benkelman - Dundy Co. Fair - (308) 423-2021
Bladen - Webster Co. Fair & Rodeo (402) 756-3404
Bloomfield - Knox Co. Fair - (402) 373-4393
Bridgeport - Morrill Co. Fair - (308) 586-2927
Broken Bow - Custer Co. Fair - (308) 935-1825
Burwell - Garfield Co. Fair & Nebraska's Big Rodeo - (308) 348-2204
Central City - Merrick Co. Fair - (308) 548-2553
Chadron - Dawes Co. Fair - (308) 432-3373
Chambers - Holt Co. Fair - (402) 925-2961
Chappell - Deuel Co. Fair - (308) 874-3260
Clay Center - Clay Co. Fair - (402) 726-2552
Columbus - Platte Co. Fair - (402) 564-0133
Concord - Dixon Co. Fair - (402) 355-2686
Crete - Saline Co. Fair - (402) 433-4138
Culbertson - Hitchcock Co. Fair - (308) 278-3107
Curtis - Frontier Co. Fair - (308) 367-4182
David City - Butler Co. Fair - (402) 367-6106
Dunning - Blaine Co. Fair - (308) 538-2227 - (308) 282-2753
Ellsworth - Sheridan Co. Fair & Rodeo - (308) 235-3122
Elwood - Gosper Co. Fair - (308) 785-2280
Eustis - Agricultural Society Fair - (308) 486-5615
Fairbury - Jefferson Co. Fair - (402) 729-5792
Fordyce - Cedar Co. Fair - (402) 357-3378
Franklin - Franklin Co. Fair - (308) 425-6250
Fremont - Fremont 4H Fair - (402) 721-2641
Fullerton - Nance Co. Fair - (308) 536-2258
Geneva - Fillmore Co. Fair - (402) 282-7372
Gordon - Sheridan Co. Fair - (308) 282-2828

Grafton - Fillmore Co. Fair - (402) 282-7372
Grand Island - Hall Co. Fair - (402) 845-2947
Grant - Perkins Co. Fair - (308) 352-2268
Gretna - Sarpy Co. Fair - (402) 332-4827
Harrison - Sioux Co. Fair - (308) 668-2428
Hartington - Cedar Co. Fair - (402) 256-3193
Hastings - Adams Co. Fairfest - (402) 462-3247
Hayes Center - Hayes Co. Fair - (308) 286-3416
Hemingford - Box Butte Co. Fair - (308) 487-5223
Holdrege - Phelps Co. Fair - (308) 995-6319
Humboldt - Richardson Co. Free Fair & Fall Festival - (402) 862-2376
Imperial - Chase Co. Fair - (308) 882-4629
Johnstown - Brown Co. Fair & Rodeo
Kimball - Kimball-Banner Co. Fair & Rodeo - (402) 722-4445
Kearney - Buffalo Co. Fair - (308) 236-1201
Keystone - Keith Co. Fair - (308) 726-8217
Leigh - Colfax Co. Fair - (402) 352-4299
Lewellen - Garden Co. Fair - (308) 772-3465
Lexington - Dawson Co. Fair - (308) 324-3600
Lincoln - Lancaster Co. Fair - (402) 441-6545
Lincoln - Nebraska State Fair - (402) 474-5371
Louisville - Cass Co. Fair - (402) 234-7288
Loup City - Sherman Co. Fair - (308) 745-1712
Madison - Madison Co. Fair & Rodeo - (402) 454-2831
Mason City - Custer Co. Fair - (308) 732-3475
McCook - Red Willow Co. Fair - (308) 345-4650
Minden - Kearney Co. Fair - (308) 832-0645
Mitchell - Scotts Bluff Co. Fair - (888) 661-3247
Mullen - Hooker Co. Fair - (308) 546-2754
Neligh - Antelope Co. Fair - (402) 887-5252
Nelson - Nuckolls Co. Fair - (402) 225-2092
New Castle - Dixon Co. Fair - (402) 355-2686
Norden - Keya Paha Co. Fair - (402) 387-2698
North Platte - Lincoln Co. Fair - (308) 534-8191
Oakland - Burt Co. Fair - (402) 685-5540

Appendix B

Ogallala - Keith Co. Fair - (308) 239-4497
Omaha - Douglas Co. Fair & Expo. - (402) 444-1948
Ord - Valley Co. Fair - (308) 728-7869
Orleans - Harlan Co. Fair - (308) 824-3452
Pawnee City - Pawnee Co. Fair - (402) 852-2200
Pierce - Pierce Co. Fair - (402) 329-6225
St. Paul - Howard Co. Agricultural Society Fair - (308) 754-5467
Scribner - Dodge Agricultural Society Fair - (402) 664-3165
Seward - Seward Co. Fair - (402) 643-3602
Sidney - Cheyenne Co. Fair & Rodeo - (308) 254-3179
South Sioux City - Dakota Co. Fair - (402) 987-3898
South Sioux City - Dakota-Thurston Co. Fair - (402) 494-5522
Spalding - Greeley Co. Free Fair - (308) 497-2416
Spencer - Boyd Co. Fair - (402) 589-1455
Springfield - Sarpy Co. Fair - (402) 332-4827

Springview - Keya Paha Co. Fair - (402) 497-3553
Stanton - Stanton Co. Fair - (402) 439-2408
Stapleton - Logan Co. Fair - (308) 636-2332
Stockville - Stockville Co. Fair - (308) 367-8337
Stromsburg - York Co. Fair - (402) 732-6737
Syracuse - Otoe Co. Fair - (402) 873-3832
Table Rock - Pawnee Co. Fair - (402) 852-2405
Taylor - Loup Co. Fair - (308) 942-3467
Tecumseh - Johnson Co. Fair - (402) 335-2382
Trenton - Hitchcock Co. Fair - (308) 334-5421
Valentine - Cherry Co. Fair & PRCA Rodeo - (402) 376-1699
Wahoo - Saunders Co. 4H Fair & Rodeo - (402) 784-2442
Wauneta - Hayes Co. Fair - (308) 286-3416
Wayne - Wayne Co. Fair - (402) 375-4635
Weeping Water - Cass Co. Fair - (402) 234-7288
West Point - Cuming Co. Fair - (402) 372-5877

Nevada

Caliente - Lincoln Co. Fair - (775) 726-3594
Carson City - RSVP Spring Fun Fair - (775) 687-4680
Elko - Elko Co. Fair - (775) 738-3616
Ely - White Pine Co. Fair - (775) 289-3074
Eureka - Eureka Co. Fair - (775) 237-5263
Logandale - Clark Co. Fair & Rodeo - (702) 398-3247

Pahrump - Pahrump Harvest Festival, Fair & Rodeo - (775) 727-1555
Reno - Nevada State Fair - (775) 688-5767
Reno - Reno Rodeo - (775) 329-3877
Winnemucca - Tri-Co. Fair - (775) 623-5071
Yerington - Lyon Co. Fair & Rodeo - (775) 463-3368

New Hampshire

Belmont - Belknap Co. Fair - (603) 524-1422
Center Sandwich - Sandwich Fair - (603) 284-7062
Contoocook - Hopkinton State Fair - (603) 746-4191
Cornish Flat - Cornish Fair - (603) 675-6417
Deerfield - Deerfield Fair - (603) 463-7421
East Swanzey - Cheshire Fair - (603) 357-4740
Lancaster - Lancaster Fair - (603) 788-4531

Milford - Hillsboro Co. Agricultural Fair - (603) 588-6106
New Boston - Hillsboro Co. Agri. Fair - (603) 641-6060
North Haverhill - North Haverhill Fair - (603) 989-3305
Rochester - Rochester Fair - (603) 332-6585
Stratham - Stratham Fair - (603) 772-4977

Appendix B

New Jersey

Augusta - New Jersey State Fair/Sussex Co. Farm & Horse Show - (973) 948-5500

Berkley Township - Ocean Co. Fair - (732) 914-9466

Blackwood - Camden Co. 4H Fair - (856) 566-2900

Bridgewater - Somerset Co. 4H Fair - (908) 526-6644

Cape May Courthouse - Cape May Co. 4H Fair - (609) 465-5115

Chester - Morris Co. 4H Fair - (973) 285-8301

East Brunswick - Middlesex Co. Fair - (732) 257-8858

East Rutherford - Meadowlands Fair - (201) 933-0199

Egg Harbor - Atlantic Co. 4H Fair - (609) 625-0056

Flemington - Hunterdon Co. 4H & Agricultural Fair - (908) 788-1340

Freehold - Monmouth Co. Fair - (732) 842-4000

Lumberton - Burlington Co. Farm Fair - (609) 267-2881

Millville - Cumberland Co. Cooperative Fair - (856) 825-3820

Mullica Hill - Gloucester Co. 4H Fair - (856) 307-6450

Oceanport - Lions Strawberry Fair - (732) 544-8424

Phillipsburg - Warren Co. Farmers Fair - (908) 859-6563

Roseland - Essex Co. 4H Fair - (973) 228-3785

Wayne - Passaic Co. 4H Fair - (973) 305-5742

West Orange - Essex Co. 4-H Fair - (9730) 228-3785

West Windsor - Mercer Co. 4H Fair - (609) 989-6830

Woodstown - Salem Co. Fair - (856) 769-0414

New Mexico

Albuquerque - New Mexico State Fair - (505) 265-1791

Belen - Valencia Co. Fair - (505) 865-4584

Clovis - Curry Co. Fair - (505) 763-6505

Estancia - Torrance Co. Fair - (505) 847-2585

Farmington - San Juan Co. Fair - (505) 325-5415

Las Cruces - So. New Mexico State Fair & Rodeo - (505) 524-8602

Los Alamos - Los Alamos Co. Fair & Rodeo - (505) 662-2656

Lovington - Lea Co. Fair & Rodeo - (800) 658-9955

Portales - Roosevelt Co. Fair - (505) 356-4417

Reserve - Catron Co. Fair - (505) 533-6430

Roswell - Ea. New Mexico State Fair - (505) 623-9411

Tucumcari - Quay Co. Fair - (505) 461-0562

New York

Afton - Afton Fair - (607) 639-1798

Albion - Orleans Co. 4H Fair - (585) 798-4265

Altamont - Altamont Fair - (518) 861-6671

Angelica - Allegany Co. Fair - (585) 466-7670

Ballston Spa - Saratoga Co. Fair - (518) 885-9701

Batavia - Genesee Co. Agricultural Society Fair - (585) 948-9609

Bath - Steuben Co. Fair - (607) 776-4801

Boonville - Oneida Co. Fair - (315) 942-2251

Brookfield - Madison Co. Fair - Madison Co. Fair - (315) 691-5858

Cairo - Greene Co. Youth Fair - (518) 622-9820

Caledonia - Livingston Co. Agricultural Society & Fair at Caledonia - (585) 538-2168

Canandaigua - Ontario Co. Fair - (585) 394-4601

Castle - Wyoming Co. Fair - (585) 493-5626

Chatham - Columbia Co. Fair - (518) 392-2121

Cobleskill - Cobleskill "Sunshine" Fair - (518) 234-2123

Cortland - Cortland Co. Jr. Fair - (607) 753-5077

Dunkirk - Chautauqua Co. Agricultural Fair - (716) 366-4752

Elmira - Chemung Co. Fair - (607) 734-1217

Floral Park - Queens Co. Fair - (718) 347-3276

Fonda - Fonda Fair - (518) 853-3313

Frankfort - Herkimer Co. Fair - (315) 895-7464

Gouverneur - Gouverneur & St. Lawrence Co. Fair - (315) 287-3010

Grahamsville - Grahamsville Little World's Fair - (845) 985-2500

Greenwich - Washington Co. Fair - (518) 692-2464

Hamburg - Erie Co. Fair & Expo - (716) 649-3900

Appendix B

Hemlock - Hemlock Fair - (585) 367-3370

Henrietta - Monroe Co. Fair - (585) 334-4000

Horseheads - Chemung Co. Fair - (607) 734-1203

Knowlesville - Orleans Co. Youth Fair - (585) 589-5561

Little Valley - Cattaraugus Co. & Agricultural Society Fair - (716) 938-6676

Lockport - Niagara Co. Fair - (716) 433-8839

Lowville - Lewis Co. Agricultural Society Fair - (315) 376-8333

Malone - Franklin Co. Agricultural Fair - (518) 483-0751

Middletown - Orange Co. Fair - (845) 343-4826

Morris - Otsego Co. Fair - (607) 263-5289

Morrisonville - The Agricultural & Industrial Fair of Clinton Co. - (518) 591-7998

New Paltz - Ulster Co. Fair - (845) 255-1380

Norwich - Chenango Co. Fair - (607) 334-9198

Old Bethpage - Long Island Fair Agricultural Society Queens, Nassau, Suffolk - (516) 572-8406

Owego - Tioga Co. Fair - (607) 687-1308

Palmyra - Wayne Co. Fair - (315) 597-5372

Penn Yan - Yates Co. Fair - (315) 536-3830

Pike - Wymoing Co. Fair - (585) 493-5626

Plattsburg - The Agricultural & Industrial Fair of Clinton Co. - (518) 561-7998

Rhineback - Dutchess Co. Fair - (845) 876-4001

Sandy Creek - Oswego Co. Fair - (315) 298-4015

Schaghticoke - Schaghticoke Fair - (518) 753-4411

Syracuse - New York State Fair - (315) 487-7711

Trumansburg - Thompkin Co. Fair - (607) 387-6504

Uniondale - Nassau Co. Fair - (321) 633-4208

Walton - Delaware Valley Agricultural Society Fair - (607) 865-4763

Warrensburg - Warren Co. Fair - (518) 623-3291

Waterloo - Seneca Co. Fair - (315) 568-9501

Watertown - Jefferson Co. Fair - (315) 782-8612

Watkins Glen - Schuyler Youth Fair - (607) 535-7141

Weedsport - Cayuga Co. Fair - (315) 834-6606

Westport - Essex Co. Fair - (518) 962-4407

Whitney Point - Broome Co. Fair - (607) 692-4149

Yonkers - Greater Westchester Co. Fair & Expo - (914) 968-4200

Yorktown Heights - Yorktown Grange Fair - (914) 962-3900

North Carolina

Ahoskie - Atlantic District Fair - (252) 333-4553

Albemarle - Stanly Co. Fair - (704) 474-3673

Burlington - Alamance - Alamance Co. Agricultural Fair - (336) 228-6106

Carthage - Moore Co. Agricultural Fair - (910) 947-3963

Clyde - Haywood Co. Fair - (828) 456-3575

Concord - Cabarrus Co. Agricultural Fair - (704) 920-EXPO

Drexel - Drexel Community Fair - (828) 438-3933

Dudley - Wayne Regional Agricultural Fair (919) 735-7277

Edenton - Chowan Co. Fair - (252) 482-4057

Fayetteville - Cumberland Co. Fair - (910) 438-4140

Fletcher - North Carolina Mountain State Fair - (828) 687-1414

Fort Bragg - Fort Bragg Fair - (910) 396-6319

Franklin - Macon Co. Fair - (828) 369-3523

Goldsboro - Wayne Regional Agricultural Fair - (919) 735-7277

Greensboro - Central Carolina Fair - (336) 433-7243

Greenville - Pitt Co. American Legion Agricultural Fair - (252) 758-6916

Hamlet - Richmond Co. Agricultural Fair - (910) 582-2223

Henderson - Vance Co. Regional Fair - (434) 348-3378

Hickory - Hickory American Legion Fair - (828) 464-5433

Hudson - Caldwell Co. Agricultural Fair - (828) 728-7050

Jacksonville - Onslow Co. Fair - (910) 346-3871

Kenansville - Duplin Co. Agribusiness Fair - (910) 296-2400

King - Stokes Co. Agriculture Fair - (336) 983-3019

Kings Mountain - Bethware Community Fair - (704) 739-7005

Kinston - Lenoir Co. Fair - (252) 523-4555

Lenoir - Caldwell Co. Agricultural Fair - (828) 728-7050

Lexington - Davidson Co. Agricultural Fair - (336) 243-2528

Lumberton - Robeson Co. Fair - (910) 738-2126

Makin - Warren Co. Agricultural Fair - (252) 257-4480

Monroe - North Carolina/South Carolina District Fair - (704) 283-5846

Morganton - Burke Co. Fair - (828) 437-8431

Morganton - Burke Co. Spring Fair - (828) 437-8431

Mount Airy - Surry Co. Agricultural Fair - (336) 786-6830

Appendix B

Newland - Avery Co. Agricultural Fair - (828) 733-3642
North Wilkesboro - Wilkes Agricultural Fair - (336) 838-4942
Pittsboro - Chatham Co. Agricultural & Industrial Fair - (919) 542-4406
Raleigh - North Carolina State Fair - (919) 821-7400
Rocky Mount - Rocky Mount Fair - (252) 977-3247
Sanford - Lions/Lee Co. Agricultural Fair - (919) 776-2714
Shelby - Cleveland Co. Fair - (704) 487-0651
Sparta - Alleghany Co. Agricultural Fair - (336) 372-5597
Statesville - Iredell Co. Agricultural Fair - (704) 528-6176
Taylorsville - Alexander Co. Agricultural Fair - (828) 632-2226
Warrenton - Warren Co. Agricultural Fair - (252) 257-4480
Waynesville - Haywood Co. Fair - (828) 456-3575
Whiteville - Columbus Co. Agricultural Fair - (910) 642-7585
Wilmington - Cape Fear Fair & Expo - (910) 313-1234
Wilson - Wilson Co. Fair - (252) 237-8443
Winston-Salem - Dixie Classic Fair - (336) 727-2236
Yanceyville - Caswell Co. & Agricultural Fair - (336) 694-6700

North Dakota

Amiden - Slope Farmers Fair - (701) 879-6270
Beach - Golden Valley Co. Fair - (701) 872-4332
Beulah - Mercer Co. Fair - (701) 873-5195
Bismarck - Missouri Valley Fair - (701) 258-6451
Bottineau - Bottineau Co. Fair - (701) 228-3702
Bowman - Bowman Co. Fair - (701) 523-3178
Carrington - Foster Co. Fair - (701) 652-2581
Carson - Grant Co. Fair - (701) 622-3470
Cooperstown - Griggs Co. Fair - (701) 797-331
Crosby - Divide Co. Fair - (701) 965-6358
Dickinson - West River Ag. Expo - (701) 225-5115
Fessenden - Wells Co. Fair - (701) 547-3834
Flaxton - Burke Co. Fair - (701) 596-3898
Forman - Sargent Co. Fair - (701) 724-3419
Grand Forks - Greater Grand Forks Fair & Exhibition - (701) 343-2862
Hamilton - Pembina Co. Fair - (701) 265-3359
Hettinger - Adams Co. Fair Days - (701) 567-2240
Jamestown - Stutsman Co. Fair - (701) 252-6868
Lisbon - Ransom Co. Fair - (701) 683-5000
Minot - North Dakota State Fair - (701) 857-7620
Mott - Hettinger Co. Fair - (701) 824-2095
New Salem - Morton Co. Fair - (701) 843-8517
Underwood - McLean Co. Fair - (701) 734-6713
Watford City - McKenzie Co. Fair - (701) 842-6411
West Fargo - Red River Valley Fair - (701) 282-2200
Williston - Upper Missouri Valley Fair - (701) 572-3338
Wishek - Tri Co. Fair - (701) 452-2149

Ohio

Albany - Albany Independent Agricultural Fair - (740) 698-6787
Ashland - Ashland Co. Fair - (419) 289-0466
Athens - Athens Co. Fair - (740) 797-4356
Atica - Atica Independent Agricultural Fair - (419) 426-7194
Bellefontaine - Logan Co. Fair - (937) 599-4178
Bellville - Bellville Independent Fair - (419) 886-4768
Berea - Cuyahoga Co. Fair - (440) 243-0090
Bowling Green - Wood Co. Fair - (419) 352-0441
Bucyrus - Crawford Co. Fair - (419) 683-2711
Burton - Great Geauga Co. Fair - (440) 834-1846
Cadiz - Harrison Co. Fair - (740) 945-2122
Caldwell - Noble Co. Fair - (740) 732-2112
Canfield - Mahoning Co. Agricultural Society/Canfield Fair - (330) 452-0621
Canton - Stark Co. Agricultural Society Fair - (330) 533-4107
Carrollton - Carroll Co. Fair - (330) 739-3524
Carthage - Hamilton Co. Fair - (513) 761-4224
Celina - Mercer Co. Fair - (419) 586-3239
Chillicothe - Ross Co. Fair - (740) 634-2921
Cincinnati - Hamilton Co. Fair - (513) 761-4224
Circleville - Pickaway Co. Fair - (740) 474-2085

Appendix B

Columbus - Ohio State Fair - (614) 644-4000
Cortland - Trumbull Co. Fair - (330) 637-6010
Coshocton - Coshocton Co. Fair - (740) 622-2385
Croton - Hartford Independent Fair - (740) 893-4881
Dayton - Montgomery Co. Fair - (937) 224-1619
Delaware - Delaware Co. Fair - (740) 362-3851
Dover - Tuscarawas Co. Fair - (330) 343-0524
Eaton - Preble Co. Fair - (937) 456-3748
Findlay - Hancock Co. Fair - (419) 423-9273
Fremont - Sandusky Co. Fair - (419) 332-5604
Gallipolis - Gallia Co. Jr. Fair - (740) 379-2785
Georgetown - Brown Co. Fair - (937) 378-3558
Greenville - Darke Co. Fair - (937) 548-5044
Hamilton - Butler Co. Fair - (513) 892-1423
Hicksville - Defiance Co. Fair - (419) 784-4194
Hilliard - Franklin Co. Fair - (614) 876-7235
Hillsboro - Highland Co. Fair - (937) 393-9975
Jefferson - Ashtabula Co. Fair - (440) 576-7626
Kenton - Hardin Co. Fair - (419) 675-2396
Lancaster - Fairfield Co. Fair - (740) 653-304
Lebanon - Warren Co. Agricultural Fair - (513) 932-2636
Lima - Allen Co. Fair - (419) 228-7141
Lisbon - Columbiana Co. Fair - (330) 337-8828
Logan - Hocking Co. Fair - (740) 385-4059
London - Madison Co. Fair - (740) 852-1654
Loudonville -Loudonville Free Street Fair - (419) 994-4391
Lucasville - Scioto Co. Fair - (740) 353-3698
Mansfield - Richland Co. Fair - (419) 747-3717
Marietta - Washington Co. Fair - (740) 373-1347
Marion - Marion Co. Fair - (740) 382-2558
Marysville - Union Co. Fair - (937) 246-5733
Maumee - Lucas Co. Fair - (419) 893-2127
McArthur - Vinton Agricultural Fair - (740) 596-4995
McConnelsville - Morgan Co. Fair - (740) 962-2709
Medina - Medina Co. Fair - (330) 723-9633
Millersburg - Holmes Co. Fair - (419) 994-3165
Montpelier - Williams Co. Fair - (419) 485-3755
Mount Gilead - Mt. Gilead Fair - (419) 947-1611
Mount Vernon - Knox Co. Fair - (740) 397-0484
Napoleon - Henry Co. Fair - (419) 592-9096
New Lexington - Perry Co. Fair - (740) 342-3047

Norwalk - Huron Co. Fair - (419) 744-2116
Oak Harbor - Ottawa Co. Fair - (419) 898-1971
Old Washington - Guernsey Co. Agricultural Society - (740) 439-2106
Ottawa - Putnam Co. Fair - (419) 523-4628
Owensville - Clermont Co. Fair - (513) 724-7834
Painesville - Lake Co. Fair - (440) 354-3339
Paulding - Paulding Co. Fair - (419) 399-2961
Pemberville - Pemberville Free Fair - (419) 287-3832
Piketon - Pike Co. Fair - (740) 947-5253
Pomeroy - Meigs Co. Fair - (740) 985-4372
Proctorville - Lawrenceville Co. Fair - (740) 886-5823
Randolph - Portage Co. Randolph Fair - (330) 325-7476
Richwood - Richwood Independent Fair - (740) 943-3235
St. Clairsville - Belmont Co. Fair - (740) 695-6265
Sandusky - Erie Co. Fair - (419) 359-1782
Sidney - Shelby Co. Fair - (937) 492-5088
Smithfield - Jefferson Agricultural Fair - (740) 765-5156
Springfield - Clark Co. Fair - (937) 323-3090
Tallmadge - Summit Co. Fair - (330) 633-6200
Tiffin - Seneca Co. Fair - (419) 447-7888
Troy - Miami Co. Fair - (937) 335-7492
Union - Richwood Independent Fair - (740) 943-3235
Upper Sandusky - Wyandot - Co. Fair - (419) 294-4320
Urbana - Champaign Co. Fair - (937) 653-2640
Van Wert - Van Wert Co. Fair - (419) 238-9270
Vinton - Vinton Agricultural Fair - (740) 384-6443
Wapakoneta - Auglaize Co. Fair - (419) 738-2515
Washington - Barlow Independent Fair - (740) 678-2138
Washington Court House - Fayette Co. Fair - (740) 335-5856
Waterford - Barlow Independent Fair - (740) 678-2138
Wauseon - Fulton Co. Fair - (419) 335-6006
Wellington - Lorain Co. Fair - (440) 647-2781
Wellston - Jackson Co. Fair - (740) 988-2631
West Union - Adams Co. Agricultural Fair - (937) 544-3202
Wilmington - Clinton Co. Agricultural Fair - (937) 382-1741
Woodsfield - Monroe Co. Fair - (740) 472-1465
Wooster - Wayne Co. Fair - (330) 262-8001
Xenia - Greene Co. Fair - (937) 372-8621
Zanesville - Muskingum Co. Fair - (740) 454-0770

Appendix B

Oklahoma

Ada - Pontotoc Co. Free Fair - (580) 310-0441
Altus - Jackson Co. Fair - (580) 482-4430
Apache - Apache District Fair & Centennial - (580) 588-3578
Ardmore - Co. Free Fair - (580) 223-2541
Chandler - Lincoln Co. Fair - (405) 258-0560
Chickasaw - Grady Co. Fair - (580) 252-2918
Clinton - Custer Co. Free Fair - (580) 323-2291
Cordell - Washita Co. Free Fair - (580) 832-3356
Duncan - Grady Co. Fair - (580) 252-5676
Duncan - Stephens Co. Fair - (580) 255-0510
El Reno - Canadian Co. Free Fair - (405) 262-0683
Enid - Garfield Co. Fair - (580) 237-0238
Guthrie - Logan Co. Fair - (405) 282-3331
Guymon - Panhandle Exposition - (580) 338-5446
Hugo - Choctaw Co. Fair - (580) 326-3359
Kellyville - Creek Co. Fair - (918) 224-7885
Kingfisher - Kingfisher Co. Fair - (405) 375-3822

Lawton - Comanche Co. Free Fair - (580) 357-1483
Norman - Cleveland Co. Fair - (405) 360-4721
Oklahoma City - Oklahoma State Fair - (405) 948-6700
Okmulgee - Okmulgee Co. Free Fair - (918) 756-1958
Pawnee - Pawnee Co. Fair - (918) 762-2735
Perry - Noble Co. Fair - (580) 336-4684
Purcell - McClain Co. Fair - (405) 527-2900
Shawnee - Pottawatomie Co. Fair - (405) 275-7020
Stillwater - Payne Co. Free Fair - (405) 377-1275
Sulphur - Murray Co. Free Fair - (580) 622-3016
Tulsa - Tulsa State Fair - (918) 744-1113
Vinita - Craig Co. Free Fair - (918) 256-7133
Walters - Cotton Co. Free Fair - (580) 875-3756
Watonga - Blaine Co. Fair - (580) 623-5243
Waurika - Jefferson Co. Fair - (580) 228-2332
Wewoka - Seminole Co. Free Fair - (405) 257-5433

Oregon

Albany - Linn Co. Fair - (541) 926-4314
Astoria - Clatsop Co. Fair - (503) 325-4600
Baker - Baker Co. Fair - (541) 523-7881
Burns - Harney Co. Fair - (541) 573-6166
Canby - Clackamas Co. Fair - (503) 226-1136
Central Point - Jackson Co. Fair - (541) 774-8270
Condon - Gilliam Co. Fair - (541) 384-4139
Corvallis - Benton Co. Fair - (541) 757-1521
Enterprise - Wallowa Co. Fair - (541) 426-4097
Eugene - Lane Co. Fair - (541) 682-4292
Fossil - Wheeler Co. Fair & Rodeo - (541) 763-4560
Gold Beach - Curry Co. Fair - (541) 247-4541
Grants Pass - Josephine Co. Fair - (541) 476-3215
Heppner - Morrow Co. Fair & Rodeo - (541) 676-9474
Hermiston - Umatilla Co. Fair - (541) 567-6121
Hillsboro - Washington Co. Fair & Rodeo - (503) 648-1416
Hood River - Hood River Co. Fair - (541) 354-2865
John Day - Grant Co. Fair - (541) 575-1900
Klamath Falls - Klamath Co. Fair - (541) 883-3796

La Grande - Union Co. Fair - (541) 963-1011
Lakeview - Lake Co. Fair & Round-up - (541) 947-2925
Lena - Morrow Co. Fair & Rodeo - (541) 676-9474
Madras - Jefferson Co. Fair Rodeo - (541) 325-5050
McMinnville - Yamhill Co. Fair & Rodeo - (503) 434-7524
Moro - Sherman Co. Fair - (541) 565-3510
Myrtle Point - Coos Co. Fair - (541) 572-2002
Newport - Lincoln Co. Fair & Rodeo - (541) 265-6237
Ontario - Malheur Co. Fair - (541) 889-3431
Portland - Multnomah Co. Fair - (503) 761-7577
Prineville - Crook Co. Fair - (541) 447-6575
Redmond - Deschutes Co. Fair - (541) 548-2711
Rickreall - Polk Co. Fair - (503) 623-3048
Roseburg - Douglas Co. Fair - (541) 957-7010
St. Helens - Columbia Co. Fair - (503) 397-4231
Salem - Marion Co. Fair - (503) 585-9998
Salem - Oregon State Fair - (503) 947-3247
Tigh Valley - Wasco Co. Fair - (541) 296-5644
Tillamook - Tillamook Co. Fair - (503) 842-2272
Veneta - Oregon Country Fair - (541) 343-4298

Appendix B

Pennsylvania

Acme - Bullskin Township Community Fair - (724) 547-4268

Albion - Albion Area Fair - (814) 756-4833

Allentown - Allentown Fair - (610) 433-7541

Altoona - Sinking Valley Fair - (814) 684-4379

Amity - Washington Co. Fair - (724) 225-7718

Beaver Falls - Big Knob Grange Fair - (724) 774-7093

Bedford - Bedford Co. Fair - (814) 623-9011

Bellwood - Bellwood-Antis Farm Show - (814) 742-8121

Bensalem -Pennsylvania Fair - (321) 633-4028

Berlin - Berlin Brothersvalley Community Fair - (814) 267-5253

Berks - Kempton Country Fair - (610) 756-6444

Biglerville - So. Mountain Fair - (717) 677-9663

Bloomsburg - Bloomsburg Fair - (570) 784-4949

Brookville - Jefferson Co. Fair - (814) 265-0640

Bushkill - Pike Co. Fair - (570) 296-8790

Butler - Butler Farm Show - (742) 482-4000

Carlisle - Cumberland Ag. Expo - (717) 249-8434

Centre Hall - Centre Co. Grange Fair - (814) 364-9212

Chambersburg - Franklin Co. Fair - (717) 369-4100

Clearfield - Clearfield Co. Fair - (814) 765-4629

Clinton - Findlay Township Community Fair - (724) 695-0500

Cochranton - Cochranton Community Fair - (814) 425-2302

Commodore - Cookport Fair - (724) 254-4613

Cookport - Green Township Community Fair - (724) 254-4613

Curryville - Morrison Cove Community Fair - (814) 793-2111

Dallas - Luzerne Co. Fair - (570) 675-FAIR

Dawson - Dawson Grange Community Fair - (724) 736-2943

Dayton - Dayton Fair - (814) 257-8332

Delta - Mason Dixon Fair - (717) 456-6000

Denver - Denver Fair - (717) 336-4072

Dillsburg - Dillsburg Community Fair - (717) 432-7361

Dunbar - Fayette Co. Fair - (724) 628-3360

Dushore - Sullivan Co. Fair - (570) 924-3205

East Smethport - McKean Co. Fair - (814) 887-5396

Ebensburg - Cambria Co. Fair - (814) 472-7491

Edinboro - Waterford Community Fair - (814) 796-6923

Elizabethtown - Elizabethtown Fair - (717) 367-0508

Emporium - Cameron Co. Fair - (814) 546-2574

Ephrata - Ephrata Fair - (717) 733-4451

Farmington - Mountain Area Fair - (724) 329-5513

Forksville - Sullivan Co. Fair - (570) 924-3843

Franklin - Venango Co. Fair - (814) 437-7716

Gettysburg - Great Gettysburg Fair - (717) 334-7724

Gilbert - West End Fair - (610) 681-4293

Gratz - Gratz Fair - (717) 365-3441

Graysville - Jacktown Fair - (724) 428-3637

Greensburg - Westmoreland Co. Fair - (724) 423-5005

Harford - Harford Fair - (570) 434-4300

Harrisburg - Keystone Int'l Livestock Expo & Fair - (717) 787-2905

Harrisburg - Pennsylvania Farm Show - (717) 783-5373

Hegins - Tri-Valley Community Fair - (570) 682-3125

Home - Ox Hill Community Agricultural Fair - (724) 397-4449

Honesdale - Wayne Co. Fair - (570) 253-1847

Hookstown - Hookstown Fair - (724) 573-4512

Howard - Centre Co. Grange Fair - (866) 236-3247

Hughesville - Lycoming Co. Fair - (570) 784-0487

Huntingdon - Huntingdon Co. Fair - (814) 643-4452

Indiana - Indiana Co. Fair - (724) 932-5140

Jamestown - Jamestown Community Fair - (724) 932-5140

Kane - McKean Co. Fair - (814) 887-5361

Kempton - Kempton Country Fair - (610) 756-6444

Kimberton - Kimberton Community Fair - (610) 933-4566

Kunkletown - West End Fair - (610) 681-4293

Kutztown - Kutztown Fair - (610) 683-7696

Lampeter - West Lampeter Community Fair - (717) 464-2476

Laurelton - Union Co. West End Fair - (570) 922-1445

Lebanon - Lebanon Area fair - (717) 273-3795

Leesport - Reading Fair - (610) 370-3473

Lemont Furnace - Uniontown Poultry & Farm Show - (724) 439-5253

Lock Haven - Clinton Co. Fair - (570) 726-4148

Mackeyville - Clinton Co. Fair - (570) 726-4148

Manheim - Manheim Community Farm Show - (717) 361-0998

Martinsburg - Morrison Cove Community Fair (814) 643-4452

McConnellburg - Fulton Co. Fair - (717) 485-5730

Meadville - Crawford Co. Fair - (814) 333-7400

Mehoopany - Kiwanis Wyoming Co. Fair - (570) 836-5502

Mercer -Jefferson Township Fair - (724) 662-3310

Mercer - Mercer Co. Grange Fair - (724) 748-4007

Meshoopen - Kiwanis Wyoming Co. Fair - (570) 836-7287

Meyersdale - Somerset Co. Fair - (814) 634-5619

Appendix B

Middleburg - Beaver Community Fair - (507) 652-4963

Millport - Potter Co. Fair - (814) 698-2368

Moscow - Greene-Dreher-Sterling Fair - (570) 676-4047

Mount Bethel - Blue Valley Farm Show - (610) 588-2818

Mount Pleasant - Bullskin Township Community Fair - (724) 887-3986

New Bethlehem - Clarion Co. Fair - (814) 275-3929

New Castle - Lawrence Co. Fair - (724) 654-2175

New Derry - Derry Township Fair - (724) 694-2175

Newfoundland - Greene-Dreher-Sterling Fair - (570) 676-4047

New Holland - New Holland Farmers Fair - (717) 354-5880

Newport - Perry Co. Fair - (717) 567-3084

New Tripoli - Schnecksville Community Fair - (610) 767-5026

Oley - Oley Valley Community Fair - (610) 944-7862

Palmerton - Carbon Co. Fair - (610) 377-6251

Petersburg - Huntingdon Co. Fair - (814) 669-4268

Philadelphia - Philadelphia Co. Fair - (321) 633-4028

Pittsburgh - Allegheny Co. Fair & Exposition - (412) 473-2540

Pittsfield - Warren Co. Fair - (814) 723-1342

Pittston Township - The NE Fair & Expo - (570) 654-2503

Planfield - Plainfield Farmers Fair - (610) 863-6816

Port Royal - Juniata Co. Fair - (717) 527-4414

Prospect - Big Butler Fair - (724) 538-9014

Quarryville - Southern Lancaster Co. Fair - (717) 786-1054

Ridgeway - Elk Co. Fair - (814) 885-8376

Rochester - Big Knob Grange Fair - (724) 774-7093

St. Marys - Elk Co. Fair - (814) 885-8376

Schnecksville - Schnecksville Community Fair - (610) 799-9467

Schuylkill - Schuylkill Co. Fair - (570) 754-3247

Shippensburg - Shippensburg Community Fair - (717) 532-3800

Skelp - Sinking Valley Fair - (814) 684-4379

Spartansburg - Spartansburg Community Fair - (814) 654-7608

Stoneboro - The Great Stoneboro Fair - (724) 370-2852

Sykesville - Sykesville Ag & Youth Fair - (814) 894-7871

Thompsontown - Beaver Community Fair - (570) 658-4963

Tionesta - Wolf's Corners Fair - (814) 755-4222

Transfer - Transfer Harvest Home Fair - (727) 962-0959

Troy - Troy Fair - (570) 297-3648

Uniontown - Fayette Co. Fair - (724) 628-3360

Unionville - Unionville Community Fair - (610) 347-1726

Washington - Washington Co. Fair - (724) 225-7718

Washingtonville - Montour-De Long Community Fair - (570) 437-2178

Waterford - Waterford Community Fair - (814) 796-6923

Wattsburg - Erie Co. Fair at Wattsburg, PA - (814) 739-2232

Waynesboro - Franklin Co. Fair - (717) 369-4100

Waynesboro - Greene Co. Fair - (724) 627-9160

Wellsboro - Tioga Co. Fair - (570) 724-3196

West Alexander - West Alexander Fair - (724) 484-7340

West Chester - Goshen Country Fair - (610) 430-1555

West Newton - Sweickley Township Fair - (724) 872-5579

Westover - Harmony Grange Fair - (814) 743-6716

Williamsburg - Williamsburg Community Farm Show - (814) 832-9443

Wind Ridge - Jacktown Fair - (724) 428-3637

Wrightstown - Middletown Grange Fair - (215) 968-2321

York - York Fair - (717) 848-2596

Rhode Island

Portsmouth - 4H Country Fair - (401) 849-8721

Richmond - Washington Co. Fair - (401) 539-7042

South Carolina

Aiken - Aiken Jaycee Western Carolina State Fair - (803) 648-8955

Anderson - Anderson Co. Fair - (864) 226-6114

Beaufort - Beaufort Co. Fair - (843) 524-8760

Columbia - South Carolina State Fair - (803) 799-3387

Florence - Ea. Carolina Agricultural Fair - (843) 665-5173

Greenville - Upper South Carolina State Fair - (864) 269-0852

Appendix B

Greenwood - Greenwood Co. Agricultural Fair - (864) 227-0533
Ladson - Coastal Carolina Fair - (843) 572-3161
Lancaster - Lancaster Co. Fair - (803) 283-3086
Laurens - Laurens Co. Fair - (864) 984-5550

Orangeburg - Orangeburg Co. Fair - (803) 534-0358
Rock Hill - York Co. Fair - (803) 366-4277
Spartanburg - Piedmont Interstate Fair - (864) 582-7042
Sumter - Sumter Co. Fair - (803) 495-8222
Union - Union Co. Agricultural Fair - (864) 427-1212

South Dakota

Aberdeen - Brown Co. Fair - (605) 626-7110
Alcester - Union Co. Fair - (605) 253-2838
Camp Crook - Harding Co. Fair - (605) 797-4451
Edgemont - Fall River Co. Fair - (605) 662-7703
Flandreau - Moody Co. Fair - (605) 997-2469
Ft. Pierre - Hughes/Stanley Co. Fair - (605) 223-7730
Hermosa - Custer Co. Fair - (605) 255-4758
Huron - South Dakota State Fair - (605) 353-7340
Martin - Bennett Co. Fair & 4H Achievement Days - (605) 685-6972
McIntosh - Corson Co. Fair - (605) 823-4771
Miller - Hand Co. Achievement Days - (605) 853-2738
Mission - Todd Co. Fair - (605) 969-3441
Mobridge - Mobridge Sitting Bull Stampede & Rodeo - (605) 845-2387

Nisland - Butte-Lawrence Co. Fair - (605) 257-2113
Onida - Sully Co. Fair - (605) 258-2776
Parker - Turner Co. Fair - (605) 297-4771
Philip - Haakon/Jackson Co. Fair - (605) 859-2840
Rapid City - Black Hills Stock Show & Rodeo - (605) 355-3861
Rapid City - Central States Fair - (605) 355-3861
Redfield - Redfield Bull-A-Rama Rodeo - (605) 472-0965
Sioux Falls - Sioux Empire Fair - (605) 367-7178
Timber Lake - Dewey Co. Fair - (605) 865-3652
Vermillion - Clay Co. Fair - (605) 677-7111
Waubay - Day Co. Fair - (605) 947-4178
Webster - Day Co. Fair - (605) 947-4178
Winner - Mid Dakota Fair - (605) 842-1533

Tennessee

Alexandria - DeKalb Co. Fair - (615) 529-2735
Ashland City - Cheatham Co. Fair - (615) 792-4885
Athens - Mid-East Tennessee Regional Fair (McMinn Co.) - (423) 745-6947
Benton - Polk Co. Fair - (423) 338-8648
Bolivar - Hardeman Co. Fair - (731) 658-2421
Camden - Benton Co. Fair - (731) 584-1514
Celina - Clay Co. Fair - (931) 243-3338
Clarksville - No. Tennessee State Fair (Montgomery Co.) - (931) 552-4681
Clinton - Anderson Co. Fair - (865) 457-1522
Columbia - Maury Co. Fair - (931) 381-2900
Cookeville - Putnam Co. Fair - (931) 526-5818
Crossville - Cumberland Co. Fair - (931) 484-4932
Decatur - Meigs Co. Fair - (423) 334-5781
Decaturville - Decatur Co. Fair - (731) 852-4270
Dickson - Dickson Co. Fair - (615) 446-2178

Dunlap - Sequatchie Co. Fair - (423) 949-2161
Dyersburg - Dyer Co. Fair - (731) 285-0072
Fayetteville - Lincoln Co. Fair - (931) 937-8376
Franklin - Williamson Co. Fair - (615) 550-7031
Gallatin - Sumner Co. Fair - (615) 452-2536
Gray - Appalachian Fair (Washington Co.) - (423) 477-3211
Greeneville - Greene Co. Fair - (423) 638-2521
Hixson - Hamilton Co. Fair - (423) 209-6210
Hohenwald - So. Ctrl. Area Fair (Lewis Co.) - (931) 796-5425
Huntington - Carroll Co. Fair - (731) 986-4872
Jackson - W. Tennessee State Fair (Madison Co.) - (731) 424-0151
Jamestown - Fentress Co. Agricultural Fair - (931) 879-4933
Jasper - Marion Co. Fair - (423) 942-3480
Jefferson City - Jefferson Co. Fair - (865) 971-2090
Knoxville - Tennessee Valley Fair (Knox Co.) - (865) 215-1470

261

Appendix B

Lafayette - Macon Co. Fair - (615) 666-4204
Lawrenceburg - Middle Tennessee Fair (Lawrence Co.) - (931) 762-1975
Lebanon - Wilson Co. Fair - (615) 443-2626
Lexington - Henderson Co. Fair - (731) 967-3988
Livingston - Overton Co. Fair - (931) 823-5070
Manchester - Coffee Co. Fair - (931) 394-2499
McMinnville - Warren Co. Fair - (931) 686-8379
Memphis - Mid-South Fair - (901) 274-8800
Nashville - Tennessee State Fair - (615) 862-8980
New Tazewell - Claiborne Co. Fair - (423) 626-7993
Newport - Cocke Co. Fair - (423) 613-5822
Oneida - Scott Co. Fair - (423) 569-6900
Paris - Henry Co. Fair - (731) 642-2412
Pikeville - Bledsoe Co. Fair - (423) 881-4598
Pulaski - Giles Co. Fair - (931) 424-4014

Rock Island - Warren Co. Fair - (931) 686-2729
Savannah - Hardin Co. Fair - (731) 925-8000
Selmer - McNairy Co. Fair - (731) 645-4754
Sevierville - Sevier Co. Fair - (865) 453-7403
Sparta - White Co. Fair - (931) 836-2248
Spencer - Van Buren Co. Fair - (931) 946-3323
Springfield - Robertson Co. Fair - (615) 382-7649
Talbott - Jefferson Co. Fair - (865) 689-3700
Tazewell - Clairborne Co. Fair - (423) 626-7993
Tracy City - Grundy Co. Fair - (931) 592-5010
Trenton - Gibson Co. Fair - (731) 855-7656
Union City - Obion Co. Fair - (731) 885-5361
Wartburg - Morgan Co. Fair - (423) 346-6847
Waverly - Hickman Co. Fair - (931) 296-3442
Waverly - Humphreys Co. Agricultural & Industry Fair - (931) 296-3442

Texas

Abilene - West Texas Fair & Rodeo - (915) 677-4376
Alice - Jim Wells Co. Fair - (361) 664-7595
Amarillo - Amarillo Tri-State Fair - (806) 376-7767
Anderson - Grimes Co. Fair - (936) 825-2066
Angleton - Brazoria Co. Fair - (979) 849-6416
Austin - Star of Texas Fair & Rodeo - (512) 919-3000
Bay City - Matagorda Co. Fair & Rodeo - (979) 245-2454
Beaumont - So. Texas State Fair - (409) 832-9991
Bellville - Austin Co. Fair - (979) 865-5995
Belton - Ctrl Texas State Fair - (254) 933-5353
Big Spring - Howard Co. Fair - (915) 267-7210
Boerne - Kendall Co. Fair - (830) 249-2839
Bonham - Fannin Co. Fair - (903) 583-7453
Brenham - Washington Co. Fair - (979) 836-4112
Caldwell - Burleson Co. Fair - (979) 567-3938
Coldspring - San Jacinto Co. Fair - (936) 767-8156
Columbus - Colorado Co. Fair - (979) 732-9266
Conroe - Montgomery Co. Fair - (936) 760-3247
Cotulla - La Salle Co. Wildhog Cook-off & Fair - (830) 879-2852
Crosby - Crosby Fair & Rodeo - (281) 328-2113
Dallas - State Fair of Texas - (214) 565-9931
Denton - No. Texas State Fair & Rodeo - (940) 387-2632
El Paso - SW Int'l Livestock Show & Rodeo - (915) 532-1401
Elm Mott - Riesel Fair - (254) 829-2383

Ft. Worth - SW Expo. & Livestock Show - (817) 877-2400
Fredericksburg - Gillespie Co. Fair - (830) 997-2359
Giddings - Lee Co. Fair & Rodeo - (979) 542-3455
Glen Rose - Somervell Co. Rodeo - (254) 897-4509
Grand Prairie - (972) 647-2331
Greenville - Hunt Co. Fair - (903) 454-1503
Hearne - Robertson Co. Fair - (979) 828-4968
Hempstead - Waller Co. Fair - (979) 826-2825
Hitchcock - Galveston Co. Fair & Rodeo - (409) 986-6010
Hondo - Medina Co. Fair - (830) 426-5406
Houston - Harris Co. Fair - (281) 550-8432
Houston - Houston Livestock Show & Rodeo - (832) 667-1000
Humble - Humble Fair & Rodeo - (281) 641-8000
Huntsville - Walker Co. Fair - (936) 295-8760
Junction - Hill Country Fair - (915) 446-3757
Kerrville - Kerr Co. Fair - (830) 257-6833
Kountze - Hardin Co. Youth Fair - (409) 246-5128
La Grange - Fayette Co. Country Fair - (979) 968-3781
Lamesa - Dawson Co. Fair - (806) 872-3444
Laredo - Laredo Int'l Fair & Expo. - (956) 722-9948
Liberty - Trinity Valley Exposition - (936) 336-8168
Longview - Longview Jaycees Gregg Co. Fair & Expo - (903) 753-4478
Lubbock - Panhandle-South Plains Fair - (806) 763-2833
Mercedes - Rio Grande Valley Livestock Show - (956) 565-2456

Appendix B

Mount Pleasant - Titus Co. Fair - (903) 577-8117
Nacogdoches - Pineywood Fair - (936) 564-0849
Navasota - Grimes Co. Fair - (936) 825-2508
New Braunfels - Comal Co. Fair - (830) 609-2860
Odessa - Permian Basin Fair & Expo - (915) 550-3232
Paris - Red River Valley Fair - (903) 785-4485
Pasadena - Pasadena Rodeo - (281) 487-0240
Port Arthur - Cavoilcade - (409) 983-1009
Refugio - Refugio Co. Fair & PRCA Rodeo - (361) 526-1605
Rio Grande City - Starr Co. Youth Fair - (956) 487-2043
Rosenberg - Ft. Bend Co. Fair - (281) 342-6171
San Angelo - San Angelo Stock Show & Rodeo - (915) 653-5622
San Antonio - San Antonio Livestock Expo, Inc. - (210) 225-5851
Seguin - Guadalupe Co. Agricultural & Livestock Show - (830) 379-6477
Stamford - Texas Cowboy Reunion - (915) 773-3614
Tyler - East Texas State Fair - (903) 597-2501
Waco - Heart O' 'Texas Fair & Rodeo - (254) 776-16601
Wharton - Wharton Co. Youth Fair & Expo. - (979) 677-3350
Wichita Falls - Texas/Oklahoma Fair - (940) 716-5500

Utah

Beaver - Beaver Co. Fair - (435) 438-6450
Castle Dale - Emery Co. Fair - (435) 687-2403
Circleville - Piute Co. Fair & Butch Cassidy Days - (435) 577-2915
Coalville - Summit Co. Fair - (435) 336-3221
Delta - Millard Co. Fair - (435) 743-7909
Duchesne - Duchesne Co. Fair - (435) 738-1191
Farmington - Davis Co. Fair - (801) 451-4080
Heber City - Mountain Valley Fair Days at Heber City - (435) 654-1654
Hinckley - Millard Co. Fair - (435) 864-3660
Junction - Piute Co. Fair & Butch Cassidy Days - (435) 577-2029
Lehi - Lehi Round Up Rodeo & Celebration - (801) 768-7124
Lehi - Utah Co. Fair - (801) 768-4902
Loa - Wayne Co. Fair - (435) 836-2650
Logan - Cache Co. Fair & Rodeo - (435) 716-7150
Manti - Sanpete Co. Fair - (435) 835-1351
Minersville - Beaver Co. Fair - (435) 387-6009
Moab - Grand Co. Fair - (435) 259-5386
Monticello - San Juan Co. Fair & Blue Mountain Roundup Rodeo - (435) 587-3239
Morgan - Morgan Co. Fair & Rodeo - (801) 876-2505
Nephi - Juab Co. Fair - (435) 623-1460
Ogden - Weber Co. Fair - (800) 44-ARENA
Panguitch - Garfield Co. Fair - (435) 676-1160
Parowan - Iron Co. Fair - (435) 477-8380
Price - Carbon Co. Fair & Rodeo - (435) 636-3233
Randolph - Rich Co. Fair & Rodeo - (435) 793-3182
Richfield - Sevier Co. Fair - (435) 893-0457
Roosevelt - Uintah Basin in Celebration-UBIC - (435) 722-3411
St. George - Washington Co. Fair - (435) 673-9522
Salt Lake City - Utah State Fair - (801) 538-8400
South Jordan - Salt Lake Co. Fair - (801) 254-0106
Tooele - Tooele Co. Fair - (435) 843-2350
Tremonton - Box Elder Co. Fair & Rodeo - (435) 744-2600
Vernal - Uintah Co. Fair - (435) 789-1660

Vermont

Barton - Orleans Co. Fair - (802) 525-3555
Bondville - The Bondville Fair - (802) 297-1882
Bradford - Connecticut Valley Fair - (802) 222-5750
East Montpelier - Washington Co. Fair & Field Days - (802) 229-4851
Essex Junction - Champlain Valley Expo - (802) 878-5545
Guilford - Guilford Fair - (802) 254-2463
Highgate - Franklin Co. Field Days - (802) 868-2514
Johnson - Lamoille Co. Field Days - (802) 635-7113
Lyndonville - Caledonia Co. Fair - (802) 626-5917
New Haven - Addison Co. Fair & Field Days - (802) 545-2557
Pawlet - Vermont State Grange Fair - (802) 296-2118
Rutland - Vermont State Fair - (802) 775-5200

Appendix B

Springfield - Windsor Co. Agricultural Fair - (802) 885-2075
Tunbridge - Tunbridge World's Fair - (800) 889-5555

Whitingham - Deerfield Valley Farmer's Day
- (802) 368-9968

Virginia

Abingdon - Washington Co. Fair - (276) 628-3789
Amelia - Amelia Co. Fair - (804) 561-3655
Arlington - Arlington Co. Fair - (703) 920-4556
Berryville - Clarke Co. Fair - (540) 955-1947
Bland - Bland Co. Fair - (276) 688-4423
Castlewood - Russell Co. Fair & Horse Show
- (276) 762-2261
Charles City - Charles City Co. Fair - (804) 829-9241
Chase City - South Central Fair - (434) 372-4545
Chesterfield - Chesterfield Co. Fair - (804) 276-9298
Clintwood - Dickenson Co. Fair - (276) 679-1101
Courtland - Franklin-Southampton Co. Fair - (757) 562-3765
Danville - Harvest Fair of Hampton Road in Danville
- (804) 569-3225
Dublin - New River Valley Fair - (540) 674-1548
Farmville - Five Co. Fair - (434) 392-7002
Fredericksburg - Fredericksburg Agricultural Fair
- (540) 373-1294
Front Royal - Warren Co. Fair - (540) 635-5827
Gate City - Scott Co. Fair - (276) 386-9524
Gloucester - Gloucester Fair - (804) 693-2729
Hamilton - Loudoun Co. Fair - (703) 777-0373
Harrisonburg - Rockingham Co. Fair - (540) 434-0005
Isle of Wight - Isle of Wight Co. Fair - (757) 357-2291
Lexington - Rockbridge Regional Fair - (540) 463-6263
Louisa - Louisa Co. Agricultural Fair - (540) 967-5926
Lucketts - Lucketts Fair - (703) 771-5281
Luray - Page Valley Agricultural & Industrial Fair
- (540) 843-3247
Lynchburg - Fair by the James - (804) 569-3244
Madison - Madison Co. Fair - (540) 948-7073

Manassas - Prince William Co. Fair - (703) 368-0173
Mechanicsville - State Fair of Virginia - (804) 569-3200
Monterey - Highland Co. Fair - (540) 468-2550
North Garden - Albemarle Co. Fair, Inc. - (434) 293-6396
Orange - Orange Co. Fair - (540) 672-2271
Powhatan - Powhatan Co. Fair - (804) 598-9808
Quinton - New Kent Co. Fair - (804) 932-3573
Richmond - State Fair of Virginia - (804) 228-3200
Ringgold - Virginia Beach Pittsylvania Co. Fair
- (434) 822-6850
Rural Retreat - Wythe Co. Fair - (276) 686-5951
Ruther Glen - Caroline Co. Agricultural Fair
- (804) 448-3111
Salem - Salem Fair - (540) 375-4013
Saltville - Rich Valley Agricultural Fair - (276) 624-3263
Scottsville - James River Valley Fair - (434) 572-3586
South Boston - Halifax Co. Fair - (434) 572-3586
Stanardsville - Greene Co. Fair - (434) 985-3333
Stuart - Patrick Co. Agricultural Fair - (276) 694-4211
Tazewell - Tazewell Co. Fair - (276) 988-7541
Toano - James City Co. Fair - (757) 566-1367
Verona - Augusta Co. Fair - (540) 245-5627
Warrenton - Greater Shenandoah Valley Fair
- (540) 943-9336
Warsaw - Richmond Co. Fair - (804) 333-3420
Wilmington - Deerfield Valley Farmers' Day Exhibition
- (802) 464-6572
Winchester - Frederick Co. Fair - (540) 667-8739
Wise - Virginia-Kentucky Dist. Fair - (276) 679-2046
Woodstock - Shenandoah Co. Fair - (540) 459-3867

Washington

Asotin - Asotin Co. Fair - (509) 243-4101
Bremerton - Kitsap Co. Fair & Rodeo - (360) 337-5350
Cashmere - Chelan Co. Fair - (509) 782-3232
Castle Rock - Castle Rock Fair - (360) 274-8422

Chehalis - Lewis Co. Spring Youth Fair - (360) 748-0280
Chehalis - SW Washington Fair - (360) 736-6072
Cheney - West Plains Community Fair - (509) 926-2176
Colfax - Palouse Empire Fair - (509) 397-3753

Appendix B

Colville - Colville PRCA Rodeo - (509) 684-4849
Colville - NE Washington Fair - (509) 684-2585
Cusick - Pend Oreille Co. Fair - (509) 445-1367
Danville - Grand Forks & District Fall Fair
 - (250) 442-3817
Davenport - Lincoln Co. Fair - (509) 725-5161
Dayton - Columbia Co. Fair - (509) 382-2370
Deer Park - Deer Park Community Fair - (509) 276-2444
Ellensburg - Kittitas Co. Fair - (509) 962-7639
Elma - Grays Harbor Co. Fair - (360) 482-2651
Enumclaw - King Co. Fair - (206) 296-8888
Friday Harbor - San Juan Co. Fair - (360) 378-4310
Goldendale - Klickitat Co. Fair - (509) 773-3900
Graham - Pierce Co. Fair - (253) 847-4754
Grandview - Yakima Valley Fair & Rodeo - (509) 882-4111
Kalama - Kalama Community Fair - (360) 673-5323
Kennewick - Benton Franklin Fair - (509) 586-9211
Key Center - Key Peninsula Community Fair
 (253) 884-4FUN
Langley - Island Co. Fair - (360) 221-4677
Longview - Cowlitz Co. Fair - (360) 577-3121
Lynden – NW Washington Fair - (360) 354-4111
Menlo - Pacific Co. Fair - (360) 942-3713
Monroe - Evergreen State Fair - (360) 805-6700
Moses Lake - Grant Co. Fair - (509) 765-3581
Mount Vernon - Skagit Co. Fair - (360) 336-9453

Okanogan - Okanogan Co. Fair - (509) 422-1621
Olympia - Capital Lake Fair - (360) 943-7344
Olympia - Thurston Co. Fair - (360) 768-5453
Othello - Adams Co. Fair - (509) 488-2871
Pomeroy - Garfield Co. Fair - (509) 843-3631
Port Angeles - Clallam Co. Fair - (360) 417-2551
Port Townsend - Jefferson Co. Fair - (360) 385-1013
Puyallup - Puyallup Spring Fair - (253) 845-1771
Puyallup - Western Washington Fair - (253) 845-1771
Republic - Ferry Co. Fair - (509) 775-3146
Ridgefield - Clark Co. Fair - (360) 397-6180
Roy - Pierce Co. Fair - (253) 843-1173
Seattle - Fremont Fair - (206) 399-9565
Shelton - Mason Co. Fair - (360) 427-7789
Skamokawa - Wahkiakum Co. Fair - (360) 795-3480
Spokane - Spokane Co. Interstate Fair - (509) 477-1766
Stanwood - Stanwood-Camano Fair - (360) 629-4121
Stevenson - Skamania Co. Fair - (509) 427-5588
Valley - Valley Community Fair - (509) 937-2054
Walla Walla - Walla Walla Fair & Frontier Days
 - (509) 527-3247
Waterville - Waterville-North Ctrl. Washington
 - (509) 745-8480
Winlock - Winlock Washington State FFA Spring Fair
 - (360) 785-3883
Yakima - Ctrl. Washington State Fair - (509) 248-7160

West Virginia

Belington - Belington Community Fair - (304) 823-1025
Cottageville - Jackson Co. Jr. Fair - (304) 372-9292
Danville - Boone Co. Fair - (304) 369-2338
Daybrook - Clay District Fair - (304) 798-3495
Eleanor - Putnam Co. Fair - (304) 586-3451
Fairlea - The State Fair of West Virginia - (304) 645-1090
Fort Ashby - Mineral Co. Fair - (304) 298-3333
Grafton - Taylor Co. Fair - (304) 265-4155
Hurricane - Hurricane Volunteer Firefighter's Fair
 - (304) 562-5663
Lewisburg - Wirt Co. Fair - (304) 275-3915
Mannington - Mannington District Fair - (304) 986-2155
Martinsburg - Berkley Co. Youth Fair - (304) 263-5869
Matewan - Magnolia Fair - (304) 426-6621
Middlebourne - Tyler Co. Fair - (304) 758-2184
Milton - Cabell Co. Fair - (304) 743-4273

Mineral - Mineral Co. Fair - (304) 298-3712
Mineral Wells - West Virginia Interstate Fair & Expo.
 - (304) 489-1301
Morgantown - Monongalia Co. Fair - (304) 291-7201
Moundsville - Marshall Co. Fair - (304) 845-8659
New Martinsville - Westzel Co. Fair & Festival (Town
 & Country Days) - (304) 455-3907
Petersburg - Tri-Co. Cooperative Fair - (304) 538-2278
Philippi - Barbour Co. Fair - (304) 457-3254
Point Pleasant - Mason Co. Fair - (304) 675-5463
Reedsville - Valley District Fair - (304) 864-6741
Ripley - Mountain State Art & Craft Fair - (304) 372-8459
Rivesville - Paw Paw District Fair - (304) 278-7042
St. George - Tucker Co. Fair - (304) 478-3820
Spanishburg - Mercer Co.'s Bluestone Valley Fair
 - (304) 425-1429
Summersville - Nicholas Co. Fair - (304) 872-1454

Appendix B

Sutton - Braxton Co. Fair - (304) 765-3300
Wadestown - Battelle District Fair - (304) 662-6265
Wayne - Wayne Co. Fair - (304) 849-4632

West Union - Doddridge Co. Fair - (304) 782-3126
Weston - Lewis Co. Fair - (304) 269-1924
Wheeling - Ohio Co. Country Fair - (304) 234-3673

Wisconsin

Amherst - Portage Co. Fair - (715) 824-5674
Antigo - Langlade Co. Fair - (715) 627-2539
Arkansaw - Pepin Co. Fair - (715) 672-5214
Athens - Athens -Fair - (715) 257-7619
Baraboo - Sauk Co. Fair - (608) 356-8913
Beaver Dam - Dodge Co. Fair - (920) 885 3586
Black River Falls - Jackson Co. Fair - (715) 984-2576
Bloomington - Blakes Prairie Jr. Fair - (608) 994-2607
Cedarburg - Ozaukee Co. Fair - (262) 377-3030
Chilton - Calumet Co. Fair - (920) 849-9803
Chippewa Falls - No. Wisconsin State Fair - (715) 723-2861
Crandon - Forest Co. Fair - (715) 649-3269
Darlington - Lafayette Co. Fair - (608) 776-4828
DePere - Brown Co. Fair - (920) 336-7292
Eagle River - Vilas Co. Fair - (715) 479-2057
Elkhorn - Walworth Co. Fair - (262) 723-3228
Ellsworth - Pierce Co. Fair - (715) 273-3531
Elroy - Elroy Fair - (608) 562-3842
Florence - Florence Co. Fair - (715) 528-5521
Fond du Lac - Fabulous Fond du Lac Co. Fair - (920) 921-0921
Friendship - Adams Co. Fair - (608) 584-5301
Galesville - Trempealeau Co. Fair - (608) 582-2604
Gays Mills - Crawford Co. Fair - (608) 326-0224
Gillett - Oconto Co. Fair - (920) 855-6290
Glenwood City - St. Croix Co. Fair - (715) 246-5272
Grantsburg - Burnett Co. Fair - (715) 689-2195
Green Bay - Brown Co. Fair - (920) 864-2570
Green Lake - Green Lake Co. Fair - (920) 294-4032
Hayward - Sawyer Co. Fair - (715) 634-2485
Hurley - Iron Co. Fair - (715) 561-4824
Iron River - Bayfield Co. Fair - (715) 373-6104
Janesville - Rock Co. 4H Fair - (608) 755-1470
Jefferson - Jefferson Co. Fair - (920) 674-7479
Ladysmith - Rusk Co. Fair - (715) 532-2639
Lancaster - Grant Co. Fair - (608) 723-2135
Lodi - Lodi Agricultural fair - (608) 592-5746
Luxemburg - Kewaunee Co. Fair - (920) 845-2941

Madison - Dane Co. Fair - (608) 224-0500
Manitowoc - Manitowoc Co. Fair - (920) 683-4378
Marengo - Ashland Co. Fair - (715) 278-3430
Marshfield - Central Wisconsin State Fair - (715) 387-1261
Mauston - Juneau Co. Fair - (608) 562-3609
Medford - Taylor Co. Fair - (715) 748-2925
Menomonie - Dunn Co. Fair - (715) 235-3467
Merrill - Lincoln Co. 4H Fair - (715) 536-5212
Mineral Point - Iowa Co. Fair - (608) 987-3490
Mondovi - Buffalo Co. Fair - (608) 323-7298
Monroe - Green Co. Fair - (608) 862-3902
Neillsville - Clark Co. Fair - (715) 669-5925
Niagara - Florence Co. Fair - (715) 589-3291
Oconto - Oconto Co. Youth Fair - (920) 855-6577
Oshkosh - Winnebago Co. Fair - (920) 231-6002
Phillips - Price Co. Fair - (715) 339-3307
Plymouth - Sheboygan Co. Fair - (920) 893-5751
Portage - Columbia Co. Fair - (920) 348-5855
Rhinelander - Oneida Co. Fair - (715) 873-4052
Rice Lake - Barron Co. Fair - (715) 736-3247
Richland Center - Richland Co. Fair - (608) 647-6859
Rosholt - Rosholt Community Fair - (715) 677-4708
St. Croix Falls - Polk Co. Fair - (715) 268-9853
Sarona - Washburn Co. Fair - (715) 469-3217
Saxon - Iron Co. Fair - (715) 561-5780
Seymour - Outagamie Co. Fair - (920) 833-2941
Shawano - Shawano Co. Fair - (715) 526-5419
Spooner - Washburn Co. Fair - (715) 469-3217
Stoughton - Stoughton Jr. Fair - (608) 835-8550
Sturgeon Bay - Door Co. Fair - (920) 856-6546
Superior - Head of Lakes Fair - (715) 394-7848
Thorp - Clark Co. Fair - (715) 669-5925
Tomah - Monroe Co. Fair - (608) 269-5283
Union Grove - Racine Co. Fair - (262) 878-3895
Viroqua - Vernon Co. Fair - (608) 634-4064
Waukesha - Waukesha Co. Fair - (262) 544-5922
Wausau - Wisconsin Valley Fair - (715) 261-1539
Wausaukee - Marinette Co. Fair - (715) 735-1782

Appendix B

Wautoma - Waushara Co. Fair - (920) 787-0416
Webster - Central Burnett Co. Fair - (715) 468-2974
West Allis - Wisconsin State Fair - (800) 884-FAIR
West Bend - Washington Co. Fair - (262) 677-5060
West Salem - La Crosse Interstate Fair - (608) 788-5506
Westfield - Marquette Co. Fair - (608) 297-9153
Weyauwega - Waupaca Co. Fair - (920) 867-3395
Wilmot - Kenosha Co. Fair - (262) 843-2106

Wyoming

Afton - Lincoln Co. Fair - (307) 886-3941
Basin - Bighorn Co. Fair - (307) 568-2968
Big Penny - Sublette Co. Fair - (307) 276-5373
Casper - Ctrl. Wyoming Fair & Rodeo - (307) 235-5775
Cheyenne - Laramie Co. Fair - (307) 633-4534
Douglas - Wyoming State Fair & Rodeo - (307) 358-2398
Evanston - Uinta Co. Fair - (307) 783-0313
Gillette - Campbell Co. Fair - (307) 687-0200
Jackson - Teton Co. Fair - (307) 733-5289
Laramie - Albany Co. Fair - (370) 742-3224
Newcastle - Weston Co. Fair - (307) 746-9906
Powell - Park Co. Fair - (307) 754-5421
Rawlins - Carbon Co. Fair - (307) 324-6866
Riverton - Fremont Co. Fair - (307) 856-6611
Rock Springs - Wyoming's Big Show - (307) 352-6789
Sheridan - Sheridan Co. Fair - (307) 672-2079
Sundance - Crook Co. Fair - (307) 283-2644
Thermopolis - Hot Springs Co. Fair - (307) 864-2466
Torrington - Goshen Co. Fair - (307) 532-2525
Wheatland - Platte Co. Fair & Rodeo - (307) 322-9504
Worland - Washakie Co. Fair - (307) 347-8989

Appendix B

Appendix B

CANADIAN FAIR LISTINGS
(Province-by-Province)

Appendix B

Appendix B

Alberta

Calgary - Calgary Exhibition & Stampede - (403) 261-0101

Edmonton - Canadian Finals Rodeo - (780) 471-8795

Edmonton - Edmonton's Klondike Days & Expo.
- (888) 800-7275

Grande Prairie - Grande Prairie Regional Fair
- (780) 532-3279

Lethbridge - Whoop-Up Days Summer Fair & Rodeo
- (403) 328-4491

Medicine Hat - Medicine Hat Exhibition & Stampede
- (403) 527-1234

Olds - Mtn. View Co. Fair & Rodeo - (403) 556-3770

Oyen - Big Country Fair - (403) 664-3622

Ponoka - Ponoka Stampede - (403) 783-0100

Red Deer - Westerner Days Fair & Exposition - (403) 343-7800

Twin Butte - Pincher District Fair & Professional Rodeo
- (403) 627-4702

Vegreville - Vegreville Co. Fair - (780) 632-3950

Vermilion - Vermilion Fair - (780) 853-4108

Wanham - Alberta Provincial Plowing Match - (780) 694-3915

Westerose - Lakedell Country Fair - (780) 586-2505

British Columbia

Abbotsford - Abbotsford Agrifair - (604) 852-6674

Agassiz - Agassiz Fall Fair & Corn Festival - (604) 796-3246

Armstrong - Interior Provincial Exhibition - (250) 546-9406

Barriere - North Thompson Fall Fair & Rodeo
- (250) 672-5672

Burns Lake - Lakes District Fall Fair - (250) 692-2200

Coombs - Coombs Fair - (250) 752-8638

Courtenay - Comox Valley Exhibition - (250) 339-6942

Creston - Creston Valley Fall Fair - (250) 428-4316

Dawson Creek - Dawson Creek Exhibition - (250) 782-8911

Duncan - Cowichan Exhibition - (250) 748-0822

Fort St. John - North Peace Fall Fair - (250) 785-4758

Kamloops - Kamloops Provincial Winter Fair - (250) 314-9645

Lillooet - Lillooet & District Fall Fair - (250) 256-7827

Maple Ridge - Maple Ridge Fair - (604) 463-6922

McBride - Robson Valley Fall Fair - (250) 569-0321

Merritt - Nicola Valley Fall Fair - (250) 378-5925

Nanaimo - Vancouver Island Exhibition - (250) 758-3247

Peachland - Peachland Fall Fair - (250) 767-2218

Port Alberni - Alberni District Fall Fair - (250) 723-9313

Prince George - P.G.X.-Prince George Exhibition
- (250) 563-4096

Princeton - Princeton & District Fall Fair - (250) 295-7639

Quesnel - Quesnel Fall Fair - (250) 992-3666

Saanichton - Saanich Fair - (250) 652-3314

Salmon Arm - Salmon Arm & Shuswap Lake Agricultural Fair
- (250) 832-0442

Salt Spring Island - Salt Spring Fall Fair - (250) 537-4755

Salt Spring Island - Salt Spring Fall Fair - (250) 537-4755

Smithers - Bulkley Valley Exhibition - (250) 847-3816

Summerland - Summerland Fall Fair - (250) 494-6064

Sunset Prairie - Kiskatinaw Fall Fair - (250) 782-1807

Surrey - Cloverdale Rodeo & Exhibition - (604) 576-9461

Vancouver - The Fair at the Pacific National Exhibition
- (604) 253-2311

Victoria - Luxton Fair - (250) 478-6625

Manitoba

Brandon - Manitoba Summer Fair - (204) 726-3590

Brandon - Royal Manitoba Winter Fair - (204) 726-3590

Carman - Carman Country Fair - (204) 754-2226

Dauphin - Dauphin Fair & Exhibition - (204) 638-4428

Morris - Manitoba Stampede & Exhibition - (204) 746-2552

Portage La Prairie - Portage Industrial Exhibition
- (204) 857-3231

Roblin - Roblin Fair & Rodeo - (204) 937-2372

Selkirk - Selkirk Triple S Fair & Rodeo - (204) 738-2305

Swan River - Swan River Fair - (204) 734-3718

Westbourne - Gladstone Fair & Rodeo - (204) 385-2847

Winkler - Winkler (Stanley) Harvest Festival & Exhib.
- (204) 325-9758

Winnipeg - Red River Exhibition - (204) 888-6990

Appendix B

New Brunswick

Fredericton - Fredericton Exhibition - (506) 458-9819
Gagetown - Queens Co. Fair - (506) 488-2954
Grand Falls - Exposition Regional du Madawaska - (506) 473-7755
Miramichi - Miramichi Agricultural Exhibition - (506) 773-1989
Miramichi - Napan Agricultural Show - (506) 773-7411
Petitcodiac - Westmorland Co. Agricultural Fair - (506) 756-9003

Port Elgin - Port Elgin Agricultural Fair - (506) 538-2326
Riverside Albert - Albert Co. Fair - (506) 882-2306
St. John - Atlantic National Exhibition - (506) 633-2020
Stanley - Stanley Fair - (506) 367-2359
Ste Marie de Kent - Kent Co. Agricultural Fair - (506) 576-8922
Sussex - Kings Co. Agricultural Fair - (506) 433-2796
Taymouth - Kings Co. Agricultural Fair - (506) 367-2339

Nova Scotia

Antigonish - Eastern Nova Scotia Exhibition - (902) 863-2781
Bridgewater - South Shore Exhibition - (902) 543-3341
Halifax - Maritime Fall Fair - (902) 876-8214
Lawrencetown - Annapolis Valley Exhibition - (902) 584-3339
Middle Musquodoboit - Halifax Co. Exhibition - (902) 384-2894

Pictou - Pictou/North Colchester Exhibition - (902) 485-5391
Shelburne - Shelburne Co. Exhibition - (902) 875-3663
Truro - Nova Scotia Provincial Exhibition - (902) 893-9222
Windsor - Hants Co. Exhibition - (902) 798-0000
Yarmouth - Western Nova Scotia Exhibition - (902) 761-3104

Ontario

Acton - Acton Fall Fair - (519) 853-4699
Almonte - Middleville Agricultural Fair - (613) 256-1368
Ancaster - Ancaster Fair - (905) 648-6198
Annan - Sydenham Fair - (519) 376-1640
Arnprior - Arnprior Fair - (613) 622-0079
Arthur - Arthur Fall Fair - (519) 848-2742
Aylmer West - Aylmer Agricultural Fair - (519) 773-3445
Barrie - Barrie Fair & National Horse Show - (705) 737-3670
Bayfield - Bayfield Fall Fair - (519) 482-3020
Beachburg - Beachburg Fair - (613) 582-3841
Beamsville - Lincoln Co. Fair - (905) 309-4554
Beaverton - Beaverton Fair - (705) 426-9444
Beeton - Beeton Agricultural Fair - (705) 435-5867
Belleville - Quinte Exhibition - (613) 968-3266
Binbrook - Binbrook Fair - (905) 692-4003
Blackstock - Blackstock Agricultural Fair - (905) 986-0035
Bobcaygeon - Bobcaygeon Agricultural Fair - (705) 793-2466
Bolton - Bolton Fall Fair - (905) 857-4805
Bonfield - Bonfield Agricultural Fair - (705) 776-2452
Bracebridge - Bracebridge Agricultural Fair - (705) 645-4223

Brampton - Brampton Fall Fair - (905) 843-0210
Brantford - Burford Agricultural Fair - (519) 753-7242
Burford - Burford Agricultural Fair - (519) 753-7242
Brechin - Carden Agricultural Fair - (705) 833-2411
Bridgden - Bridgden Fair - (519) 864-1197
Brooklin - Brooklin Spring Fair - (905) 723-8602
Brussels - Brussels Fall Fair - (519) 887-2664
Burk's Falls - Burk's Falls Agricultural Fair - (705) 382-2167
Caledon - Caledon Fall Fair - (519) 941-6163
Caledonia - Caledonia Agricultural Fair - (905) 765-6861
Cambridge - Cambridge Fall Fair - (519) 621-9140
Campbellford - Campbellford Fair - (705) 632-1278
Carp - Carp Fair - (613) 839-2172
Cavan - Milbrook Fair - (705) 745-7322
Charlton - Charlton Agricultural Fair - (705) 544-8358
Chatsworth - Chatsworth Fair - (519) 794-2523
Chatsworth - Desboro Fair - (519) 794-3586
Chesley - Chesley Agricultural Fair - (519) 363-5742
Chesterville - Chesterville & District Agricultural Fair - (613) 448-3546
Clarksburg - Beaver Valley Agricultural Fair - (519) 599-5226

Appendix B

Clearview Township - Great Northern Exhibition - (705) 444-0308
Clinton - Clinton Spring Fair - (519) 482-7925
Cobden - Cobden Fair - (613) 646-2426
Cochrane - Cochrane Agricultural Fair - (705) 272-3964
Coe Hill - Coe Hill Agricultural Fair - (613) 337-5504
Coldwater - Coldwater Fall Fair - (705) 686-7847
Comber - Comber Agricultural Fair _ (519) 687-3607
Cookstown - Cookstown Agricultural Fair - (705) 458-1387
Delhi - Houghton Agricultural Fair - (519) 582-3661
Delta - Delta Fair - (613) 928-2800
Deseronto - Mohawk Fair - (613) 396-3800
Dobbington - Arran-Tara Fair - (519) 934-2357
Dorchester - Dorchester Fair - (519) 268-3544
Drayton - Drayton Fair - (519) 638-2449
Dresden - Dresden Exhibition - (519) 683-6194
Drumbo - Drumbo Agricultural Fair - (519) 463-5228
Dryden - Dryden & District Fall Fair - (807) 223-6766
Dunchurch - Dunchurch Agricultural Fair - (705) 389-2370
Dundalk - Dundalk Agricultural Fair - (519) 923-3051
Dungannon - Dungannon Agricultural Fair - (519) 529-3130
Dunnville - Dunnville Agricultural Fair - (905) 774-8199
Durham - Neustadt Agricultural Fair - (519) 369-5712
Dutton - Wallacetown Fair - (519) 762-3635
Echo Bay - North Shore Agricultural Fair - (705) 248-2800
Elmira - Elmira Fair - (519) 669-5351
Elmvale - Elmvale Agricultural Fair - (705) 322-1136
Embro - Embro & Zorra Fall Fair - (519) 462-2389
Emsdale - Emsdale Agricultural Fair - (705) 638-0058
Englehart - Englehart Fall Fair - (705) 544-8916
Erin - Erin Fall Fair - (519) 855-4682
Exeter - Exeter Fair - (519) 235-1284
Fenelon Falls - Fenelon Fair - (705) 887-1614
Feversham - Feversham Agricultural Fair - (519) 922-2792
Fordwich - Howick-Turnberry Agricultural Fair - (519) 335-3269
Forest - Forest & District Agricultural Fair - (519) 786-6062
Fournier - Riceville Fair - (613) 524-5284
Georgetown - Georgetown Fall Fair - (905) 873-6157
Glencoe - Glencoe Fair - (519) 287-5311
Gloucester - Gloucester Fair - 9613) 744-2671
Grand Valley - Grand Valley Agricultural Fair - (519) 928-5754
Guelph - Int'l Plowing Match & Machinery Show - (519) 767-2928
Hanover - Hanover Fair - (519) 364-5766
Harriston - Harriston-Minto Fair - (519) 338-3111
Harrow - Harrow Fair - (519) 738-3262

Hensall - Hensall Fair - (519) 262-2247
Highgate - Highgate Agricultural Fair - (519) 678-3997
Huntsville - Huntsville Fair - (705) 789-6284
Huntsville - Stisted Fair - (705) 789-6578
Ilderton - Ilderton Fair - (519) 666-0658
Indian River - Norwood Fair - (705) 639-5283
Ingersol - Embro Fair - (519) 485-0668
Inwood - Brooke, Alvinston & Watford Agricultural Fair - (541) 844-2325
Iriquois Falls - Porquis Fair - (705) 232-6600
Iron Bridge - Iron Bridge - Agricultural Fair - (705) 843-0425
Kakabeka Falls - Hymers Agricultural Fair - (807) 767-1087
Kenora - Kenora Agricultural Fair - (807) 548-5612
Kincardine - Kincardine Agricultural Fair - (519) 395-5160
Kingston - Kingston Agricultural Fair - (613) 542-6701
Kinmount - Kinmount Agricultural Fair - (705) 488-3182
Kirkton - Kirkton Agricultural Fair - (519) 229-8151
Lakefield - Lakefield Agricultural Fair - (705) 652-8213
Lansdowne - Lansdowne Fair - (613) 659-2399
Leamington - Leamington District Fair - (519) 326-8082
Lindsay - Lindsay Central Exhibition - (705) 324-5551
Listowel - Listowel Agricultural Fair - (519) 291-2776
Little Britain - Oakwood Agricultural Fair - (705) 786-2748
London - Western Fair - (519) 438-7203
Long Sault - Stormont Co. Agricultural Fair - (613) 936-9132
Lucknow - Lucknow Agricultural Fall Fair - (519) 528-3528
Maberly - Maberly Fair - (613) 268-2291
Madoc - Madoc Fair - (613) 473-2686
Manitowaning - Manitowaning Fall Fair - (705) 859-2691
Markdale - Markdale Agricultural Fair - (519) 986-4516
Markham - Markham Agricultural Fair - (905) 642-3247
Marmora - Marmora Fair - (613) 472-5403
Massey - Massey Agricultural Fair - (705) 865-2070
Merrickville - Merrickville Fair - (613) 838-1219
Maxville - Maxville Fair - (613) 527-5346
McDonalds Corners - McDonalds Corners Agricultural Fair - (613) 278-2362
McKellar - McKellar Agricultural Fair - (705) 389-2622
Meaford - Meaford & St. Vincent Fair - (519) 538-2173
Meaford - Rocklyn Agricultural Fair - (519) 538-1759
Melbourne - Melbourne Fair - (519) 438-7613
Metcalfe - Metcalfe Fair - (613) 821-0591
Mildmay - Mildmay-Carrick Agricultural Fair - (519) 367-5821
Milton - Milton Fall Fair - (905) 878-5689
Milverton - Milverton Agricultural Fair - (519) 595-8688
Minden - Haliburton County Fair - (705) 286-2270
Mindemoya - Providence Bay Agricultural Fair - (705) 377-4876

Appendix B

Mitchell - Mitchell Fair - (519) 345-2450
Mount Forest - Mount Forest Fall Fair - (519) 323-4622
Mountain Grove - Parham Fair - (613) 335-3221
Murillo - Murillo Fair - (807) 767-2365
Napanee - Napanee Agricultural Fair - (613) 354-3973
Navan - Navan Fair - (613) 835-2766
Neustadt - Neustadt Fair - (519) 799-5517
New Liskeard - New Liskeard Fair - (705) 647-8492
Norwood - Norwood Thanksgiving Fall Fair - (705) 639-5283
Ohsweken - Six Nations Agricultural Fair & Pow-Wow - (519) 445-0783
Orangeville - Orangeville Fair - (519) 942-9597
Orillia - Orilla Fall Fair - (705) 325-0353
Orillia - Ramona Agricultural Fair - (705) 325-8526
Oro Station - Oro World's Fair - (705) 487-2348
Orono - Durham Ctrl Agricultural Fair - (905) 983-9510
Ottawa - Avonmore Faire - (613) 741-4333
Ottawa - Central Canada Exhibition - (613) 237-7222
Ottawa - Gloucester Agricultural Fair - (613) 744-2671
Owen Sound - Owen Sound Agricultural Fair - (519) 371-1720
Paisley - Paisley Fall Fair - (519) 353-5559
Palmerston - Palmerston Agricultural Fair - (519) 343-5421
Parham - Parham Fair - (613) 374-1826
Paris - Paris Fall Fair - (519) 442-2823
Parkhill - Parkhill Fair - (519) 294-6684
Parry Sound - Foley Fair - (705) 378-2823
Perth - Perth Fair - (613) 267-4104
Peterborough - Peterborough Exhibition - (705) 742-5781
Petrolia - Petrolia & Enniskillen Fall Fair - (519) 844-2531
Picton - Prince Edward Co. Agricultural Fair - (613) 476-6154
Porquis Junction - Porquis Agricultural Fair - (705) 232-6600
Port Hope - Port Hope Fall Fair - (905) 885-8261
Port Perry - Port Perry Agricultural Fair - (905) 985-3819
Powassan - Powassan Agricultural Fair - (705) 724-6933
Ramore - Matheson & District Agricultural Fair - No #
Renfrew - Renfrew Fair - (613) 432-5331
Richmond - Richmond Fair - (613) 838-3420
Ridgetown - Ridgetown Agricultural Fair - (519) 678-3059
Ripley - Ripley Huron Agricultural Fair - (519) 395-5732
Rockton - Rockton World's Fair - (519) 647-2502
Rockwood - Fergus Fall Fair - (519) 856-9621
Rodney - Rodney-Aldborough Agricultural - (519) 768-1348
Roseneath - Roseneath Fall Fair - (905) 352-3778
Russell - Russell Fair - (613) 445-3079
St. Marys - St. Marys Agricultural - (519) 349-2740
Schomberg - Schomberg Agricultural Spring Fair - (905) 939-7761

Severn Bridge - Severn Bridge Agricultural Fair - (705) 689-6428
Shannonville - Shannonville Agricultural Fair - (613) 477-2254
Simcoe - Donnybrook Agricultural Fair - (519) 582-1708
Simcoe - Norfolk Co. Fair - (519) 426-7280
Smiths Falls - Lombardy Fair - (613) 284-2640
Smithville - Smithville Fair - (905) 957-6207
South Porcupine - Porcupine Agricultural Fair - (705) 235-3050
South River - South River-Machar Agricultural Fair - (705) 499-3148
Spencerville - Spencerville Agricultural Fair - (613) 658-3333
Staples - Comber Agricultural Fair - (519) 687-3607
Stayner - Stayner & District Community Fair - (705) 428-2280
Stirling - Stirling Agricultural Fair - (613) 395-5579
Stratford - Stratford Fall Fair - (877) 717-FAIR
Strathroy - Strathroy Agricultural Fair - (519) 245-2306
Sunderland - Sunderland Agricultural Fall Fair - (705) 432-8661
Sundridge - Strong Agricultural Fair - (705) 384-5450
Sutton West - Sutton Fair and Horse Show - (905) 722-3165
Tara - Arran-Tara Fair - (519) 934-2357
Tavistock - Tavistock Agricultural Fair - (519) 655-2691
Teeswater - Teeswater Fair - (519) 357-2365
Thorndale - Thorndale Fall Fair - (519) 461-1936
Thunder Bay - Summer Fair at Canadian Lakehead Exhibition - (519) 842-5964
Tilsonburg - Tilsonburg Tri-Co. Agricultural Fair - (807) 622-6473
Timmins - Porcupine District Fair - (705) 268-5994
Toronto - Canadian National Exhibition - (416) 263-3800
Toronto - The Royal Agricultural Winter Fair - (416) 263-3400
Trout Creek - Trout Creek Agricultural Fair - (705) 723-5564
Tweed - Tweed Fair - (613) 478-3903
Uxbridge - Uxbridge Fair - (905) 852-7003
Vankleek Hill - Vankleek Hill Agricultural Fair - (613) 527-2822
Walkerton - Hanover Fair - (519) 881-3341
Walkerton - Walkerton Little Royal Fair - (519) 881-3413
Warkworth - Warkworth Agricultural Fair - (705) 924-2561
Washago - Severn Bridge Fair - (705) 689-6428
Welland - Niagara Regional Agricultural Fair - (905) 735-6413
Wiarton - Wiarton & District Agricultural Fair - (519) 534-0283
Wilberforce - Wilberforce Agricultural Fair Society - (705) 448-2683
Woodbridge - Woodbridge Fall Fair - (905) 265-1782
Woodstock - Woodstock Fair - (519) 537-8212
Wyoming - Wyoming Fair - (519) 845-0150
Yarker - Centreville Agricultural Fair - (613) 358-2282

Appendix B

Prince Edward Island

Charlottetown - Old Home Week - (902) 629-6623

Crapaud - Crapaud Exhibition - (902) 658-2787

Dundas - PEI Plowing Match & Agricultural Fair (902) 583-2340

Souris - Ea. Kings Exhibition - (902) 687-3284

Strachcona - PEI Plowing Match & Agricultural Fair - (902) 583-2113

Quebec

Amqui - Exposition Agricole de la Vallee - (418) 629-4542

Ayer's Cliff - Stanstead Exposition - (819) 876-73117

Bedford - Bedford Fair - (450) 248-2817

Berthierville - Expo Agricole de Berthierville - (450) 836-6667

Brome - Brome Fair - (450) 242-3976

Cookshire - Cookshire Fair - (819) 875-3771

Lachute - Expo Lachute Fair - (450) 562-3741

Montmagny - Montmagny Fair - (418) 248-3418

Ogden - Ayer's Cliff Exposition - (819) 876-7317

Ormstown - Ormstown Fair - (450) 829-2776

Quebec - Expo Quebec - (418) 691-7110

Richmond - Richmond Fair - (819) 826-3198

Rimouski - Exposition Regionale de Rimouski - (418) 723-1666

St. Agaoit - Lotbiniere Exposition - (418) 888-4628

St. Bruno De Guigues - Temiscaminque Fair - (819) 629-6214

St. Felicien - St. Felicien Fair - (418) 679-4554

St. Giles - Lotbinere - (418) 596-2688

St. Honore de Shenley - Beauce Fair (418) 485-6507

St. Hyacinthe - St. Hyacinthe Fair - (450) 773-9307

Shawville - Shawville Fair - (819) 647-3213

St. Marc des Carrieres - Portneuf Fair - (418) 285-0086

Trois-Rivieres - Quebec Center Fair - (819) 374-2714

Saskatchewan

Abernathy - Abernathy Agricultural Fair - (306) 333-4407

Alameda - Alameda Agricultural Society Summer Fair - (306) 489-4415

Arcola - Arcola Fair & Stampede - (306) 455-2375

Biggar - Biggar Rodeo - (306) 948-3672

Broadview - Broadview Fall Fair - (306) 696-2884

Central Butte - Central Butte District Agricultural Fair - (306) 796-2193

Churchbridge - Churchbridge Agricultural Summer Fair - (306) 896-2988

Coronach - Coronach Agricultural Fair - (306) 267-6034

Creelman - Creelman Summer Fair - (306) 722-3505

Denzil - Denzil Fall Fair - (306) 358-2067

Elstow - Elstow Celebration - (306) 257-3674

Estevan - Estevan Pro Rodeo - (306) 634-5595

Glenavon - Glenavon Fair & Sports Day - (306) 698-2776

Hanley - Hanley & Dist Agricultural Fair - (306) 544-2566

Invermay - Invermay Fair - (306) 593-4557

Kelliher - Parkland Agricultural Society Fair - (306) 675-6100

Kelvington - Kelvington Fair - (306) 327-4206

Lloydminster - Colonial Days - (306) 825-5571

Maryfield - Maryfield Summer Fair - (306) 646-4505

Melfort - Melfort Fair - (306) 752-2240

Melville - Melville Fair & Rodeo - (306) 728-5277

Moose Jaw - Moose Jaw Hometown Fair - (306) 692-2723

Moosomin - Fairmede Agricultural Fair - (306) 435-3512

Nipawin - Nipawin Exhibition - (306) 862-4080

North Battleford - NW Territorial Days - (306) 445-2024

Perdue - Perdue Fair - (306) 237-4737

Prince Albert - Prince Albert Summer Fair - (306) 764-1712

Redvers - Redvers Community Fair - (306) 452-3766

Regina - Buffalo Days - (306) 781-9200

Rosthern - Rosthern Town & Country Fair - (306) 232-4661

St. Walburg - St. Walburg Agricultural Fair Days - (306) 248-3778

Saskatoon - Saskatoon Exhibition - (306) 931-7149

Silver Stream - Connaught Fair - (306) 873-5224

Appendix B

Swift Current - Frontier Days Regional Fair & Pro Rodeo - (306) 773-2944

Tisdale - Connaught Agricultural Society Fair - (306) 873-4860

Vanscoy - Vanscoy & District Annual Summer Fair - (306) 978-4481

Turtleford - Turtleford Agricultural Fair - (306) 845-2482

Unity - Unity Fall Fair - (306) 228-3935

Weyburn - Weyburn Fair & Exhibition - (306) 842-4052

Yorkton - Yorkton Exhibition Summer Fair - (306) 783-4800

Appendix B

U.S. FESTIVAL LISTINGS
(State-by-State)

Appendix B

Appendix B

Alabama

Arab - Poke Salat Festival - (256) 586-9913

Birmingham - City Stages, A Birmingham Festival - (205) 251-1272

Calvert - Mowa Choctaw Annual Powwow - (251) 829-5500

Childersburg - DeSoto Caverns Park Indian Dance Festival - (800) 933-2283

Childersburg - Desoto Caverns Park Fall Indian Dance & Crafts Festival - (800) 933-2283

Danville - Lawrence Co. Indian Festival - (256) 905-2494

Decatur - Rocking Horse Spring & World Celebration - (256) 353-7225

Florence - Alabama Renaissance Faire - (256) 768-3031

Florence - W.C. Handy Music Festival - (256) 766-7642

Gadsden - Gadsden Area Riverfest - (256) 543-3472

Greenville - Watermelon Jubilee Arts & Crafts Festival - (334) 382-2174

Gulf Shores - National Shrimp Festival - (251) 968-6904

Mobile - Bayfest - (251) 208-7835

Mobile - Festival of Flowers - (251) 639-2050

Mobile - Mardi Gras - (251) 208-2018

Montgomery - Jubilee CityFest - (334) 834-7220

Mount Vernon - Choctaw Indian Pow-Wow - (251) 829-5500

Muscle Shoals - Songfest International Music - (800) 941-6762

Oneonta - Covered Bridge Festival - (205) 274-2153

Springville - Homestead Hollow Spring Festival - (205) 836-8483

Springville - Homestead Hollow Harvest Festival - (205) 836-8483

Stevenson - Stevenson Depot Days - (256) 437-3012

Alaska

Anchorage - Anchorage Fur Rendezvous - (907) 274-1177

Cordova - Cooper River Delta Shorebird Festival - (907) 424-7260

Eagle River - Bear Paw Festival - (907) 694-4702

Fairbanks - Festival of the Native Arts - (907) 474-6889

Fairbanks - Golden Days - (907) 452-1105

Girdwood - Aleyska Resort Winterfest - (907) 754-2219

Girdwood - Aleyska Spring Carnival - (907) 754-1111

Homer - Kachemak Bay Shorebird Festival - (907) 235-7740

Juneau - Juneau Jazz & Classics - (907) 463-3378

Ketchikan - The Blueberry Arts Festival - (907) 225-2211

Ketchikan - Fourth of July Celebration - (907) 225-3184

Ketchikan - The Winter Arts Faire - (907) 225-2211

Kodiak - Koniag's Kodiak Crab Festival - (907) 486-5557

North Pole - Winter Festival - (907) 488-2242

Palmer - Colony Christmas - (907) 745-2880

Palmer - Colony Days - (907) 745-2880

Petersburg - Fourth of July Community Celebration - (907) 772-3646

Petersburg - Little Norway Festival - (907) 772-3646

Seward - Seward Polar Bear Jump-Off Festival - (907) 224-4049

Soldotna - Soldotna Progress Days - (907) 262-9814

Arizona

Apache Junction - Arizona Renaissance Festival - (520) 463-2600

Chandler - Ostrich Festival - (480) 963-4571

Flagstaff - Flagstaff Wool Festival - (928) 774-6272

Flagstaff - Independence Day Festival - (928) 774-6272

Glendale - Glendale Jazz & Blues Festival - (623) 930-2963

Glendale - Glendale World Music Festival - (623) 930-2963

Glendale - Thunderbird Balloon Classic - (602) 978-7330

Holbrook - Old West Days - (928) 524-6407

Kingman - Arizona's Route 66 Fun Run - (928) 753-5001

Peoria - San Gennaro Fair/Area Street Fair - (702) 286-4944

Phoenix - Devonshire Renaissance Faire - (602) 246-2125

Phoenix - Latino Book & Family Festival-Phoenix - (760) 434-0798

Pinetop - White Mountain Bluegrass Music Festival - (928) 367-4290

Appendix B

Prescott - Fall Fest in the Park - (928) 445-2000
Prescott - Faire On The Square - (928) 778-1926
Prescott - Territorial Days - (928) 778-2193
Sedona - Sedona Jazz on the Rocks Festival - (928) 282-1985
Snowflake - Pioneer Days Celebration - (928) 536-4331
Taylor - Sweet Corn Festival - (928) 536-7366
Tempe - Tempe Fall Festival of the Arts - (480) 967-4877
Tempe - Tempe Spring Festival of the Arts - (480) 967-4877
Tucson - La Fiesta De Los Chiles - (520) 326-9686
Tucson - La Fiesta De Los Vaqueros (Tucson Rodeo) - (520) 294-8896
Tucson - Trail Dust Days - (520) 296-4551
Tucson - Tucson Celtic Festival & Scottish Highland Games - (520) 888-1058
Wickenburg - Gold Rush Days - (928) 684-5479
Williams - Rendezvous Days - (928) 635-1418
Yuma - Yuma Co. Fair Fourth of July Celebration - (928) 726-4420

Arkansas

Altus - Altus Autumn Fest - (479) 468-4684
Altus - Altus Grape Fest - (479) 468-4624
Altus - Altus Springtime Gala - (479) 468-4191
Banks - Buck Fever Festival - (870) 465-2217
Batesville - Arkansas Scottish Festival - (870) 698-4382
Batesville - White River Carnival - (870) 793-2378
Booneville - July 4th Celebration & Fireworks Display - (479) 675-2666
Cave City - Watermelon Festival - (870) 283-5959
Clarksville - Johnson Co. Peach Festival - (479) 754-9152
Conway - Toad Suck Daze - (501) 327-7788
Dardanelle - Free State of Yell Fest - (479) 229-3328
Dardanelle - Mount Nebo Chicken Fry - (479) 229-3328
Dermott - Crawfish Festival - (870) 538-5656
Dierks - Pine Tree Festival - (870) 286-2131
Dumas - Ding Dong Daddy Days - (870) 382-5447
El Dorado - Fantastic Fourth Celebration - (870) 863-6113
El Dorado - MusicFest El Dorado - (870) 862-4747
Eureka Springs - Eureka Springs Jazz Festival - (479) 253-6258
Eureka Springs - Original Ozark Folk Festival - (479) 253-7788
Fairfield Bay - Oktoberfest - (501) 884-3324
Felsenthal - Felsenthal Bream Festival - (870) 862-6508
Fordyce - Fordyce on the Cotton Belt Festival - (870) 352-3520
Fort Smith - Oktoberfest - (479) 785-1231
Fort Smith - Riverton Blues & American Music Festival - (479) 785-0115
Fountain Hill - Frontier Days Festival - (870) 853-5201
Glenwood - Caddo River Sawmill Days - (870) 356-3947
Hampton - Hogskin - Holidays - (870) 798-2100
Harrisburg - Homestead Festival - (870) 578-9251
Harrison - Crawdad Days Music Festival - (870) 741-2659
Harrison - NW Arkansas Bluegrass Festival - (870) 427-3342
Heber Springs - Old Soldiers Reunion - (501) 362-5802
Heber Springs - Ozark Trout Festival - (501) 362-2444
Heber Springs - Springfest Festival - (501) 362-2444
Helena - King Biscuit Blues Festival - (870) 338-8798
Hope - Hope Watermelon Festival - (870) 777-3640
Horseshoe Bend - Dogwood Days - (870) 670-5433
Hot Springs - Hot Springs Arts & Crafts Fair - (501) 623-5756
Lakeview - Troutfest - (870) 431-5521
Lincoln - Arkansas Apple Festival - (479) 824-FEST
Little Rock - Greek Food Festival - (501) 664-6290
Little Rock - Riverfest - (501) 255-3378
Magnolia - Magnolia Blossom Festival - (870) 234-4352
Malvern - Brickfest - (501) 332-2721
Mammoth Springs - Old Soldiers Reunion - (870) 625-7364
Marianna - Autumn on the Square - (870) 295-2439
Marion - Esperanza Bonanza Festival - (870) 739-4421
Maynard - Maynard Pioneer Days - (870) 647-2701
Maynard - Old Folks Singing Days - (870) 647-2701
Mena - Quachita Heritage Days - (479) 394-2912
Morrilton - Great Arkansas Pig-Out Festival - (501) 354-2393
Mountain View - Arkansas Beanfest & Championship
Outhouse Race - (870) 269-8068
Mountain View - Arkansas Folk Festival - (870) 269-8068
Mountain View - Old Time Gathering on the Square & 4th of July Celebration - (870) 269-8068
Newport - Portfest Rollin' on the River - (870) 523-3618
Paragould - Caboose Festival - (870) 240-0544
Paris - Old Fashioned Independence Day - (479) 963-3936
Pocahontas - Fourth on the Black Festival - (870) 892-3924
Prairie Grove - Clothesline Fair - (479) 846-2990
Prescott - Chicken & the Egg Festival - (870) 887-2101
Rector - Labor Day Weekend Celebration - (870) 595-3551

Appendix B

Salem - Fulton Co. Homecoming Festival - (870) 895-3217
Sheridan - Timberfest - (870) 942-3021
Stephens - Deer Dog Festival - (870) 596-2634
Stuttgart - Grand Prairie Festival of the Arts - (870) 673-1781
Tonitown - Tonitown Grape Festival - (479) 361-2615
Trumann - Wild Duck Festival - (870) 483-5424
Tuckerman - Hometown Days - (870) 349-5380
Warren - Bradley Co. Pink Tomato Festival - (870) 226-5225
Washington - Jonquil Festival - (870) 983-2684

California

Anderson - Shasta Highlands Renaissance & Celtic Faire - (530) 246-2834
Angels Camp - Calaveras Celtic Festival - (209) 588-9314
Angels Camp - Mark Twain Days - (209) 754-3521
Antioch - Delta Blues Festival - No #
Aptos - Santa Cruz Blues Festival - (831) 426-8435
Avalon - Catalina Island Jazz Trax Festival - (818) 346-4063
Barstow - Calico Days - (800) TOCALICO
Barstow - Spring Festival - (760) 254-2122
Bishop - Millpond Festival - (760) 873-8014
Borrego Springs - Borrego Days - (760) 767-5555
Borrego Springs - Borrego Springs Grapefruit Festival - (760) 767-5555
Borrego Springs - Cinco de Mayo Fiesta - (800) 559-5524
Brentwood - Brentwood ComFest - (925) 634-7789
Bridgeport - Bridgeport 4th of July Celebration - (760) 932-7500
Calexico - Mariachi Festival - (760) 357-1166
Camp Mather - Strawberry Music Festival - (209) 553-0191
Carlsbad - Del Mar Renaissance Festival - (760) 434-3499
Castroville - Castroville Artichoke Festival - (831) 633-2465
Coalinga - Horned Toad Derby - (800) 854-3885
Corning - Olive City Festival - (530) 824-5550
Corona - European Renaissance Festival - (909) 735-0101
Corona - Palm Springs Renaissance Festival - (909) 735-0101
Devore - Renaissance Pleasure Faire (Southern California) - (909) 880-0122
Eureka - Rhododendron Festival - (707) 442-3738
Fair Oaks - Fair Oaks - Fair Oaks Renaissance Tudor Fayre - (916) 965-8463
Folsom - Folsom Renaissance Faire & Tournament - (916) 355-7285
Fremont - Fremont Festival of the Arts - (510) 795-2244
Fresno - Fresno City College Renaissance Faire - (559) 226-5341
Fresno - St. Paul Newman Center Renaissance Festival - (559) 436-3434
Gilroy - Gilroy Garlic Festival - (408) 842-1625

Graeagle - Mohawk Valley Independence Day Celebration - (530) 832-5444
Grass Valley - California Worldfest - (530) 891-4098
Grass Valley - Country Christmas Fair - (530) 273-6217
Guerneville - Jazz on the River - (510) 655-9471
Guerneville - Russian River Blues Festival - (510) 655-9471
Hanford - Renaissance of tKings Cultural Arts Faire - (559) 585-2525
Hayward - Hayward Zucchini Festival - (510) 264-9466
Hollister - Renaissance Pleasure Faire (Northern California) - (408) 846-6446
Inland Empire - Latino Book & Family Festival-Inland Empire - (760) 434-0798
Isleton - Isleton Crawdad Festival - (916) 777-5880
Kernville - Whiskey Flat Days - (760) 376-2629
La Canada Flintridge - Holiday Festival at Descanso Gardens - (818) 949-4200
La Canada Flintridge - Pumpkin Festival at Descanso Gardens - (818) 949-4200
La Canada Flintridge - Spring Festival - (818) 949-4200
Laguna Beach - Sawdust Art Festival's Winter Fantasy - (949) 494-3030
Lancaster - California Poppy Festival - (661) 723-0685
Lodi - Lodi Wine & Sausage Festival - (209) 810-5230
Long Beach - Long Beach Bayou Festival - (562) 427-3713
Long Beach - Long Beach Blues Festival - (562) 985-5566
Long Beach - Queen Mary Scottish Festival - (562) 499-1650
Long Beach - Grecian Festival by the Sea - (714) 220-0730
Loomis - Loomis Eggplant Festival - (916) 652-7252
Los Angeles - Fiesta Broadway - (310) 914-0015
Los Angeles - Latino Book & Family Festival - Los Angeles - (760) 434-0798
Mendocino - Mendocino Music Festival - (707) 937-2044
Monterey - Monterey Jazz Festival - (831) 373-3366
Morro Bay - Morro Bay Harbor Festival - (805) 772-1155
Mount Shasta - Fourth of July Celebration - (530) 926-6004
Newman - Newman Fall Festival - (209) 862-3612
Novato - Heart of the Forest Renaissance Faire - (415) 897-4555

Appendix B

Oakhurst - Okhurst Fall Festival - (559) 683-7766
Oakhurst - Oakhurst Mtn. Peddler's Fair - (559) 683-7766
Orangevale - Orangevale Pow Wow Days - (916) 988-0175
Palmdale - Palmdale Fall Festival - (661) 267-5611
Patterson - Patterson Apricot Fiesta - (209) 892-3118
Petaluma - Petaluma Summer Music Festival - (707) 763-8920
Piercy - Reggae on the River - (707) 923-4599
Placerville - El Dorado Co. Harvest Fair - (530) 621-5520
Porterville - Dutch Oven Cook Off - (559) 784-3775
Portola - Feather River Railroad Days Festival - (530) 832-4216
Quincy - High Sierra Music Festival - (510) 420-1529
Rancho Cucamonga - Rancho Cucamonga Grape Harvest Festival - (909) 987-1012
Ridgecrest - High Desert Spring Festival (760) 375-8000
Riverside - Stater Bros. Riverside Orange Blossom Festival - (909) 715-3400
Sacramento - Gold Rush Days - (800) 292-2334
Sacramento - Sacramento Jazz Jubilee - (916) 327-5277
San Bernardino - Renaissance Pleasure Faire - (909) 880-6211
San Bernardino - Route 66 Rendezvous - (909) 889-3980
San Clemente - San Clemente Fiesta Street Festival - (949) 492-1131
San Diego - Latino Book & Family Festival-San Diego - (760) 434-0798
San Diego - Thunderboat Regatta - (619) 225-9160
San Francisco - Cherry Blossom Festival - (415) 563-2313
San Francisco - North Beach Festival - (415) 989-2220
San Francisco - San Francisco Blues Festival - (415) 447-1241
San Jose - Hoi He Summer Festival - (408) 294-3247
San Jose - Hoi Tet Festival-Vietnamese New Year - (408) 294-3247
San Jose - San Jose - American Festival - (888) 726-5673
San Jose - San Jose Jazz Festival - (831) 457-1141
San Luis Obispo - Central Coast Renaissance Festival - (800) 688-1477
San Luis Obispo - San Luis Obispo Mozart Festival - (805) 781-3008

Sanger - Sanger Harvest Fest - (559) 875-4575
Santa Barbara - Santa Barbara Renaissance Faire & Midsummer Market - (805) 925- 8824
Santa Maria - Santa Maria Valley Strawberry Festival - (805) 692-6722
Santa Rosa - Health & Harmony Music & Arts Festival - (707) 575-9355
Santa Rosa - Spirit of the Holidays Gift Faire - (707) 861-2035
Sausalito - Sausalito Art Festival - (415) 332-3555
Seaside - Monterey Bay Blues Festival - (831) 394-2652
Sebastopol - Sebastopol Celtic Festival - (707) 829-7067
Selma - Selma Raisin Festival - (559) 896-3315
Shaftner - Mayfest - (661) 746-2600
Solvang - Taste of Solvang - (805) 688-6144
South Gate - Azalea Festival - (323) 563-5443
Stanford - Stanford Powwow - (650) 723-4078
Stockton - Stockton Asparagus Festival - (209) 644-3740
Taft - Boom Town Days - (661) 765-2165
Tahoe City - Snowfest - (530) 581-1283
Tehachapi - Tehachapi Mountain Festival & P.R.C.A. Rodeo - (661) 822-4180
Temecula - Temecula Valley Balloon & Wine Festival - (951) 676-6731
Thousand Oaks - Ojai Renaissance Faire & Shakespeare By The Lake- (805) 496-6036
Tracy - California Dry Bean Festival - (209) 835-2131
Victoville - Huck Finn's Jubilee - (909) 780-8810
Visalia - Tulare Co. Renaissance Festival - (559) 688-0540
Walnut Creek - Walnut Festival - (925) 935-6766
Weaverville - Independence 4th of July Celebration - (530) 623-3215
Yermo - Calico Civil War - (760) 254-2122
Yermo - Calico Ghost Haunt - (760) 254-2122
Yermo - Calico Heritage Fest - (760) 254-2122
Yuba City - California Dried Plum Festival - (530) 671-3100
Yucca Valley - Grubstake - Days - (760) 365-6323

Colorado

Aspen - Jazz Aspen Snomass - (970) 704-9312
Boulder - Boulder Creek Festival - (303) 449-3825
Breckenridge - Breckenridge Music Festival - (970) 453-2120
Breckenridge - Breckenridge Int'l Snow Sculpture Championships - (970) 453-2913
Breckenridge - Ullr Fest - (970) 453-2913

Castle Rock - Colorado Renaissance Faire - (303) 688-6010
Central City - Madam Lou Bunch Festival - (303) 580-5251
Colorado Springs - Colorado Springs Balloon Classic - (719) 471-4833
Crested Butte - Crested Butte Wildflower Festival - (970) 349-2571

Appendix B

Denver - American Red Cross Fat Tire Classic
- (303) 722-7474

Denver - Cinco de Mayo "Celebrate Culture" Festival
- (303) 534-8342

Denver - Festival of Mtn. & Plain/A Taste of Colorado
- (303) 295-6300

Denver - Oktoberfest on Larimer Square - (303) 534-2367

Durango - Animas River Days Whitewater Festival
- (800) 426-7637

Estes Park - Long Peaks Scottish/Irish Festival
- (970) 586-6308

Fort Collins - NewWest Fest - (970) 224-FEST

Fruita - Fruita Fall Festival - (970) 858-3894

Glenwood Springs - Strawberry Days Festival
- (970) 945-6589

Grand Junction - Country Jam USA-Colorado
- (800) 530-3020

Grand Junction - Grand Valley Renaissance Faire
- (970) 523-7841

Lamar - Sand & Sage Roundup - (719) 336-7734

Las Animas - Bent Co. Harvest Show - (719) 456-0764

Littleton - Western Welcome Week - (303) 794-4870

Lyons - Rocky Mountain Bluegrass Festival-Rocky Grass
- (800) 624-2422

Mack - Country Jam USA-Colorado - (715) 839-7500

Mack - Rock Jam - (715) 839-7500

Meeker - Range Call Celebration - (970) 878-5510

Nederland - NedFest - (303) 415-5665

Olathe - Olathe Sweet Corn Festival - (970) 323-6006

Ordway - Crowley Co. Days - (719) 267-3134

Pagosa Springs - Four Corners Folk Festival - (971) 731-5582

Pueblo - Sand & Sage Round up - (719) 336-7734

Silverton - Great Western Rocky Mtn. Brass Band Festival
- (970) 325-4080

Telluride - Telluride Blues and Brews Festival
- (970) 728-8037

Telluride - Telluride Bluegrass Festival - (800) 624-2422

Telluride - Telluride Jazz Celebration - (970) 728-7009

Telluride - Telluride Wine Festival - (970) 728-3178

Trinidad - Trinidad Roundup & Rodeo - (719) 846-7921

Connecticut

Branford - Branford Festival - (203) 488-1255

Bristol - Bristol Chrysanthemum Festival - (860) 584-4718

East Norwalk - Norwalk Seaport Assn. Oyster Festival
- (203) 838-9444

Enfield - Enfield July 4th Celebration - (860) 537-0566

Guilford - The Great Connecticut Jazz Fest - (203) 562-3378

Hartford - Hartford Festival of Jazz - (866) 943-JAZZ

Litchfield - A Taste of Litchfield Hills - (860) 738-3801

Mystic - Mystic Seaport Lobsterfest - (860) 572-0711

Mystic - Sea Music Festival - (888) 9SEAPORT

Mystic - Taste of Conn. Food Festival - (860) 536-3575

New Haven - St. Andrews Italian Feast - (203) 776-0693

New London - Sailfest - (860) 444-1879

Preston - Cajun & Zydeco Blast from the Bayou
- (860) 886-1944

Putnam - The Connecticut Renaissance Faire
- (860) 928-0600

Simsbury - Septemberfest - (860) 651-7307

Uncasville - Pillar Polkabration - (860) 848-8171

West Hartford - Apple Harvest Festival - (860) 920-5330

West Hartford - Taste of Hartford - (860) 920-5330

West Hartford - Elizabeth Park Rose Weekend
- (860) 231-9443

Delaware

Bridgeville - Bridgeville Apple-Scrapple Festival
- (302) 337-7135

Dewey Beach - Dewey Beach Music Conference & Festival
- (717) 234-4342

Dover - Old Dover Days - (302) 724-1736

Millsboro - World Championship Punkin Chunkin
(302) 684-8196

Milton - LambJam - (302) 337-7876

Newark - Oktoberfest - (302) 366-9495

Rehoboth - World Championship Punkin' Chunkin'
- (302) 945-9062

Rehoboth Beach - Sea Witch Halloween & Fiddler's
Festival - (302) 227-2233

Wilmington - Clifford Brown Jazz Festival - (302) 567-2100

Wilmington - Greek Festival - (302) 654-4447

Appendix B

Wilmington - Riverfront Blues Festival - (320) 576-2100
Wilmington - St. Anthony's Italian Festival - (302) 888-4600

Wintethur - The Craft Festival at Wintethur - (302) 888-4600

District of Columbia

Washington - National Cherry Blossom Festival
- (202) 547-1500

Washington - Saints Constantine & Helen Greek
- (202) 829-2910

Florida

Boca Raton - Boca Festival Days - (561) 395-4433
Bradenton - De Soto SeaFood Fest - (941) 747-1998
Bradenton - Florida Heritage Festival - (941) 747-1998
Clearwater - Clearwater Jazz Holiday - (727) 461-5200
Cocoa - Cocoa Village Mardi Gras - (321) 633-4028
Cocoa - Cocoa Village Oktoberfest & Street Party
- (321) 633-4028
Coconut Grove - The Italian Renaissance Festival
- (305) 758-4595
Coconut Grove - Miami / Bahamas Goombay Festival
- (305) 372-9966
Crestview - Crestview Music Fest - (850) 682-6121
Daytona Beach - Halifax Art Festival - (800) 544-0415
Deerfield Beach - Florida Renaissance Festival
- (954) 771-7117
DeLand - St. Peter's Oktoberfest - (386) 822-6000
Delray Beach - Hatsume Fair - (561) 495-0233
Englewood - Pioneer Days - (941) 475-2380
Fernandina Beach - Isle of Eight Flags Shrimp
- (800) 226-3542
Floral City - Floral City Strawberry Festival - (352) 726-2801
Fort Lauderdale - Cajun/Zydeco Crawfish Festival
- (954) 828-3255
Fort Lauderdale - July 4th Family Celebration
- (954) 828-3255
Fort Lauderdale - The McDonalds Air & Sea Show
- (954) 527-5600
Fort Lauderdale - Sound Advice Blues Festival
- (954) 828-3255
Fort Myers - Edison Festival of Light - (239) 334-2999
Fort Walton Beach - Billy Bowlegs Pirate Festival
- (850) 244-8191
Gainesville - Downtown Festival & Art Show and JazzFest
- (352) 334-5064
Gainesville - Hoggetowne Medieval Faire - (352) 334-5064
Hialeah - Hialeah Spring Festival - (305) 828-9898

Homestead - Redland Renaissance Faire - (954) 680-0180
Indiantown - Indiantown Spring Festival - (772) 597-3987
Jacksonville Beach - Beaches Festival - (904) 247-6236
Jupiter - ArtsGras Arts Festival - (561) 694-2300
Key West - Cuban American Heritage Festival
- (305) 295-9665
Largo - Fright Fest - (800) 779-4910
Largo Bay - Renaissance Festival - (800)
Live Oak - Blue Grass Festival - (386) 364-1683
Live Oak - Fall Suwannee River Jubilee - (386) 364-1683
Live Oak - Florida Renaissance Festival (North)
- (954) 776-1642
Live Oak - Hot Air Balloons Classic - (386) 364-1683
Live Oak - The Old Tyme Farm Days - (386) 364-1683
Live Oak - Spring Bluegrass Festival - (386) 364-1683
Live Oak - Spring Sewannee River Jubilee - (386) 364-1683
Melbourne - Melbourne Jumbalaya Jam - (321) 633-4028
Melbourne - Melbourne Oktoberfest - (321) 633-4028
Miami - Calle Ocho - (305) 644-8888
Miami - Discovery of America Day - (305) 541-5023
Miami - Festival of the Americas - (305) 541-5023
Miami Beach - Art Deco Weekend Festival - (305) 672-2014
Middleburg - First Coast Ham Jam - (904) 284-4728
Naples - American Street Craft Festival - (239) 435-3742
Naples - Firecracker Festival & Sale - (239) 435-3742
Naples - Mother's Day Weekend Festival & Sale
- (239) 435-3742
Naples - Naples Dowtown Octoberfest & Sidewalk Sale
- (239) 435-3742
Naples - Naples Downtown Festival of the Arts & Showcase
- (239) 435-3742
Naples - Naples Downtown New Year's Art Festival
- (239) 435-3742
Naples - Naples July 4th Craft Festival & Sales
- (239) 435-3742

Appendix B

Navarre - Navarre Fun Fest - (850) 939-3267
Niceville - Boggy Bayou Mullet Festival - (850) 729-4545
Orlando - Orlando Int'l Fringe Festival - (407) 648-0077
Panama City Beach - Indian Summer Seafood Festival - (850) 233-4346
Patalka - Patalka Bluegrass Festival - (706) 864-7203
Pensacola - Pensacola Crawfish Creole Fiesta - (850) 433-6512
Pensacola - Pensacola JazzFest - (850) 433-8382
Pensacola - Pensacola Seafood Festival - (850) 433-6512
Perry - Florida Forest Festival - (850) 584-8733
Port Canaveral - SeaFest - (321) 454-2026
St. Petersburg - St. Petersburg Festival of States - (727) 898-3654
Sarasota - Sarasota Jazz Festival - (941) 366-1552
Sarasota - Sarasota Music Festival - (941) 953-4252
Sunrise - Woodstock Arts & Crafts Festival, Inc. - (954) 370-8651
Tampa - Fiesta Day - (813) 248-0721
Tampa - Gasparilla Extravaganza - (813) 353-8070
Tampa - Gasparilla Pirate Fest - (813) 353-8070
Tampa - Ybor City Bikefest - (813) 248-0721
Tampa - Ybor City Main Street Arts & Crafts Series - Fall - (813) 248-0721
Tampa - Ybor City Main Street Arts & Crafts Series - Winter - (813) 248-0721
Tampa - Ybor City's Big Bam Boom - (813) 621-7121
Tampa - Ybor City's Guavaween - (813) 621-7121
Tampa - Ybor City's "Taking It To The Streets" - (813) 621-7121
Titusville - Indian River Festival - (321) 267-3036
Trenton - Down Home Days Arts & Crafts Festival - (352) 463-3467
West Palm Beach - Palm Beach Seafood Festival - (561) 832-6397
West Palm Beach - SunFest of Palm Beach Co. - (561) 659-5980

Georgia

Alma - Georgia Blueberry Festival - (912) 632-5859
Atlanta - Atlanta Dogwood Festival - (404) 329-0501
Atlanta - Festival of Trees - (404) 264-9348
Atlanta - Music Midtown-An Atlanta Festival - (404) 233-8889
Athens - Athfest: Athens, GA Music & Arts Festival - (706) 548-1973
Camilla - Gnat Days Summer Festival - (229) 336-5255
Columbus - Riverfest Weekend - (706) 323-7979
Conyers - Conyers Cherry Blossom Festival - (770) 602-2606
Cordele - Watermelon Days Festival - (229)) 273-1668
Dahlonega - Wildflower Festival of the Arts - (706) 867-6829
Dalton - Prater's Mill Country Fair - (706) 694-MILL
Darien - Scottish Heritage Days - (912) 437-4770
Fairburn - Georgia Renaissance Festival - (770) 964-8575
Hahira - Hahira Honey Bee Festival - (229) 794-2330
Helen - Oktoberfest - (706) 878-1908
Hiawassee - Georgia Mtn. Fall Festival - (706) 896-4191
Hiawassee - Rhododendron Festival - (706) 896-4191
Jekyll Island - New Year's Bluegrass Festival - (706) 864-7203
Kingsland - Labor Day Weekend Catfish Festival - (912) 729-4382
Lincolnton - Lewis Family Homecoming & Bluegrass Festival - (706) 864-7203
Lumpkin - Harvest Festival - (229) 838-6310
Macon - Macon, GA's Int'l Cherry Blossom Festival - (478) 751-7429
Maysville - Maysville Autumn Leaf Festival - (706) 652-2334
Stone Mountain - Atlanta Fest - (615) 771-1818
Stone Mountain - Fantastic 4th Celebration - (770) 498-5690
Stone Mountain - Yellow Daisy Festival - (770) 498-5633
Sylvester - Georgia Peanut Festival - (229) 776-7718
Tyrone - Tyrone Founders Day - (770) 487-4694
Varnell - Prater's Mill Country Fair - (706) 694-MILL

Hawaii

Hilo - Merrie Monarch Festival - (808) 935-9168
Honolulu - Aloha Festivals - (808) 589-1771
Honolulu - King Kamehameha Celebration - (808) 586-0333
Kaanapali - Maui Music Festival - (800) 628-4767

Appendix B

Idaho

Boise - Boise River Festival - (208) 338-8887
Emmett - Cherry Festival - (208) 365-3485
Grangeville - Grangeville Border Days - (208) 983-2485
Hailey - Northern Rockies Folk Festival - (208) 788-0183
Lava Hot Springs - Somerville Manor's Medieval Faire - (208) 776-5429
Lewiston - Dogwood Festival of the Lewis-Clark Valley - (208) 792-2243
McCall - McCall Winder Carnival - (800) 260-5130
Moscow - Lionel Hampton Jazz Festival - (208) 885-6765
Moscow - Rendezvous in the Park - (208) 882-1178
Payette - Apple Blossom Festival - (208) 642-2362
Rexburg - Idaho Int'l Folk Dance Festival - (208) 356-5700
Rodeberry - McCall Summer Folk Festival - (208) 634-3642
Salmon - Sacajawea Heritage Days - (800) 727-2540
Salmon - Salmon River Days - (208) 756-2100
Sandpoint - The Festival at Sandpoint - (208) 265-4554
Sandpoint - Sandpoint Winter Carnival - (208) 263-0887
Sun Valley - Ketchum Wagon Days - (800) 634-3347
Twin Falls - Western Days - (208) 735-3254

Illinois

Beardstown - Beardstown Fall Fun Festival - (217) 323-5166
Brimfield - Jubilee College Olde English Faire - (309) 243-9489
Brookfield - BrookFest - (773) 868-3010
Canton - Canton Friendship Festival - (309) 647-3744
Chester - Popeye's Picnic - (618) 826-2700
Chicago - Andersonville Midsommarfest - (773) 665-4682
Chicago - Backyard Bash - (773) 665-4682
Chicago - Belmnont/Sheffield Music Festival - (773) 868-3010
Chicago - Celtic Chicago Fest - (312) 744-3315
Chicago - Chicago Air & Water Show - (312) 744-0631
Chicago - Chicago Blues Festival - (312) 744-3370
Chicago - Chicago Country Music Festival - (312) 744-3315
Chicago - Chicago Gospel Music Festival - (312) 744-3315
Chicago - Chicago Jazz Music Festival - (312) 744-3315
Chicago - Italian Market Days - (312) 744-3315
Chicago - Latino Book & Family Festival-Chicago - (760) 434-0798
Chicago - Lincoln Park West Festival - (773) 868-3010
Chicago - Northalsted Market Days - (773) 868-3010
Chicago - Oyster Festival - (773) 868-3010
Chicago - Taste of Chicago - (312) 744-3315
Chicago - Venetian Night - (312) 744-3315
Chicago - Viva Chicago Latin Music Festival - (312) 744-3315
Cicero - Latino Book & Family Festival - (760) 434-4484
Davenport - A Taste of the Quad Cities @ Molines Riverfest - (563) 344-7068
Decatur - Decatur Celebration - (217) 423-4222
Decatur - Fallfest - (217) 422-7300
Decatur - SummerStart Festival & Power Boat Races - (217) 422-2867
DeKalb - DeKalb Corn Fest - (815) 748-2676
Dixon - Dixon Petunia Festival - (815) 284-3361
Downers Grove - Heritage Festival Street Fair - (630) 434-5555
Effingham - Corvette Funfest - (217) 347-5591
Effingham - Funfest for Beetle - (217) 347-5591
Effingham - Funfest for Porsche - (217) 347-5591
Evanston - Custer's Last Stand Festival of the Arts - (847) 328-2204
Frankfort - Frankfort Fall Festival - (815) 469-3356
Grayville - Grayville Days - (618) 375-3671
Hanover Park - Harvest Fest - (630) 372-4200
Herrin - HerrinFesta Italiana - (618) 942-8445
Istaca - Itascafest - (630) 773-5571
Kankakee - Kankakee River Valley Regatta & River Festival - (309) 852-2537
Kewanee - Hog Capital of the World Festival - (815) 935-7390
LaHarpe - LaHarpe Summerfest - (217) 659-3793
LeRoy - LeRoy Fall Festival - (309) 962-9687
Lisle - Eyes to the Skies Balloon Festival - (630) 963-4281
Long Grove - Strawberry Festival - (847) 634-0888
Marissa - Marissa Coal Festival - (618) 295-2562
McHenry - McHenry Area Chamber of Commerce Fiesta Days - (815) 385-4300
Mendota - Mendota Sweet Corn Festival - (815) 539-6507
Moline - Taste of the Quad Cities - (563) 344-7068

Appendix B

Monmouth - Warren Co. Prime Beef Festival - (309) 734-3181

Morris - Grundy Co. Corn Festival - (815) 942-2676

Morton - Morton Pumpkin Festival - (309) 263-2491

Oregon - Stronghold's Olde English Faire - (815) 732-6111

Peoria - Peoria Fall Festival & Ribfest - (309) 681-0696

Peoria - Peoria Steamboat Festival - (309) 681-0696

Pekin - Pekin Marigold Festival - (309) 346-2106

Rockford - Civil War Days - (815) 397-9112

Rockford - On The Waterfront Festival - (815) 964-4388

Rock Island - Gumbo Ya Ya Festival - (309) 788-6311

Rock Island - Quad City Arts Festival of Trees - (563) 324-FEST

St. Charles - Pride of the Fox RiverFest, St. Charles - (630) 557-2575

St Charles - St. Charles Scarecrow Festival - (630) 377-6161

Shorewood - Shorewood Crossroads Festival - (815) 725-2900

Stillman Valley - Stillman Valley Fall Festival - (815) 645-2590

Thomson - Thomson Melon Days - (815) 259-5705

Washington - Cherry Festival - (309) 444-9921

Indiana

Attica - Potawatomi Festival - (765) 762-6656

Auburn - Auburn Cord Duesenberg Festival - (260) 925-3600

Auburn - TruckFest - (260) 925-3600

Aurora - Aurora Farmer Fair - (812) 926-1300

Aurora - Aurora Firecracker Festival - (812) 926-1593

Bean Blossom - Bean Blossom Blues Fest - (812) 988-6422

Bean Blossom - Bean Blossom Gospel Jubilee - (812) 988-6422

Bean Blossom - Bean Blossom Olde Tyme Music - (812) 988-6422

Bean Blossom - Bill Monroe Bean Blossom Bluegrass Festival - (812) 988-6422

Bean Blossom - Bill Monroe Hall of Fame/Uncle Pen Days Festival - (812) 988-6422

Bean Blossom - Central Indiana Bluegrass Festival - (765) 674-5117

Bloomington - Lotus World Music & Arts Festival - (812) 336-6599

Brazil - Brazil Rotary July 4th Celebration - (812) 835-3775

Chesterton - Wizard of Oz Festival - (219) 926-5513

Clinton - Little Italy Festival Town - (765) 832-9744

Columbus - Bluegrass Music Festival - (812) 375-2723

Columbus - Ethic Expo - (812) 376-2520

Columbus - Gospel Music Festival - (812) 379-2789

Columbus - Jazz Festival - (812) 375-2723

Crown Point - Hometown Square Festival - (219) 663-1600

Dillsboro - Dillsboro Homecoming Festival - (812) 432-5654

Dunkirk - Dunkirk Glass Days Festival - (765) 768-6193

Elkhart - Elkhart Jazz Festival - (574) 295-8701

Elkhart - Mainstreet Showcase of Art - (574) 295-8701

Evansville - Evansville Freedom Festival - (812) 421-1120

Fort Wayne - Germanfest - (800) 767-7752

Fort Wayne - Greekfest - (260) 489-0774

Fort Wayne - Three Rivers Festival - (260) 426-5556

Greenfield - Riley Festival - (317) 462-2141

Hope - Hope Heritage Days - (812) 546-4707

Huntingburg - Herbstfest - (812) 683-221

Indianapolis - Indy Jazz Fest - (317) 635-6630

Jasper - Jasper Strassenfest - (812) 482-6866

Kendallville - Apple Festival - (260) 347-4035

Kendallville - Bluegrass Festival - (574) 858-9308

Kokomo - Haynes/Apperson Festival - (800) 456-1106

La Porte - Oktoberfest - (219) 874-8927

Lafayette - A Taste of Tippecanoe - (765) 423-2787

Linton - Linton Freedom Festival - (812) 847-4846

Logansport - Brass Ring Festival - (574) 722-4766

Marion - James Dean Fest - (765) 668-4488

Mitchell - Persimmon Festival - (812) 849-4441

Nappanee - Amish Acres Arts & Crafts Festival - (574) 773-4188

Nappanee - Nappanee Apple Festival - (574) 773-7812

New Castle - Farmers Pike Festival - (765) 332-2134

New Haven - New Haven Canal Days Festival - (260) 749-2972

Odon - Odon Old Settlers - (812) 636-4460

Peru - Circus City Festival - (765) 472-3918

Plymouth - Marshall Co. Blueberry Festival - (888) 936-5020

Rockville - Parke Co. Covered Bridge Festival - (765) 569-5226

Salem - Fodder Festival - (812) 883-5750

Salem - Maxwell Days - (812) 883-5750

Salem - Old Settlers Days - (812) 883-3281

Shelbyville - Bears of Blue River Festival - (317) 398-6011

South Bend - South Bend Summer in the City Festival - (574) 299-4768

Tipton - Tipton Co. Pork Festival - (765) 675-2342

Union Mills - Mill Pond Festival - (219) 767-2370

Appendix B

Valparaiso - Valparaiso Popcorn Festival - (219) 464-8332
Van Buren - Van Buren Popcorn Festival - (765) 934-4888
Vevay - Swiss Wine Festival - (800) 435-5688
Wabash - Wabash Canal Days - (800) 563-1169
Warren - Salamonie Summer Festival - (260) 375-2454
Whiting - Pierogi Fest - (219) 659-0292
Whitig - Whitig Fourth of July Parade & Festival - (219) 659-7700

Iowa

Albia - Albia Restoration Day - (641) 932-5108
Amana - Maifest - (800) 579-2294
Bonaparte - Wybreg Village Renaissance Festival-Fall - (888) 243-4340
Burlington - Burlington Steamboat Days - (319) 754-4334
Burlington - Land of Mark Twain Bluegrass Music Festival - (573) 853-4344
Cedar Falls - Sturgis Falls Celebration - (319) 277-0751
Cedar Rapids - Cedar Rapids Freedom Festival - (319) 365-8313
Charles City - America's Homecoming Celebration - (641) 228-4234
Clear Lake - Clear Lake 4th of July Celebration - (641) 357-2159
Clear Lake - Int'l May Festival - (641) 357-5177
Clear Lake - Iowa Renaissance Festival & Harvest Faire - (641) 357-5177
Clear Lake - Nebraska Renaissance Fair - (641) 357-5177
Clinton - Riverboat Days - (563) 593-0910
Creston - 10,000 Crestonians - (641) 782-7021
Davenport - Mississippi Valley Blues Fest - (563) 322-5837
Davenport - Quad City Arts Festival of Trees - (800) 747-7800
Elk Horn - Jule Fest - (712) 764-7472
Elk Horn - Tivoli Fest - (712) 764-7472
Fort Madison - Family Spring Bluegrass Music Weekend - (573) 853-4344
Fort Madison - Fort Madison Tri-State Rodeo - (319) 372-2550

Gladbrook - Gladbrook Corm Carnival - (641) 473-2802
Grandview - Biggest Small Town Celebration 4th of July - No Phone
Harrison - National Old-Time Country Music Contest, Festival & Expo - (712) 762-4363
Iowa City - Iowa Arts Festival - (319) 337-7944
Iowa City - Iowa City Jazz Festival - (319) 358-9346
Iowa Falls - Riverband Rally - (641) 648-5549
Jefferson - Bell Tower Festival - (515) 386-2155
Little Amana - Splinter Fest - "A Festival of Woodcrafting" - (563) 875-2701
Missouri Valley - National Old-Time Music Festival & Pioneer Ag. Expo - (712) 762-4363
Mount Pleasant - Heritage Cityfest - (319) 385-3101
Mount Pleasant - Midwest Old Threshers Reunion - (319) 385-8937
Muscatine - Great River Days - (563) 263-1711
Orange City - Orange City Tulip Festival - (712) 707-4510
Pella - Pella Tulip Festival - (641) 628- 4311
Red Oak - Red Oak Junction Days - (712) 623-4821
Sac City - Chautauqua Days - (712) 662-7383
Schaller - Pop Corn Days - (712) 275-4229
Sioux City - River-Cade Festival - (712) 277-4226
Spencer - Flagfest - (712) 262-5680
Story City - Scandinavian Days - (515) 733-4214
Tama - Meskwaki Bluegrass Music Festival - (573) 853-4344
Waterloo - My Waterloo Days - (319) 233-8431

Kansas

Atchison - Amelia Earhart Festival - (913) 367-2427
Atchison - Int'l Forest of Friendship Celebration - (913) 367-1419
Bonner Springs - Kansas City Renaissance Festival - (800) 373-0357
Coffeyville - New Beginning Festival - (620) 251-2550

Columbus - Columbus Day Festival & Hot Air Balloon Regatta - (620) 429-1492
Dodge City - Dodge City Days - (620) 227-3119
El Dorado - El Dorado Prairie Port Festival - (316) 321-1841
Ellinwood - Ellinwood After Harvest Festival - (620) 564-3300
Ellsworth - Cowtown Festival - (785) 472-3491

Appendix B

Ellsworth - Star Spangled Spectacular - (785) 472-3186
Hays - Wild West Festival - (785) 623-4476
Holton - Glory Days Festival - (785) 364-3963
Hutchinson - Hutchfest - (620) 663-7448
Independence - Neewollah Fest - (620) 331-1800
Leavenworth - Leavenworth River Fest - (913) 682-2313
Logan - Hansen Arts & Craftss Fair - (785) 689-4846
Logan - Labor Day Celebration - (785) 689-4846
Manhattan - Country Stampede - (785) 539-2222
North Newton - Bethel College Fall Festival - (316) 284-5252
Olathe - Old Settlers Celebration - (913) 782-5252
Ottawa - Yule Fest Weekend - (785) 242-1411

Phillipsburg - Kansas' Biggest Rodeo - (785) 543-9073
Pittsburg - 4th of July Celebration - (620) 231-8310
Pittsburg - Little Balkans Days - (620) 231-1000
Topeka - Fiesta Mexicana - (785) 232-5088
Topeka - Sunflower Music Festival - (785) 231-1010
Victoria - Herzogfest - (785) 735-2352
Wellington - Kansas Wheat Festival - (620) 326-7466
Wichita - Mid-America All-Indian Center's Pow Wow
 - (316) 262-5221
Wichita - Wichita River Festival - (316) 267-2817
Winfield - Walnut Valley Festival - (620) 221-3250

Kentucky

Ashland - Festival of Trees - (606) 324-3175
Ashland - Poage Landing Days - (800) 377-6249
Bardstown - Kentucky Bourbon Festival - (502) 348-3623
Burnside - Burnside Catfish Festival - (606) 561-4026
Cadiz - Trigg Co. Country Ham Festival - (270) 522-3357
Carlisle - Blackberry Festival - (859) 289-2384
Corbin - Corbin Nibroc Funfest - (606) 528-6390
Covington - Maifest - (859) 491-0458
Covington - Oktoberfest - (859) 491-0458
Dixon - Freedom Days Festival - (270) 639-5186
Elizabethtown - Kentucky Heartland Festival - (270) 765-4334
Falmouth - Kentucky Wool Festival of Pendleton Co.
 - (859) 654-3378
Fulton - Pontotoc Weekend - (270) 472-9000
Grayson - Grayson Memory Days - (606) 474-9522
Hardin - Hot August Blues Festival - (800) 325-0143
Harlan - Poke Sallet Festival & Homecoming
 - (606) 573-4717
Henderson - Big River Arts & Crafts Festival - (270) 926-4433
Henderson - Tri-Fest - (270) 831-1560
Jamestown - Lakefest - (270) 343-4594

Lexington - Festival of the Bluegrass - (859) 846-4995
Lexington - Lexington's Fourth of July Festival
 - (859) 258-3123
London - World Chicken Festival - (800) 348-0095
Louisa - Lawrence Co. Septemberfest - (606) 673-3387
Louisville - Buechel-Bash Festival - (502) 634-1167
Louisville - IBMA's Bluegrass Fan Fest - (888) GET-IBMA
Louisville - Kentucky Derby Festival - (502) 584-6383
Louisville - Strassenfest - (502) 561-3440
Morehead - Appalacian Celebration - (606) 784-6221
Owensboro - Int'l Barbeque Festival - (270) 926-6938
Paducah - Paducah Summer Festival - (800) PADUCAH
Prestonsburg - Jenny Wiley Pioneer Festival - (606) 886-6539
Renfro Valley - Appalachian Harvest Festival - (606) 256-2638
Renfro Valley - Old Joe Clark Bluegrass Festival
 - (606) 256-2638
Somerset - Master Musicians Festival - (606) 677-2933
Tyner - Stringbean Memorial Bluegrass Festival
 - (606) 287-0600
Tyner - Stringbean Memorial Mt. Music Festival
 - (606) 287-0600
Winchester - Daniel Boone Pioneer Festival - (859) 744-0556

Louisiana

Abbeville - Louisiana Cattle Festival - (337) 893-6328
Alexandria - Cenlabration - (318) 473-1127
Alexandria - Uncle Sam Jam - (318) 443-7454

Amite - Amite Oyster Festival - (985) 748-5161
Baker - Baker Buffalo Festival - (225) 278-0300
Baldwin - Garfish Festival - (337) 923-7781

Appendix B

Basile - Louisiana Swine Festival - (337) 432-5251

Baton Rouge - Louisiana Original Music Festival - (225) 925-0288

Bogalusa - Independence Day Festival - (985) 732-3791

Breaux Bridge - Breaux Crawfish Festival - (337) 332-6655

Bridge City - Bridge City Gumbo Festival - (504) 436-4712

Bunkle - Louisiana Corn Festival - (318) 346-2575

Buras - Plaquemines Parish Fair & Orange Festival - (905) 657-7083

Cameron - Louisiana Fur & Wildlife Festival - (337) 538-2411

Chackbay - Louisiana Gumbo Festival - (985) 633-7789

Church Point - Church Point Buggy Festival - (337) 684-2739

Colfax - Louisiana Pecan Festival - (318) 627-5196

Crowley - Int'l Rice Festival - (337) 783-3067

Delcambre - Delcambre Shrimp Festival - (337) 685-2653

DeQuincy - Louisiana Railroad Days Festival- (337) 786-2722

DeRidder - DeRidder Dayd in the Park - (337) 462-2121

Des Allemands - Louisiana Catfish Festival - (985) 758-7542

Donaldsonville - Sunshine Festival - (225) 473-4814

Dubach - Louisiana Chicken Festival - (318) 777-3221

Erath - Erath Fourth of July Celebration - (337) 937-5861

Forest Hill - Louisiana Nursery Festival - (318) 748-6803

Franklinton - Washington Parish Watermelon Festival - (985) 839-3094

Gheens - Gheens Bon Mange' Festival - (985) 532-6755

Gretna - Gretna Heritage Festival - (504) 361-7748

Gueyden - Gueyden Duck Festival - (337) 536-9328

Hammond - Louisiana Renaissance Festival - (985) 429-9992

Harahan - St. Rita Pecan Festival - (504) 737-2915

Houma - Louisian Freedom Festival - (985) 851-3000

Iowa - Iowa Rabbit Festival - (337) 582-4423

La Place - St. John Andouille Festival - (985) 652-9569

Lafayette - Festival Int'l de Louisiane - (337) 232-8086

Lafayette - Festivalis Acadiens - (800) 346-1958

Lafayette - Mardi Gras in Cajun Country - (800) 346-1958

Lake Charles - Contraband Days - (337) 436-5508

Lake Charles - Mardi Gras of Imperial Calcasieu - (337) 475-7393

Larose - Family FunFest - (985) 693-7355

Larose - French Food Festival - (985) 693-7355

Logansport - Perier City Fest - (318) 692-5498

Madisonville - Madisonville Wooden Boat Festival - (985) 845-9200

Mandeville - Greater Mendeville Seafood Festival - (985) 845-9200

Mansfield - Louisiana Blueberry Festival - (318) 872-1310

Mansura - Cochon De Lait Festival - (318) 964-2771

Marthaville - Good Ole Days Festival - (318) 352-4107

Meraux - Louisiana Shrimp Festival - (504) 279-1921

Monroe - Folklife Festival - (318) 324-1665

Morgan City - Louisian Shrimp & Petroleum Festival - (985) 385- 0703

New Iberia - Louisiana Sugar Cane Festival - (337) 369-9323

New Orleans - Christmas New Orleans Style - (504) 522-5730

New Orleans - Essence Music Festival - (504) 410-4100

New Orleans - French Quarter Festival - (504) 522-5730

New Orleans - New Orleans Jazz & Heritage Festival - (504) 522-4786

New Orleans - Satchmo Summerfest - (504) 522-5730

Pine Prairie - Boggy Bayou Festival - (337) 599-2031

Ponchatoula - Ponchatoula Strawberry Festival - (985) 386-6677

Port Barre - Port Barre Cracklin Festival - (337) 585-6673

Rayne - Rayne Frog Festival - (337) 334-2332

Rayne - Roberts Cove Germanfest - 337) 334-8354

Robert - Louisiana Renaissance Festival - (985) 429-9992

Ruston - Louisiana Peach Festival - (318) 255-2031

Shreveport - Celebration of Spring Bloom - (318) 938-5402

Shreveport - Christmas in Roseland - (318) 938-5402

Shreveport - Fall Bloom Celebration - (318) 938-5402

Shreveport - Holiday in Dixie - (318) 865-5555

Shreveport - Mudbug Madness Festival - (318) 222-7403

Shreveport - Red River Revel Arts Festival - (318) 424-4000

Sorrento - Sorrento Lions Boucherie Festival - (225) 647-9966

Starks - Starks Mayhaw Festival - (337) 743-6297

Sulphur - Carlyss Cajun Bon-ton Festival - (337) 583-4800

Thibodoux - Thibodeauxville Fall Festival - (985) 446-1187

Ville Platte - Louisiana Cotton Festival - (337) 363-7348

West Monroe - Foxlife Festival - (800) 843-1872

Maine

Auburn - Great Falls Balloon Festival - (800) 639-6331

Bath - Bath Heritage Days - (207) 443- 9751

Belfast - Belfast Bay Festival - (207) 338-5719

Biddeford - La Kermesse Franco-Americaine Festival - (207) 282-2894

Appendix B

Boothbay Harbor - Windjammer Days - (207) 633-2353

Brunswick - Maine Festival - (207) 336-3833

Brunswick - Thomas Point Beach Bluegrass Festival - (209) 725-6009

Fort Fairfield - Maine Potato Blossom Festival - (207) 472-3802

Machias - Wild Blueberry Festival - (207) 255-6665

Madawaska - Acadian Festival - (207) 728-7000

New Gloucester - Maine Renaissance Faire - (207) 926-5693

Rockland - North Atlantic Blues Festival - (207) 596-6055

Rockland - Maine Lobster Festival - (207) 596-0376

York - Harvestfest - (207) 363-4422

Maryland

Annapolis - Maryland Renaissance Festival - (410) 266-7304

Annapolis - Maryland Seafood Festival - (410) 268-7682

Baltimore - Fell's Point Fun Festival - (410) 675-6756

Bethesda - London Azalea Garden Festival - (301) 320-3200

Bethesda - Taste of Bethesda - (301) 215-6660

Bowie - Safeway's National Capital Barbecue Battle - (301) 860-0630

Columbia - Capital Jazz Fest - (301) 322-8100

Crisfield - National Hard Crab Derby & Fair - (410) 968-2500

Cumberland - Heritage Days Festival - (301) 777-2787

Frederick - Frederick Festival of the Arts - (301) 694-9632

Grantsville - Summer Festival & Craft Show - (301) 895-3332

Hagerstown - Western Maryland Blues Fest - (301) 739-8577

Havre de Grace - Havre de Grace Decoy & Wildlife Art Festival - (410) 939-3739

Ocean City - Springfest - (410) 250-0125

Ocean City - Sunfest - (410) 250-0125

Reisterstown - Reister's Towne Festival - (410) 356-0688

Towson - Towsontown Spring Festival - (410) 825-1144

Westminster - Fall Harvest Days - (800) 654-4645

Westminster - Fallfest - (410) 848-9393

Massachusetts

Baltimore - Artscape-Baltimore's Festival of the Arts - (410) 752-8632

Boston - Boston Harborfest - (617) 227-1528

Carver - King Richard's Faire - (508) 866-5391

Charlemont - Yankee Doodle Days-Charlemont's Hometown Fair - (413) 339-8746

Cummington - Massachusetts Sheep & Woolcraft Fair - (413) 624-5562

Dorchester - Boston Folk Festival - (671) 287-6910

Fitchburg - Autumn Air Fest Air Show - (978) 345-9695

Harwich Port - Harwich Cranberry Festival - (508) 430-2811

Holyoke - Celebrate Holyoke - (413) 536-4611

New Bedford - New Bedford Summerfest - (508) 999-5231

New Bedford - Whaling City Festival - (508) 996-3348

Pittsfield - Festival of Trees at The Berkshire Museum - (413) 443-7171

Salem - Salem Heritage Days - (877) SALEM-MA

Weymouth - Tedeschi & Li'l Peach Balloon Festival - (973) 882-9896

Wilbraham - Wilbraham Peach Festival - (413) 599-0010

Michigan

Alma - Alma Highland Festival & Games - (989) 463-8979

Alpena - Great Lakes Lighthouse Festival - (989) 595-3632

Ashley - Trading Days - (989) 847-2474

Battle Creek - International Festival of Lights - (269) 962-4076

Battle Creek - Team US National Hot Air Balloon Championship & Air Show - (269) 962-0592

Bay City - Bay City River Roar - (989) 891-7627

Bay City - Labadie Pig Gig - (989) 624-8410

Benton Harbor - Blossomtime Festival - (269) 926-7397

Appendix B

Boyne City - National Morel Mushroom Festival - (231) 582-2197

Boyne Falls - Boyne Falls Polish Festival - (231) 549-2623

Cadillac - North American Snowmobile Festival - (231) 775-0657

Carson City - Frontier Days - (989) 584-3515

Chesaning - Chesaning Showboat Festival - (800) 255-3055

Clare - Clare Irish Festival - (989) 366-2442

Colon - Colon Magic Festival - (269) 432-3235

Dearborn Heights - Spirit Festival - (313) 277-7900

Detroit - Detroit Festival of the Arts - (313) 577-5088

East Jordan - Sno-Blast Festival - (231) 536-7351

Elsie - Elsie Dairy Festival - (989) 834-2132

Evart - Non-Electric Musical Funfest - (231) 832-2605

Frankenmuth - Frankenmuth Bavarian Festival - (989) 652-8155

Frankenmuth - Frankenmuth Oktoberfest - (989) 652-3378

Fremont - National Baby Food Festival - (231) 924-0770

Galesburg - Silver Leaf Renaissance Faire - (269) 343-9090

Grand Rapids - Festival of the Arts - (616) 459-1300

Hillsdale - American Legion 4th July Celebration - (517) 437-2876

Holland - Tulip Time Festival - (616) 396-4221

Holly - Michigan Renaissance Festival - (800) 601-4848

Howell - Michigan Challenge Balloonfest - (517) 546-3920

Kalkaska - National Trout Festival - (231) 258-9103

Lapeer - Lapeer Days Summer Festival - (810) 664-6641

Landing - Common Ground Music Festival - (517) 267-1502

Livonia - Livonia SPREE - (734) 427-8190

Mackinac Island - Lilac Festival - (906) 847-6418

Marine City - Maritime Days - (810) 765-0508

Marine City - Scarecrow Festival - (810) 765-4501

Marine City - Vintage Festival Marine City Home Tour - (810) 765-4501

Mesick - Mushroom Festival - (231) 885-2679

Midland-Matrix - Midland Festival - (989) 631-8250

Millington - Millington Old Fashioned Summer Festival - (989) 871-4939

Mount Pleasant - Mt. Pleasant Summer Festival - (989) 773-3378

Munger - Munger Potato Festival - (989) 659-3270

Muskegon - Muskegon Summer Celebration - (231) 722-6520

Niles - Four Flags Area Apple Festival - (269) 683-8870

Owosso - Curwood Festival - (989) 723-2161

Pigeon - Farmer's Festival - (989) 453-0130

Rogers City - Nautical City Festival - (989) 734-4656

Saint Joseph - Venetian Festival on St. Joseph River - (269) 983-7917

Sault Sainte Marie - Maritime Days - (800) 647-2858

Sebewaing - Michigan Sugar Festival - (989) 883-2150

Shelby - National Asparagus Festival - (231) 861-8110

Taylor - Taylor - (734) 459-6969

Three Oaks - Flag Day Weekend - (269) 756-5621

Three Rivers - Three Rivers Water Festival - (269) 278-8193

Traverse City - National Cherry Festival - (231) 947-4230

Twin Lakes - Country Thunder USA - (480) 966-9920

Vassar - Vassar Riverfest - (989) 823-2601

Walhalla - Michigan Womyn's Festival - (231) 757-4766

Wayland - Winterfest - (269) 792-4396

Webberville - Firemen's Field Day & Ox Roast - (517) 521-3654

Wyandotte - Wyandotte Street Art Fair - (734) 324-4505

Wyandotte - Wyandotte Winterfest - (734) 324-4505

Ypsilanti - Ypsilanti Heritage Festival - (734) 434-0136

Minnesota

Albert Lea - Big Island Rendezvous & Festival - (507) 373-3939

Albert Lea - Minnesota Storytelling Festival - (507) 373-4748

Austin - Austin Community Festival - (507) 437-3448

Austin - SPAMTOWN USA - (507) 437-3448

Brooklyn Park - Brooklyn Park Tater Daze - (763) 493-8181

Canby - Hat Days - (507) 223-7775

Champlin - Father Hennepin Festival - (763) 421-2820

Chatfield - Chatfield Western Days - (507) 867-4772

Chisholm - Polkafest - (218) 254-7959

Clarissa - Clarissa Summerfest - (218) 756-2185

Detroit Lakes - Spirit Fest - (218) 847-1681

Detroit Lakes - We Minnesota Country Music Fest - (218) 847-1681

Duluth - Bayfront Blues Festival - (715) 394-6831

Eagan - Minnesota Scottish Fair & Highland Games - (651) 687-9666

East Grand Forks - Heritage Days Festival - (218) 773-0406

Elbow Lake - Flekkefest - (218) 685-5380

Ely - Blueberry/Art Festival - (218) 365-6123

Ely - Harvest Moon Festival - (218) 365-6123

Appendix B

Ely - Voyageur Winter Festival - (218) 365-5131

Forest Lake - Forest Lake Independence Day Celebration - (651) 464-2600

Franklin - Catfish Derby Days - (507) 557-2259

Fulda - Wood Duck Festival - (507) 425-2351

Goodview - Goodview Days - (507) 452-1630

Grand Marais - Grand Marais Lions Club Fisherman's Picnic - (800) 835-1293

Grand Rapids - Judy Garland Festival - (218) 326-1900

Hastings - Rivertown Days - (651) 437-6775

Hayfield - Hey Days - (507) 477-3535

Henderson - Sauerkraut Days - (507) 248-3544

Holley - Western Minnesota Steam Threshers Reunion - (701) 232-4484

Hopkins - Hopkins Rasbrry Festival - (952) 931-0878

Houston - Houston Hoedown Days - (507) 896-3010

Hutchinson - Hutchinson Jayvee Water Carnival - (320) 587-2128

Inver Grove Heights - South St. Paul Kaposia Days - (651) 451-2266

Jordan - Old Time Harvest - (952) 492-2062

Litchfield - Litchfield Watercade - (320) 693-8184

Long Prairie - Prairie Days Heritage Festival - (320) 732-2514

Minneapolis - Basilica Block Party - (612) 317-3422

Minneapolis - Metris Uptown Art Fair - (812) 823-4581

Minneapolis - Minneapolis Aquatennial - (612) 338-3807

Minneapolis - Rockin Ribfest - (612) 673-1300

Minneapolis - Winter Bluegrass Weekend - (800) 635-3007

Montgomery - Kolacky Days - (507) 364-5577

Moorhead - Scandinavian Hjemkomst Festival - (218) 299-5452

Moose Lake - Agate Days - (218) 485-0145

Moose Lake - Art in the Park - (218) 485-4522

Moose Lake - Crazy Corn Days - (218) 485-4522

Moose Lake - 4th of July - (218) 485-4522

Morris - Prairie Pioneer Days - (320) 589-1242

Nevis - Muskie Days - (218) 652-3115

New Brighton - New Brighton Stockyard Days - (651) 638-2045

New Ulm - Heritagefest - (507) 354-8850

Norwood Young America - Stiftungfest-Minnesota's Oldest Celebration - (952) 467-2313

Olivia - Corn Capital Days - (320) 523-1350

Ortonville - Corn Festival - (320) 839-3284

Perham - Pioneer Days - (218) 346-7710

Perham - Turtle Fest - (218) 346-7710

Red Wing - River City Days - (651) 388-4719

Richmond - Minnesota Bluegrass & Old-Time Music Festival - (715) 635-2479

Richmond - Minnesota Homegrown Kickoff - (800) 635-3037

Rochester - Rochesterfest - (507) 285-8769

St. Cloud - Wheels, Wings & Water Festival - (320) 251-0083

St. Paul - Festival of Nations - (651) 647-0191

St. Paul - St. Paul Winter Carnival - (651) 223-4700

St. Paul - Scottish Country Fair - (651) 696-6239

St. Peter - Rock Bend Folk Festival - (507) 934-3269

Shakopee - Medieval Fair - (800) 966-8215

Shakopee - Minnesota Renaissance Festival - (952) 445-7361

South St. Paul - South St. Paul Kaposia Days - (651) 451-2266

Spring Valley - Wilder Fest - (507) 346-1015

Walker - Moondance Jam - (218) 836-2598

Walker - Old Fashioned 4th of July Celebration - (218) 547-1515

Wells - Wells Kernel Days - (507) 553-6450

Willmar - Willmar Fests - (320) 220-1869

Winsted - Winstock Country Music Festival - (612) 338-1051

Mississippi

Biloxi - Biloxi Seafood Festival - (228) 374-2717

Biloxi - Mississippi Coast Coliseum Country Cajun Crawfish Festival - (228) 594-3700

Clarksdale - The Sunflower River Blues & Gospel Festival - (662) 624-5772

Greenville - Holiday Fest - (662) 378-2617

Greenville - Spring Fest - (662) 378-2617

Gulfport - Mississippi Deep Sea Fishing Rodeo - (228) 863-2713

Jackson - CelticFest - (601) 607-6441

Tupelo - Elvis Presley Festival - (862) 841-6598

Vicksburg - Riverfest - (601) 218-1363

Appendix B

Missouri

Altenburg - East Perry Community Fair - (573) 824-5513

Blue Springs - Blue Springs Fall Fun Fest - (816) 554-7794

Boonville - Big Muddy Folk Festival - (888) 588-1477

Branson - Festival of American Music & Craftsmanship - (417) 338-8207

Branson - National Kid Fest - (417) 338-8282

Branson - An Old Time Christmas - (417) 338-8282

Branson - World-Fest - (417) 366-7706

Brookfield - Summer Fun Days - (660) 258-7255

Brunswick - Brunswick Lewis & Clark Bicentennial Commemoration - (660) 548-9771

Brunswick - Brunswick Pecan Festival - (660) 548-3141

Buckner - Lewis & Clark Trail Days - (816) 650-9701

Bucklin - Bucklin Homecoming - (660) 695-3694

Carthage - Maple Leaf Festival - (417) 358-2373

Carthage - Midwest Gathering of Artists - (417) 358-7163

Centralia - Centrailia Anchor Festival - (573) 682-2272

Chillicothe - Old Time Harvest Days - (660) 646-2795

Clarence - Clarence Homecoming - (660) 699-3832

Clinton - Emancipation Celebration - (660) 885-8738

Clinton - Olde Glory Days - (660) 885-8166

Columbia - Heritage Festival - (573) 874-7460

Concordia - Concordia Fall Festival - (660) 463-1346

Deepwater - Labor-Harvest Picnic - (660) 696-2545

El Dorado Springs - El Dorado Springs Picnic - (417) 876-2691

Fair Grove - Fair Grove Heritage Reunion - (417) 759-2807

Farmington - Farmington Country Days - (573) 756-3615

Festus - Festus Firecracker Festival - (636) 937-6646

Florissant - Valley of Flowers Festival - (314) 837-0033

Fulton - Callaway Heritage Festival - (573) 642-3055

Gladstone - Gladfest - (816) 436-4523

Grain Valley - Grain Valley Fair Daze - (816) 224-8808

Hannibal - National Tom Sawyer Days - (573) 248-1237

Hannibal - River Arts Festival - (573) 221-6545

Hannibal - TSBA Winter Bluegrass Festival - (573) 853-4344

Hardin - Skeeter Fest - (660) 398-4833

Houstonia - Hamlet of Sedalia Festival Mid-Missouri - (660)568-3586

Huntsville - Randolph Co. Old Settlers & Fall Fair - (800) 622-2070

Independence - Santa-Cali-Gon Days Festival - (816) 252-4745

Jameson - Jameson Picnic - (660) 828-4338

Jamesport - Summer Festival - (660) 684-6146

Kahoka - Meskawaki Bluegrass Music Festival - (573) 853-4344

Kahoka - TSBA Kahoka Festival of Bluegrass Music - (573) 853-4344

Kansas City - Ethnic Enrichment Festival - (816) 513-7652

Kansas City - Kansas City Blues & Heritage Festival - (816) 221-4444

Kansas City - Kansas City Renaissance Festival - (800) 373-0357

Kearney - Jesse James Festival - (816) 628-6420

Lake Ozark - Annual Lake of the Ozarks "Dixieland" Jazz Festival - (573) 964-2200

Lake Ozark - Lake Lights Festival - (573) 964-1008

Lake Ozark - Osage Mtn. Man Rendezvous - (573) 964-1008

Lebanon - Farmfest - (417) 588-3256

Lebanon - Hillbilly Days - (417) 588-3256

Lee's Summit - Festival of the Arts - (816) 246-6598

Lee's Summit - Oktoberfest - (816) 524-2424

Lee's Summit - Old Tyme Days - (816) 246-6598

Liberty - Liberty Fall Festival - (816) 781-5200

Mansfield - Missouri Renaissance Faire - (417) 924-2222

Mansfield - Wilder Days - (417) 924-3719

Neosho - Thomas Hart Benton Arts & Crafts Festival - (417) 451-8090

Nevada - Bushwhacker Days - (417) 667-5300

New Cambria - New Cambria Fall Festival - (660) 226-5211

New Melle - New Melle Festival - (636) 828-5158

Nodaway - Hopkins Picnic - (660) 778-3555

O'Fallon - Heritage & Freedomfest - (636) 240-2000

Parkville - Jazz & Fine Arts River Jam - (816) 505-2227

Piedmont - Ozark Heritage Festival - (573) 223-4046

Poplar Bluff - Black River Festival - (573) 686-6866

Raytown - Raytown Round-Up Days - (816) 353-8500

St. Charles - Festival of the Little Hills - (636) 723-9681

St. James - St. James Grape Festival - (573) 265-3480

St. Joseph - Trails West! - (816) 232-1912

St. Louis - Fair St. Louis - (314) 434-3434

St. Louis - The Japanese Festival - (314) 577-9540

Salem - Dent Co. Fall Festival - (573) 729-5629

Salem - Dent Co. Spring Festival - (573) 729-5629

Salisbury - Salisbury Steak Festival - (660) 388-6273

Sedalia - Scott Joplin Ragtime Festival - (866) 218-6258

Sikeston - Cotton Carnival - (573) 471-9956

Sikeston - Springfest - (573) 471-2498

Slater - Slater Fall Festival - (660) 529-2271

Springfield - Festival of Lights - (417) 862-5567

Springfield - Greater Ozarks Blues Festival - (417) 869-8558

Stanton - Fall Festival of Gospel Music - (314) 772-3048

Appendix B

Stockton - Stockton Black Walnut Festival - (417) 276-5213

Sweet Springs - Sweet Springs Festival - (660) 335-9944

Urich - Urich Reunion - (660) 638-4849

Warsaw - Heritage Days - (800) WAR-SAW4

Warsaw - Warsaw Jubilee Days - (660) 438-5057

Wentzville - Greater St. Louis Renaissance Faire - (636) 916-1643

West Plains - Heart of the Ozarks Arts & Crafts Show - (417) 256-9640

West Plains - Heart of the Ozarks Bluegrass - (417) 256-5154

Montana

Billings - Festival of Cultures - (406) 657-1042

Billings - Skyfest Hot Air Balloon Rally - (406) 256-0466

Bozeman - SeptoberFest - (406) 582-3270

Bozeman - Wild West Winterfest - (406) 582-3270

Culbertson - Culbertson Frontier Days - (406) 787-5821

Great Falls - Montana Traditional Jazz Festival - (406) 454-1305

Hardin - Little Big Horn Days - (406) 665-1672

Helena - Mt. Helena Music Festival - (406) 447-1535

Kalispell - Artists & Craftsmen of the Flathead Summer Show - (406) 881-4288

Libby - Libby Logger Days - (406) 293-4167

Libby - Libby Nordicfest - (406) 293-2440

Livingston - Festival of the Arts - (406) 222-2300

Red Lodge - Red Lodge Mountain Man Rendevous - (406) 843-5833

Virginia City - Victorian Ball & Heritage Days - (406) 843-5833

Wolf Point - Wolf Point Wild Horse Stampede - (406) 653-2012

Nebraska

Ainsworth - Middle of Nowhere Carnival Days - (402) 387-2740

Ainsworth - National Country Music Festival - (402) 387-2844

Alliance - Heritage Days - (308) 762-1520

Arcadia - Arcadia Fall Festival - (308) 789-6528

Bayard - Chimney Rock Pioneer Days - (308) 586-2002

Chadron - Fur Trade Days - (308) 432-4401

Clarkson - Clarkson Czech Festival - (402) 892-3331

Columbus - Columbus Days - (402) 564-2769

Comstock - Comstock Windmill Festival - (800) 658-4443

Crete - Crete Blue River Festival - (402) 826-2136

Diller - Diller Picnic & Parade - (402) 793-5396

East City Park - National Country Music Festival - (402) 387-2844

Fairbury - Germanfest - (402) 729-3000

Fairbury - Rock Creek Trail Days - (402) 729-5777

Fairbury - Rock Island Rail Days - (402) 729-5131

Falls City - Cobblestone Festival - (402) 245-4228

Fremont - John C. Fremont Days - (402) 727-9428

Gering - Oregon Trail Days - (308) 436-4457

Gordon - Willow Tree Festival - (308) 282-1582

Gothenburg - Harvest Festival - (308) 537-3505

Gothenburg - Pony Express Rodeo & 4th of July Celebration - (308) 385-5444

Grand Island - Central Nebraska Ethnic Festival - (308) 537-3505

Hastings - Cottonwood Festival - (402) 461-8412

Hemingford - Family Fun Days - (308) 487-5599

La Vista - La Vista Days Celebration - (402) 339-2078

Milligan - Milligan June Jubilee - (402) 629-4446

Nebraska City - Arbor Day Celebration - (402) 873-3000

Nebraska City - Fourth of July Celebration - (402) 873-3000

Neligh - Neligh Old Mill Days - (402) 887-4456

Norfolk - LaVitsef Time - (402) 371-7845

North Platte - NEBRASKAland DAYS - (308) 532-7939

O'Neill - Summerfest - (402) 336-2355

Ogallala - Ogallala Indian Summer Rendezvous - (308) 284-4066

Omaha - LaFesta Italiana - (402) 341-9562

Omaha - Omaha Summer Arts Festival - (402) 341-5881

Omaha - River City Roundup Fair & Festival - (402) 554-9610

Omaha - Septemberfest-Salute to Labor - (402) 346-4800

Omaha - Taste of Omaha - (402) 346-8003

Palisade - Palisade Pioneer Days - (308) 285-3404

Appendix B

Papillion - Papillion Days - (402) 331-3917

Plattsmouth - Kass Kounty King Korn Karnival - (402) 296-4155

St. Paul - Grover Cleveland Alexander Days - (308) 754-5309

South Sioux City - South Sioux City Sports Days - (800) 793- 6327

Sumner - Sumner's July 4th Celebration - (308) 752-3465

Sutton - Dugout Days - (402) 773-5504

Valentine - Old West Days - (402) 376-3834

Verdigre - Kolach Days - (402) 668-2305

Wilber - Wilber Czech Festival - (888) 494-5237

Wymore - Sam Wymore Days - (402) 645-3693

Nevada

Austin - Gridley Days - (775) 964-2200

Carson City - July 4th Cavalcade of Spectaculars - (775) 687-4680

Carson City - Nevada Days Celebration - (775) 687-4680

Elko - Elko National Basque Festival - (775) 738-9691

Fallon - Hearts of Gold Cantaloupe Festival - (775) 423-2544

Gardenville - Carson Valley Days - (775) 265-2807

Genoa - Candy Dance - (775) 782-8696

Henderson - Henderson Days - (702) 565-8951

Incline Village - Lake Tahoe Shakespeare Festival - (775) 832-1616

Las Vegas - Age of Chivalry Renaissance Festival - (702) 455-8838

Las Vegas - Summerlin Street Fair - (702) 286-4944

Pahrump - Spring Fling - (775) 727-1555

Reno - Artown - (775) 322-1538

Sparks - Hot August Nights - (775) 356-1956

Sparks - Numaga Days Celebration - (775) 425-0775

Valley View - San Gennaro Fest - (623) 487-7774

New Hampshire

Concord - League of New Hampshire Craftsmen - (603) 224-3375

Concord - New Hampshire Highland Games - (603) 229-1975

Hampton - Seafood Festival - (603) 926-8718

Hillsborough - Hillsborough Balloon Festival - (603) 428-8337

Lincoln - SoulFest - (978) 346-4577

Manchester - Riverfest - (603) 623-2623

Portsmouth - Market Square Day - (603) 431-5388

Sandown - The Festival of the Lion Renaissance Faire - (603) 887-4034

New Jersey

Asbury Park - Asbury Park Jazz Festival - (732) 502-5703

Augusta - Crawfish Fest - (202) 539-8830

Belmar - New Jersey Seafood Festival - (732) 681-3700

Blairstown - Blairstown 4th of July Celebration - (570) 897-5007

Bridgeton - Bridgeton Folk Festival - (856) 451-9208

Cape May - Cape May Food & Wine Festival - (609) 884-5404

Cape May - Cape May Music Festival - (800) 275-4278

Cape May - Cape May's Spring Festival - (609) 884-5404

Cape May - Victorian Fair - (609) 884-5404

Cape May - Victorian Week Festival in Cape May - (609) 884-5404

Elmer - Appel Farm Arts & Music Festival - (800) 394-1211

Hoboken - St. Ann's Street Festival - (201) 659-1114

Jackson - Jackson Day - (732) 928-1200

Long Branch - Oceanfest - (732) 946-2711

New Brunswick - New Jersey Folk Festival - (732) 932-5775

Point Pleasant Beach - Festival of the Sea - (732) 899-2424

Readington - Quick Chek New Jersey Festival of Ballooning - (973) 882-5464

Appendix B

Seaside Heights - Ocean Co. Italian Festival/Columbus Day Parade - (732) 477-6507

Somerset - New Jersey Renaissance Kingdom - (732) 271-1119

South Orange - New Jersey Renaissance Kingdom - (732) 271-1119

Trenton - Heritage Days Festival - (609) 989-3353

Wildwood - Wildwood Music Festival - (609) 729-6818

Woodstown - Delaware Valley Bluegrass Festival - (302) 234-1771

New Mexico

Albuquerque - Gathering of Nations - (505) 836-2810

Albuquerque - Kodak Albuquerque Int'l Balloon Fiesta - (505) 821-1000

Angel Fire - World Shovel Race Championships - (505) 911-4351

Bernalillo - Bernalillo Wine Festival - (505) 867-3311

Fall River - Fall River Celebrates America Waterfront Festival - (508) 676-8226

Farmington - Freedom Days - (505) 326-7602

Farmington - Totah Festival Indian Market & Pow Wow - (800) 448-1240

Fort Sumner - Old Fort Days - (505) 355-7705

Gallup - Gallup Inter Tribal Indian Ceremonial - (505) 863-3896

Hillsboro - Hillsboro Apple Festival - (505) 895-5686

La Cruces - Cowboy Days - (505) 522-4100

Red River - Aspencade Arts & Crafts Fair - (505) 754-2366

Red River - Mardi Gras in The Mountains - (800) 348-6444

Santa Fe - Native Roots & Rhythm - (505) 989-8898

Santa Fe - Santa Fe Jazz Festival - (505) 989-8442

Silver City - The Silver City Renaissance Faire - (505) 534-0790

Taos - Taos Fall Arts Festival - (505) 758-3873

Taos - Taos Spring Arts Celebration - (800) 732-8267

Taos - Yuletide in Taos - (505) 758-3873

Truth or Consequences - Fiesta - (505) 894-2946

New York

Albany - Fabulous Fourth Festivities - (518) 474-5986

Albany - Fleet Bluesfest - (518) 474-5986

Albany - Int'l Food Festival - (518) 474-5986

Altamont - Old Songs Festival of Traditional Music & Dance - (518) 765-2815

Ancramdale - Grey Fox Bluegrass Festival - (603) 523-8330

Croton on Hudson - Great Hudson River Revival/Music & Environmental Festival - (845) 454-7673

Dansville - New York State Festival of Balloons - (585) 335-8794

Darien Center - Kingdom Bound - (716) 633-1117

Eden - Eden Corn Festival - (716) 992-9141

Guilderland - Old Songs Festival of Traditional Music & Dance - (518) 765-2815

Hillsdale - Falcon Ridge Folk Festival - (860) 364-0366

Hunter - German Alps Festival - (888) HUNTERMTN

Hunter - Int'l Celtic Festival - (888) HUNTERMTN

Ithaca - Ithaca Festival - (607) 273-3646

Jamesville - Balloon Fest - (315) 435-5252

Lake George - Lake George Winter Festival - (518) 688-5771

New York - Harlem Jazz & Music Festival - (212) 862-8473

New York - Harlem Week - (212) 862-8477

New York - Latino Book & Family Festival-New York - (760) 434-0798

North Tonawanda - Canal Fest of the Tonawandas - (716) 692-3292

Oswego - Oswego Harborfest - (315) 343-6858

Phelps - Sauerkraut Festival - (315) 548-2222

Rochester - Lilac Festival - (585) 546-3070

Salamanaca - Falling Leaves Festival - (716) 945-3110

Saranac Lake - Saranac Lake Winter Carnival - (518) 891-1990

Saugerties - Hudson Valley Garlic Festival - (845) 246-3244

Sterling - Sterling Renaissance Festival - (315) 947-5782

Syracus - New York State Blues Festival (315) 469-1723

Syracus - Syracus Arts & Crafts Festival - (315) 422-8284

Syracuse - Syracuse Winterfest - (315) 676-2496

Trumansburg - Finger Lakes Grass Roots Festival - (607) 387-5098

Tuxedo - New York Renaissance Faire - (845) 351-5171

Appendix B

North Carolina

Arden - Fall Harvest Days/Antique Engine & Tractor Show - (828) 683-0853
Asheville - Bele Chere - (828) 259-5811
Asheville - Goombay! Festival - (828) 252-4614
Asheville - Mountain Dance & Folk Festival - (828) 258-6101
Asheville - Fiesta Latina - (828) 277-1797
Bakersville - Rhododendren Festival - (800) 227-3912
Benson - Benson Mule Days - (919) 894-3825
Black Mountain - Lake Eden Arts Festival - (828) 68-MUSIC
Black Mountain - Sourwood Festival - (828) 669-2300
Charlotte - Festival in the Park - (704) 338-1060
Charlotte - Food Lion Speed Street - (704) 455-6814
Cherokee - Cherokee Bluegrass Festivall - (706) 864-7203
Cherokee - North Carolina State Bluegrass Festival - (706) 864-7203
Davidson - Carolina Renaissance Festival - (704) 896-5555
Durham - Bull Durham Blues Festival - (919) 683-1709
Fort Bragg - Oktoberfest Internationale - (910) 396-3919
Franklin - Lotus Flower Festival - (828) 524-3264
Hendersonville - North Carolina Apple Festival - (828) 697-4557
Hickory - Oktoberfest - (828) 781-1960
Holden Beach - North Carolina Festival-by-the-Sea - (910) 842-6485

Huntersville - Carolina Renaissance Festival - (704) 896-5555
Monroe - Blooming Arts Festival - (704) 283-2784
Morehead City - North Carolina Seafood Festival - (252) 726-6273
Morganton - The Historic Morganton Festival - (828) 438-5252
Morganton - Sunfest - (828) 438-5252
Mount Airy - Autumn Leaves Festival - (800) 948-0949
Ocean Isle Beach - North Carolina Oyster Festival - (800) 426-6644
Raeford - North Carolina Turkey Festival - (910) 875-5929
Raleigh - July 4th Celebration - (919) 831-6640
Raleigh - North Carolina Renaissance Faire - (919) 755-8004
Salisbury - Autumn Jubilee - (704) 636-2089
Shallotte - North Carolina Oyster Festival - (910) 754-6644
Southport - North Carolina 4th of July Festival - (910) 457-5578
Tabor City - North Carolina Yam Festival (910) 653-2031
Washington - Washington Summer Festival - (252) 946-9168
Waynesville - Folkmoot USA - (828) 452-2997
Wilkesboro - MerleFest - (800) 343-7857
Wilmington - North Carolina Azalea Festival at Wilmington - (910) 794-4650

North Dakota

Center - Oliver County Old Settler's Days - (701) 794-8711
Dickinson - Holiday Craft Show - (701) 225-5115
Dickinson - Northern Plains Heritage Festival - (701) 225-5115
Dickinson - Parade of Lights - (701) 483-4479
Dickinson - Roughrider Days - (701) 225-5115
Fargo - Fargo Blues Festival - (218) 287-9601
Fargo - Island Park Show - (701) 241-8160
Fargo - Red River Street Fair - (701) 241-1570
Fargo - Rib Fest & More - (701) 241-9100
Grafton - SummerFest - (701) 352-0781
Grand Forks - Sertoma 4th of July Festival & Fireworks - (701) 775-4626
Hebron - Hebron Watermelon Day - (701) 878-4494
Jamestown - Buffalo City Bull-A-Rama - (701) 252-4835
Jamestown - Cabin Fever Festival - (701) 252-4835

Jamestown - "White Cloud's" Birthday Celebration - (701) 252-8648
Kenmare - Goosefest - (701) 385-4857
Lisbon - Happy Days - (701) 683-5680
Minot - Norsk Hostfest - (701) 852-2368
Mooreton - Labor Day Celebration - (701) 671-2308
New Leipzig - Oktoberfest - (701) 584-2920
Oakes - Oakes Irrigation Days - (701) 742-3508
Rolla - Western Minnesota Steam Threshers Reunion - (701) 232-4484
Stanton - Knife River Days - (701) 745-3267
Valley City - Sheyenne Valley Community Days - (701) 845-1891
Valley City - Snoball Arts & Crafts Festival (Sponsored by Faith in Action) - (701) 845-6491
Washburn - Lewis & Clark Days - (701) 462-8535

Appendix B

Ohio

Alliance - Carnation City Festival - (330) 823-6260

Bainbridge - Fall Festival of Leaves - (740) 634-2085

Barnesville - Barnesville Pumpkin Festival - (740) 425-2593

Bay Village - Baycrafters Renaissance Fayre - (440) 871-6543

Belpre - Belpre Area Invitational Homecoming - (740) 423-8934

Bidwell - Bob Evans Farm Festival - (740) 245-5305

Bowling Green - Black Swamp Arts Festival - (419) 354-2723

Bradford - Bradford Pumpkin Show - (937) 448-2710

Bucyrus - Bratwurst Festival - (419) 562-2728

Cambridge - SE Ohio Renaissance Faire - (740) 435-3271

Canton - Pro Football Hall of Fame Festival - (330) 456-7253

Chillicothe - Farmers Fall Festival - (740) 775-4966

Chillicothe - Feast of the Flowering Moon - (740) 775-2121

Cincinnati - Queen City Blues Fest - (513) 569-5466

Cincinnati - Taste of Blue Ash - (513) 745-8553

Cincinnati - Tall Stacks Music, Arts & Heritage Festival - (513) 721-0104

Circleville - Circleville Pumpkin Show - (740) 474-6611

Cleveland - Great American Rib Cook-Off & Music Festival - (440) 247-2722

Cleveland - KidsFest - (440) 247-2722

Cleveland - Midwest BrewFest - (440) 246-2722

Cleveland - Taste of Cleveland - (440) 247-2722

Columbus - Columbus Arts Festival - (614) 224-2606

Columbus - Festival Latino - (614) 645-6449

Columbus - German Village Oktoberfest - (614) 221-8888

Coshocton - Apple Butter Stirrin' Festival - (800) 877-1830

Coshocton - Civil War Reenactment - (740) 622-9310

Coshocton - Coshocton Canal Festival - (740) 622-9310

Coshocton - Coshocton Hot Air Balloon Festival - (740) 622-5411

Coshocton - Heritage Craft & Olde Time Music Festival - (740) 622-9310

Crooksville - Crooksville-Roseville Pottery Festival - (740) 697-7021

Fort Loramie - Country Concert at Hickory Hill Lakes - (419) 628-3571

Grove City - Big Bear Balloon Festival - (877) 9FUNFEST

Harveysburg - British Isles Festival - (513) 897-7000

Jackson - Jackson Co. Apple Festival - (740) 286-1339

Kingston - Kingston Summer Festival - (740) 642-5220

Lorain - Lorain International Festival - (440) 282-6263

Loudonville - Mohican Blues Festival - (419) 368-3090

Maria Stein - Maria Stein Country Fest - (419) 925-4151

Marietta - Ohio River Sternwheel Festival - (740) 373-5178

Marion - Marion Popcorn Festival - (740) 387-FEST

Middletown - Middfest International - (513) 425-7707

Milan - Milan Melon Festival - (419) 499-2766

Millersport - Sweet Corn Festival - (740) 246-5680

Morristown - Jamboree in the Hills - (304) 232-1170

Nelsonville - Parade of the Hills - (740) 753-3525

New Philadelphia - Tuscarawas Co. Italian-American Festival- (330) 339-6405

New Straitsville - Moonshine Festival - (740) 394-2838

North Ridgeville - North Ridgeville Corn Festival - (440) 327-5144

Norwalk - Prairie Peddler Festival-Fall - (419) 663-1818

Norwalk - Prairie Peddler Festival-Spring - (419) 663-1818

Painesville - Lake Co. Perch Fest - (440) 354-2424

Port Clinton - Port Clinton Walleye Festival - (419) 732-2864

Portsmouth - Portsmouth River Days - (740) 354-8807

Ripley - Ohio Tobacco Festival - (937) 392-1590

Rock Creek - Great Lakes Medieval Faire - (888) 633-4382

Serport Harbor - Lake Co. Perch Fest - (440) 354-2424

Toledo - The Pharm/Light the Night - (419) 249-4086

Toledo - Riverfest - (419) 249-5018

Toledo - Toledo Blues Fest - (419) 249-0486

Troy - Troy Strawberry Festival - (937) 339-7714

Trumbull Township - Great Lakes Medieval Faire (888) 633-4382

Twinsburg - Twins Days Festival - (330) 425-3652

Utica - Utica Ice Cream Festival - (740) 892-4272

Wilmington - Ohio Renaissance Festival - (513) 897-7000

Woodsfield - Black Walnut Festival - (740) 472-1465

Oklahoma

Broken Arrow - Rooster Days Festival - (918) 251-1518

Claremore - Bluegrass & Chili Festival - (918) 341-2818

Claremore - Will Rogers Arts & Crafts Show - (918) 341-5881

Enid - Cherokee Strip Days - (580) 237-2494

Appendix B

Enid - Tri-State Music Festival - (580) 237-4964
Eufaula - Whole Hawg Days - (918) 689-2791
Guthrie - '89er Day Celebration - (405) 282-2589
Guthrie - Guthrie Jazz Banjo Festival - (800) OKB-ANJO
Guthrie - Oklahoma Int'l Bluegrass Festival - (405) 282-4446
Norman - Chocolate Festival - (405) 329-4523
Norman - Holiday Gift Gallery - (405) 329-4523
Norman - Medieval Fair - (405) 288-2536
Norman - Midsummer Nights Fair - (405) 329-4523
Oklahoma City - Aerospace America - (405) 685-9546
Oklahoma City - Chuck Wagon Gathering & Children's Cowboy Festival - (405) 478-2250
Oklahoma City - Festival of the Arts - (405) 270-4848
Oklahoma City - Red Earth Native American Cultural - (405) 427-5228
Okmulgee - Okmulgee Pecan Festival - (918) 756-6172
Perry - Cherokee Strip Celebration - (580) 336-4684
Perry - Spring Heritage Festival - (580) 336-4684
Sallisaw - Grapes of Wrath Festival - (918) 775-2558
Sand Springs - Labor Day Festival - (918) 246-2561
Sapulpa - Route 66 Blowout - (918) 224-0170
Seminole - Seminole Gusher Day - (405) 382-3640
Tulsa - Oktoberfest - (918) 744-9700
Tulsa - Tulsa International Mayfest - (918) 582-6435
Wilburton - Robbers Cave Fall Festival - (918) 465-2565
Yukon - Chisholm Trail Festival - (405) 354-1895

Oregon

Astoria - Astoria-Warrenton Crab & Seafood Festival - (503) 325-6311
Baker City - Miner's Jubilee - (541) 523-5855
Bend - Cascade Festival of Music - (541) 382-8381
Boardman - Boardman 4th of July Celebration - (541) 481-3014
Canyonville - Canyonville Pioneer Days - (541) 839-4733
Charleston - Charleston Seafood Festival - (541) 888-2548
Coos Bay - Oregon Coast Music Festival - (541) 267-0938
Corvallis - Corvallis Falls Festival - (541) 757-6363
Corvallis - Da Vinci Days - (541) 757-6363
Dallas - Dallas Summerfest - (503) 623-2564
Eugene - Eugene Celebration - (541) 681-4108
Florence - 4th of July Celebration - (541) 997-3128
Florence - Rhododendron Festival - (541) 997-3128
Gladstone - Gladstone Chautauqua Festival - (503) 656-5225
Gresham - Mt. Hood Jazz Festival - (503) 665-3827
Joseph - Chief Joseph Days Rodeo - (541) 432-1015
Junction City - Scandinavian Festival - (541) 998-9372
Kings Valley - Shrewsbury Renaissance Faire - (541) 929-4897
Lakeview - Festival of Free Flight - (877) 947-6040
Lebanon - Lebanon Strawberry Festival - (541) 258-4444
McMinnville - Turkey Rama - (503) 472-6196
Mount Angel - Mount Angel Oktoberfest - (503) 845-6882
Newberg - Old Fashioned Festival - (503) 538-9455
Newport - Glastonbury Faire - (541) 265-ARTS
Newport - Newport Seafood & Wine Festival - (541) 265-5883
North Bend - South Coast Dixieland Clambake Jazz Festival - (541) 396-5373
Pendleton - Pendleton Round-Up - (541) 276-2553
Philomath - Philomath Frolic & Rodeo - (541) 929-2611
Portland - Bite of Portland Festival - (503) 297-2700
Portland - Cinco de Mayo Festival - (503) 222-9807
Portland - The Grotto's Christmas Festival of Lights - (503) 254-7371
Portland - Portland Rose Festival - (503) 227-2681
Portland - Waterfront Blues Festival - (503) 297-2700
Salem - Oregon Dayes of Olde Renaissance Festival - (503) 371-4362
Salem - Salem Art Fair & Festival - (503) 581-2228
Springfield - Springfield Filbert Festival - (541) 343-3586
Sublimity - Sublimity Harvest Festival - (503) 769-3579
Sunriver - Sunriver Music Festival - (541) 593-1084
Sweet Home - Sportman's Holiday/Sweet Home Rodeo - (541) 367-6186
Tillamook - June Dairy Festival & Parade & Tillamook Co. Rodeo - (503) 842-7525
Veneta - Oregon Country Fair - (541) 343-4298

Appendix B

Pennsylvania

Allentown - Pennsylvania Dutch Folk Festival - (215) 679-9610

Altona - Hoss's Keystone Country Festival - (814) 949-7275

Bensalem - Fall Festival - (215) 633-3636

Bethel Park - Ligonier Highland Games - (412) 851-9900

Bethlehem - Christkindlmarkt Bethlehem - (610) 861-0678

Bethlehem - Musikfest - (610) 861-0678

Blakeslee - Gathering on the Mountain - (800) 468-2442

Blakeslee - Jack Frost Celtic Fest - (570) 443-8425

Blakeslee - Pocono Blues Festival - (570) 443-8425

Blakeslee - Pocono's Greatest Irish Festival - (570) 443-8425

Clarion - Autumn Leaf Festival - (814) 226-9161

Cornwall - A Celtic Fling - (717) 665-7021

Cornwall - Blast From The Past - (716) 665-7021

Erie - Celebration Erie - (814) 870-1269

Erie - Erie Area Summer Festival of the Arts - (814) 838-1431

Erie - St. Paul's Italian Festival - (814) 456-9391

Franklin - Applefest - (814) 432-5823

Gettysburg - Gettysburg Civil War Heritage Days - (717) 334-6274

Greenburg - Westmoreland Arts & Heritage Festival - (724) 834-7474

Harbor Creek - Harborfest - (814) 899-9173

Harrisburg - Central PA Jazz Festival - (717) 540-1010

Harrisburg - Kipona Celebration - (717) 256-3030

Harrisburg - American Musicfest - (717) 255-3020

Hazelton - Funfest - (570) 455-1508

Intercourse - Rhubarb Festival - (717) 768-8261

Jersey Shore - Jersey Shore Town Meeting July 4th Celebration - (570) 398-4545

Johnstown - Johnstown FolkFest - (814) 539-1889

Kane - Kanefest - (814) 837-6565

Kennett Square - The Mushroom Festival - (610) 693-3203

Kutztown - Kutztown Pennsylvania German Festival (610) 683-1597

Lake Harmony - Pocono Blues Festival - (570) 443-8425

Lock Haven - Labor Day Regatta - (570) 748-5782

Lock Haven - Riverfest - (570) 748-5782

Lock Haven - Sentimental Journey - (570) 748-8283

Manheim - A Celtic Fling - (717) 665-7021

Manheim - Blast From the Past Rock and Roll Festival - (717) 665-7021

Manheim - Pennsylvania Rennaissance Faire - (717) 665-7021

Mansfield - Fabulous 1890's Weekend - (570) 662-4846

McClure - McClure Bean Soup Festival - (800) 338-7389

McConnellsburg - Fulton Fall Folk Festival - (717) 485-4064

Meadville - Thurston Classic-Hot Air Balloon & Night Glo- (814) 634-0213

Meyersdale - Pennsylvania Maple Festival - (814) 634-0213

Milton - Milton Harvest Festival - (570) 742-7341

Montrose - Blueberry Festival - (814) 336-4000

Mount Pleasant - Mount Pleasant Glass & Ethic Festival (724) 547-7738

North East - North East Firemen's Cherry Festival - (814) 725-4336

North East - Wine Country Harvest Festival - (814) 725-4262

Oil City - Oil Heritage Festival - (814) 676-6296

Philadelphia - Jam on the River - (215) 629-3200

Philadelphia - Sunoco Welcome America! - (215) 683-2201

Pittsburgh - Pittsburgh Three Rivers Regatta - (412) 875-4841

Pittsfield - Wild Wind Folk Art & Craft Festival - (818) 723-0707

Reading - Berks Jazz Festival - (610) 655-6374

Renovo - Pennsylvania State Flaming Foliage Festival - (570) 923-2411

Rochester - Riverfest - (724) 775-1200

Schaefferstown - Cherry Fair & Early American Crafts Show - (717) 949-2244

Schaefferstown - Pennsylvania GERMAN Folklife Festival - (717) 949-2244

Schwenksville - Philadelphia Folk Festival - (215) 247-1300

Scranton - LaFiesta Italiana of Lackawanna Co. - (570) 342-8281

Somerset - Somerfest - (814) 443-2433

South Park - Allegheny Co. Rib Cook-Off - (412) 678-1727

State College - Central Pennsylvania Festival of the Arts - (814) 237-3682

Stroudsburg - Shawnee Fall Foliage Balloon Festival - (570) 421-4433

Tionesta - Tionesta Indian Festival - (814) 755-4591

Wellsboro - Pennsylvania State Laurel Festival - (570) 724-1926

West Newton - Pittsburgh Rennaissance Festival - (724) 872-1670

Whitehall - Lehigh Valley Blues Fest - (610) 261-2888

Appendix B

Rhode Island

Middletown - Newport Music Festival - (401) 846-1133
Newport - Christmas in Newport - (401) 849-6454
Newport - Newport Folk Festival - (401) 846-1600
Newport - Sunset Music Festival - (401) 486-1600
Warwick - Gaspee Days Arts & Crafts Festival - (401) 781-1772
Woonsocket - Autumnfest - (401) 762-9072

South Carolina

Aiken - Aiken's Makin' - (803) 641-1111
Aiken - Battle of Aiken - (803) 642-2500
Anderson - Freedom Weekend Aloft - (864) 222-0051
Batesburg-Leesville - SC Poultry Festival - (888) 427-7273
Beaufort - Festival of Trees - (843) 525-6257
Beaufort - 4th of July Flying Pig Kite Festival - (843) 986-5400
Beaufort - Gullah Festival - (843) 986-5400
Beaufort - Shrimp Festival - (843) 986-5400
Beaufort - Water Festival - (843) 524-0600
Belton - Belton Standpipe Festival - (864) 847-7111
Bishopville - Lee Co. Cotton Festival - (803) 484-5145
Blacksburg - Pioneer Days - (803) 222-3209
Branchville - Raylrode Daze Festival - (803) 274-8831
Carlisle - Piggie on the Rock - (864) 427-1505
Charleston - MOJA Arts Festival:A Celebration of African -American & Caribbean Art - (843) 724-7305
Charleston - Spoleto Festival USA - (843) 579-3100
Columbia - KidsDay Columbia - (803) 343-8750
Columbia - 3 Rivers Music Festival - (803) 401-8990
Easley - City of Easley-4th of July Festival - (864) 859-2693
Gaffney - South Carolina Peach Festival - (864) 489-9066
Greenville - BellSouth Red, White & Blue - (864) 467-5780
Greenville - Fall For Greenville - (864) 467-5780
Greenville - RiverPlace Arts Festival - (864) 467-5781
Greenwood - SC Festival of Flowers - (864) 223-8411
Hampton - Hampton Co. Watermelon Festival - (803) 643-4978
Lake City - SC Tobacco Festival - (843) 374-8611
Laurens - Laurens Co. POP Jubilee - (864) 682-4156

Little River - Blue Crab Festival - (843) 249-6604
Mannig - Striped Bass Festival - (803) 435-4405
Mullins - Golden Leaf Festival - (843) 464-5200
Myrtle Beach - Canadian-American Days Festival - (843) 626-7444
Myrtle Beach - Dickens Christmas Show & Festivals - (843) 448-9483
Myrtle Beach - South Carolina State Bluegrass Festival - (716) 864-7203
Myrtle Beach - Sun Fun Festival-A Celebration of Summer - (843) 626-7444
Orangeburg - South Carolina Festival of Roses - (803) 534-6821
Pageland - Pageland Watermelon Festival - (843) 672-6401
Pelion - SC Pelion Peanut Party - (803) 263-4050
Pendleton - Historic Pendleton Spring Jubilee - (864) 646-3782
Port Royal - 4th of July Flying Pig Kite Festival - (843) 986-5400
Rock Hill - Come-See-Me Festival - (803) 329-7625
St. George - World Grits Festival - (843) 563-7943
Simpsonville - Simpsonville Labor Day Festival - (864) 963-3781
Summerville - Flowertown Festival - (843) 871-9622
Sumter - Iris Festival - (800) 688-4748
Wagener - Wagons to Wagener - (803) 564-3412
Walhalla - Oktoberfest - (864) 638-2727
Walterboro - Colleton Co. Rice Festival - (843) 549-1079
Westminster - South Carolina Apple Festival - (864) 647-7223
Williamston - Belton Standpipe Festival - (864) 847-7111
Woodruff - Bubbafest - (864) 582-7042

Appendix B

South Dakota

Armour - Douglas Co. Achievement Days - (605) 724-2719
Belle Fourche - Black Hills Roundup - (605) 892-2676
Brookings - Brookings Festival of Lights - (605) 692-6125
Deadwood - Days of '76 Rodeo & Parade - (800) 999-1876
Deadwood - Kool Deadwood Nites - (605) 578-1876
Madison - Prairie Village Jamboree - (605) 256-3846
Milbank - A August Celebration - (605) 432-6656

Mitchell - Corn Palace Festival - (605) 995-8427
Philip - 4H Achievement Days/Co. Fair - (605) 859-2645
Redfield - July Fourth Celebration - (605) 472-0965
Sioux Falls - Sioux Falls Jazz & Blues Fest: JazzFest - (605) 335-6101
Sturgis - Sturgis Motorcycle Rally - (605) 347-9190
Tabor - Czech Days - (605) 463-2476

Tennessee

Brownsville - Brownsville Blues Festival - (731) 772- 2193
Byrdstown - Shrimp Festival - (931) 864-7195
Chattanooga - Chattanooga Traditional Dixieland Jazz Festival - (423) 266-0944
Chattanooga - Riverbend Festival (423) 756-2212
Clarksville - Clarksville Oktoberfest - (931) 358-2280
Coker Creek - Autumn Gold Festival - (423) 261-2242
Columbia - Mule Day - (931) 381-9557
Cookeville - Fall FunFest - (931) 528-4612
Dayton - Tennessee Strawberry Festival - (423) 775-0361
Dover - Pickin' Party - (270) 924-2000
Dyer - Dyer Station Celebration - (731) 855-0973
Elizabethton - Covered Bridge Celebration - (423) 547-3851
Erwin - Erwin/Unicoi Co. Apple Festival - (423) 743-3000
Franklin - Main Street Festival - (615) 595-1239
Gatlinburg - Gatlinburg Games & Scottish Festival - (865) 922-3790
Henderson - Chester Co. Bar-B-Que Festival - (731) 989-5222
Humboldt - W. TN Strawberry Festival - (731) 784-1842
Huntsville - Huntsville Firemen 4th - (423) 663-3471
Jonesborough - Jonesborough Days - (423) 753-5281
Jonesborough - National Storytelling Festival - (423) 753-2171
Jonesborough - Quiltfest - (423) 753-6644
Kenton - Kenton White Squirrel Celebration - (731) 749-5767
Kingsport - Fun Fest - (423) 392-8806
Knoxville - Dogwood Arts Festival - (865) 637-4561
Knoxville - Fantasy of Trees - (865) 541-8385
Loudon - Smoky Mtn. Fiddlers Convention - (865) 458-9020
Manchester - Bonnaroo Music Festival - (865) 523-2665
Maryville - Smoky Mtn. Artist & Hanscrafters Festival - (865) 982-3457
Memphis - Beale Street Music Festival - (901) 525-4611

Memphis - Bluestock Int'l Music Festival - (901) 526-4280
Memphis - Elvis Week - (901) 332-3322
Memphis - Great Southern Food Festival - (901) 525-4611
Memphis - King Biscuit Blues Festival - (870) 338-8101
Memphis - Memphis in May Int'l Week - (901) 525-4611
Memphis - World Championship Barbecue Cooking Contest - (901) 525-4611
Murfreesboro - Uncle Dave Macon Days Old Time Music & Dance Festival - (615) 893-6565
Nashville - Australian Festival - (615) 460-1401
Nashville - Fan Fair - (615) 244-2840
Nashville - Nashville River Stages - (615) 346-9000
Nashville - World of Bluegrass - (888) GET-IBMA
Norris - Tennessee Fall Homecoming - (865) 494-0514
Oak Ridge - Mayfest - (865) 482-3450
Oneida - Scott Co. Sorghum Festival - (800) 645-6905
Paris - World's Biggest Fish Fry - (731) 642-3431
Pigeon Forge - Dollywood Harvest Celebration/Southern Gospel Jubilee - (865) 428-9563
Ripley - Lauderdale Co. Tomato Festival - (731) 635-9541
Rugby - Christmas at Rugby - (423) 628-2441
Rugby - Festival of British & Appalachian Culture - (423) 628-2441
Rutherford - Davy Crockett Day - (731) 665-7253
Shelbyville - Tennessee Walking Horse National Celebration - (931) 684-5915
South Pittsburg - National Cornbread Festival - (423) 837-0022
Trade - Trade Days Festival - (828) 297-2200
Trenton - Trenton Teapot Festival - Teapot Festival - (731) 855-2013
Yorkville - Yorkville Int'l Washer Pitchin' Contest - (731) 543) 6110

Appendix B

Texas

Albany - Fort Griffin Fandangle - (915) 762-2525
Alvarado - Pioneers & Old Settlers Reunion - (817) 790-3503
Anahuac - Texas Gatorfest - (409) 267-4190
Arkansas Pass - Official Shrimporee of Texas - (800) 633-3028
Arkansas Pass - Shrimporee - (361) 478-7211
Athens - Black-Eyed Pea Fall Harvest - (903) 675-5181
Austin - Austin City Limits Music Festival - (512) 303-3801
Austin - Republic of Texas Biker Rally - (972) 386-7619
Bastnop - Excalibur Fantasy Faire - (512) 303-3801
Bay City - Bay City Lions Club Rice Festival - (979) 245-0717
Beaumont - Neches River Festival - (409) 835-2443
Bergheim - Boeme BergesFest - (830) 336-2997
Boerne - Boerne BergesFest - (830) 249-8173
Brownsville - Charro Days Fiesta - (956) 542-4245
Burton - Burton Cotton Gin Festival - (979) 289-FEST
Center - East Texas Poultry Festival - (936) 598-3682
Clute - Great Texas Mosquito Festival - (979) 265-8392
Comanche - Comanche Co. Pow-Wow - (915) 356-3233
Conroe - Conroe Cjun Catfish Festival - (936) 539-6009
Corpus Christi - Bayfest - (361) 887-0868
Corpus Christi - Buccaneer Days Celebration - (361) 882-882-3242
De Leon - De Leon Peach & Melon Festival, Inc. - (254) 893-6600
Dublin - Dublin St. Patrick Festival - (254) 445-3422
Emory - Eagle Fest - (903) 473-3913
Ennis - National Polka Festival - (972) 878-2625
Euless - Actor Daze - (817) 685-1669
Flatonia - Czhilispiel - (361) 865-3920
Fort Worth - Chisholm Trail Round-Up - (817) 625-7005
Fort Worth - MAIN ST. Fort Worth Arts Festival - (817) 870-1692
Fort Worth - Mayfest - (817) 332-1055
Fredericksburg - Night in Old Fredericksburg - (830) 997-6523
Galveston - Dickens on The Strand - (409) 765-7834
Galveston - Mardi Gras! Galveston - (409) 763-6564
Galveston Island - Mardi Gras Galveston - (409) 763-6564
Gilmer - Cherokee Rose Festival - (903) 843-2413
Gilmer - East Texas Yamboree - (903) 843-2413
Grand Prairie - Caribbean Music Weekend - (972) 647-2331
Grand Prairie - Mountain Man Weekend - (972) 647-2331
Grand Prairie - National Championship Indian Pow-Wow - (972) 647-2331
Grapevine - Grapefest - (817) 410-3185

Grapevine - Grapevine New Vintage Wine Festival - (972) 647-2331
Grapevine - Main Street Days - (817) 410-3185
Harlington - Riofest - (956) 425-2705
Hico - Hico Old Settlers Reunion - (254) 796-4221
Hildago - Borderfest - (956) 843 -2303
Houston - Bayou City Cajun Festival - (281) 890-5500
Houston - CY-Fair Houston Livestock Show & Rodeo BBQ - (281) 890-5500
Houston - Festival de la Familia - (281) 890-5500
Houston - Houston International Festival - (713) 654-8808
Houston - Latino Book & Family Festival-Houston - (760) 434-0798
Houston - Pickin' & Peddlin' Bluegrass Festival - (281) 890-5500
Huntsville - General Sam Houston Folk Festival - (936) 294-1832
Kerrville - Texas Arts & Crafts Fair - (830) 896-5711
Lake Worth - Bullfrog Festival - (817) 237-237-0060
Laredo - Washington's Birthday Celebration - (956) 722-0589
Lubbock - 4th on Broadway Celebration - (806) 749-2929
Lubbock - Lubbock Arts Festival - (806) 744-2787
Lubbock - The National Cowboy Symposium & Celebration - (806) 795-2455
Lifkin - Texas State Forest Festival - (936) 634-6644
Luling - Luling Watermelon Thump - (830) 875-3214
Marshall - Fire Ant Festival (903) 935-7868
Marshall - Stagecoach Days - (903) 935-7868
Nederland - Nederland Heritage Festival - (409) 724-2269
New Braunfels - Wurstfest - (830) 625-9167
Pasadena - Pasadena Strawberry Festival - (281) 991-9500
Plantersville - The Texas Renaissance Festival - (281)-356-2178
Port Arthur - Mardi Gras of Southeast Texas - (409) 721-8717
Poteet - Poteet Strawberry Festival - (830) 742-8144
San Antonio - Fiesta San Antonio - (210) 227-5191
San Antonio - Fiesta San Antonio - (201) 227-5191
San Antonio - Texas Folklike Festival - (210) 458-2249
South Padre Island - South Padre Island Bikefest - (956) 668-7484
Stanton - Old Sorehead Trade Days - (915) 756-2006
Sulphur Springs - Hopkins Co. Fall Festival & Fair - (903) 885-1534
Sweetwater - World's Largest Rattlesmake Roundup - (915) 235-5488
Texarkana - Quadrangle Festival - (903) 793-4831
Tyler - Texas Rose Festival - (903) 597-3130

Appendix B

Waxahachie - Scarborough Faire Renaissance Festival - (972) 938-3247

Wichita Falls - FallsFest - (940) 682-9797

Yorktown - Yorktown Western Days - (361) 564-2661

Utah

American Fork - American Fork Steel Days - (801) 763-3000

Brian Head - Brian Head Resort Spring Carnival - (435) 677-2035

Brigham City - Brigham City Peach Days - (405) 723-3931

Cedar City - Paiute Restoration Gathering & Pow Wow - (435) 586-1112

Cedar City - Utah Midsummer Renaissance Faire - (435) 586-1124

Eureka - Tintic Silver Festival - (435) 433-6921

Garland - Garland Wheat & Beet Days - (435) 257-6881

Ogden - Hot Rock'n 4th - no phone

Ogden - Pioneer Days Celebration - (801) 629-8214

Park City - Park City Jazz Festival - (435) 940-1362

Payson - Payson Scottish Festival - (801) 465-2933

Price - International Days - (435) 636-3184

Provo - America's Freedom Festival - (801) 370-8055

Riverton - Riverton City Town Days Celebration - (801) 208-3121

Salt lake City - Folk & Bluegrass Festival - (801) 532-5218

Salt Lake City - Greek Festival - (801) 328-9681

Salt Lake City - Utah Arts Festival - (801) 322-2428

Snowbird - Snowbird Jazz & Blues Festival - (801) 933-2110

Snowbird - Snowbird Oktoberfest - (801) 933-2110

Springville - Springville Art City Days Celebration - (901) 489-2726

Springville - Springville World Festival - (801) 489-2726

Wellsville - Festival of The American West - (435) 245-6050

Vermont

Bellows Falls - Vermont Renaissance Festival - (802) 463-2565

Bennington - Mayfest Arts Festival - (802) 442-5758

Bennington - Midnight Madness - (802) 442-5758

Bennington - Summer Under the Tent Festival For the Arts - (802) 442-5758

Burlington - Burlington Discover Jazz Festival - (802) 663-7992

Enosburg Falls - Vermont Dairy Festival - (802) 933-5921

Essex Junction - Vermont Sheep & Wool Festival - (802) 446-3325

Guilford - Vermont Renaissance Festival - (802) 463-2565

Middlebury - Middlebury Festival on the Green - (802) 388-0216

Quechee - Quechee Hot Air Balloon Festival & Crafts Fair - (802) 295-7900

St. Albans - Vermont Maple Festival - (802) 524-8500

Sheldon - Vermont Dairy Festival - (802-933-5921)

South Hero - So. Hero Applefest & Crafts - (802) 372-5566

Stowe - Stowe Winter Carnival - (802) 253-9437

Swanton - Swanton Summer Festival - (802) 868-7200

Woodstock - Wassail Celebration - (888) 496-6378

Virginia

Abingdon - Virginia Highlands Festival - (276) 623-5266

Alexandria - Alexandria Red Cross Waterfront Festival - (703) 549-8300

Big Island - Bluegrass Festival - (434) 299-5080

Big Island - Celtic Festival - (434) 299-5080

Blacksburg - Steppin' Out - (540) 951-0454

Chesapeake - Chesapeake Jubilee - (757) 482-4848

Clarksville - The Virginia Lake Festival - (434) 374-2436

Colonial Beach - Potomac River Festival - (804) 224-8145

Appendix B

Danville - Danville Harvest Jubilee - (434) 773-8160
Danville - Festival in the Park - (434) 773-8160
Edinburg - Ole' Time Festival - (540) 984-8286
Emporia - Virginia Peanut Festival - (434) 634-9441
Fairfex - Celebration Festival - (703) 324-3247
Floyd - Floydfest - (540) 745-3378
Fredericksburg - Heritage Festival - (540) 373-1776
Galax - Old Fiddler's Convention - (276) 236-8541
Hampton - Hampton Bay Days - (757) 727-1132
Hampton - Hampton Jazz Festival - (757) 838-4203
Lymchburg - Christmas at the Market - (434) 847-1499
Marion - Hungry Mother Festival - (276) 783-2901
Mathews - Mathews Market Days - (804) 725-7196
Mineral - Mineral Bluegrass Festival - (706) 864-7203
Norfolk - Bayou Boogaloo & Cajun Food Festival - (757) 441-2345

Norfolk - Harborfest - (757) 441-2345
Norfolk - Norfolk's Int'l Azalea Festival - (757) 282-2801
Norton - Best Friend Festival - (276) 679-0961
Poquoson - Poquoson Seafood Festival - (757) 868-3580
Portsmouth - Seawall Festival - (276) 393-9933
Port Townsend - Centrum's Port Townsend Blues & Heritage Festival - (360) 385-3102
Richmond - Greek Festival - (804) 355-3687
Roanoke - Roanoke Festival in the Park - (540) 342-2640
Saltville - Saltville Labor Day Celebration - (276) 496-4212
Suffolk - Suffolk Peanut Fest - (757) 539-6751
Virginia Beach - American Music Festival - (757) 425-3111
Virginia Beach - Blues at the Beach - (757) 425-3111
Virginia Beach - Neptune Festival - (757) 498-0215
Winchester - Shenandoah Apple Blossom Festival - (540) 662-3863

Washington

Anacortes - Anacortes Waterfront Festival & Boat Show - (360) 293-7911
Auburn - Auburn Good Ol' Days - (253) 939-3389
Bellevue - Bellevue Art Museum Fair - (425) 519-0742
Bellevue - 6th Street Arts & Crafts Fair - (425) 453-1223
Bellingham - Ski To Sea Festival - (360) 734-1330
Bremerton - Holidazzle - (306) 337-5350
Camas - Camas Days - (360) 834-2472
Carnation - Camlann Medieval Faire - (425) 788-8624
Chelan - Lake Chelan Bach-Fest - (509) 667-0904
Chewelah - Chewelah Chataqua - (509) 935-8991
Colville - Colville Rendevous - (509) 684-6312
Edmonds - A Taste of Edmonds - (425) 670-1496
Ephrata - Sage N Sun Festival - (509) 754-0766
Everett - Everett Salty Sea Days - (425) 339-1113
Everett - Everett Sausage Fest - (425) 349-7014
Gig Harbor - Washington Renaissance Fantasy Faire in Gig Harbor - (800) 359-5948
Grand Coulee - Colorama Festival & Pro-West Rodeo - (509) 633-3074
Grand Coulee - Fourth of July Festival - (509) 633-3074
Grand Coulee - Laser Light Festival - (509) 633-3074
Issaquah - Issaquah Salmon Days Festival - (206) 270-2532
Kennewick - Ye Merrie Greenwood Renaissance Faire - (509) 783-7727
Kent - Kent Cornucopia Days - (253) 852-5466
Lake Stevens - Lake Stevens Aquafest - (425) 379-3477

Leavenworth - Wenatchee River Salmon Festival - (509) 548-7641
Mercer Island - Mercer Island Summer Celebration! - (206) 236-7285
Mount Vernon - Skagit Valley Tulip Festival - (360) 428-5959
Nine Mile Falls - NW Renaissance Festival - (509) 276-9169
Ocean City - Fire O'er The Water - (360) 289-4552
Olympia - Olympia Harbor Days (800) 788-8847
Pasco - Pasco Fiery Food Festival - (509) 545-0738
Port Angeles - The Dungeness Crab & Seafood Faire (360) 457-6110
Port Townsend - Rhododendron Festival - (360) 385-2722
Port Townsend - Wooden Boat Festival - (360) 385-3628
Puyallup - Meeker Days - (253) 840-2631
Richland - Ye Merrie Greenwood Renaissance Faire - (509) 783-7727
Seattle - Bite of Seattle - (206) 232-2982
Seattle - Greenspire Faire - (206) 732-8359
Seattle - Magnolia Summer Festival - (206) 284-5836
Seattle - Northwest Folklife Festival - (206) 684-7300
Seattle - SEAFAIR - (206) 728-0123
Seattle - Seattle Int'l Children's Festival - (206) 684-7338
Sedro-Woolley - Sedro-Woolley Loggerodeo - (360) 826-4310
Sequin - Sequin Irrigation Festival - (360) 683-6197
Silverdale - Silverdale Whaling Days - (360) 692-1107
Spokane - Spokane Lilac Festival - (509) 535-4554

Appendix B

Springdale - Frontier Days Rodeo & Celebration - (509) 258-7110

Tacoma - Tacoma Freedom Fair & Airshow - (253) 761-9433

Tacoma - Tall Ships Tacoma Festival - (253) 682-1446

Tacoma - Taste of Tacoma - (206) 232-2982

Walla Walla - Walla Walla Balloon Stampede - (509) 525-0850

Walla Walla - Walla Walla Sweet Onion Blues Fest - (509) 525-1031

Wenatchee - Washington State Apple Blosson Festival/Arts & Crafts Fair - (509) 662-3616

Winthrop - Winthrop Rhythm & Blues Festival - (206) 595-3220

Yakima - Yakima Folklife Festival - (509) 348-0747

West Virginia

Alderson - Alderson 4th of July Celebration - (304) 445-7730

Berkeley Springs - Uniquely West Virginia: A Celebration of Wine & Food - (800) 447-8797

Bluefield - Mountain Festival - (304) 327-7184

Buckhannon - WV Strawberry Festival - (304) 472-9036

Burlington - Burlington Old-Fashioned Apple Harvest Festival - (309) 788-2342

Burnsville - WV Autumn Festival - (304) 765-7602

Chapmanville - Apple Butter Festival - (304) 855-4582

Charleston - Charleston Sternwheel Regatta - (304) 343-5153

Clarksburg - West Virginia Italian Heritage Festival - (304) 622-7314

Clay - Clay Co. Golden Delicious Festival - (304) 587-4455

Cliftop - Appalachian String Band Music Festival - (304) 438-3005

Cowen - Cowen Historical Railroad Festival - (304) 847-2312

Cox's Mill - WV State Folk Festival - (304) 462-8427

Craigsville - Craigsville Fall Festival - (304) 742-3802

Davis - Leaf Peepers Festival - (304) 259-5315

Durbin - Durbin Days - (304) 456-4281

Elkins - Mountain State Forest Festival - (304) 636-1824

Fairmont - Three Rivers Festival - (304) 363-2625

Fayetteville - New River Gorge Bridge Day Festival - (304) 465-5617

Hinton - WV State Water Festival - (304) 466-5332

Huntington - Juneteenth Festival - (304) 525-3352

Ireland - Irish Spring Festival - (304) 452-8962

Kingwood - Preston Co. Buckwheat Festival - (304) 329-0021

Knob Fork - Autumnfest - (304) 775-2805

Marlinton - Pioneer Days - (304) 799-4315

Martinsburg - Mountain State Apple Harvest Festival - (304) 263-2500

Meadow Bridge - Meadow Bridge Homecoming Festival - (304) 484-7250

Morgantown - The Florence Merow Mason-Dixon Festival of W. Virginia - (304) 599-1309

Mullens - Dogwood Festival - (304) 294-6470

Mullens - Lumberjackin' Bleugrassin' Jamboree - (304) 294-4000

Parkersburg - Mid-Ohio Valley Multi-Cultural Festival - (740) 423-9314

Parkersburg - Parkersburg Homecoming Festival - (304) 422-9970

Parkersburg - WV Honey Festival - (304) 424-1960

Pennsboro - Pennsboro Country Roads Festival - (304) 659-2989

Petersburg - Spring Mountain Festival - (304) 257-2722

Philippi - Blue & Gray Reunion - (304) 457-4265

Pickens - WV Maple Syrup Festival - (304) 924-5096

Pinch - Pinch Reunion Week - (304) 965-1233

Pineville - Wyoming Co. Labor Day Festival - (304) 732-7695

Point Pleasant - Battle Days - (304) 675-3844

Point Pleasant - Country Music Festival Chicken B.B.Q. - (304) 675-5737

Point Pleasant - Fall Country Festival - (304) 675-5737

Point Pleasant - Point Pleasant Sternwheel Regatta & River Festival - (304) 675-3440

Princeton - Princeton Summerfest - (304) 487-1502

Quiet Dell - Fall Frolic - (304) 622-3304

Quiet Dell - Spring Frolic - (304) 622-3304

Ronceverte - Ronceverte River Festival - (304) 647-3825

Salem - Salem Apple Butter Festival - (304) 782-3565

Sistersville - WV Oil & Gas Festival - (304) 652-2939

Spencer - WV Black Walnut Festival - (304) 927-5616

Summersville - Music in the Mountains - (304) 872-3145

Terra Alta - Terra Alta July 4th Celebration - (304) 789-2431

Webster Springs - Webster Co. Woodchopping Festival - (304) 847-7291

Weston - Fourth of July Celebrtation - (304) 269-2349

Weston - Stonewall Jackson Heritage Arts & Crafts Jubilee - (304) 243-269-1863

Wheeling - Oglebayfest - (304) 243-4132

Appendix B

Wisconsin

Arcadia - Broiler-Dairy Days - (608) 323-3366

Beloit - Riverfest - (608) 365-4838

Burlington - ChocolateFest - (262) 763-3300

Cadott - Chippewa Valley Country Fest - (715) 720-7110

Cadott - Chippewa Valley Rock Fest - (715) 720-7110

Cumberland - Cumberland Rutabaga Festival - (715) 822-3378

Eau Claire - Country Jam USA-Wisconsin - (715) 839-7500

Fond du Lac - Fond du Lac's Walleye Weekend Festival - (920) 923-6555

Grantsburg - Snowmobile Watercross - (715) 463-5466

Green Bay - Bayfest - (920) 336-6123

Horicon - Marsh Days Festival - (920) 485-3200

Kenosha - Bristol Renaissance Faire - (262) 396-4320

Keshena - Menominee Ice Challenge - (800) 343-7778

La Crosse - Great River Jazz Fest - (608) 784-7575

La Crosse - La Crosse Riverfest - (608) 782-6000

La Crosse - Oktoberfest - (608) 784-3378

Lake Mills - Festival Days - (920) 648-5115

Little Chute - Great Wisconsin Cheese Festival - (920) 788-7390

Madison - Art Fair on the Square - (608) 257-0158

Marinette - Porterfield Country Music Festival - (920) 834-2465

Marshfield - Dairyfest - (800) 422-4541

Menasha - Country USA - (920) 969-2270

Merrill - Winterfest - (715) 536-9474

Middleton - Middleton Good Neighbor Festival - (608) 831-6350

Milwaukee - Annunciation Greek Fest - (414) 461-9400

Milwaukee - Bastille Days Festival - (414) 271-1416

Milwaukee - Festa Italiana - (414) 223-2193

Milwaukee - German Fest - (414) 464-9444

Milwaukee - Holiday Folk Fair Int'l - (414) 225-6220

Milwaukee - Mexican Fiesta - (414) 383-7066

Milwaukee - Milwaukee Irish Fest - (414) 476-3378

Milwaukee - Polish Fest - (414) 529-2140

Milwaukee - Summerfest - (414) 273-2680

Monroe - Cheese Days - (608) 325-7771

Muskego - Muskego Community Festival - (262) 679-2800

Neenah - CommunityFest - (920) 722-7758

New Glarus - Wilhelm Tell Festival - (608) 527-2370

New Richmond - Fun Festival - (715) 246-2900

Oregon - Oregon Summer Fest - (608) 835-3697

Oshkosh - Country USA - (920) 969-2270

Oshkosh - Oshkosh Sawdust Days - (920) 235-5584

Park Falls - Flambeau Rama - (715) 762-2703

Prairie Du Chien - Prairie Dog Blues Festival - (608) 326-4024

Racine - Harbor Fest - (262) 639-2665

Racine - Salmon-A-Rama - (262) 636-1860

Reedsburg - Reedsburg Butter Festival - (608) 524-3208

Rhinelander - Hodag Country Festival - (715) 369-1300

Rice Lake - Rice Lake Aquafest - (715) 234-6060

Richland Center - Star Spangled Celebration - (608) 647-6341

Ripon - Cookie Daze - (920) 748-6764

Ripon - Dickens of a Christmas - (920) 748-6764

Ripon - Pumpkin Fest - (920) 748-7466

Ripon - Ripon Fest - (920) 748-6764

Ripon - Ripon Jazz Festival - (920) 748-7466

Shawano - Old Time Music & Craft Festival - (715) 799-3688

Sheboygan - Bratwurst Festival - (920) 451-2300

Sheboygan Falls - Jaycee's Fall Fest - (920) 467-9450

Siren - 4th of July - (715) 349-5000

Siren - Harvestfest - (715) 349-5000

Siren - Summerfest - (715) 349-5000

Sparta - Sparta Butterfest - (608) 269-4932

Sun Prairie - Sun Prairie Sweet Corn Festival - (608) 837-4547

Warrens - Cranberry Festival - (608) 378-4200

West Allis - West Allis Western Days - (414) 541-1846

West Bend - West Bend Germanfest - (262) 338-3909

Wisconsin Dells - Automotion - (800) 223-3557

Wisconsin Dells - Autumn Harvest Fest - (800) 223-3557

Wisconsin Dells - Flake Out Festival - (608) 254-8088

Wisconsin Dells - Wisconsin Dells Polish Fest - (608) 253-4451

Wisconsin Dells - Wo-Zha-Wa Days Fall Festival - (608) 254-8088

Appendix B

Wyoming

Alta - Grand Targhee's Bluegrass Festival - (800) 827-4433

Cheyenne - Cheyenne Frontier Days - (307) 778-7200

Cody - Plains Indian Museum Powwow - (307) 578-4049

Gillette - Cam-Plex Winter Western - (307) 682-0552

Lander - Lander Pioneer Days Parade & Rodeo - (307) 332-2365

Pinedale - Green River Rendezvous - (877) 686-6266

Appendix B

Appendix B

CANADIAN FESTIVAL LISTINGS
(Province-by-Province)

Appendix B

Appendix B

Alberta

Banff - Banff/Lake Louise Winter Festival - (403) 762-0270
Calgary - Calgary Blues & Roots Festival - (403) 670-0460
Calgary - Calgary Folk Music Festival - (403) 233-0904
Calgary - TD Canada Trust Jazz Festival - (403) 262-1500
Calgary - Calgary Winterfest - (403) 543-5480
Camrose - Big Valley Jamboree - (888) 404-1234
Canmore - Canmore Folk Music Festival - (403) 678-2524
Canmore - Canmore Heritage Days - (403) 678-2524
Edmonton - Edmonton Heritage Festival - (780) 488-3378
Edmonton - Jazz City Int'l Music Festival - (780) 432-7166
Edmonton - Edmonton Folk Music Festival - (780) 429-1899
Edmonton - Edmonton Int'l Street Performers Festival - (780) 425-5162
Jasper - Jasper in January - (780) 852-5247
Strathmore - Strathmore Heritage Days - (403) 934-5811
Twin Butte - Pincher Creek Cowboy Poetry Gathering - (403) 627-4702
Vegreville - Ukrainian Pysanka Folk Festival - (780) 632-2777

British Columbia

Bella Coola - Discovery Coast Music Festival - (250) 799-5670
Cumberland - Vancouver Island Music Fest - (250) 336-7981
Duncan - Island Folk Festival - (250) 748-3975
Harrison Hot Springs - Harrison Festival - (604) 796-3664
Hope - Hope Brigade Days - (604) 869-2744
Kelowna - Okanagan Fall Wine Festival - (250) 861-6654
Kelowna - Okanagan Summer Wine Festival - (250) 861-6654
Kelowna - Icewine Festival - (250) 861-6654
Kelowna - Okanagan Spring Wine Festival - (250) 861-6654
Kimberley - Julyfest - (250) 427-3666
Mission - Mission Folk Music Festival - (604) 826-5937
New Westminster - Hyack Festival - (604) 522-6894
Salmon Arm - Salmon Arm Roots & Blues Festival - (403) 670-0460
Vancouver - Vancouver Fringe Festival - (604) 257-0350
Vancouver - Vancouver International Jazz Festival - (604) 872-5200
Vancouver - Vancouver Folk Music Festival - (604) 602-9798
Victoria - Folkfest - (250) 414-0006
Victoria - JazzFest International - (250) 388-4423
Victoria - Vancouver Island Blues Bash - (250) 338-4423

Manitoba

Altona - Manitoba Sunflower Festival - (204) 324-9005
Austin - Manitoba Threshermen's Reunion & Stampede - (204) 637-2354
Birds Hill Park - Winnipeg Folk Festival - (204) 231-0096
Brandon - Int'l Ham Festival - (701) 263-4390
Dauphin - Dauphin's Countryfest - (204) 622-3700
Dauphin - Canada's National Ukrainian Festival - (204) 622-4600
Frederickton - Harvest Jazz & Blues Festival - (888) 688-5837
Gimli - Icelandic Festival of Manitoba - (204) 642-7417
Kilarney - Prairie Pioneer Days (Flywheel Days) - (204) 523-8614
Lockport - Lockport Children's Winter Festival - (204) 757-2222
Morden - Morden Corn & Apple Festival - (204) 822-5630
Neepawa - Neepawa & Area Lily Festival - (204) 476-8811
Russell - Beef & Barley Festival - (204) 773-2456
Steinbach - Pioneer Days Mennonite Heritage Village - (204) 326-9661
St. Pierre - Jolys-St. Pierre Frog Follies - (204) 433-3516
St. Rose du Lac - Hoof &Holler Days - (204) 447-3047
The Pas - Northern Manitoba's Trappers Festival - (204) 623-2912
Winkler - Pembina Thresherman's Reunion Days - (204) 325-7497
Winnipeg - Folklorama-Canada's Cultural Celebration - (204) 982-6210
Winnipeg - Winnipeg Fringe Theatre Festival - (204) 956-1340
Winnipeg - Festival du Voyageur - (204) 237-7692

Appendix B

Winnipeg - Jazz Winnipeg Festival - (204) 956-1340
Winnipeg - Winnipeg International Children's Festival - (204) 958-4730
Winnipeg - Winnipeg Oktoberfest - (204) 957-4521

New Brunswick

Caraquet - Acadian Village: Acadian National Holiday - (506) 726-2600
Caraquet - Le Festival Acadien De Darequet- (506) 727-2787
Edmundston - Youth Fair (Salon de la Jeunesse) - (506) 737-6927
Edmundston - La Foire Brayonne - (506) 739-6608
Fredericton - New Brunswick Summer Music Festival - (506) 453-4697
Lameque - Festival International de Musique Baroque - (506) 344-5846
Miramichi - Miramichi Folksong Festival - (506) 662-1780
Miramichi - Canada's Irish Festival - (506) 778-8810
Petit Rocher - Festival des Rameurs - (506) 783-8365
Petit Roche - Rendez-Vous Acadian - (506) 542-2686
Salisbury - Salisbury Community Days - (506) 372-3230
St. John - Festival by the Sea - (506) 632-0086
St. Stephen - Chocolate Fest - (506) 465-5616
Shediac - Shediac Lobster Festival - (506) 532-1122
Sussex - Atlantic Balloon Fiesta - (506) 432-9444

Newfoundland

Grand Falls - Windsor-Exploits Valley Salmon Festival - (703) 489-0407

Northwest Territories

Paultuk - Paultuk-Ikhalukpik Jamboree - (867) 580-3531
Yellowknife - Caribou Carnival - (867) 766-3865

Nova Scotia

Antigonish - Antigonish Highland Games - (902) 863-3179
Canso - Stan Rogers Folk Festival - (902) 336-2475
Cape Breton Island - Celtic Colours International Festival - (902) 539-8800
Halifax - Nova Scotia International Tattoo - (902) 420-1114
Kentville - Annapolis Valley Apple Blossom Festival - (902) 678-8322
Lower Wedgeport - Festival Acadian Day Wedgeport (Canada Day Weekend) - (902) 663-2745
Pictou - New Scotland Days - (902) 485-6057
Sydney - Celtic Colours International Festival - (902) 562-6700

Appendix B

Ontario

Barrie - Grand Prix of Barrie - (705) 737-9793

Brampton - Brampton Folk Festival - (905) 796-3957

Burlington - Lilac Festival - (905) 527-1158

Caledon - Canada Day Strawberry Festival - (519) 927-5607

Fort Erie - Friendship Festival - (905) 871-6454

Goderich - Celtic Roots Festival - (519) 584-8221

Guelph - Hillside Festival - (519) 763-6396

Hamilton - Festival of Friends - (905) 525-6644

Hamilton - RBC Aquafest - (905) 546-2424

Have Lock - Have Lock Country Jamboree - (705) 778-3353

London - Fiesta Del Sol - (519) 672-6614

London - Home Co. Folk Festival - (519) 432-4310

London - Sunfest - (519) 672-1522

Mississaugua - Streetsville Founder's Bread & Honey Festival (905) 816-1640

North Bay - North Bay Heritage Festival & Airshow - (705) 474-0626

Oakville - Oakville Waterfront Festival - (905) 847-7975

Ottawa - Canada Day Festival - (613) 239-5594

Ottawa - Canadian Tulip Festival - (613) 567-5757

Ottawa - Ottawa Blues Festival - (613) 247-1188

Ottawa - Ottawa Folk Festival - (613) 230-8234

Ottawa - Fringe Festival - (613) 232-6162

Ottawa - Ottawa International Jazz Festival - (613) 241-2633

Perth - Stewart Park Festival - (613) 264-1190

Renfrew - Valley Bluegrass Festival - (613) 623-8545

St. Catharines - Niagara Grape & Wine Festival - (905) 688-0212

St. Thomas - Iron Horse Festival - (519) 633-2535

Thunder Bay - Canada Day Multi-Cultural Festival - (807) 473-2343

Thunder Bay - Ojibwa Keeshigun Native Festival - (807) 473-2344

Toronto - Beaches International Jazz Festival - (416) 698-2152

Toronto - NXNE (North by Northeast Music Festival & Conference) - (416) 863-6963

Windsor - International Freedom Festival - (519) 252-7264

Prince Edward Island

Borden Carleton - Bridgefest - (902) 437-4386

Charlottetown - Festival of Lights - (902) 629-1864

Charlottetown - Festival of the Fathers - (902) 629-1864

Kensington - Kinsington Harvest Festival - (902) 836-3509

Summerside - Summerside Lobster Carnival - (902) 436-3650

Tignish - Tignish Irish Moss Festival - (902) 882-2600

Wellington - L' Exposition agricole et le Festival acadiean de la region E - (902) 854-3300

Quebec

Beauce - Festival Beauceron de l'erable (Maple Festival) - (418) 228-7476

Drummondville - Mondial des cultures de Drummondville - (819) 472-1184

Montmagny - Snow Goose Festival - (418) 248-3954

Montreal - Montreal International Jazz Festival - (514) 523-3378

Montreal - Festival International de Jazz de Montreal - (514) 523-3378

Montreal - Just For Laughs Festival - (514) 845-3155

Orford - Festival Orford - (418) 843-9871

Quebec - Quebec Winter Carnaval - (418) 626-3716

Quebec - Quebec City Summer Festival - (418) 523-4540

Sillery - Woodstock en Beauce - (877) 411-5151

Thetford Mines - Thetford North American Snowmobile Festival - (418) 335-9138

Appendix B

Saskatchewan

Balcarres - Fall Fair Days - (306) 334-2566
Regina - Mosaic-A Festival of Cultures - (306) 757-5990
Saskatoon - Folkfest - (306) 931-0100

Saskatoon - Saskatchewan Jazz Festival - (306) 652-1421
Weyburn - Country Music Jamboree - (306) 842-8080

Yukon Territory

Dawson City - Dawson City Music Festival - (867) 993-5584
Dawson City - Dawson City Discovery Days
 - (867) 993-5575
White Horse - Yukon River Bathtub Race
 - (867) 667-2148

Whitehorse - Yukon International Storytelling
 - (867) 633-7550
Whitehorse - Yukon Sourdough Rendezvous Festival
 - (888) 386-6766

Appendix B

FAIR & FESTIVAL MEETINGS CONTACT DATA

Appendix B

Appendix B

Agricultural Fair Assn. of **New Jersey** - (609) 292-5536

Alberta Assn. of Agricultural Societies - (780) 427-2174

Arizona Fairs Association - (602) 252-6771

Arkansas Fair Managers Association - (870) 628-6943

Assn. Des Expo Agricoles Du **Quebec** - (418) 248-8824

Associated **Alaskan** Fairs - (907) 766-2476

Association of **Alabama** Fairs - (205) 221-3100

Association of **Connecticut** Fairs - (860) 599-8498

Association of **Iowa** Fairs - (563) 547-4996

British Columbia Assn. of Agricultural Fairs & Exhibitions - (250) 7944224

Calfest - (530) 583-5605

Canadian Assn. of Fairs & Exhibitions - (613) 233-0012

Colorado Association of Fairs & Shows - (719) 275-4842

Colorado Festivals & Events Association - (303) 904-1521

Exhibition Association of **Nova Scotia** - (902) 384-2836

Festivals & Events Assn. of **Oklahoma** - (405) 736-0313

Florida Federation of Fairs - (813) 685-7924

Florida Festivals & Events Association - (561) 736-7071

Georgia Association of Agricultural Fairs - (478) 477-2334

Georgia Festivals & Events Association - (770) 592-7180

Illinois Association of Agricultural Fairs - (815) 692-2400

Indiana Association of Co. & District Fairs - (317) 398-2888

Int'l Association of Fairs & Expositions - (417) 862-5771

Kansas Fairs Association - (620) 669-8386

Kentucky Assn. of Fairs & Horse Shows - (606) 451-0404

Louisiana Association of Fairs & Festivals - (985) 446-1462

Louisiana Festivals & Events Association - (504) 865-1087

Maine Association of Agricultural Fairs - (307) 268-4631

Manitoba Assn. of Agricultural Societies - (204) 746-8186

Maryland Association of Agricultural Fairs & Shows - (301) 932-1234

Massachusetts Agricultural Fairs Assn. - (781) 834-6629

Michigan Assn. of Fairs & Exhibitions - (517) 371-2000

Michigan Festival & Events Association - (989) 845-2080

Mid-Atlantic Festivals & Events Assn. - (215) 567-2621

Mid-West Fairs Association - (785) 233-4037

Minnesota Federation of Co. Fairs - (507) 523-2468

Minnesota Festivals & Events Association - (507) 359-3378

Mississippi Assn. of Agricultural Fairs - (601) 825-5482

Missouri Association of Fairs & Festivals - (573) 334-9250

Nebraska Association of Fair Managers - (402) 854-3275

New Brunswick Fairs & Exhibitions Assn. - (506) 454-1053

New Hampshire Association of Fairs & Expositions - (603) 271-2404

New York Festivals & Events Association - (315) 781-0820

New York State Assn. of Agricultural Fairs - (518) 753-4956

North Carolina Assn. of Agricultural Fairs - (919) 467-8810

North Carolina Association of Festivals & Events Inc. - (336) 956-2952

North Dakota Association of Fairs - (701) 265-8446

North Dakota Festival & Events Assn. - (701) 241-8160

Ohio Fair Managers Association - (419) 648-8106

Ohio Festivals & Events association - (740) 852-8890

Oklahoma Association of Fairs & Festivals - (405) 672-5193

Ontario Assn .of Agricultural Societies - (905) 986-0238

Oregon Fairs Association - (503) 370-7019

Oregon Festivals & Events Association - (503) 620-3153

Pennsylvania State Association of Co Fairs - (866) 723-2477

Prince Edward Island Assn. of Exhibitions - (902) 368-4848

Rocky Mountain Association of Fairs - (406) 734-5395

Rocky Mountain Festivals & Events Assn. - (801) 322-2428

Saskatchewan Assn. of Agricultural Societies & Exhibitions - (306) 664-6654

South Carolina Association of Fairs - (803) 799-3387

South Dakota Fairs Association - (605) 397-8333

Southwestern Festivals & Events Assn. - (505) 281-3755

Tennessee Association of Fairs - (931) 438-7242

Tennessee Festivals & Events Association - (931) 684-5915

Texas Association of Fairs & Events - (979) 245-4549

Texas Festival & Events Association - (830) 997-0741

Utah Association of Fairs & Shows - (801) 538-8445

Vermont Agricultural Fairs Association - (802) 388-3335

Virginia Association of Fairs - (301) 869-4387

Virginia Festival & Events Association - (757) 635-7597

Washington Festivals & Events Association - (360) 452-7019

Washington State Fair Association - (360) 740-6479

West Virginia Assn. of Fairs & Festivals - (888) 982-3247

Western Fairs Association - (916) 927-3100

Wisconsin Association of Fairs - (608) 584-5327

Wisconsin Festivals & Events Association - (608) 836-5021

Wyoming Association of Co. Fairs - (307) 358-2398

Appendix B

Appendix C

RECORDING STUDIOS

SOUND ENGINEERS

CARTAGE COMPANIES

STUDIO MUSICIANS

BACK-UP SINGERS

Appendix C

Appendix C

Nashville Recording Studios

615 Music Studios	(615) 244-6515	**OUD Recording Studio**	(615) 321-5683
Audio Productions	(615) 321-3612	**Quad Studios**	(615) 321-9500
Audio Services	(615) 327-9040	**Sony Tree Studios**	(615) 726-8300
Dark Horse Recording	(615) 791-5030	**Sound Emporium, Inc.**	(615) 383-1982
East Iris Studios	(615) 777-9080	**Sound Stage Studios**	(615) 256-2676
Emerald Studios	(615) 846-5200	**Soundshop Recording Studios**	(615) 244-4149
Hilltop Recording Studios	(615) 865-5272	**Spotland Studios**	(615) 385-2957
IV Music Studios	(615) 320-1444	**Starstruck Studios**	(615) 259-5400
Jamsync Studios	(615) 320-5050	**The Castle Recording Studios**	(615) 791-0810
New Reflections Studios	(615) 269-0826	**The Money Pit**	(615) 256-0311
Ocean Way Studios	(615) 320-3900	**The Orchard Recording Studio**	(615) 778-5762
Omni	(615) 321-5526	**The Sound Kitchen**	(615) 370-5773
Orchard Recording Studios	(615) 776-5762		

Sound Engineers
-partial list with "platinum credits" - contact through above listed studios -

Chuck Ainlay	**Grant Greene**
Jeff Balding	**Mike Hanson**
Mike Bradley	**Julian King**
Mark Capps	**John Kunz**
Bob Bullock	**Gary Paczosa**
Ben Fowler	**Billy Sherrill**

Cartage Companies

Nashville Cartage	(615) 242-7871
SIR Cartage	(615) 255-4500
Session Services	(615) 242-7300
Soundcheck	(615) 726-1165
Tennessee Stage & Supply	(615) 242-9545

Appendix C

Studio Musician's
-partial list of Nashville's top session players-
call musician's union for contact numbers

Guitar

Bobby All
Pat Buchanan
Gary Burnett
Mark Caff Stevens
Jerry Kimbrough
Jeff King
Chris Leuzinger
Brent Mason
Brent Rowan
Michael Spriggs
John Willis

Piano/Keyboards

David Briggs
Tony Harrell
John Hobbs
Jimmy Nichols
Bobby Ogdin
Gary Prine
Matt Rawlins
"Pig" Robbins
Mike Rojas
Gary Smith
Rees Wynans

Harp(Harmonica)

Mike Douchette
Jelly Roll Johnson
Charlie McCoy

Bass

Mike Brignardello
Jimmy Carter
John Howard
Larry Paxton
Jackie Street
Bob Wray

Drums

Eddie Bayers
Steve Brewster
Jerry Kroon
Paul Liem
Kenny Malone
Greg Morrow
Milton Sledge
Chuck Tilley
Tommy Wells

Appendix C

Fiddle

- Glenn Duncan
- Stuart Duncan
- Larry Franklin
- Rob Hajacos
- Aubrey Haynie
- Tammy Rogers
- John Yudkin

Steel/Dobro

- Mike Douchette
- Buddy Emmons
- Paul Franklin
- Sonny Garrish
- Mike Johnson
- Russ Pahl
- Scott Sanders

Backup Singers
-partial list of Nashville's top session vocalists-
call AFTRA for contact numbers

- Bob Bailey
- Michael Black
- Perry Coleman
- Matt Dame
- Thom Flora
- The Jordanaires
- Wesley Hightower
- Gene Miller
- John Wesley Ryles
- Jason Sellers
- Russell Terrell
- Dennis Wilson
- Curtis Wright
- Curtis Young

- Lisa Blackman
- Becka Bramlett
- Margie Cates
- Lisa Cochran
- Joanna Cotton
- Melody Crittenden
- Kim Fleming
- Vicki Hampton
- Joanna Janet
- Lianna Manis
- Kim Parent
- Lisa Silver

Appendix C

Appendix C

RECORD LABELS

PERFORMANCE RIGHTS SOCIETIES

Appendix C

Appendix C

Record Labels

Acony Records Nashville
P.O. Box 40100
Nashville, TN 37204
(615) 269-9072

Arista Records
1400 18th Ave. South
Nashville, TN 27212
(615) 301-4488

Artemis Records
130 Fifth Avenue, 7th Floor
New York, NY 10011
(212) 414-1700

Back Porch Records
4650 North Port Washington Rd.
Milwaukee, WI 53212
(414) 961-8350

Bandit Records
635 West Iris Dr.
Nashville, TN 37204
(615) 242-1234

Blue Hat Records
17060 Central Pike
Lebanon, TN 37090
(615) 443-2112

BNA Records
1400 18th Ave. South
Nashville, TN 37212
(615) 301-4400

Broken Bow Records
209 10th Ave. South, Ste. 220
Nashville, TN 37203
(615) 244-8600

Capitol Nashville
3322 West End Ave., 11th Floor
Nashville, TN 37203
(615) 269-2000

Cleopatra Label Group
1831 Pontius Ave.
West Los Angeles, CA 90025
(310) 477-4000 Ext 102

Columbia Records
1400 18th Av. South
Nashville, TN 37212
(615) 858-1300

Curb/Asylum Records
48 Music Square East
Nashville, TN 37203
(615) 321-5080

Curb Records
48 Music Square East
Nashville, TN 37203
(615) 321-5080

Destiny Row Records
P.O. Box 128168
Nashville, TN 37212
(615) 292-2435

Dualtone Records
1614 17th Ave. South
Nashville, TN 37203
(615) 320-0620

Epic Records
1400 18th Ave. South
Nashville, TN 37203-4323
(615) 858-1300

Equity Music Group
1222 16th Ave., South, 2nd Floor
Nashville, TN 37212
(615) 695-2350

IME Records
2 Music Circle S. Ste 101
Nashville, TN 37203
(615) 944-2230

Lost Highway Records
60 Music Square East
Nashville, TN 37203
(615) 524-7500

Lyric Street Records
1100 Demonbreun St., Ste. 100
Nashville, TN 37203
(615) 963-4848

MCA/UMG
60 Music Square East
Nashville, TN 37203
(615) 524-7500

Mercury/UMG
60 Music Square East
Nashville, TN 37203
(615) 524-7500

Nonesuch Records
1290 Ave of the Americas, 27th Floor
New Yorjk, NY 10104
(212) 707-2900

NSD Records
2 Music Circle S., Suite 101
Nashville, TN 37203
(615) 944-2230

Appendix C

RCA Records
1400 18th Ave. South
Nashville, TN 37212
(615) 301-4300

Redeemer Records
2 Music Circle S, Ste 101
Nashville, TN 37203
(615) 944-2230

RMG Records
P.O. Box 2476
Hendersonville, TN 37077
(615) 452-7878

Rounder Records
1 Camp Street
Cambridge, MA 02140
(617) 218-4497

Selectone Records
320 Main Street, Ste. 210
Franklin, TN 37064
(615) 591-8930

Skaggs Family Records
329 Rockland Rd.
Hendersonville, TN 37075
(615) 264-8877

Sugar Hill Records
120 31st Ave North
Nashville, TN 37203
(625) 297-6890

Universal South
40 Music Square West
Nashville, TN 37203
(615) 259-5300

Vanguard Records
2700 Pennsylvania Ave.
Santa Monica, CA 90404
(310) 829-9355

Warner Bros. Records
20 Music Square East
Nashville, TN 37203
(615) 748-8000

Western Beat Records
P.O. Box 128105
Nashville, TN 37212
(615) 248-5026

Performing Rights Societies

ASCAP
2 Music Square West
Nashville, TN 37203
(615) 742-5000
www.ascap.com

BMI
10 Music Square East
Nashville, TN 37203
(615) 401-2000
www.bmi.com

SESAC
55 Music Square East
Nashville, TN 37203
(615) 320-0055
www.sesac.com

Appendix C

PUBLICISTS

RECORD PROMOTERS

RADIO SYNDICATORS

RODEO COMPANIES

Appendix C

Appendix C

Publicists

Alabama Promotions
101 Glen Blvd.
Ft. Payne, AL 35967
(256) 845-4283

Alison Auerbach Public Relations
3314 West End Avenue, Ste 503
Nashville, TN 37203
(615) 269-6440

Alliance
3805 Rolland Road
Nashville, TN 37205
(615) 292-5804

AristoMedia
P.O. Box 22765
Nashville, TN 37202
(615) 269-7071

The Brokaw Company
9255 Sunset Blvd., Ste. 804
West Hollywood, CA 90069
(310) 273-2060

Century II Promotions, Inc.
2813 Dogwood Pl.
nashville, TN 37204
(615) 385-5700

D. Baron Media Relations
1411 Cloverfield Blv.d
Santa Monica, CA 90404
(310) 315-5444

Dept. 56
22410 Colins St
Woodland Hills, CA 91367
(818) 702-6253

Erickson Public Relations
54 Brookhill Cir
Nashville, TN 37215
(615) 665-5950

FrontPage Publicity
P.O. Box 90168
Nashville, TN 37209
(615) 383-0412

The Gabriel Group
2 Music Circle S., Suite 101
Nashville, TN 37203
(615) 944-2230

Gold & Gold Productions
63 Chinook Heights S.
Lethbridge, AB T1K 6T6
(403) 327-6680

The Hofer Company
2121 Fairfax Ave, Ste 3
Nashville, TN 37212
(615) 269-7479

The Holley-Guidry Company
2714 Westwood Dr, Ste 102
Nashville, TN 37204
(615) 460-9550

Hot Schatz PR
1024 16th Avenue South, 2nd Floor
Nashville, TN 37212
(615) 782-0078

Jim Havey Public Relations
30 Music Square West
Nashville, TN 37203
(615) 251-8802

Joe's Garage
4405 Belmont Park Terrace
Nashville, TN 37215
(615) 269-3238

Karen Byrd Public Relations
2020 Fieldstone Pkwy., Ste. 900-219
Franklin, TN 37069
(615) 595-1500

KSA
138 West 25th, 7th Floor
New York, NY 10001
(212) 582-5400

LGB Media-Lisa Gladfelter Bell
1228 Pineview Ln.
Nashville, TN 37211
(615) 834-4944

LC Media
P.O. Box 965
Antioch, TN 37011
(615) 331-1710

Lotos Nile Media
P.O. Box 23050
Nashville, TN 37202
(615) 298-1144

Luck Media
8090 Olympic Blvd.
Beverly Hills, CA 90211
(310) 860-9170

Morris Entertainment International
202-478 River Ave.
Winnipeg, MB R3L 0C8
(204) 452-0052

Appendix C

Morris Public Relations
P.O. Box 210588
Nashville, TN 37221
(615) 952-9250

Nancy Seltzer & Associates, Inc.
6220 Del Valle Dr.
Los Angeles, CA 90048
(323) 938-3562

Palmer Publicity, Inc., Ltd.
461 East King's Rd.
North Vancouver, BC V7N1J1
(604) 988-6757

PFA
451 Greenwich St., Ste 503
New York, NY 10013
(212) 334-6116

PLA Media
1303 16th Ave., South
Nashville, TN 37212
(615) 327-0100

Press Office
P.O. Box 159006
Nashville, TN 372015
(615) 269-3670

The Publicity House
P.O. Box 121551
Nashville, TN 37212
(615) 297-7002

PYR Public Relations
6725 Sunset Blvd, Ste 570
Los Angeles, CA 90028
(323) 957-0730

Rogers & Cowan/LA
8687 Melrose Ave, 7th Floor
Los Angeles, CA 90069
(310) 854-8100

RPI Entertainment & Media Group
1031 N. Laurel Ave., Ste Three
Hollywood, CA 90046
(323) 960-904

Sacks & Co.
427 W. 14th Street
New York, NY 10014
(212) 741-1000

Sandie Rogers
47 Autumn View Dr.
Windham, ME 04062
(877) 438-5646

Saviano Media
1313 16th Ave. South
Nashville, TN 37212
(615) 385-1233

Schmidt Relations
2214 Elliston Pl, Ste 300
Nashville, TN 37203
(615) 846-3878

Shock Ink
14260 Ventura Blvd, Ste 202
Sherman Oaks, CA 91423
(818) 385-1051

Shore Fire Media
32 Court St, Ste 1600
Brooklyn, NY 11201
(718) 522-7171

William Smithson
1027 17th Ave., South
Nashville, TN 37212
(615) 329-8800

Star Keeper PR/Inflyght, Inc.
P.O. Box 128195
Nashville, TN 37212
(615) 833-3000

Starstruck Entertainment
40 Music Square West
Nashville, TN 37203
(615) 259-0001

Sunshine Consultants
149 5th Ave, 7th Floor
New York, NY 10010
(212) 691-2800

Susan Collier Public Relations
6204 Jocelyn Hollow Road
Nashville, TN 37205
(615) 356-0375

Tenacious Entertainment
1815 Division St., Ste 305
Nashville, TN 37203
(615) 340-0882

Tracy Bufferd
826 Broadway, Ste 411
New York, NY 10003
(212) 777-5110

United Management
3325 N. University Ave., Ste 150
Provo, UT 84604
(801) 373-3600

Webster & Associates Public Relations
P.O. Box 23015
Nashville, TN 37202
(615) 777-6995

Wolf, Paulette Events & Entertainment
3300 W. Franklin Blvd.
Chicago, IL 60624
(773) 475-4300

Appendix C

Record Promoters

Sam Cerami
(615) 256-0420

Jerry Duncan
(615) 251-0905

Grass Roots Promotions
(615) 661-6577

Marco Promotions
(615) 269-7074

Debbie Gibson Palmer
(St. Regis International, Ltd.)
(818) 783-6886

Jack Pride
(615) 302-0072

Diane Richey
(615) 320-7618

Chris Taylor
(615) 792-4753

Alan Young
(818) 597-0303

Satellite Radio & Radio Syndicators

ABC Radio Networks
  444 Madison Avenue
  New York, NY 10022
  (212) 735-1700

Amerimusic Broadcasting
  2334 CR 2265
  Telephone, TX 75488
  (903) 664-3741

FamilyNet Radio
  6350 West Freeway
  Forth Worth, TX 76116
  (800) 433-5757

Jim Owens Entertainment
  624 Grassmere Park Drive, Suite 16
  Nashville, TN 37211
  (615) 256-7700

MOR Media International, Inc.
  P.O. Box 683
  New York, NY 10108
  (800) 827-1722

Motor Racing Network
  1801 West International Speedway Blvd.
  Daytona Beach, FL 32114
  (386) 947-6400

Performance Racing Network
  P.O. Box 600
  Concord, NC 28026
  (704) 455-4488

Premiere Radio Networks
  15260 Ventura Boulevard
  Sherman Oaks, CA 91403
  (818) 377-5300

Pro Rodeo News Network
  P.O. Box 1272
  Pendleton, OR 97801
  (541) 276-8233

Sirius
  1221 Avenue of the Americas
  New York, NY 10020
  (212) 584-5100

United Stations Radio Network
  25 W. 45 St., 11th Floor
  New York, NY 10036-4902
  (212) 869-1111

Westwood One Radio Network
  8965 Lindblade
  Culver City, CA 90302
  (310) 840-4203

Appendix C

Rodeo Companies

Barnes PRCA Rodeo	Bill Hall Entertainment & Events - (215) 357-5189 William B. Hall, III
Int'l Championship Rodeo	World Classic Productions, Inc. - (615) 876-6100 George Runquist
King Bro. IXL Ranch Rodeo	Starcrest Entertainment Corp. - (740) 452-6162 Tom Workman
Longhorn World Championship Rodeos	Longhorn World Championship Rodeo, Inc. - W. Bruce Lehrke
Dave Martin's Championship Rodeo & Bullrideramania	Variety Attractions, Inc. - (740) 453-0394 Dave Martin

Appendix C

SONG PUBLISHERS

Appendix C

Appendix C

Song Publishers

Affiliated Publishers
P.O. Box 120615
Nashville, TN 37212
(615) 291-5008

Aim High Music/Zomba-BMG Publishing
1214 16th Ave South
Nashville, TN 37212
(615) 3210600

AristoMedia
1620 16th Ave. S
Nashville, TN 37212
(615) 269-7073

Black & White Music/Al Jolson
116 17 Ave. S
Nashville, TN 37203
(615) 244-5656

BMG Music Publishing
1600 Division St., Ste 225
Nashville, TN 37203
(615) 687-5839

Bob Montgomery Productions
P.O. Box 120967
Nashville, TN 37212
(615) 309-4948

Bocephus Music, Ince.
P.O. Box 40929
Nashville, TN 37204
(615) 297-3134

Bourne Co.
5 West 37th Street
New York, NY 10018
(212) 391-4300

Bradley Music Management
535 Wilson Hollow Rd
Dickson, TN 37055
(615) 3203220

Brock Music, Inc.
2937 Berry Hill Dr.
Nashville, TN 37204
(615) 298-2200

Buckhorn Music
1022-A 18th Ave. S
Nashville, TN 37204
(615) 327-0032

Buzz Cason Publishing
2804 Azalea Place
Nashville, TN 37204
(615) 383-8682

Cal IV Entertainment
808 19th Avenue South
Nashville, TN 37203
(615) 321-2700

CDB Music, LLC
1217 16th Ave S
Nashville, TN 37212
(615) 327-5474

Cherry Lane Music Publishing, Co.
6 E 32nd St., 11th Floor
New York, NY 10016
(212) 561-3000

Chrysalis Music Group
8500 Melrose Ave., Ste. 207
West Hollywood, CA 90069
(310) 652-0066

Cornelius Companies/Gateway Entertainment
1719 West End Ave., Ste. 805 E
Nashville, TN 37203
(615) 321-5333

Crutchfield Music Group
1106 17th Ave. S
Nashville, TN 37212
(615) 321-5558

Curb Music
48 Music Square East
Nashville, TN 37203
(615) 321-5080

Disney Music Publishing
500 S. Buena Vista St.
Burbank, CA 91521-6174
(818) 569-3223

Drake Music Group
P.O. Box 40945
Nashville, TN 37204
(615) 297-4345

EMI Music Publishing
35 Music Sq. East
Nashville, TN 37203
(615) 742-8081

Famous Music Publishing
65 Music Sq. East
Nashville, TN 37203
(615) 329-0500

Fox Music Publishing
10201 W. Pico Blvd.
Los Angeles, CA 90035
(310) 369-2541

Appendix C

Gabriel Music Group
2 Music Circle S, Suite 101
Nashville, TN 37203
(615) 944-2230

Harlan Howard Songs
1902 Wedgewood Ave.
Nashville, TN 37212
(615) 321-9098

Heart Chart Music
1103 B 17th Ave South
Nashville, TN 37212
(615) 327-0031

Horipro Entertainment
1819 Broadway
Nashville, TN 37203
(615) 329-0890

House of Fame, Inc.
603 East Avalon Ave.
Muscle Shoals, AL 35661
(256) 381-0801

Island Bound Music, Inc.
1204 17th Avenue S
Nashville, TN 37212
(615) 320-5440

KMG Entertainment, Inc.
1010 17th Ave South
Nashville, TN 37212
(615) 269-7000

Knox/Hi Lo Music
639 Madison Ave.
Memphis, TN 38103
(901) 523-2251

Life Music Group
P.O. Box 128288
Nashville, TN 37212
(615) 292-6363

Major Bob
1111 17th Ave. S
Nashville, TN 37212
(615) 329-4150

Makin' Music/Makin' Friends
1230 17th Ave S
Nashville, TN 37212
(615) 269-6770

Malaco Music
33 Music Square West
Nashville, TN 37203
(615) 327-0440

McLachlan-Scruggs Music
2821 Bransford Ave.
Nashville, TN 37204
(615) 292-0099

MGM Music/United Artists
2500 Broadway, 5th Floor
Santa Monica, CA 90404
(310) 449-3000

Monk Family Music Group
P.O. Box 150768
Nashville, TN 37215
(615) 292-6811

Morning Music
5200 Dixie Rd, Ste 203
Mississauga, Ontario L4W1E4
(905) 625-2676

Murrah Music
1109 16th Ave. S
Nashville, TN 37212
(615) 329-4236

Muy Bueno Music Group
1000 18th Ave. S
Nashville, TN 37212
(615) 327-9229

Painted Desert Music Corp.
488 Madison, 12th Floor
New York, NY 10022
(212) 588-0878

Peermusic
1207 16th Ave. South
Nashville, TN 37212
(615) 329-0603

R Gant Music Group
3190 Distillery Road
Greenbrier, TN 37073
(615) 329-0890

Randy Scruggs Music
2828 Azalea Place
Nashville, TN 37204
(615) 298-1238

Ray Baker Productions
199 The Hollows Court
Hendersonville, TN 37075
(615) 826-2725

Sherrill Music
1022 B 18th Ave. S
Nashville, TN 37212
(615) 321-4544

Sony/ATV
8 Music Sq. W
Nashville, TN 37203
(615) 726-8300

Southern Writers Group USA
2804 Azalea Pl.
Nashville, TN 37204
(615) 383-8682

Appendix C

Starstruck Writers Group
40 Music Sq. W
Nashville, TN 37203
(615) 259-0001

Talbot Music Group
7528 Staffordshire Dr
Nashville, TN 37221
(615) 244-6200

Ten Ten Music Group
33 Music Sq. W, #110
Nashville, TN 37203
(615) 255-9955

Tom Collins Productions
P.O. Box 121407
Nashville, TN 37212
(615) 255-5550

Universal Music Publishing
1904 Adelicia St
Nashville, TN 37212
(615) 340-5400

Warner/Chappell
20 Music Sq. East
Nashville, TN 37203
(615) 733-1880

Western Beat Entertainment
P.O. Box 128105
Nashville, TN 37212
(615) 248-5026

Wrensong Publishing Corp.
1229 17th Ave. S
Nashville, TN 37212
(615) 321-4487

Appendix C

Appendix C

MANAGERS

COMPILATION CD DISTRIBUTORS

TALENT (BOOKING) AGENTS

Appendix C

Appendix C

Managers

Al Bunetta Management
33 Music Sq. W., Ste. 102B
Nashville, TN 37203
(615) 742-1250

Al Embry International
P.O. Box 206
Old Hickory, TN 37138
(615) 847-0123

Artists Management International
P.O. Box 671837
Marietta, GA 30006-0031
(770) 428-5484

azoffmusic Management
1100 Glendon Ave, Ste 2000
Los Angeles, CA 90024
(310) 209-3100

Beach Street Artist Management
5200 Old Harding Rd.
Franklin, TN 37064
(615) 799-2229

Beau Davis Entertainment
515, 505 56th Ave. SW
Calgary, AB T2V 0G6
(403) 258-0248

Big Picture Entertainment
2820 Erica Place
Nashville, TN 37204
(615) 292-7440

Bill Anderson Enterprises
P.O. Box 888
Hermitage, TN 37076
(615) 889-8920

Birds of a Feather
P.O. Box 2476
Hendersonville, TN 37077
(615) 230-8216

Blair, Lou Management, Inc.
1653 Columbia St.
North Vancouver, BC V7J 1A5
(604) 689-7070

Bob Doyle & Associates
1111 17th Avenue South
Nashville, TN 37212
(615) 329-1040

Bobby Roberts Co.
P.O. Box 1547
Goodlettsville, TN 37070-1547
(615) 859-8899

Bobbye Sonnier
P.O. Box 13253
Lake Charles, LA 70612
(337) 217-8863

Borman Entertainment
1222 16th Ave. South, Ste. 23
Nashville, TN 37212
(615) 320-3000

Brick Wall Management
648 Amsterdam Ave., Suite 4A
NY, NY 10025
(212) 501-0748

Bruce Allen Talent
425 Carrall Street, Ste. 500
Vancouver, BC V6B 6E3
(604) 688 7274

Carter & Co. Artist Management
P.O. Box 128195
Nashville, TN 37212
(615) 641-9415

Cathy Kerr Management
9079 Nemo St
West Hollywood, CA 90069
(310) 273-9437

CDB, Inc.
17060 Central Pike
Lebanon, TN 37090
(615) 443-2112

Cecca Productions
3198 Royal Lane, Ste. 200
Dallas, TX 75229
(214) 350-8477

Chuck Morris Entertainment
1658 York St.
Denver, CO 80206
(303) 329-9292

The Consortium
704 18th Ave., South
Nashville, TN 37203
(615) 327-3004

DMG Public Relations/Sa'mall Management
10 Universal City Plz., Suite 830
Universal City, CA 91426
(818) 506-8533

Appendix C

Direct Management Group, Inc.
947 N. LaCiengega Blvd., Ste. G
Los Angeles, CA 90069
(310) 854-3535

DS Management
P.O. Box 121499
Nashville, TN 37212
(615) 385-3191

Elizabeth Travis Management
1610 16th Ave., South
Nashville, TN 37212
(615) 383-7258

Erv Woolsey Company
1000 18th Avenue South
Nashville, TN 37212
(615) 329-2402

Express Entertainment
18800 Aerial Rd
Edmond, OK 73003
(405) 844-6766

Etc. Etc.
7920 Sunset Blvd., Ste 460
Los Angeles, CA 90046
(323) 874-6464

Fast Lane Management
P.O. Box 150006
Nashville, TN 37215
(615) 371-0257

Fitzgerald Hartley Co.
56 Lindsley Avenue
Nashville, TN 37210
(615) 244-3080

Fitzgerald Hartley Company/CA
34 North Palm Street, Ste. 100
Ventura, CA 93001
(805) 641-6441

Gabriel Music Group
2 Music Circle South, Ste 101
Nashville, TN 37203
(615) 944-2230

Gayle Enterprises, Inc.
51 Music Square East
Nashville, TN 37203
(615) 327-2651

Gold Mountain Management
2 Music Circle South, Ste. 212
Nashville, TN 37212
(615) 255-9000

Graham Music Management, LLC
1016 17th Ave
Nashville, TN 37212
(615) 238-0234

Greg Hill Management
P.O. Box 159310
Nashville, TN 37215
(615) 248-7866

Hallmark Direction, CO.
713 18th Ave South
Nashville, TN 37203
(615) 320-7714

Image Marketing
91 Erin Lane
Nashville, TN 37221
(615) 353-8822

International Management Services
818 19th Avenue South
Nashville, TN 37203
(615) 321-0655

J.A.G. Management
41 Music Square East
Nashville, TN 37203
(615) 726-3230

James Dowell Management
50 Music Square West, Ste 207
Nashville, TN 37203
(615) 777-0068

Jerry Bentley
1025 16th Ave. South, Ste. 301
Nashville, TN 37212
(615) 320-3201

The JMM Company
2817 West End Ave, Ste 126-257
Nashville, TN 37203
(615) 804-6739

John Conlee Enterprises
38 Music Square East, Ste. 117
Nashville, TN 37203
(615) 726-3676

Judy Seale International
109 Rivers Edge Court
Nashville, TN 37214
(615) 872-2122

Keith Case & Associates
1025 17th Ave. South, 2nd Floor
Nashville, TN 37212
(615) 327-4646

Kragen & Co.
14039 Aubrey Road
Beverly Hills, CA 90210
(310) 854-0328

Ladd Management
533 Haggan St.
Nashville, TN 37203
(615) 244-3441

Appendix C

Level Four
304 South Trenton
Tulsa, OK 74120
(918) 599-7418

Lytle Management Group
24 Music Square West
Nashville, TN 37203
(615) 770-2688

M. Hitchcock Management
5101 Overton Road
Nashville, TN 37220
(615) 333-0015

Madison House, Inc.
4760 Walnut St., Ste. 106
Boulder, CO 80301
(303) 544-9900

Mark Rothbaum & Associates, Inc.
P.O. Box 2689
Danbury, CT 06813
(203) 792-2400

McGhee Entertainment
8730 Sunset Blvd, Ste 200
West Hollywood, CA 90069
(310) 358-9200

McLachlan-Scruggs International
2821 Bransford Ave.
Nashville, TN 37204
(615) 292-0099

Mike Robertson Management
P.O. Box 120073
Nashville, TN 37212
(615) 329-4199

Modern Management, Inc.
1625 Broadway, 6th Floor
Nashville, TN 37203
(615) 742-0099

Morey Management
9255 Sunset Blvd., Ste. 600
Los Angeles, CA 90069
(310) 205-6100

Morningstar Management
P.O. Box 1770
Hendersonville, TN 37077
(615) 824-9439

Morris Management Group
818 19th Ave South
Nashville, TN 37203
(615) 321-5025

New Frontier Management
1921 Broadway, 2nd Floor
Nashville, TN 37203
(615) 321-3810

OJ Productions
4321 Reyes Drive
Tarzana, CA 91356
(818) 708-9337

Pacific Group
1744 South 4th Street, Ste. 195
Chickasha, OK 73018
(405) 222-2446

Parallel Entertainment
9255 W. Sunset Blvd., Ste 1040
West Hollywood, CA 90069
(310) 279-1123

Possum Tracks
500 Wilson Pike Circle
Brentwood, TN 37027
(615) 329-9566

Q Prime
729 7th Avenue, 16th Floor
New York, NY 10019
(212) 302-9790

Quantum Management
5340 Forrest Acres Drive
Nashville, TN 37220
(615) 370-2426

Ray Stevens Music
1707 Grand Avenue
Nashville, TN 37212
(615) 327-4629

Refugee Management, Inc.
9005 Overlook Blvd.
Brentwood, TN 37027
(615) 256-6615

Renaissance Management
320 Main Street, Ste. 210
Franklin, TN 37064
(615) 591-8930

Rick Alter Management
1018 17th Avenue South, Ste 12
Nashville, TN 37212
(615) 320-8700

RGK Entertainment Group
219 Duffrain St., Ste. 302C
Toronto, ON M6K 3J1
(416) 410-4482

RPM Management, LLC
2214 Elliston Pl., Ste. 304
Nashville, TN 37203
(615) 256-1980

Appendix C

RS Entertainment
329 Rockland Rd.
Hendersonville, TN 37075
(615) 264-8877

Russell Carter Management
315 West Ponce De Leon
Decatur, GA 30030
(404) 377-9900

Savannah Music, Inc.
205 Powell Place, Ste. 214
Brentwood, TN 37027
(615) 369-0810

Scott Dean Management
612 Humboldt Street
Reno, NV 89509
(775) 322-9426

Serenity Career Direction
5545 Peninsula Park Landing
Hermitage, TN 37076
(615) 885-6803

SHO Artist Management
864 Pinnacle Hill Rd.
Kingston Springs, TN 37082
(615) 652-5300

Starstruck Entertainment
40 Music Square West
Nashville, TN 37203
(615) 259-0001

Strategic Artist Management
1100 Glendon Ave, Ste 1000
Los Angeles, CA 90024
(310) 208-7882

T.K.O. Artist Management
1107 17th Avenue South
Nashville, TN 37204
(615) 383-5017

Tip Top Entertainment
P.O. Box 41689
Nashville, TN 37204
(615) 292-8132

TLE, Inc. Artist Management
2 Music Circle South, Ste 202
Nashville, TN 37203
(615) 242-7000

Tom T. Hall Enterprises
P.O. Box 1246
Franklin, TN 37065-1246
(615) 591-2032

Turner & Nichols
40 Music Sq. West
Nashville, TN 37203
(615) 369-0318

United Management
3325 North University Avenue, #150
Provo, UT 84604
(801) 373-3600

Universal South Artist
40 Music Square West
Nashville, TN 37203
(615) 259-5300

Vector Management
P.O. Box 120479
Nashville, TN 37212
(615) 269-6600

Walker Management
12021 Wilshire Blvd., Ste. 911
Los Angeles, CA 90025
(310) 457-5040

Wynonna, Inc.
1610 17th Avenue South
Nashville, TN 37212
(615) 790-8300

Compilation CD Distributors

Overseas

International Music Express
2 Music Circle S., Suite 101
Nashville, TN 37203
(615) 944-2230
www.gabrielmusicgroup.com

Domestic

National Music Express
2 Music Circle S., Suite 101
Nashville, TN 37203
(615) 944-2230
www.gabrielmusicgroup.com

CDX
2603 Westwood Dr.
Nashville, TN 37204
(615) 292-0123

Appendix C

Talent (Booking) Agents

The Agency Group
8490 Sunset Blvd., Ste. 403
West Hollywood, CA 90069
(310) 360-0771

ACTS Nashville
1103 Bell Grimes Ln.
Nashville, TN 37207
(615) 254-8600

Al Bunetta Management
33 Music Sq. W, #102B
Nashville, TN 37203
(615) 742-1250

Al Embry International
P.O. Box 206
Old Hickory, TN 37138
(615) 847-0123

Art Fegan Entertainment
1307 Long Hunter Lane
Nashville, TN 37217
(615) 399-7054

Artist Management International
P.O. Box 671837
Marrietta, GA 30006-0031
(770) 514-9701

Bobby Roberts Co.
P.O. Box 1547
Goodlettsville, TN 37070-1547
(615) 859-2200

BSC Management
P.O. Box 368
Tujunga, CA 91043
(818) 487-9803

Buddy Lee Attractions
38 Music Square East, Ste. 300
Nashville, TN 37203
(615) 244-4336

Cecca Productions
3198 Royal Lane, #200
Dallas, TX 75229
(214) 350-8477

Center Stage Booking
6114 Little Brandywine
San Antonio, TX 78233
(210) 637-71419

Creative Artists Agency
3310 West End Avenue, 5th Floor
Nashville, TN 37203
(615) 383-8787

Dale Morris & Associates, Inc.
818 19th Avenue South
Nashville, TN 37203
(615) 327-3400

Entertainment America Agency
464 Second Street
Excelsior, MN
(715) 543-8250

Erv Woolsey Agency
1000 18th Avenue South
Nashville, TN 37212
(615) 327-4917

Gabriel Music Group
2 Music Circle South, Ste 101
Nashville, TN 37203
(615) 944-2230

Gerald Murry Music
2903 Woodward Ave.
Muscle Shoals, AL 35661
(256) 381-0432

Great American Talent
P.O. Box2476
Hendersonville, TN 37077
(615) 452-7878

High Road Touring
751 Bridgeway, Fl. 3
Sausalito, CA 94965
(415) 332-4692

ICM
8942 Wilshire Blvd.
Beverly Hills, CA 90211
(310) 550-4000

International Management consultants
1445 Lambert Closse, 2nd Floor
Montreal, PQ H3H 1Z5
(514) 939-0100

Joe Taylor Artist Agency
2802 Columbine Place
Nashville, TN 37204
(615) 385-5666

Appendix C

Key Entertainment Group
513 8th Ave SW, Suite 305
Calgary, AB T2P 1G3
(403) 262-2245

Lustig Talent Enterprises, Inc.
P.O. Box 70850
Orlando, FL 32877
(407) 816-8960

Lutz, Richard Entertainment Agency
145 N. 46th St., Suite 1
Lincoln, NE 68503
(402) 475-1900

Mascioli Entertainment Corporation
2202 Curry Ford Rd., Ste E
Orlando, FL 32806
(407) 897-8824

Monterey Peninsula Artists
124 12th Avenue South, Ste. 410
Nashville, TN 37203
(615) 251-4440

Music City Artists
2723 Berrywood Dr.
Nashville, TN 37204
(615) 383-4862

Simply Entertainment, Inc.
707 18th Ave., South
Nashville, TN 37203
(615) 327-0444

Third Coast Talent
P.O. Box 110225
Nashville, TN 37222-0225
(615) 333-7235

United Management
3325 North University Avenue, #150
Provo, UT 84604
(801) 373-3600

William Morris Agency
1600 Division St., Ste 300
Nashville, TN 37203
(615) 963-3000

INDEX

A

A & R Department 52, 53, 54, 148
AFTRA 57, 62, 141
ASCAP 47, 83, 141
accompaniment tracks 91
"Achy Breaky Heart" 52
act (definition of) 151
"adds" radio 76
Adkins, Trace 67
advertising agencies 19, 120
affiliation (with performance societies) 48
aftermarket 14, 94 (See also *Fairs*)
agents (See *Booking Agents*)
airplay (See *Radio Airplay*)
Alabama (group) 9, 56
Alabama (listings)
    country radio 177
    fairs 233
    festivals 279
    convention data 319
Alaska (listings)
    country radio 177
    fairs 233
    festivals 279
    convention data 319
Alberta (listings)
    country radio 205
    fairs 271
    festivals 313
    convention data 319

American Federation of Musicians (See *musician's union*)
American Federation of Television and Radio Artists (See *AFTRA*)
"American Idol" 114, 115
American Legion 116
American Society of Composers, Authors and Publishers (See *ASCAP*)
Ampex distributor (Nashville) 59
Amusement Business Magazine 99, 125
appearance (See *stage presence*)
Argentina (radio listings) 211
Aristo Media Associates 124
Arizona (listings)
    country radio 177
    fairs 233
    festivals 279
    convention data 319
Arkansas (listings)
    country radio 178
    fairs 234
    festivals 280
    convention data 319
artist pack 5, 23-31, 88, 103, 112, 113, 123, 131, 132, 134
    booking agents require 131, 132, 134
    demo 24
    narrative bio 25, 26
    photos 25

Index

posters 29-31
press (newspaper) info 27, 112, 113
stick to the facts 26
showcasing 123
sources 28
video 28, 29
artwork 79
Atlantic City 101, 102
attitude 2
attorneys 120, 129, 137, 138, 141 (See also *entertainment attorneys*)
"Audition" Sham 141
Australia 105, 107
Australia (radio listings) 211
Austria (radio listings) 212
auto tune 68, 151

B

BMI 47, 83, 141
back-lighting 93
back-up singers (listings) 325
backer 152 (See *investors*)
backing (See *investors*)
"bailout" clause 16, 152
Baldknobbers 101
bands (finding one) 91
bar coding 79, 152
bars 24, 33-35, 65, 87, 131
negative, positive aspects 34
Belgium (radio listings) 213
Bentley, Dierks 144
Big & Rich 20
Billboard 75, 76, 77, 99, 125, 152
bio 152 (See *biography*)
biography 25, 26, 179
elements of 26
format 26, 27
samples of 165, 166
Black Hills Opry 115
"blocks" (of time recording) 57, 152
Bluegrass (vocals) 66

"blurbs" (media) 112
"body language" (images) 20
Bogáncs Music 47
Bojtorján 106
"book" 152
booking agents 5, 23, 123-125, 131-135
booking yourself 132-135 (See also *fairs*)
developing selling skills 134
draw factor, your 131
finding an agent 131, 132
general background 131
influencing an agent's interest 132
listing of 349
"pitching" yourself 133, 134
two types of agents (agencies) 131
booking yourself (See chapters on *Booking Agents* and *Fairs*)
"borrowed" equity 120
Boxcar Willie 105
Bradley, Harold 43
Brandt, Paul 108
Branson (MO) 101-103
development of 101
finding backers 102
opportunities 101-103
Brazil (radio listings) 213
British Columbia (listings)
country radio 205
fairs 271
festivals 313
convention data 319
Broadcast Music Incorporated (See *BMI*)
Brooks, Garth 21
Bulgaria (radio listings) 214
business cards 133

C

CD distributors (compilation) listing of 348
"CD Mail Direct to Radio" Sham 145
CD's 71-74, 76, 78, 79, 84, 85, 97, 144, 147
advantages of 71

Index

costs of manufacturing 72
CMA 141, 152
CPA 11
cable t.v. 29, 98
California (listings)
    country radio 178
    fairs 235
    festivals 281
    convention data 319
Canada 108-110
    airplay (American in Canada) 109, 110
    airplay (Canadian in U.S.) 110
    artists, Canadian 66, 108
    Cancon 108, 109
        requirements to qualify 109
    contrast in country music (from U.S.) 108
    MAPL system 109
    regional flavors 108
    writers 109
Canadian content 152 (See *Cancon*)
Cancon 108, 109, 152
Canyon, George 108
"captive" audience 87, 98
career-launching (efforts) 45, 134
cartage 59, 152
cartage company (See *cartage*)
cartage companies (listings) 323
Cash, Johnny 82
CashBox 152
cassettes 71, 72, 79, 84, 97
    advantages of 71
    cost of manufacturing 71
catalogs (publishing) 46, 152
    administration of 46
Cavalcade of Acts and Attractions 125
chain stores 79
Chamber of Commerce 115, 116
character (images) 21
charts (radio) 84, 152
charts (session) 57, 62, 152
Chesney, Kenny 20
Chevy trucks 119

churches 116
city editor 113
Clark Kent/Superman 133
Clark, Terri 108
Cline, Patsy 65
clubs (See *bars*)
"code" 152
college communications course 29
Colorado (listings)
    country radio 179
    fairs 236
    festivals 282
    convention data 319
"competition" 74
competition (with yourself) 73, 84
compilation CD (& services) 74, 107, 152, 348
compilation "with names" CD 74
confidence 33-35
Connecticut (listings)
    country radio 180
    fairs 236
    festivals 283
    convention data 319
"connections" 3
consignment (sales) 97, 99
"Consultation" Sham 143
contract riders 95
contractor 57, 153
contractor's fee 57
contracts 16, 46, 95, 135, 138
    samples of 170, 171
"copy" song (See *"cover" songs*)
cosmetic value (PA systems) 92
"cover" (songs) 5, 48, 49, 153
Crawford, Cindy 119
Croatia (radio listings) 214
custom labels 73, 97, 153
Cyrus, Billy Ray 20, 52
Czech Republic (radio listings) 214

D

Index

DAT (See *Digital Audio Tape*)
DAW (See *Digital Audio Workstation*)
DVD   29, 71, 72, 153
daily rates (studio)   59
Davis, Skeeter   106
"deal" (record)   153
Delaware (listings)
    country radio   180
    fairs   237
    festivals   283
    convention data   319
demo   24, 49, 54, 56, 153
    for club bookings   24
    for record labels   24
    for talent buyers   24
demo scale (See *scale, union scale*)
Denmark   106, 107
Denmark (radio listings)   214
Digital Audio Tape   59, 153
Digital Audio Workstation   153, 156, 157
digital hard drives   59
digital multi-track tape   59
Digital Performer   153
digital studios   58
District of Columbia (listings)
    country radio   180
    festivals   284
    convention data   319
Dixie Chicks   19
"Don't Be Cruel"   49
"double scale"   56, 153
draw (attraction)   89
"drops" (radio)   76, 153
"drummer trick"   91

E

Eastern Europe   105
electrical service (stages)   93
Electro Voice   92
electronic (digital) pitch correction   68
Elks (club)   116

e-mail (labels)   52
emotions (singing)   67
endorsements   14, 119-122, 138, 153
    getting a "deal"   119, 120
    how they work   121
    local possibilities   122
    what stimulates interest   121, 122
    what they provide   122
engineer (recording/sound)   59, 153
    duties of   59
    fees   59
    listing of   323
England (See also *United Kingdom*)   105
Enquirer, The   111
entertainment attorneys   137, 138
    acting as door openers   138
    fees   138
    finding an entertainment attorney   137, 138
    their mission   137
entertainment editor   113
Entertainment Tonight   111
envelopes   133
escrow account (See *musician's union*)
"established" artist   49
Estonia (radio listings)   215
Europe (See *overseas market*)
"Evaluation" Sham   143
Evans, Sara   144
exclusive writer's contract   46, 49

F

fair & festival meetings (annual), listing of   317
fairs   87-95
    after-market sales   94
    booking yourself (See also *Booking Agents*)
        88-90, 132-135
    factors to consider   94, 95
    family oriented   88
    finding a backup band   91
    lighting (stage)   93
    listings (Canada)   269

Index

    listings (US) 231
    negotiating your booking 89, 90
    overcoming objections 89, 90
    sample contract (booking) 95 A
    sound systems (stage) 92, 93
    what they're looking for 88
    working with accompaniment tracks 90, 91
    worlds of opportunities 87
    your fee 94, 95
fair conventions 125
fan clubs 114
Faroe Islands (radio listings) 215
festivals (See *Fairs*)
    listings (Canada) 311
    listings (US) 277
financial backing (See *investors*)
finding investors 9-17
Finland (radio listings) 216
Florida (listings)
    country radio 180
    fairs 237
    festivals 284
    convention data 319
Ford, Henry 129
Ford trucks 119
Fox, George 108
Fox, Harry (Agency) 47
Fox Network 114
France 105
France (radio listings) 216

G

G.A.C. (Great American Country) 61
"Gambler, The" 43, 50
Garrish, Sonny 56
Gavin 75, 77, 147, 154
Georgia (listings)
    country radio 181
    fairs 238
    festivals 285
    convention data 319

Germany 105
Germany (radio listings) 217
Gill, Vince 20, 67
Gilley, Mickey 101
gimmicks 21
Globe, The 111
goals 2-7
    defining 3
    long-term 4
    short-term 4
Gong Show 114
Gracin, Josh 115
Grand Ole Opry 39, 115
Greece (radio listings) 218
Greenwood, Lee 65
Guide to Fairs, Festivals & Expositions 125

H

Haggard, Marty 3
Haggard, Merle 3
Hall, Dr. Richard 2
hard drive 59, 154
Harris, Emmylou 106
Hawaii (listings)
    country radio 181
    fairs 238
    festivals 285
    convention data 319
Higgins, Bill 19, 87
high school communications course 29
Hill, Faith 19, 20, 49, 87
"hillbilly" 66
Holland (See *Netherlands*)
"honky-tonks" (See *bars*)
human interest editor 113
humane society 27, 28, 113
Humperdink, Englebert 67
Hungary 106, 107
Hungary (radio listings) 218

I

Index

Iceland (radio listings) 219
Idaho (listings)
    country radio 181
    fairs 239
    festivals 286
    convention data 319
Illinois (listings)
    country radio 182
    fairs 239
    festivals 286
    convention data 319
illusions 19-22, 102
    difference between (images & illusion) 20
    what they are based on 20
image-driven sponsorships 120, 121
images 19-22
    character 21
    finding yours 21, 22
    how images work 19-21
    physical looks 21
    right combination of 21
independent approach 69-79, 131, 140
    advantages of pursuing 69, 70
    artwork 79
    bar coding 79
    "big" picture 70
    costs 70
    "custom" vs. "independent" labels 73, 97
    distribution 77-79
    high-visibility venues 70
    mailings 73, 74
    manufacturing 71, 72
    marketing 77-79
    promotions 72-77
        costs of 74, 75
    radio 75, 77
    radio promotions (techniques of) 75-77, 81-84
    recognition factor 73
    releasing product 71, 72
        costs of 71, 72
    self marketing 78

    spending your own money 69, 70
    vital areas 70
independent labels 73, 75, 78, 154
independently manufactured "product" (CD's and cassettes) 13
Indiana (listings)
    country radio 183
    fairs 240
    festivals 287
    convention data 319
"indie" (See *independent label*)
infringement lawsuits 138
initiating airplay (radio) 83
Inside Edition 111
International Music Express 74, 107
investors 9-17, 55, 102
    appeal to invest 11
    backer "prospectus" 169
    business proposals 9
    customizing your proposal 15
    dealing with strangers 16
    don't "over-commit" 16
    finding one 9, 11, 55, 102
    making concessions 16
    percentages and timeframes 15, 16
    project needs 10
    reasons to look for 10
    returns on investment 12-17
    suggested approach 11
    where to look 10, 11
Iowa (listings)
    country radio 183
    fairs 241
    festivals 288
    convention data 319
Ireland (radio listings) 219
Italy (radio listings) 219

J

JBL 92
J-card 71, 154

Index

Jackson, Alan   35, 49, 66, 119, 144
jamborees   115
Japan   105
Japan (radio listings)   220
jewel box   154
Jewell, Buddy   115
Johnson, Carolyn Dawn   108
Jones, Tom   67
Jordan, Michael   119
Jordanaires   57
Judd, Wynonna   21, 35, 66
Judds, The   49
jukeboxes   117, 118
   benefits of   117, 118
   getting added   117, 118
   locating supplier   117
   why your CD?   118
   your fee   118

K

Kansas (listings)
   country radio   184
   fairs   243
   festivals   288
   convention data   319
karaoke (See also *accompaniment tracks*)   24, 35, 65
   benefits/drawbacks   35
Keith, Toby   14, 66, 119
Kentucky (listings)
   country radio   184
   fairs   244
   festivals   289
   convention data   319
Kenya (radio listings)   220
Kristofferson, Kris   39

L

label   154
label roster   154
labels (See *major labels, independent labels, custom labels*)
lang, k.d.   108
Las Vegas   101, 102
Latvia (radio listings)   220
lawyers (See *attorneys*)
lease deal (records) overseas   105, 107
letter of recommendation   31, 164
   sample of   160
licensing (See also *licensing agencies* and *mechanical licensing*)   83, 84, 154
   for radio airplay   83
licensing agencies   47
licensing (retail)   99
"life of the record"   74, 75
lighting (stage) (See also *PAR-64's*)   93, 124
limited pressing scale   56, 154
Lions   116, 134
Lithuania (radio listings)   220
Lonestar   144
Louisiana (listings)
   country radio   185
   fairs   245
   festivals   289
   convention data   319
Luxembourg (radio listings)   221
Lynn, Loretta   3, 26

M

MAPL system   109, 154
mp3 file   52
Mackie   92
mail order   99
Maine (listings)
   country radio   186
   fairs   246
   festivals   290
   convention data   319
major labels   13, 14, 17, 23, 39, 51-54, 62, 63, 69, 74, 81, 82, 97, 102, 118, 123-125, 128, 137, 140, 154, 329, 330
   advantages they offer   51, 52

Index

   how "backing" helps 17
   importance in airplay 81
   influence of attorneys 137
   showcasing 123-125
   submitting material to 52
Malta (radio listings) 221
marketing (See *merchandising*)
managers 6, 90, 127-129, 137, 154
   another Col. Parker? 128
   finding your manager 129
   functions of 127, 128
   how managers earn their money 127
   listing of 345
   managing yourself for now 127, 129
   qualities to look for 128
   "think tank" concept 129
   what interests a good manager 127
Manitoba (listings)
   country radio 205
   fairs 271
   festivals 313
   convention data 319
Marlboro Man 120
Maryland (listings)
   country radio 186
   fairs 246
   festivals 291
   convention data 319
Massachusetts (listings)
   country radio 186
   fairs 247
   festivals 291
   convention data 319
master session 13, 14, 56, 154
mastering 58, 71, 154
mastering studio 58, 59
McBride, Martina 56
McCoy, Charlie 106
McEntire, Pake 3
McEntire, Reba 3, 14, 20
McGraw, Tim 20, 34, 87, 114
mechanical licensing 48, 49

mechanical royalties (See *royalties*)
merchandising 6, 12-16, 97-99
   building "national" recognition 6
   considerations in self-merchandising 98, 99
   dealing with "backers" 12-16
   dealing with stores 99
   strategies 97-99
      advertising 99
      consignment 97
      "give-aways" 99
   live performances 98
   pricing 99
      quality of merchandise 98
   radio 98
      sell direct 97
      T.V. 98
      web page 98
merchants (local) 89
Messina, JoDee 114
Mexico (radio listings) 221
Michigan (listings)
   country radio 186
   fairs 247
   festivals 291
   convention data 319
Minnesota (listings)
   country radio 187
   fairs 248
   festivals 292
   convention data 319
Mississippi (listings)
   country radio 188
   fairs 250
   festivals 293
   convention data 319
Missouri (listings)
   country radio 188
   fairs 250
   festivals 294
   convention data 319
mixing 58, 153, 154
money 3, 6, 7, 9-17

Index

acquiring investors 3, 6, 9-17
    making money with your talent 7
    necessity of 9-17
    repayment (to "backers") 12, 13
    various proposals 13-17
Montana (listings)
    country radio 189
    fairs 251
    festivals 295
    convention data 319
Montgomery Gentry 67
Morris, Gary 67
Moose 116, 134
motivation 2, 3
multi-track 59, 154
musical calls (radio promotions) 83, 155
music charts 57, 62, 155
Music City 37, 155
music director 82-84, 114, 129, 144, 155
Music Row 38, 79, 125
Music Row Magazine 75, 77, 147, 155
musicians 55-57, 62, 124
    "road" musicians 55, 56
    "session" (studio) musicians 55, 56, 57, 157
    studio musicians (listings) 324
musician's union 56, 62, 141

N

NSD Records 73
"name" 3, 155
Namibia (radio listings) 221
narrative biography (See *biography*)
Nashville 37-40
    moving to 37-40
    reasons for 37, 38
    reasons against 38, 39
    rejections 39
    preparation for 39, 40
Nashville "quality" (recordings) 70, 82, 118, 147
Nashville recording artist 24, 29, 30
Nashville Star 115

Nashville Songwriters Association 46
national act (pursuing) 6
National Music Express 75
Nebraska (listings)
    country radio 190
    fairs 252
    festivals 295
    convention data 319
negotiate (prices) 89
Netherlands (radio listings) 221
Nevada (listings)
    country radio 190
    fairs 253
    festivals 296
    convention data 319
New Brunswick (listings)
    country radio 205
    fairs 272
    festivals 314
    convention data 319
New Hampshire (listings)
    country radio 190
    fairs 253
    festivals 296
    convention data 319
New Jersey (listings)
    country radio 190
    fairs 254
    festivals 296
    convention data 319
New Mexico (listings)
    country radio 191
    fairs 254
    festivals 297
    convention data 319
New York (listings)
    country radio 191
    fairs 254
    festivals 297
    convention data 319
New Zealand 105, 107
New Zealand (radio listings) 222

Index

Newfoundland (listings)
    country radio   206
    festivals   314
    convention data   319
news (See *publicity*)
news director   114
newsletter   5
newspaper write-ups   27, 28, 112
    samples of   167
Nike (sneakers)   119
"non-reporter" (radio)   75, 155
North Carolina (listings)
    country radio   192
    fairs   255
    festivals   298
    convention data   319
North Dakota (listings)
    country radio   192
    fairs   256
    festivals   298
    convention data   319
Northern Ireland (radio listings)   223
Norway (radio listings)   223
Northwest Territories (listings)
    country radio   206
    festivals   314
    convention data   319
Nova Scotia (listings)
    country radio   206
    fairs   272
    festivals   314
    convention data   319

O

Ohio (listings)
    country radio   193
    fairs   256
    festivals   299
    convention data   319
Oklahoma (listings)
    country radio   193

fairs   258
    festivals   299
    convention data   319
Ontario (listings)
    country radio   206
    fairs   272
    festivals   315
    convention data   319
"On the Other Hand"   65
"one-nighter"   134, 155
open-mike   38, 155
Oprys   115
Oregon (listings)
    country radio   194
    fairs   258
    festivals   300
    convention data   319
over-dub studio   58, 155
overseas market   105-110
    background   105
    benefits it offers   105-107
    European radio (differences from U.S.)   106
    getting airplay   7, 109, 110
    "lease" deal   107
    making contacts   106, 107
    most popular styles   108

P

PA Systems   92, 98
    brand names   92
    cosmetic value   92
    self-contained   92
    size   92
PAR-64   93, 155
PR firms   111, 112, 123, 124
    functions of   112
Paisley, Brad   87
"paper ads" (radio)   77, 84, 155
Parker, Colonel Tom   128
Parton, Dolly   3
Parton, Randy   3

Index

Parton, Stella 3
Peavey 92
Pennsylvania (listings)
    country radio 194
    fairs 259
    festivals 301
    convention data 319
per inquiry 78, 155
performance fees 94
performance rights societies 47, 48, 83
    joining 48
    listings 330
    performance royalties 47, 48
    purpose of 48
photographs 25, 30, 52
    promotional, samples of 168
physical beauty (images) 21
"pickers" (See *musicians*) 155
"Piece of My Heart" 49
playlist (See *radio airplay*)
Poland (radio listings) 224
"politics" (inside "connections") 3
Portugal (radio listings) 224
posters 29-31
    elements of 29, 30
    format 29, 30
    samples of 163, 164
    where to obtain 31
presenter 106, 156
Presley, Elvis 19, 50, 66, 67, 115, 127
Presley's Jubilee Theater 101
press info (See *publicity*)
press kit (See *artist pack*) 156
press releases 112
Pride, Charley 101
Prince Edward Island (listings)
    country radio 206
    fairs 275
    festivals 315
    convention data 319
printers (See *artist pack*)
Pro Tools 59, 156

producer 61-64, 141, 142, 148, 156
    acquiring a producer 61, 62
    fees 64
    qualities to look for 62
    scams 141, 142
    what to avoid 63
"product" 156
program director 114, 129, 156
project coordinator (record release) 73
promo pack (See *artist pack*) 156
promotional flyer (See also *press release)*
    sample of 161, 162
promotions (See *record promoters*, *Radio Airplay*,
    Independent Approach)
promotions (beer) 121
promotions (soft drinks) 121
pseudonyms 133
publicists (listings) 333
publicity 6, 27, 28, 97, 98, 111-116, 118, 121,
    123, 128
    American Legion 116
    attention as a commodity 111
    chamber of commerce 115
    churches 116
        dances 116
        festivals 116
        lawn fetes 116
    circuses 116
    concerts in park 116
    Elks (F.B.O.E.) 116
    exhibitions 116
    fan clubs 114
        starting your own 114
    fire departments 115
    generating publicity 111
    humane society 27
    jamborees 115
    Lions club 116
    magazines 111
    Moose club 116
    newspaper write-ups 27, 28, 112, 113
        who to contact 28, 113

Index

oprys 115
PR firms 111, 112
radio interviews 113, 114
    who to contact 113
Rotary International 116
self-publicizing 27, 112-116
talent contests 114, 115
    benefits of 114
    shortcomings 114, 115
T.V. shows (& news) 27, 29, 111, 113
    creating interest 113
V.F.W. (Veterans of Foreign Wars) 116
publisher (See *publishing*)
"Publisher" Sham 146
publishers (music/song), listing of 339
publishing 39, 45-50, 63, 83, 137, 138, 146
    "assignment" of songs 46
    attorneys, advantages of 138
    door-opening strategies 49, 50
    how publishers work 45, 46
    landing a job 39
    mechanical licensing 48
    mechanical royalties 47
    ownership of songs (See *assignment of*)
    performance rights societies 47, 48
        joining one 48
    "publisher sham" 146
    publishing rights 46
    singers who write 45, 46
    splitting royalties 47, 157
    starting your own publishing company 48
    what publishers look for 49
    soliciting material 49
    writers only 46
publishing company (See *publishing*) 156
publishing house (See *publishing*)
publishing royalties 14, 47

Q

quality recordings (See *Nashville quality*)
quality, "star" 19

concentrating on strong points 21
Quebec (listings)
    country radio 206
    fairs 275
    festivals 315
    convention data 319

R

R&R (trade magazine) 75, 77, 147
RADAR 156
radio (airplay) 6, 30, 75, 76, 81-85, 118, 145-147
    "adds" (radio) 76
    ballad or "up tempo" 82
    format 82
    label 82
    playlist 74, 75, 76, 155
    promotions 75, 76, 82
    qualifying for 81, 82
    "quality" recording 81
    relating to jukeboxes 118
    "reporters" 75, 77, 83, 156
    self-promoting 82-85, 98
    time of year 82
Radio & Records (See R&R)
radio airplay 83
radio interviews 113, 114
radio stations, Canada (listings) 201
radio stations, overseas (listings) 205
radio stations, U.S. (listings) 175
"Radio Station Talent Scout" Sham 146
radio syndicators (listings) 335
Rapid City (South Dakota) 115
Rascal Flatts 56
"record" 156
record companies (See *major labels, independent labels*)
record companies/labels (listings) 329
record labels (See *record companies*)
record promoters 72, 74-77, 82, 83, 156
    importance of 74
    listing of 335

Index

    options (costs) 74
    radio regarding promotions (See *Radio*)
record releases 14
Record World 156
recording "cover" (copy) material 48, 49
recording session 14, 55-59
    AFTRA 57
    backup singers 57
        acquiring them 57
        contractor 57
        rates 57
    "blocks" of time 57
    cartage 59
    engineer 59
        rates 59
    musicians 55-57
        acquiring them 56
        demo scale 56
        limited pressing scale 56
        master scale 56, 154
        rates 56
        session leader 57
    musician's union 56
        health & welfare fund 56
        pension fund 56
    road musicians (vs. studio musicians) 55, 56
    studios 58, 59
        day rate 59
        hourly rate 59
        mastering studio 58, 59
        overdub studio 58
        tracking studio 58
    tape 59
recording studios 58, 59
    listings 323
recording (vocal performance) 65-68
    approach to ballads 67, 82
    approach to up-tempo songs 67, 82
    capturing enthusiasm 66, 67
    dealing with emotions 66, 67
    defining your style 66, 67
    importance of spontaneity 66, 67

Redlin, Terry 1
references 31
regional editor (newspaper) 113
"reporters" (radio) 75, 77, 83, 156
reversion clause 46, 156
Rhode Island (listings)
    country radio 195
    fairs 260
    festivals 302
    convention data 319
"rider" (contract) 95, 156
Rimes, LeAnn 20
road musicians (see *musicians*) 156
rodeo companies (listings) 336
rodeos (See *fairs*)
Rogers, Kenny 50
Romania (radio listings) 224
Rotary 116, 134
royalties 45-48, 50, 157
    incentive 47, 50
    mechanical 47, 154
    performance rights societies 47
    performance royalties 47, 48, 50
    publisher's portion 47
    splitting of 47
    writer's portion 47
    "200%" royalty 48
Russia (radio listings) 225

S

SESAC 47, 83, 141, 157
sales-driven sponsorship 120, 121
Saskatchewan (listings)
    country radio 207
    fairs 275
    festivals 316
    convention data 319
satellite broadcasting 76, 157
satellite radio providers 335
Sawyer Brown 115
scale (See *union scale*) 157

Index

scams & shams 139-148
    always consider source 141
    "Audition" Sham 141, 142
    beware independent trade mags 146
    checking out names/reputations 141
    "Computer" Sham 147
    "Consultation/Evaluation" Sham 143, 144
    deceptive big prizes 142
    easy targets 139
    "Internet CD Promo" Sham 146
    "It's a hit" 148
    Mailing "Direct to Radio" Sham 145
    misleading names 141
    money/cost always a reality 140, 141
    "Paying Fees to Enter Talent Contest" Sham 145
    "producers"/"counselors" 142
    "Publisher" Sham 145
    "Radio Station Talent Scout" Sham 145
    rules of thumb 140
    "Scholarship" Sham 147
    "Selling Tickets" Sham 142
    "Seminar" Sham 147
    "Showcase" Sham 146
    "sin of omission" 139, 140
    "Talent Contest" Sham 141, 142
    "Talent Contest on Internet" Sham 146
    "Trade Magazine" Sham 144
    "Video" Sham 143
    "We'll Pay Half" Sham 145
    "Win a Recording in Nashville" Sham 146
Scandinavia 105, 107
Schlitz, Don 43, 50
"Scholarship" Sham 147
Scotland (radio listings) 225
secondary stations (radio) 75, 157
Secord, "Uncle" Hank 1, 2
Seger, Bob 119
"self-contained" 89, 92, 157
"Seminar" Sham 147
sensuality (images) 20
session leader 56, 57, 62, 157

session musician (See *musicians*)
"Showcase" Sham 146
showcasing 6, 15, 112, 123-125, 129, 132, 157
    aimed at record labels 124, 125
    aimed at talent buyers (i.e. Fairs) 125
    helpful publications 125
    hiring a PR firm 123, 124
    publicizing event 124
    putting it together yourself 124
        backup band 124
        logistics of event 124
    qualifying for fair associations 125
    who to contact 125
show host (see *presenter*) 157
shrink-wrapping 71
"side" 157
"side"-lighting 93
Simmons, Richard 120
Simpson, Jessica 120
Sinatra, Frank, Jr. 3
singers, studio back-up, listing of 325
singing (See *recording*)
single act 90
Sioux Falls (South Dakota) 27, 28
Slovakia (Slovak Republic) (radio listings) 225
Slovenia (radio listings) 225
Smirnoff, Yakov 101
solicited material 53, 157
"Somethin' Like That" 65
SONAR 157
"song plugger" 49
song publishers (See *publishers music/song*)
song-writing 41-43
    anatomy of 41-43
        chorus/refrain 43
        "payoff" 42
        theme 42
        title 42
        unfolding of story 42, 43
    misconceptions of 41
    typical beginnings of 41
sound engineers (listings) 323

Index

sound systems (See also *PA* Systems) 89, 91-93, 124
South Africa (radio listings) 226
South Carolina (listings)
    country radio 195
    fairs 260
    festivals 302
    convention data 319
South Dakota (listings)
    country radio 195
    fairs 261
    festivals 303
    convention data 319
Spain (radio listings) 226
"split" publishing (See *publishing*) 157
sponsorships 14, 89, 119-122, 157
    benefits provided by 121
    borrowed equity, how it works 120
    car dealerships 89
    finding sponsorships 120
    general info 119
    getting a "deal" 119, 120
    how sponsorships work 119, 120
    image driven 121
    matching "the fit" 120
    sales driven 121
    steps to pursue 120
    supermarkets 89
spotlight 93
Sri Lanka (radio listings) 226
Stafford, Terry 50
stage 89
stage presence 5
starter stations 75, 76, 147, 157
    advantages for new artists 75, 76
stationery (letterheads) 133
Strait, George 19, 20, 67, 119
studios (See *recording studios*)
success 5-7
    as a club act 5
    as a national act 6, 7
"Summertime Blues" 49

"Suspicion" 50
Sweden (radio listings) 226
"Sweet Dreams" 65
Switzerland 105
Switzerland (radio listings) 227

T

T.V. 27, 29, 111-115, 143
talent 1, 3, 7
talent/booking agents (listings) 349
talent buyers 88, 89, 90, 123, 125
talent contests 114, 115, 140, 141, 142, 146
    "Large Fee to Enter Talent Contest" Sham 115, 146
talk shows 113
    creating "causes" 113
tape (recording tape) 59
"tech" 92
    how to get one 92
Tennessee (listings)
    country radio 196
    fairs 261
    festivals 303
    convention data 319
Texas (listings)
    country radio 197
    fairs 262
    festivals 304
    convention data 319
tracking studio 58
"tracks" (music) 90, 91, 157
    working with a drummer 91
"Trade Magazine" Sham 145
trade magazines 7, 75, 158
Travis, Randy 21, 65
tray card 158
Tritt, Travis 20, 66
Twain, Shania 20, 108
Twitty, Conway 3
Twitty, Kathy 3
Twitty, Mike 3

Index

Tyson, Ian 108

U

Underwood, Carrie 87, 115
union scale 56, 57, 157
    double scale 56
    health, welfare, pension fees 58
    limited pressing, demo scale 56, 57
    master scale 56
United Arab Emirates (radio listings) 227
United Kingdom (radio listings) 227
United Record Pressing 71
United States (radio listings) 175
Universal Product Code (UPC) 79
"unsolicited" material 53, 158
up-tempo (songs) 66, 67, 158
Uruguay (radio listings) 229
Urban, Keith 56, 70, 114
Utah (listings)
    country radio 199
    fairs 263
    festivals 305
    convention data 319

V

VCR 21
V.F.W. 116
VHS 71, 72
Van Shelton, Ricky 67
Vermont (listings)
    country radio 199
    fairs 263
    festivals 305
    convention data 319
vibrato 66, 67, 158
video 14, 28, 29, 71, 143
    alternate (budget) approaches 28, 29
    costs 28, 72
    purpose of 71, 72
"Video" Sham 143

vinyl (records) 71, 158
Virginia (listings)
    country radio 199
    fairs 264
    festivals 305
    convention data 319
vocal performance (See *recording*)
vocal talent
    development of 1, 2, 5
    interpretation of 1
vocalists (back-up) (See also *AFTRA*) 57
    (See also *singers, studio backup*)
voltage (electrical) 93
volunteer fire departments 27, 115

W

WYRK Radio 115
Walker, Jeff (agency) 125
war 42
Washington (listings)
    country radio 200
    fairs 264
    festivals 306
    convention data 319
web (websites) 5, 23, 31, 79, 98, 119, 129, 137
    backup vocalists (AFTRA) 57
    commercial/graphic artists 79
    marketing 119
    musician's union 56
    MySpace.com 98
    promotional 5, 23
    record production 79
    self-merchandising 98
    UPC 79
"We'll Pay Half" Sham 145
West Virginia (listings)
    country radio 200
    fairs 265
    festivals 307
    convention data 319
Whitman, Slim 105

Index

wholesale prices   78, 118
Williams, Hank, Sr.   66, 82
Wilson, Gretchen   20, 35, 82
"Win a Recording in Nashville" Sham   147
Wisconsin (listings)
    country radio   201
    fairs   266
    festivals   308
    convention data   319
Wrangler jeans   119
Wright, Michelle   108
writer's night   38
writer's portion (publishing)   46
Wynette, Tammy   66
Wyoming (listings)
    country radio   201
    fairs   267
    festivals   309
    convention data   319

Y

Yamaha   92
Yearwood, Trisha   21
youth (images)   21
Yukon Territory (listings)
    festivals   316
    convention data   319

Index